THE DEVIL IN BABYLON

THE DEVIL IN BABYLON

FEAR OF PROGRESS AND

THE BIRTH OF MODERN LIFE

ALLAN LEVINE

Library and Archives Canada Cataloguing in Publication

Levine, Allan, 1956-
The Devil in Babylon : fear of progress and the
birth of modern life / Allan Levine.

ISBN 0-7710-5273-1

1. United States–History–20th century. 2. Canada–History–20th century.
3. United States–History–20th century–Biography.
4. Canada–History–20th century–Biography. I. Title.

E45.L49 2005   973   C2005-900435-5

We acknowledge the financial support of the Government of Canada through the Book Publishing Industry Development Program and that of the Government of Ontario through the Ontario Media Development Corporation's Ontario Book Initiative. We further acknowledge the support of the Canada Council for the Arts and the Ontario Arts Council for our publishing program.

Photo on page ii: The Manhattan skyline in 1913, looking north towards the towers of the Woolworth and Singer buildings.

Typeset in Janson by M&S, Toronto
Printed and bound in Canada

This book is printed on acid-free paper that is 100% ancient-forest friendly (100% post-consumer recycled).

McClelland & Stewart Ltd.
The Canadian Publishers
481 University Avenue
Toronto, Ontario
M5G 2E9
www.mcclelland.com

1 2 3 4 5   09 08 07 06 05

For my niece Megan,
a courageous young woman

The only reasonable ground for true optimism . . . is to accept the reality of Satan, and the only solid ground for hope is to believe that the devil, the arch enemy of God and man, has promoted, inspired, and now directs all of the wickedness of the world, and that he may be resisted, overcome and finally defeated, through faith in God.

– John Roach Straton, *Fighting the Devil in Modern Babylon* (1929)

Contents

Acknowledgements

I would like to thank many of the usual suspects who have contributed so much to my writing career during the past few years. Hilary McMahon, my literary agent, continues to look after my best interests – and answer my numerous e-mails in a timely fashion. I am delighted that this is my second book with Alex Schultz, my wise and gifted editor at McClelland & Stewart. His talents and efforts are much appreciated, as are those of copy editor Jenny Bradshaw and Marilyn Biderman, director of rights and contracts.

My gratitude goes as well to University of Manitoba historian Jack Bumsted and to Sheppy Coodin, my former colleague at St. John's-Ravenscourt School, for taking the time to comment on several chapters. Thanks, too, to Bonnie Bodner of the Inter-Library Loan Department of the Winnipeg Public Library for tracking down many books.

My wife, Angie, and our children, Alexander and Mia, as always offered unquestioning support. Even if I do not always acknowledge this, I greatly appreciate their love and encouragement. And I would be remiss if I did not mention the newest member of our family, Maggie, our energetic beagle, who on our daily walks together usually permits me time for some much-needed reflection.

This book is dedicated to my seventeen-year-old niece, Megan Morrison. She has faced adversity with a courage and resolve I can only admire. I wish her good health and much happiness always – and for years to come.

AL

INTRODUCTION

The City

The city is not all bad nor all good. It is humanity compressed, the best and worst combined, in a strangely composite community.

– Reverend Lyman Abbott, 1892

Urban Nights and Magical Powers

To be a New Yorker in 1913 was to experience everything the modern world had to offer. From the glittering lights on Broadway to the Model-T Ford automobiles putt-ing their way down Fifth Avenue, few cities in the world embraced invention and innovation like New York. The question most often heard from Harlem to the financial district around Wall Street was, "What will they think of next?" New Yorkers greeted each new development with awe and wonder, convinced beyond all doubt that they were the true messengers of progress.

In the spring of 1913, the attention of the entire city was riveted on the corner of Broadway and Park Row, close to New York City Hall. For months, crowds had gathered to watch the rising of the Woolworth Building, the dream of Frank W. Woolworth, the original "five-and-dime" merchant and self-made multi-millionaire. When completed, it was to eclipse every other skyscraper in the city, adding a new dimension to the already glorious Manhattan skyline.

In the early evening of April 24, President Woodrow Wilson, in an impressive display of the latest technology, threw a switch at the White House. Instantly, hundreds of miles away, a bell rang in the basement engine room of the new $13.5 million Woolworth Building as well as in the banquet hall, twenty-seven floors up, where Frank Woolworth was entertaining nine hundred guests – dignitaries, politicians, wealthy friends, and a who's who of Wall Street. At that moment, eighty thousand lights lit up the building. The sight was dazzling, like "an immense ball of fire," as one spectator recalled, "giving the effect of a gorgeous jewel resplendent in its setting of rich gold, and [visible] to mariners forty miles out to sea."

Towering sixty stories high over Manhattan, Woolworth's skyscraper, with its "Gothic-inspired architecture," was the tallest building in the world – a rank it would hold for seventeen years, until the Chrysler Building surpassed it. It was soon christened the "Cathedral of Commerce," one of the city's star attractions – especially its observation deck on the 54th floor – and a symbol of modernity. "The Woolworth Building will be New York's true fame," the Reverend S. Parkes Cadman declared at the opening ceremonies. "It does not scrape the sky; it greets it."

The erection of the Woolworth Building was, in fact, the culmination of three decades of dramatic industrial and technological change. If ever the adage that "progress is inevitable" was true, it was in New York City. First was the advent of electricity and the incandescent light bulb, the significant and enduring contribution of the brilliant inventor Thomas Alva Edison. By the end of the 1880s, the "dim flicker of gas," reported the *New York Herald*, had been replaced with the "steady glare of electric light."

Next was the Brooklyn Bridge, an engineering feat of genius, fourteen years in the making. When it was finished in 1883, the bridge spanned nearly one-third of a mile across the East River, linking Manhattan and Brooklyn. With its giant masonry towers and spiderweb of steel cables, lit up at night by seventy electric arc lamps, it was a shining gateway to the future, where the union of "electricity and steel" meant anything was possible. Thereafter, the bridge became one of the city's great icons, immortalized in books, poems, plays, and motion pictures.

Other landmarks soon followed: Madison Square Garden and the New York Public Library, along Fifth Avenue. The library, graced with impressive columns and twin marble lion statues, would have been at home in Paris. In 1904, the *New York Times* relocated to a new twenty-five-storey building on 42nd Street between Broadway and Seventh Avenue. The spot was officially known as Long Acre Square, but people soon started calling it "Times Square." Almost overnight, it became the "crossroads of the world," New York's mecca of culture and entertainment, boasting theatres with electric marquees, expensive restaurants, luxury hotels – and, for the more adventurous, high-class brothels.

On New Year's Eve 1904, to celebrate the newspaper's auspicious new home, Adolph Ochs, the *Times'* publisher, threw a party complete with midnight fireworks show. "Broadway had been waiting for the signal," the paper reported the next day. "The instant the first flash on the Times Tower showed [the new year] a great shout went up and ear-splitting blast was sounded from the horns of the myriad of merrymakers in the streets below. . . . Never was a New Year's Eve more joyously celebrated." The tradition stuck. Two years later, as thousands of New Yorkers crowded in and around Times Square to ring in 1907, Ochs installed "a large illuminated four-hundred-pound glass ball [that] lowered from the tower flagpole precisely at midnight to signal the end of one year and the beginning of the next."

The birth of Times Square as the city's central gathering place coincided with the opening of the New York Subway system. Like the Brooklyn Bridge, it ranked as another example of engineering brilliance. Owing mainly to the efforts of financier August Belmont, the city had acquired an electric-powered rapid transport system that would become a "New York institution."

Belmont (who also established New York's Belmont Park race-track) employed close to 10,000 immigrant labourers who toiled day and night for four and a half years, tunnelling and building miles of track, much of it underground. On its first day of operation, in October 1904, 150,000 New Yorkers gladly paid the nickel fare to experience this revolutionary mode of transportation. Now it was possible to travel from City Hall, in Lower Manhattan, to Harlem (still a white and isolated neighbourhood) north of Central Park – a distance of approximately eight miles – in about fifteen minutes. Nearly a million people a day soon depended on the subway to move them around in New York's worsening congestion. It was a modern convenience they could not do without.

Above it all was the New York skyline. Well before the Woolworth Building, the city had acquired a taste for ever-taller skyscrapers. "The skyline of New York is changing so rapidly," journalist Lincoln Steffens wrote in 1903, "that the American traveller who goes abroad can recognize with more certainty the profiles of foreign cities he approaches than that of his own metropolis as he sees it from the deck of the steamer on his return."

Property and office space in Lower Manhattan was at a premium – by 1910, frontage on Wall Street was selling for an astonishing twenty-five thousand dollars a foot – yet every major corporation and business wanted to be located there. Hence, as Steffens put it, "the only way out was up." Skyscrapers owed their birth to the use of steel-frame construction and the invention of the elevator (the creation of Elisha Graves Otis in 1853), combined with architectural talent and a vision of what the modern world should look like. "The skyscraper," writes historian Paul Johnson, "represented the application of science at its frontiers and imaginative intelligence in the art of building in precisely the way a great Renaissance architect like Michelangelo would have instantly appreciated."[*]

Skyscrapers may have been born in Chicago with the Home Life Insurance Building in 1884–85, but it was in New York where they transformed a city in a matter of a few decades. Beyond their architectural beauty, however, skyscrapers were "statements," expressions of a fierce and escalating rivalry involving money, ego, and "corporate glory" – a feud among the city's business tycoons and financiers. (In 1907 alone, $178 million was spent on new buildings in New York City.)

Each time a new skyscraper rose up, people asked how much higher the next one would be. Was there no limit? "It is as if some mighty force were astir beneath the ground, hour by hour," *Harper's Weekly* observed in 1902, "pushing up structures that a dozen years ago would have been inconceivable."

The Tower Building on Broadway, erected in 1889, is recognized as New York's first true skyscraper. Yet it was a mere eleven stories. The gold-domed New York World Building, the headquarters of Joseph Pulitzer's newspaper, followed, and at sixteen stories it was considered a remarkable achievement. One visitor "stepped off the elevator at the top floor and asked in a loud voice, 'Is God in?'"

The Fuller Building on 23rd Street where Broadway crosses Fifth Avenue – more commonly called the "Flatiron" because of its unique triangular design – stopped New Yorkers and visitors alike in their tracks. From the right vantage point, the building, which opened in 1902, "seemed to be nothing but a flat wall." Five years later, the Singer sewing machine company's Singer Tower rose forty-seven stories "into air above Broadway." Two years after that, in

---

[*] This fascination with reaching the clouds was given new impetus in mid-December 1903, when Orville and Wilbur Wright successfully got their flying machine off the ground at Kitty Hawk, North Carolina. It would be decades before airplanes became a part of day-to-day life, but the aviation industry was about to take off.

1909, the Metropolitan Life Insurance Company at Madison Square became the "tallest structure on earth." Until the Woolworth Building came along.

Walking the streets of New York was an experience few people could forget. "[Is] New York the most beautiful city in the world?" asked the poet and critic Ezra Pound in 1913. "It is not far from it. No urban nights are like the nights there. I have looked down across the city from high windows. It is then that the great buildings lose reality and take on magical powers. Squares and squares of flame, set and cut into the ether. Here is our poetry, for we have pulled down the stars to our will."

Physical Evils Produce Moral Evils

As magical, wondrous, and modern as the Woolworth Building and other skyscrapers were, they possessed an illusory quality. True, these mammoth structures testified to the spirit of progress that epitomized the age. But not everyone in the early decades of the twentieth century shared in the "American Dream" they seemed to promise. Not everyone lived in the manner of the great millionaire moguls of the time – William Henry Vanderbilt, Andrew Carnegie, Henry Frick, Philip Armour, and John D. Rockefeller – in palatial mansions on Fifth Avenue, luxurious apartment houses on the Upper West Side, or in country homes fit for royalty. Not everyone was able to attend plays at Broadway theatres and shop at Macy's Department Store, Lord & Taylor, Brooks Brothers, and Tiffany's.

"It's only a matter of three miles from Madison Square to Hester Street," wrote E.S. Martin in *Harper's Magazine* in 1898, "but who would dream, who had not seen it, that the same town held within so short a distance scenes and people so contrasted?" No one had to convince the social philosopher Henry George or the journalist Jacob Riis that there was a gulf between rich and poor in North America. It was one of the many by-products of capitalism: Inequality was as harsh a reality in the new world as it had been in the old. "Material progress does not merely fail to relieve poverty – it actually produces it," concluded George in 1884. "This association of progress with poverty is the great enigma of our times. It is the central fact from which spring industrial, social, and political difficulties that perplex the world."

Jacob Riis's experience was more personal. Born in Denmark in 1849, he arrived in New York City in 1870 at the age of twenty-one. After working as a carpenter and coal miner, he landed a job as a reporter with a newspaper in Brooklyn and was eventually hired by the New York *Tribune*. His talent and energy impressed his bosses, and he was soon named the *Tribune*'s police reporter, a position at which he excelled.

Accompanying the police, he gained entry into the hectic and destitute world of New York's Lower East Side and came to know well its ever-growing population of eastern and southern European immigrants – Italians, Poles, Jews, Bohemians, Galicians who joined the Irish and small number of "Negroes" already living in the neighbourhood that extended from the bottom of Manhattan north to 10th Street and east past the Bowery. Day after day, he reported on their various struggles in short, sharp stories and photographs depicting their "physical wretchedness, [and] moral and spiritual degradation."

Above all, it was the hopelessness and despair in their faces, even more than the filth and dilapidated state of their tenement homes, that Riis captured so brilliantly in his photographs and sketches of East Side residents. These powerful portrayals – of men and women toiling long hours in sweatshops; children in ragged clothes, dirty and hungry; the streets filled with peddlers hawking rags and bottles; young homeless boys or "street arabs" (as Riis called them) trying to survive by their wits; prostitutes as young as fifteen years old selling their bodies so their families could eat – moved Riis to chronicle their collective tales in his book *How the Other Half Lives* (1890), a vivid and devastating portrait of late nineteenth century

North American urban life. It was a world far removed from the modern conveniences of Fifth Avenue.

But Riis was not content to be merely a storyteller. He continually recommended ways to relieve this misery. President Theodore Roosevelt later called him "the most useful citizen of New York." Lincoln Steffens, who as a young journalist looked to "Jake" Riis for guidance, recalled that he had "hot emotions" and "worked through despair to set the wrong right."

By the mid-1880s, New York City's population was approximately 1.5 million people, and according to Riis, almost one in three was "driven, or chose, to beg for food, or to accept it in charity." In the same period, one out of every ten people who died in New York received a pauper's burial in Potter's Field. Who was to blame for this tragic state of affairs? In Riis's view, responsibility lay with civic officials and anyone else who had permitted the construction of thousands of tenement houses.

Congestion in the tenements, Riis and others argued, spread disease and was largely responsible for the crime, corruption, alcoholism, vice, immorality, and abject poverty that plagued the city. "If 'Mr. Millions' had to suffer through life in a cramped tenement apartment," editor Charles Wingate declared in 1885, he would find a bottle of whisky or rum and "solace himself with the great East Side comforter." In their report on the tenements of New York prepared in the mid-1890s, Robert DeForest and Lawrence Veiller designated the Lower East Side as "the most densely populated spot in the world."

Yet as sympathetic as Riis was to the plight of New York's poor, he was not above making critical moral judgments about them. Yes, life in the tenements was dreadful, but the people who lived in them were weak and hence partially responsible for their own predicament. That most of those living in New York's slums and elsewhere in North America after 1880 were immigrants merely reinforced this view. "Typhus fever and small-pox are bred here," Riis related, "and help solve the [population problem]. Filth diseases both, they sprout naturally among the hordes that bring the germs with them from across the sea."

Away from the slum, looking down from the observation deck of the Woolworth Building and from the confines of stately homes along Fifth Avenue, the situation appeared hopeless. (It had for some time. "Physical evils produce moral evils," the New York Association for Improving the Condition of the Poor stated in the 1840s. "Degrade men to the condition of brutes, and they will have brutal propensities and passions.")

What had gone wrong? The city, in the United States and Canada, was seen at first as a promoter of culture and the "cradle of progress," where modern engineering and marvels like electricity, streetcars, subways, telephones, and skyscrapers would enhance the quality of life. In the modern metropolis, it was possible to find the best of everything – schools, churches, newspapers, libraries, bookstores, art galleries, and theatres. Then, as had happened in London, Paris, and other European cities, industrialization, immigration, squalor, greed, exploitation, crime, and political corruption – there was, wrote historian Arthur M. Schlesinger in 1933, "a cesspool under nearly every city hall" – took their toll.[*] Only the brave or foolish ventured into New York's Chinatown or into the saloons on the Bowery and down by the waterfront, where rogues,

---

[*] New York City's Tammany Society, which controlled the local Democratic Party and civic government during the late nineteenth century, was notorious for its corruption and graft. During the reign of William "Boss" Tweed, who headed the society in the 1860s and 1870s, millions of dollars were siphoned off into the pockets of Tweed and his friends. After an investigation in 1884 into the operations of Tammany, noted Arthur Schlesinger, "three aldermen were sentenced to prison, six fled to Canada, three turned state's evidence and ten others were indicted, but not brought to trial. According to the New York *Evening Post* of April 3, 1890, the Tammany executive committee at that time consisted of twenty-seven 'professional politicians,' including: 'convicted murderer, 1; acquitted of murder, 1; convicted of felonious assault, 1; professional gamblers, 4; former dive-keepers, 5; liquor dealers, 4 . . . former pugilists, 3; former toughs, 4; members of Tweed gang, 6.'"

thieves, opium and cocaine dealers, and prostitutes ruled the streets and alleys.*

Progress had its dark side.

From the peace and serenity of the countryside, the city looked sinister, gloomy, and bleak. It was the "jungle" of novelist Upton Sinclair's landmark 1906 exposé about Chicago, where corrupt bosses and unscrupulous capitalists exploited vulnerable workers daily, and the city's famous slaughterhouses spawned unimaginable viciousness and disease. Politician and crusader William Jennings Bryan called the city "enemy territory," while automobile magnate Henry Ford maintained that "the modern city concentrates within its limits the essence of all that is wrong, artificial, wayward and unjust in our social life." In his novel *Looking Backward* (1888), Edward Bellamy likened urban society to the Black Hole of Calcutta. The "press of maddened men," he wrote, "struggle to win a place at the breathing holes." With his story set in Boston, Bellamy painted a dismal picture of its "black and fetid" streets and "half-clad brutalized children" fighting and tumbling in the garbage. In short, when it came to the city, there was nothing redeeming or positive about it.

This view was in part a reaction to the dramatic pace of North America's transformation from an essentially rural society to one dominated by cities. In 1880, only twelve million Americans, or approximately 25 per cent of a total population of about fifty million, lived in towns and cities of more than four thousand people. Yet within two decades, the urban population had more than doubled. By 1900, nearly twenty-eight million Americans, or 40 per

---

* The most daunting saloon in the city might well have been Gallus Mag's Hole in the Wall on Water Street. She was, as historians Edwin Burrows and Mike Wallace point out in their history of New York, "a ferocious six-plus-footer who held up her skirt with galluses (suspenders). In addition to her considerable abilities as a mugger, Mag ran a tight ship at the Hole in the Wall. Seizing the ear of an excessively rowdy gangster in her teeth, she would drag him to the street or bite it off altogether and add it to the collection of pickled ears she kept in a jar behind the bar."

cent of a total population of seventy million, now resided in cities.

New York City had fewer than two million people in 1880; by the turn of the century this figure had jumped to 3.5 million. Chicago was a Midwestern town of 440,000 in 1880 and a growing metropolis of 1.7 million by 1900. More disconcerting to middle-class Americans (as we shall see in Chapter One) was the fact that in both cities much of this growth was due to massive immigration.

By 1890, for example, nearly 70 per cent of Chicago's population was foreign-born, and another 10 per cent were American-born children of immigrants. As one writer noted after analyzing census data in the mid-1890s, "only two cities in the German Empire, Berlin and Hamburg, have a greater German population than Chicago; only two in Sweden, Stockholm and Göteborg, have more Swedes." British novelist and poet Rudyard Kipling, for one, was not impressed. After visiting Chicago in 1899, he wrote, "This place is the first American city I have encountered. It holds rather more than a million people with bodies, and stands on the same sort of soil as Calcutta. Having seen it, I urgently desire never to see it again. It is inhabited by savages. Its water is the water of the Hughli, and its air is dirt."

In Canada, the story was the same. Although on a smaller scale, urbanization produced similar results. Winnipeg, for instance, was a small frontier town of barely eight thousand people in 1881, yet by 1911 it had grown to a prairie metropolis of 136,000. The city's commercial elite promoted Winnipeg as the "Chicago of the North," a bustling prairie grain and transportation hub, but it also suffered the same growing pains: "Unsanitary housing, poisonous sewage, contaminated water, infant mortality at alarming rates, the spread of contagion, adulterated food, impure milk, smoke-laden air, ill-ventilated factories, dangerous occupations, juvenile crime, unwholesome crowding, prostitution, and drunkenness."

Inadequate water facilities and poor sewage systems may have been ultimately responsible for the disastrous situation in Winnipeg and other cities. However, civic leaders, social reformers, physicians, and journalists, searching for a scapegoat, blamed not just "slum conditions" – a term frequently used generically to describe the squalor, vice, and degeneration – but also those who dwelled in them. The poor, who were thought to have a choice about where and how they lived, contributed to the physical decay of the cities they inhabited and helped destroy the moral atmosphere.

"Underneath the seemingly moral surface of our national life," declared a Canadian Salvation Army journal in 1887, "there is a terrible undercurrent of unclean vice with all its concomitant evils of ruined lives, desolated hearth-stones, prostituted bodies, decimated conditions, and early dishonoured graves." For Reverend S.W. Dean, who ran a mission house in Toronto in the early 1900s, the slum was "the lurking place of disease and impaired health, the hiding place of crime, the haunt of immorality." Quoting from the Bible, he added for good measure that "men love darkness rather than light because their deeds are evil." Even someone as sensible as Dr. Charles Hastings, Toronto's medical officer, noted in a report from 1911 that the unsanitary conditions he discovered were, "a danger to public morals, and in fact, an offence against public decency." In Dr. Hastings's opinion – a view that was widely shared among the North American elite and middle-classes – "criminals and moral lepers are born in the atmosphere of physical and moral rottenness pervading the slums of large cities."

A Moral Conflict

Beginning in the latter part of the nineteenth century and for the next several decades, the city was the focal point of an often bitter debate, a moral conflict, about what the modern world would look like, who would be its leaders, and what values it would embrace. What was meant by the term "progress" and whose definition was to be used as a guide? The search for these answers continues to the present day, pitting Christian conservatives against liberals and producing sharp divisions, particularly on such moral issues as abortion, stem-cell research, and same-sex marriage. Individual choice, personal background, social and economic considerations, and the issues in question produced a variety of responses and reactions in the early decades of the twentieth century – as they still do.

Middle-class Americans and Canadians, for example, might have agreed that vice and prostitution endangered their cities, but men and women differed, sometimes sharply, on the precise role women should play in remedying this situation. Would society be better off if women were given the vote and a small degree of political power? Even women themselves were uncertain. Were labour unions morally destructive and dangerous? Was the prohibition of alcohol a requirement towards the building of a morally superior quality of life? Was the admission of immigrants who were unable to speak English threatening the purity of western society? Did the automobile, despite its convenience, lower community standards by allowing young people a new-found freedom? Was censorship an affront to liberty or an absolute necessity in protecting children from the evils of literature, art, and film?

Politicians, reformers, religious officials, writers, lawyers, and businessmen wrestled with and fought over these questions, and no more so than in the period from the late 1890s to the early 1930s. In North America, it was the era of the progressives, social gospel, muckrakers, and suffragettes. There were the bloody battles of the First World War, the rise of the anarchists and Communists, who unleashed general strikes and challenged the existing order. And, for fun and entertainment, people enjoyed the Model-T and silent movies, while flappers danced the Charleston.

In the middle of these events and movements was an array of personalities, traditionalists as well as progressives, the powerful and the powerless, who, for better or worse, shaped the contours of and gave birth to modern society. Among them were Emma Goldman, a Jewish immigrant and a radical who was deemed the "most dangerous woman in America," and who believed in "free love" in an age of sexual repression; Nellie McClung, a prairie farm girl from Manitoba who became a devoted temperance advocate and led women's struggle for the vote; William Jennings Bryan, a three-time losing candidate for the American presidency, a superb orator whose legion of supporters dubbed him the "Great Commoner," and who stood in a Tennessee courtroom in 1925 to condemn Charles Darwin's theory of evolution as blasphemy; Henry Ford, whose automobile initiated a transportation revolution and altered forever the lives of millions of people, yet who also waged a vicious campaign against Jews, who he claimed were trying to take over the world; Al Capone, the flamboyant and bombastic son of Italian immigrants, who established one of the most notorious crime syndicates in U.S. history, and who owing to the numerous loopholes in Prohibition laws raked in millions of dollars; Margaret Sanger, who, even when faced with the prospect of going to jail, refused to give up her fight to legalize birth control; Daniel A. Lord, a Jesuit priest who grasped the enormous impact Hollywood films would have on North American cultural values and attempted to control their influence; and finally, Jane Addams, who dedicated her life to helping the poor and needy, and who argued when it was highly unpopular to do so that the European immigrants had cultures worth preserving in the New World.

It is their controversial stories along with those of many others that are the main focus of this book. Always, however, these personal experiences are set against the heated morality debate about society's future – including the impact of immigration, the role of women, the conflict between science and religion, the place of radicalism in a democracy, and the changing attitudes about sex – that preoccupied, and even consumed, North Americans of all classes and creeds during the early decades of the twentieth century.

This book, for the most part, takes a North American perspective. Canadians, in particular, have gone to great lengths over the years to point out the many differences between themselves and their American neighbours. Today, Canadians can boast about the superiority of their (generally workable) health-care system and a foreign policy that seeks compromise over war. They can claim, too, and with a certain justification, to have created a more tolerant and less violent society. Yet, linked closely by geography and connected through the enormous power of the media and Internet, Canadians and Americans share many of the same cultural values. Perhaps it has always been so.

In the late nineteenth and early twentieth centuries, Canadian politicians, academics, businessmen, and others viewed themselves as a bastion of Anglo civilization, an integral part of the British Empire proudly upholding the mother country's high standards of morality. At the same time, the issues and problems confronting Canadians in their cities were often identical to those experienced by Americans a decade or so earlier. For that reason, Canadians, sometimes hoping to avoid the same mistakes, studied American solutions, read the works of American experts, and looked to the United States for advice and direction. It goes without saying that each country, influenced by and reacting to local conditions and factors, did not always respond in the same way. In general, when it came to conflicts over morality, values, and the expectations for the modern world, and whether it was about immigrants, political radicalism, or the decline of religion, Americans tended to be more extreme, dogmatic, puritanical, and, on many occasions, violent. "The central paradox of American history," U.S. historian Lawrence Levine has commented, "has been a belief in progress coupled with the dread of change." The same might be said of Canada.

The Devil in Babylon

The reformers who first tackled the apparently insurmountable social and economic problems posed by life in the cities were motivated by a profound sense of urgency and fear about the moral degradation they believed was threatening their world. But like most liberal-minded (and many conservative) individuals of the era – most notably the middle-class politicians, the so-called progressives, who gave the period its name and who successfully campaigned for reform legislation to protect ordinary Americans against the abuses of monopolies, trusts, and government corruption – they accepted that progress was both natural and positive. The challenge facing them was to "reconcile a belief in eternal moral truth with the belief in the desirability of change."

In the years after 1880, their immediate task was to transform the city from the "Babylon" it had become, a place of sin and temptation, into a "New Jerusalem," where life was pure and righteous. Or, put slightly more eloquently by Reverend W.T. Gunn, a Canadian Methodist leader, "every city has been a Babylon, and every city has been a New Jerusalem; and it has always been a question whether the Babylon would extirpate the New Jerusalem, or the New Jerusalem would extirpate the Babylon." Few orators and writers of the era spoke as passionately about this apparently dire state of affairs as did John Roach Straton. He was certain of whom his enemies were: big business, jazz music, Hollywood films, liquor, Darwinism, and knee-length skirts for women. "We are now witnessing the wildest wave of immorality in the history of the human race," he declared in 1920.

Born in Evansville, Indiana, in 1875, Straton became known far and wide as the "Fundamentalist Pope." While he typically sanctified rural life as sacred and city life as "godless," he opted to live alongside "the devil," as he put it.

He reached the height of his fame in the twenties, at the Calvary Baptist Church in New York, where his weekly sermons frequently attracted crowds of 2,500 people. And although he castigated the evils of the modern world, he effectively used the radio – a very new form of technology – to broadcast his fundamentalist dogma. As the

New Republic magazine observed in his obituary in 1929, "in spirit [Straton] was a Baptist of the old school . . . in technique, he was a New Yorker of the twentieth century."

His Biblical-style message nevertheless remained constant: The survival of western civilization depended on the reform of the city. It was a theme he elaborated on in his last book, *Fighting the Devil in Modern Babylon*, published in the year of his death. He bemoaned the greed of consumer culture, the changing relationship between men and women, and the pursuit of pleasure for its own sake. New York was the "modern Babylon" – teeming with foreigners, dance halls, movie theatres, and other "diabolical influences." "We must either Americanize and Christianize New York," he wrote, "or New York will speedily Europeanize and paganize us!"

Straton and others like him aimed ultimately to purify the city and create a "homogeneous" middle-class culture. As historian Alison Parker emphasizes, this "was to be a culture that all Americans could share, a culture that reinforced and valorized a particular Protestant-based morality that privileged purity, social responsibility, and piety. It had to be accessible to average people, not just to elites or to the lower classes."

At the dawn of the twentieth century, one of the chief obstacles to attaining this lofty goal was the presence in the cities of thousands of foreigners, strangers and aliens lurking in urban ghettos, who appeared to pose a grave moral threat. At risk, so the reformers argued, was the very future of western civilization.

CHAPTER ONE

Strangers and Reformers

Previous page: Immigrants arriving in New York on the S.S. *Patricia* in 1902.

Out of the remote and little known region of northern, eastern, and southern Europe forever marches a vast and endless army. Nondescript and ever changing in personnel, without leaders or organization, this great force, moving at the rate of nearly 1,500,000 each year, is invading the civilized world.

– James D. Whelpley,
The Problem of the Immigrant, 1905

The Promised Land

They came wave after wave. The London writer James D. Whelpley called it in 1905 "a mighty stream," "a vast procession of varied humanity . . . gaining in volume and momentum with each passing year." Among the multitude were Nykola Humeniuk, from the Galician village of Ghermakivka, who relocated with his wife, Anastasia, and their two small children to farm at a homestead in Manitoba in 1897; eight-year-old Joseph Wilder, who with his family in 1904 left Ploeşti, a town in Rumania, for a new life in Winnipeg on the Canadian prairies; Tessie Riegleman, a twelve-year-old from Barafka, near Odessa, Russia, who with her parents found a new home in New York's Lower East Side in 1905; and in 1921 Peter Mossini, aged twenty-one years, who made the journey alone from his village of Santa Teresa di Riva in southern Italy in search of work in the coal mines of Pennsylvania.

Like millions more, they and their families were pushed out of their homelands by a shortage of land, lack of employment, the mechanization of labour, and religious persecution – and pulled by economic opportunity, rich available farmland, a hope of liberty, and the myth of America as the "Promised Land." They boarded steamships in Hamburg, Bremen, and Liverpool and headed across the Atlantic, or departed from Hong Kong and Macao via the Pacific. Between 1870 and 1914, more than 29.5 million immigrants (or more accurately, migrants) arrived in the United States and another 4.6 million in Canada. In the fifty-year period from 1870 to 1920, the total populations of each country increased by more than 200 per cent – the United States from 40 million to 106 million and Canada from 4 million to 9 million. Among this multitude were: 7.9 million Britons, 7.3 million Italians, 2.8 million Germans, and 2 million East European Jews.

The newcomers had an enormous impact on North American society and were themselves transformed by the immigration experience. While many opted to toil as pioneer farmers in the American and Canadian frontiers, many, too, gravitated towards the cities and almost overnight altered the urban landscape.

In the short term, this massive influx of people led to many of the problems of the cities. But the immigrants also brought with them a diverse "cultural baggage." This included different, even radical, ideas about labour and the role of the working class, nationalism, religion, women's rights, and morality, all of which soon challenged the accepted and cherished beliefs and values of the ruling classes. If this was what the modern world was to be, then some Americans and Canadians wanted no part of it.

Most immigrants wanted nothing more at first than to survive. They worked hard and struggled to build a better life not merely for themselves, but also for their children and grandchildren. They had a hunger for education and success that ultimately was passed on to each succeeding generation. In *The Promised City*, his superb 1962 study of Jewish immigrant life in New York in the early years of the twentieth century, Moses Rischin observed that the "quest for community" by the East European Jews of the Lower East Side "made them builders of a city that itself was striding toward new urban dimensions." The same might be said of other immigrant groups as well.

Suddenly, neighbourhoods of Jews, Italians, Greeks, and Chinese sprang up in New York, Chicago, Philadelphia, San Francisco, Toronto, and Montreal, creating a cultural, religious, and ethnic dynamic whose ramifications are still evident today. Whether the citizens of these and other cities were prepared, the modern world in North America was not going to be white, Protestant, and Anglo-Saxon.

Hamilton Wright Mabie, an American writer and critic who lived in New York, understood this trend more than most. "This great city of ours, with its diversities of race, of religion, of social and political and personal ideals – has a unity which the country has as yet failed to recognize, a genius which belongs to the future rather than to the past," he wrote in 1904. "We forget that New York is not only one of the first cities of modern birth . . . but also a city of a new type. Its very diversities are creating here a kind of city which men have not seen before; in which a unity of a more inclusive . . . [o]rder is slowly forming itself; a city . . . which has the light of prophecy in it."

Above all, the immigrants sought acceptance. They learned to speak English, changed their dress and dietary habits, and tailored their religious practices to the faster pace of the New World. Still, despite the overwhelming pressure to conform, this adaptation and assimilation was in the end on the immigrants' terms – a lengthy and often emotionally charged process that produced debate, conflict, anger, and at times a virulent hatred.

The Jews who arrived originated for the most part in the Russian Pale of Settlement (roughly present-day western Russia, Belarus, eastern Poland, and Lithuania), where they had been victims of brutal pogroms and repressive laws following the assassination of Czar Alexander II in March 1881. They arrived in the New

World with their families and intended to stay to rebuild their lives. So, too, did skilled tradesmen from Britain and Scotland, and Ukrainians, Poles, and Galician peasants from Russia and the Austro-Hungarian Empire. For others, mainly men – Italians from Calabria and Sicily, Chinese from Kwangtung province, and Japanese workers toiling in Honolulu, Hawaii – their voyage to North America was intended to be a temporary sojourn. By taking on back-breaking work in mines, laying track for railways, or building roads out of the muck and mud in the cities, they planned to earn enough money to return to the old country, provide for their wives and children, perhaps even live in style. (From 1890 to 1920, the return rate was approximately 30 to 50 per cent for some groups.)

Facilitating this mass movement of humanity was a fleet of relatively safe steamships, with third-class steerage tickets to North American ports costing twenty to twenty-five dollars – affordable to most peasant farmers or lower middle-class European tradesmen and unskilled labourers. Aiding the steamship companies were thousands of agents and subagents, labour recruiters like Italian *padroni*,[*] and a remarkable chain migration system in which the strong links between relatives and friends attracted one family after another so that in some cases entire towns from the Old World were transplanted to the new one.

The letters back home promised streets paved with gold. "America was in everybody's mouth," remembered Mary Antin,

---

[*] In the late nineteenth century, *padrone* was initially the name given to labour bosses in Italy who recruited indentured children, mainly to work as street musicians. As a consequence, according to historian John Zucchi, "hundreds of 'Italian slave children' inhabited the Little Italies of Europe and America, in places such as Five Points, New York, Saffron Hill, London, the Panthéon in Paris. One tenement on Crosby Street in Manhattan was reputed to have put up close to 100 children in 1873. Eighteen *padroni* and 100 children lived in another building near Place Maubert in Paris. After playing their instruments and begging in the streets, the little slaves would hand over their day's earnings to the *padrone* and share their room with their young colleagues, monkeys and instruments."

about her childhood in a Russian Jewish shtetl. "Businessmen talked of it over their accounts; the market women made up their quarrels that they might discuss it from stall to stall . . . all talked of it, but scarcely anybody knew one true fact about this magic land." In small Italian villages, peasants watched with awe the young men, the *americani*, who returned for a visit but were now dressed in fine clothes and patent leather shoes. "People used to jump at the mention of an *americano*," recalled one woman from the southern town of Rende in Calabria. "It was like Christ himself was coming home."

Getting to and surviving in the Promised Land was, in fact, a far less wondrous experience. Travelling to North America during the early 1900s was a miserable experience. There were hucksters and corrupt and abusive government agents at every port waiting to fleece the newcomers before they boarded the ships. More were waiting when they arrived on the other side. Seemingly friendly *landsmann* and *paesano* who welcomed the weary travellers with offers of places to live and jobs at the docks in New York or Halifax were more often than not rogues in the employ of unscrupulous labour bosses and hotel owners.

Once they left the ships, they were herded like cattle and interrogated by immigration and medical inspectors on the lookout for physical or mental defects and illnesses, which meant quarantine or deportation back to Europe. Abraham Cahan, the pre-eminent Yiddish journalist of his day, who arrived in New York in 1882, compared them to Cossacks.

On many occasions, there was tremendous disappointment. In January 1910, Stanislaus Bialeski, who had emigrated to the United States by himself from Hungary and settled in Brooklyn, stood weeping on the harbour pier as he watched his wife and two young children, who had recently arrived, being sent back to Europe aboard the steamer *President Lincoln*. A few days earlier, the children had been quarantined with a contagious scalp disease and medical officers had then ordered their deportation. No amount of pleading by Bialeski made the least bit of difference. There is no record to show they were ever reunited.

In the great hall at Ellis Island, in the shadow of the Statue of Liberty, officials used chalk to mark the immigrants who required further checking by physicians: the letter *H* denoted a heart problem, *K* was for hernia, *Sc* for scalp, and *X* for suspected mental problems. The new arrivals faced a barrage of questions about the amount of money they carried and whether a job awaited them. An 1885 law prohibited importation of contract labour, so even if they had guaranteed employment it was often better to lie. It usually took an entire day to get through the ordeal on Ellis Island, assuming you had no serious health problems.

From there the newcomers went in search of shelter and work. If they wanted to remain in a city, and thousands did, they could find a room in the burgeoning foreign quarters that had taken root in New York's Lower East Side, Chicago's West Side, Toronto's St. John's Ward, and Winnipeg's North End, among many others. These ramshackle neighbourhoods contained not only affordable housing in tenements and wood shanties, but also friends and family from the old country who spoke the same language, shops and stores where the newcomers could buy familiar food on credit, churches, synagogues, and social clubs, and plenty of labour opportunities in garment factories, sweatshops, or road gangs. Whether it was Hester Street in New York, Maxwell Street in Chicago, or Selkirk Avenue in Winnipeg, these were the locales where the vibrancy as well as misery of immigrant life unfolded.

In his novel *The Rise of David Levinsky* (1917), Abraham Cahan described his first experience in the Lower East Side (or "Jewish East Side") like this: "The streets swarmed with Yiddish-speaking immigrants. The signboards were in English and Yiddish, some of them in Russian. The scurry and hustle of the people were not merely overwhelmingly greater, both in volume and intensity, than in my native town. It was of another sort. The swing and step of the pedestrians, the voices and manner of the street peddlers, and a hundred and one other things seemed to testify to far more self-confidence and energy, to larger ambitions and wider scopes than did the appearance of the crowds in my birthplace."

The outsider's perception was far more negative. "Little idea can be given of the filthy and rotten tenements, the dingy courts and tumble-down sheds, the foul stables and dilapidated outhouses, the broken sewer pipes, the piles of garbage fairly alive with diseased odors, and of the number of children filling every nook, working and playing in every room," observed Agnes Holbrook, a Chicago social worker. "Fruit-stands help to fill up the sordid streets, and ice-cream carts drive a thriving trade. One hears little English spoken, and the faces and manners met with are very foreign." Add to this the dire outcomes of poverty and destitution already listed – a proliferation of brothels, prostitutes on the street, vagabonds, pickpockets, drunkenness, opium dens, distraught women whose husbands had deserted them, dishevelled and dirty children playing in the streets – and it is easy to understand why reformers and local officials believed their cities and civilization itself were under attack.

Ridding the cities of prostitution, "the social evil," was one of the first orders of business. Prostitution was (and is) a highly visible trade. Negotiations took place on the streets, and liaisons were conducted in parks and other public places. Married men who partook in this sinful activity risked contracting syphilis and infecting their "pure" wives. Eliminating it, however, proved difficult, if not impossible. "Prostitution always has been, is everywhere, and always will be," the adage of the times went. Still, the reformers and police (some of them, at any rate) were vigilant in their efforts to stamp it out, or at the very least to segregate and control it.

North American cities were no different from Paris or London – where by the 1850s, there were upwards of fifty thousand prostitutes in each city – so that in many neighbourhoods, along with churches, schools, and banks, there were also brothels. In New York, brothels were everywhere, and after 1880 especially in the Lower East Side, where "prostitutes, pimps, and madams plied their trade." Novelist Michael Gold, who grew up in the East Side, remembered that "on sunshiny days the whores sat on chairs along the sidewalks. They sprawled indolently, their legs taking up half the pavements. . . . The girls gossiped and chirped like a jungle of parrots. Some knitted shawls and stockings. Others hummed. Others chewed Russian sunflower seeds and monotonously spat out the shells." The women helped earn New York its reputation as "the wickedest city in the country."

In the early 1890s, Reverend Charles Parkhurst, the pastor of the Madison Square Presbyterian Church and president of the Society for the Prevention of Crime, emerged as the city's most vocal opponent of prostitution and condemned the police and Tammany Hall officials (the powerful Democratic municipal administration) for accepting payment in exchange for looking the other way. One madam later claimed at hearings held to investigate the corruption that she was forced to pay thirty thousand dollars annually to the police to remain in business.

Parkhurst, described by journalist and pioneering muckraker Lincoln Steffens as "tall, slim, quiet, determined, fearless and humorous," was a brilliant orator. In sermon after sermon, he demonstrated the links between graft and the police. New York, he declared, was "rotten with a rottenness which is unspeakable and indescribable."

To prove his point, one evening, wearing a disguise and soaping his hair to make himself look like a tough, he visited a saloon near the East River, an opium den in Chinatown, and several brothels, including "Nigger" Johnson's coloured dance house, where it was permissible for whites and blacks to dance together. At one of the fancier establishments he was entertained by a group of women cavorting naked in what he called "a sort of gymnastic performance." At another, a scantily clad nineteen-year-old girl asked him, "Hey, whiskers, going to ball me off?" He took it all in stride. In

1894, owing largely to Parkhurst's diligence, the New York State Legislature launched an investigation, chaired by Senator Charles Lexow, which exposed police bribery, brutality, and corruption and eventually broke Tammany's hold on the city's government.

Further north in Montreal, where, as in Paris, the Quebec authorities were slightly more tolerant, several thousand women worked a red-light district in the area south of the Ste. Catherine Street business district. In 1917, a group of concerned citizens formed the Committee of Sixteen, and with the assistance of Catholic Church officials waged a war for the "suppression, prevention and if possible the final extermination of commercialized vice." In the end, they succeeded in having just one corrupt police chief fired and several brothels closed down.

In Winnipeg, the city's chief of police, "Big" John McRae, decided that he would never permanently solve the prostitution problem and concluded that segregation was the answer. "There is no city I know which is free from it," he later testified at a provincial Royal Commission on vice. "It is like the poor, evil is always with us." In 1909, he sent for Minnie Woods, the head madam in the city, affectionately known as "Queen of the Harlots," and after lengthy negotiations it was decided that the new red-light district would be on two streets in the north-end, working-class neighbourhood of Point Douglas. Neither the chief nor Woods bothered to ask the residents in the area what they thought about this idea. Within days, a real-estate agent named John Beaman, apparently on a tip from Chief McRae, bought up many of the inexpensive houses on these two streets. He then proceeded to sell them back to Woods and her friends for an enormous seventy-thousand-dollar profit.

While Minnie Woods managed to stay in business well into the 1930s, Winnipeg's more upstanding citizens were hardly impressed by McRae's initiative or the poor publicity the city received because of it. Winnipeg was soon labelled "the wickedest city in the Dominion."

In the view of many moral reformers, vice was not acceptable under any circumstances. Adding to the sense of urgency was a panic about the white slave trade. Sordid tales, most of which were false, circulated from city to city about the abduction of innocent young white girls who were forced into prostitution in Chicago and as far away as South Africa and Argentina. The Canadian federal government issued a warning to girls not "to loiter in public places, and remember that there are women as well as men in strange cities, or travelling by train, who are watching for chances to decoy the innocent."

The truth of the matter was, as journalist George Kibbe Turner had earlier discovered in a 1907 investigation of Chicago's prostitution problems published in *McClure's Magazine*, that most women who chose to work in brothels did so out of desperation and poverty. Many were indeed destitute immigrant girls with few other options. Once involved in the trade, some became alcoholics or addicted to cocaine or morphine, cutting their wretched lives short. In any event, starting in 1910, many cities across the United States convened vice commissions and official inquiries, which eventually led to the shutting down of several red-light districts.[*] None of these efforts, of course, halted the sex trade; they merely drove it underground, out of the sight of the police, moral reformers, and other upstanding citizens. No matter, for many reformers the link between vice, prostitution, filth, poverty, and foreign immigrants was indisputable.

---

[*] This included San Francisco's infamous Barbary Coast area (now known as the Jackson Square Historic District). Established in the 1850s to meet the "needs" of gold miners flocking to San Francisco, it was home to more than eighty brothels and one thousand prostitutes. Few sexual services could not be purchased in the Barbary Coast. There were three classes of brothel, "the crib, cowyard and high-end parlour house." In the early years, the inexpensive prostitutes worked in small cubicles or "cribs." For ten cents, customers could fondle one breast of the women dancing near the entrance, two breasts cost fifteen cents, and twenty-five cents gained you admission. The "cowyard" was a larger building with hundreds of cubicles. The women rented cubicles for five dollars a day in order to conduct their business. Customers were also able to pay ten cents to watch the activities.

This was a point not lost on the Chicago social reformer Robert Hunter, who observed that it was a "peculiar fact" that nearly all of the poor in many of the great American cities were foreign-born. "To live in one of these foreign communities," he added, "is actually to live on foreign soil. The thoughts, feelings, and traditions which belong to the mental life of the colony are often entirely alien to an American."

A Laxity of Morals

"Give me your tired, your poor. / Your huddled masses yearning to breathe free," Emma Lazarus, a New York Sephardi Jew had written in 1883 in her poem "The New Colossus." So powerful was this image of America as a refuge for the world's downtrodden that in 1903 Lazarus's words were engraved at the base of the Statue of Liberty. (She had died of cancer at thirty-eight years old in 1887.) Indeed, both the United States and Canada offered freedom and opportunity, opening their doors wide not only to "desirable" immigrants from northern and western Europe – many of whom spoke English and shared Anglo-Saxon Protestant values – but also to "undesirable" and "unassimilable" immigrants from southern and eastern Europe, and, even more disconcerting, from Asia and China. Detested most of all, the Chinese, depicted for decades as the "Yellow Peril," faced severe immigration restrictions and head taxes. African-American immigrants were viewed in a similar negative light in Canada.[*]

---

[*] In 1897, Clifford Sifton became the Canadian federal minister of the Interior responsible for immigration. Out of a desire to fill up the Prairies with farmers, he actively pursued immigrants in every corner of Europe. He later described his ideal immigrant, one who would farm the land, rather than live in the city, as follows: "When I speak of quality I have in mind, I think, something that is quite different from what is in the mind of the average writer or speaker upon the question of immigration. I think a stalwart peasant in a sheep-skin coat, born on the soil, whose

From an economic perspective, the importation of thousands of unskilled labourers and industrious peasant farmers seemed to make good sense as a way to provide a ready workforce for factories and people to fill up the western frontier. Yet looking at the period from 1880 to 1930 as a whole, the general assessment was not positive. In the eyes of many politicians, church leaders, reformers, academics, and journalists, these undesirable newcomers were primitive, unciv- ilized, dirty, immoral, and degenerate, and in the case of Jews and some Asians not even Christian. "Foreign trash," "heathens," "vermin," and "foreign scum" – were just a few of the names used in speeches, government documents, and newspaper and magazine articles. "Many of our non-Anglosaxon [sic] population are amongst the best of the people from their native lands," noted a 1915 report from the Canadian Methodist Department of Temperance and Moral Reform. "It is lamentable that such large numbers have come to Canada during the last decade bringing a laxity of morals, an ignorance, a superstition and an absence of high ideals of personal character or of national life. . . . [They] may constitute a danger to themselves and a menace to our national life." Speaking in the House of Commons in early 1914, E.N. Lewis, a member of Parliament from Ontario, was more succinct: "We do not want a nation of organ-grinders and banana sellers in this country."

Much of this animosity (as will be discussed in more detail in Chapter Three) was based on popular notions of Anglo-Saxon racial superiority. From the mid-nineteenth century onward, mass immi- gration was linked with introducing impurities into the racial

---

forefathers have been farmers for ten generations, with a stout wife and a half-dozen children, is good quality. A Trades Union artisan who will not work more than eight hours a day and will not work that long if he can help it, will not work on a farm at all and has to be fed by the public when his work is slack is, in my judgement, quantity and very bad quantity. I am indifferent as to whether or not he is British-born. It matters not what his nationality is; such men are not wanted in Canada, and the more of them we get the more trouble we shall have."

makeup of North America. "Thousands [of immigrants] are being imported annually of Russians, Finns, Italians, Hungarians, Belgians, Scandinavians, etc.," wrote Charles Hastings. "The lives and environments of a large number of these have, no doubt, been such as is well calculated to breed degenerates. Who would think of comparing for a moment, in the interests of our country, mentally, morally, physically or commercially, a thousand of these foreigners with a thousand of Canadian birth?"

Clearly, mixing races was dangerous and stereotypes were commonly accepted among the most liberal-minded Canadians or Americans. Jews were dishonest and greedy – "With his clear brain sharpened in the American school, the egotistic, conscienceless young Jew constitutes a menace," stated respected U.S. sociologist Edward Alsworth Ross in 1914 – Galicians were prone to violence; Italians were idle or involved with organized criminal gangs like the Black Hand or the Mafia; the "heathen" Chinese were dirty, corrupt, and guilty of luring white women into slavery and opium dens; and African-American men were sexual predators. Reverend Samuel D. Chown, the General Superintendent of the Methodist Church in Canada, expressed a typical reaction. "The immigration question is the most vital one in Canada today, as it has to do with the purity of our national life-blood," he wrote in 1910. "It is foolish to dribble away the vitality of our country in a vain endeavour to assimilate the world's non-adjustable, profligate, and indolent social parasites. . . . It is most vital to our nation's life that we should ever remember that quality is of greater value than quantity and that character lies at the basis of national stability and progress." No one who heard Chown's speech, as historian Mariana Valverde points out, could fail to identify which "parasites" the reverend was referring to. He meant immigrants who were Jewish, Chinese, and black.

Immigration for many was nothing less than an "alien invasion" that foretold the future demise of the majority. The integration of such a vast number of people into North American society, especially from southern and eastern Europe, was almost impossible to contemplate. Even more alarming was the myth, accepted as fact, that these impoverished immigrants from Russia and Italy were having children at a faster rate than native-born Americans and Canadians. How could the Anglo-Saxon race possibly survive, innumerable scholars and writers wondered?

"We are overwhelmed, submerged and almost drowned out by a great flood-tide of European riff-raff, the refuse of almost every nation on the continent, paupers, criminals, beggars and the muddy residuum of foreign civilizations," stated the editor of the *New York Herald* early in the 1900s. "The sooner we take a decided stand and shut down the gates the better." The United States eventually did that, in 1924; while Canada kept its doors open slightly wider, but imposed more restrictions during the twenties. Earlier, the *Calgary Herald* had echoed the same view. "This policy of building a nation on the lines of the Tower of Babel, where the Lord confounded the language so that the people might not understand one another's speech," one editorial declared, "is hardly applicable to the present century."

Not surprisingly, these attitudes led to many instances of violence. One of the worst occurred in New Orleans in 1891, when nine Italians, who had been implicated in the shooting of a police official, were lynched and shot. All the men were innocent. The leader of the mob who killed them, William Parkerson, proudly told a reporter that he had done a public service. No legal action was taken against him or anyone else involved in the incident.

America Does Not Consist of Groups

In such an environment, often marked by prejudice, discrimination, and hatred, was it possible to transform the newcomers into acceptable North Americans? The Anglo-Jewish writer Israel Zangwill thought so. In early October 1908, his play *The Melting Pot* opened in the Columbia Theater in Washington, D.C., and a year later at a Broadway theatre in New York.

The dramatic production told the story of a Russian-Jewish family adapting to life in New York and the relationship between their young son, David, and his Christian lover, Vera. The play's critical moment was when David expressed his vision for the future of the United States and the emergence of a new race of people. "Now understand that America is God's crucible, the great Melting Pot, where all races of Europe are melting and reforming," he declaimed. "Celt and Latin, Slave and Teuton, Greek and Syrian, black and yellow, Jew and Gentile. . . . How the great Alchemist melts and fuses them with his purging flame! . . . Here shall they all unite to build the Republic of Man and the Kingdom of God. Peace, peace unto ye unborn millions fated to fill this giant continent – the God of our children give you peace." The play had a lengthy run in both cities, yet many of the critics were not enthusiastic. It was too "idyllic," some said, and certainly too "utopian." (The Jewish community was not pleased that the play predicted the eventual "melting" away of Jewish religion and culture.)

When it came down to it, however, most Americans and Canadians demanded that the newcomers conform and assimilate. Notions of multicultural tolerance had a few advocates – like social worker Jane Addams and U.S. philosopher Horace Kallen, who in 1924 coined the term "cultural pluralism," in which there was "unity in diversity" – but until well after the Second World War such sentiments were drowned out. The chief goal was "Americanization" and "Canadianization," and the message given to the immigrants was the same: Submit and accept an Anglo-Saxon culture and Protestant value system, or leave. "America does not consist of groups," President Woodrow Wilson said simply in 1915. "A man who thinks of himself as belonging to a particular national group in America has not yet become an American."[*]

For the immigrants, it was a no-win situation. Almost immediately, the very ability of groups such as the Jews, Chinese, and Italians to assimilate was questioned. And if they did assimilate, embracing – in the language of sociologists – the culture and identity of the "host society," they were confronted with prejudice and discrimination that kept them at a distance. In a study done in the late twenties, U.S. sociologist Emory Bogardus found that the vast majority of the American-born, middle-class sample he polled did not want Italians, for example, to marry their children or siblings. Only slightly more than 25 per cent would have them as members in their clubs or as their "personal chums." And 65 per cent did not want them as neighbours, although most did believe they should be eligible for U.S. citizenship. Other groups from southern and eastern Europe and Asia "were viewed less favourably."

As for Jews, institutional and social anti-Semitism was for decades the norm. Universities, clubs, beach resorts, and professional organizations restricted their admission. It was next to impossible before 1940, for instance, for a Jew to become an engineer or be appointed to many university faculties.

Affected as well were German-Jewish immigrants who had arrived prior to 1881 and had worked diligently to transform themselves into "Israelites," different from their fellow Christian Americans only in their religion. But this did not make them any more welcome in

---

* As historian Salvatore Mondello points out, "Writing for the *American Journal of Sociology* in 1905, G.E. DiPalma Castiglione, the manager of the U.S. Labor Information Office, supported by the Society for Italian Immigrants, asserted that the abysmal life of the Italians in the cities produced 'a reciprocal psychological state of mind' which was 'a powerful obstacle in the way of assimilation.' He pointed out that the cost of living was high in the cities, while salaries were low. This compelled the Italian migrants to make 'large material sacrifices,' which endangered their health and debased them 'socially.'"

Gentile society. On the contrary, the more they tried to exchange their "Jewishness" for an American identity and outlook, the greater the resistance from the Gentile elite. The Jewish answer eventually was to build their own resorts in such places as the Catskills and organize their own fraternal societies and social clubs.

The greatest antagonism was reserved for the migrants and sojourners who visited North America merely to make money and then depart. They were condemned for making no effort to learn the English language or local customs. Their refusal to assimilate (which in any event was difficult) was considered offensive. According to the report of the 1911 United States Immigration Commission chaired by Senator William Dillingham, they took American money "for the subsequent consumption of 'porridge, bloaters, macaroni and sauerkraut' on the other side of the Atlantic."

The 1902 Canadian Royal Commission on Chinese and Japanese Immigration was equally critical of the large number of Chinese in British Columbia, whose presence, whether temporary or not, was deemed dangerous. "They form, on their arrival," the commissioners wrote, "a community within a community, separate and apart, a foreign substance within, but not of our body politic, with no love for our laws and institutions; a people that will not assimilate or become an integral part of our race and nation. With their habits of overcrowding, and utter disregard of all sanitary laws, they are a continual menace to health. From a moral and social point of view, living as they do without home life, schools or churches, and so nearly approaching a servile class, their effect upon the rest of the community is bad." A year later, the head tax on Chinese immigrants was raised from the one hundred dollars set in 1900 (it had originally been fifty dollars, in 1885) to five hundred dollars.

If the future moral well-being of Canada and the United States indeed depended on assimilating its immigrants, then those responsible for this task had a key role to play. This significant duty was assumed by

a small army of church leaders, philanthropists, public-school teachers, librarians, doctors, nurses, social workers, community advocates,
and politicians. Their goal, in theory at least, was not simply to impart
Puritanism in a negative sense or teach immigrant children to speak
English, but more importantly to "raise the moral tone" of North
American urban life. This meant shaping immigrants' character and
values: teaching them respect for law and order and having them
embrace "thrift, punctuality, and hygiene." As one Toronto public-
school teacher put it, "Canadians are 'tidy, neat and sincere' –
foreigners are not." In short, it was about the newcomers learning and
adopting proper behaviour and submissiveness in a capitalist society.

There were many ways to accomplish this objective. Canadian
teachers routinely rewarded their foreign students for speaking
English and punished them for using their native languages.
Education was seen "not just as the process of learning but, perhaps
more importantly, as the process of becoming," explain historians
Robert Harney and Harold Troper. "Under [the teachers'] watchful
eye children were marked for transformation from foreigners into
useful young Canadians." This included teaching the children
North American ideas of cleanliness and, for girls, how to sew and
cook. Such attitudes pushed provincial politicians in Canada to
establish compulsory school laws in the first decade of the twentieth
century and to speak out against private ethnic or religious schools
as an impediment to assimilation.

In Manitoba, for instance, a federal-provincial compromise from
1897 had allowed publicly funded schools in which immigrant
languages could be used as the language of instruction. In an investigation conducted in 1907, John W. Dafoe, the respected editor of
the *Manitoba Free Press*, was shocked to discover that "some thirteen
different languages" were being used in the provincial schools in this
manner. Several years later, in the *Winnipeg Tribune*, a Ukrainian
teachers' association and its journal were declared to be "subversive
and destructive of Canadian citizenship and nationality."

These "alien" youngsters, particularly boys who would one day be able to vote, also required "pure" books to read, argued the members of the American Library Association in 1900. "It is for the boy . . . the child of foreign parents, who, in the first blush of patriotism, inspired by the sight of the school flag, comes to the library for a United States history, that we want books, the right kind of wholesome, joyous books, that shall bring sweetness and light into their lives, and ideals of virtue and civic morality to their minds." To the librarians, it only made sense that "patriotism, love of truth and beauty are best cultivated by the reading of good literature."

In other instances, the reformers' tone and message were more negative. Toronto Presbyterian minister Reverend John G. Shearer was as serious and sober an individual as any. "Shearer comes closer than any other figure," writes Mariana Valverde, "to the stereotype of the moral reformer keen on prohibiting pleasures and uninterested in people's welfare."

For more than two decades, first as the general secretary of the Lord's Day Alliance – which successfully campaigned for the Lord's Day Act, instituted in Canada in 1907, restricting Sunday business and fun – and later as the head of the Presbyterian Department of Temperance and Moral Reform, he staunchly defended his vision of a puritan country. In 1909, he also helped organize the Moral and Social Reform Council of Canada and led the Council's committee for the suppression of white slavery. There was much to learn from the Puritans' "respect for righteousness, law, order, religion, and the Lord's Day," he argued. "Let [our] Puritanism be that of the twentieth century – wise, tolerant, gracious and inflexible . . . let us go ahead in the present crusade unterrified by all sneering cries of 'puritanical legislation' raised by cavilling newspapers that would cater to an evil-minded crowd." He devoted much of his time to trying to stamp out vice and vigorously denounced any legal toleration of prostitution, as the police in Winnipeg had done in 1909 when they prescribed a red-light district in the North End.

In his battle against sin and depravity, immigrants became a convenient scapegoat. During his fight for the Lord's Day Act, he had focused part of his attack on Orthodox Jews and Seventh-day Adventists who had challenged Sunday observance laws as an infringement on their freedom of religion. Shearer found such an attitude galling. "Is it too much to ask," he wrote, "that having sought our land FOR THEIR OWN GOOD, they should conform to our laws, and recognize the civil customs prevailing in the life of our own people?" Then, on a rampage against corruption and vice after his tour of Western Canada in 1910, he unfairly blamed Chinese and Japanese immigrants for operating "most of the dens of vice."

Shearer died at the age of sixty-six in 1925, never satisfied that his moral reform work was complete or that his efforts to control and shape undesirable immigrants was successful. Jane Addams in Chicago and social gospeller James S. Woodsworth in Winnipeg took much different approaches – indicative of the complexities and demands created by industrialization and mass immigration and the responses they generated.

Salon of Democracy

Newspapers hailed her as the country's "only American saint." A century later, Jane Addams's list of achievements on behalf of the impoverished in Chicago is still impressive. She established the first social settlement in the city; the first public baths; the first public playground and gymnasium; the first citizenship classes for immigrants to the United States; and she initiated official investigations into everything from factory laws to the social value of the saloon. "She was larger than life. White hair. Black dresses down to the floor. And big, big eyes. She always was a lady," remembered Ruby Jane Deicandro, who as a young woman knew Addams. One newspaper profile about her from the late 1890s described her as "a woman of indomitable energy and persistence, of enthusiasm and adaptability." Mary Jo Deegan, one of her many biographers adds that, "she had a seminal mind, political acumen, administrative brilliance, and moral leadership, she was one of the greatest American leaders of her day, and she is one of the most influential and famous women in [U.S.] history."

If anyone lived by her convictions, it was Addams. She believed in progress and in justice and democracy for all – no matter if you were born in Illinois or a shtetl outside of Kiev. Motivated more by a good heart than by faith in the Almighty, she spent her life as a social worker in pursuit of the highest ideals of humanity.

Jane Addams was born in 1860 in Cedarville, a small town in northern Illinois, south of the Wisconsin border. She was the eighth child in a family of nine children. Her father, John, a Quaker and a major influence in her life, was a state senator and a successful banker and real-estate dealer. He was also a friend to Abraham Lincoln, who often referred to him as "Double-D'ed Addams." Jane's mother, Sarah, died when she was very young, and her father later married Anna Haleman, a widow with two children of her own.

Jane was often ill as a child but survived tuberculosis of the spine. The disease "left her with a slightly curved back and a pigeon-toed walk." She attended the Rockford Female Seminary in Rockford, Illinois, specialized in biology, and graduated in 1881. (A year later, when the seminary became Rockford College, she officially obtained a bachelor's degree in science.) As a young woman, Addams was uncertain what to do with her life. Her father died the year she graduated, which left her lost and depressed. She thought about becoming a doctor, entered Women's Medical College in Philadelphia, but then dropped out before the year was up. She returned home to Cedarville to live with her stepmother, travelled to Europe in 1883, and resisted her family's wishes that she find a husband and become a society lady. In 1887, she again journeyed to Europe, accompanied by a close friend from college, Ellen Gates Starr.*

In London, Addams visited the city's well-known settlement house Toynbee Hall in Whitechapel, which had been established in 1884 as a way for the educated to live among the poor and help them cope with the squalor, destitution, crime, and other by-products of industrialization. She and Starr saw first-hand, as well, the superb recreation facilities, including library, gymnasium, swimming pool, and classrooms, at the new People's Palace, opened in 1887 for the downtrodden in East London. These institutions impressed Addams to such an extent that she now knew her life's purpose. She returned to the United States with plans to open her own settlement house in Chicago.

Toynbee Hall had also inspired Dr. Stanton Coit, of the Society for Ethical Culture, who had opened America's first settlement house in 1886 in tenement rooms in New York City's Lower East Side. Originally it was called the Neighbourhood Guild, but later became the University Settlement under the directorship of Charles Stover, who understood more than most social reformers the complex dynamics of the immigrant quarter. His small apartment, recalled Lillian Wald, who ran the nearby Henry Street Settlement, "became a Mecca to people with problems. I remember tall and high-booted callers, lusty husky men from Rumania or some unhappy corner of the earth, filling his room to ask for help or interpretation." Stover influenced Eleanor Roosevelt, who as a girl volunteered for two years at the University Settlement.

---

* Despite their lifelong companionship, there is no evidence of a sexual relationship between Addams and Starr. The two women did love each other, as their correspondence indicates. "Let's love each other through thick and thin and work out a salvation," Addams wrote to Starr in 1889 during one separation. "Of course, I miss you all the time and never wanted you more than the last few days when everything seemed to be moving at once."

Returning to the United States in late 1888, Addams and Starr moved to Chicago. Within a few months they found a two-storey dilapidated brick mansion on Halsted Street in the impoverished nineteenth ward in the west side of the city. Built in 1856, the house had once been owned by real-estate magnate Charles Hull. The neighbourhood, however, had changed dramatically since Hull's days. It was now home to thousands of immigrants who had flocked to Chicago and were struggling to survive each day. Irish and German newcomers had first occupied the area, but by the time Addams moved in, the majority of its population were Russian Jews, Italians, and Greeks. It was an eyesore.

"The streets are inexpressibly dirty, the schools inadequate, sanitary legislation unenforced, the street lighting bad, the paving miserable and altogether lacking in the alleys and smaller streets, and the stables foul beyond description," Addams later wrote. "The older and richer inhabitants seem anxious to move away as rapidly as they can afford it. They make room for newly arrived immigrants who are densely ignorant of civic duties. . . . Many houses have no water supply save the faucet in the backyard, [and] there are no fire escapes, the garbage and ashes are placed in wooden boxes which are fastened to the street pavements." Nevertheless, she and Starr rented the Halsted property, renovated it, and named it Hull-House (Addams always hyphenated its name, although the hyphen was eventually dropped). On their first night there, Addams forgot to lock the front door, without any problems. From then on, the doors of Hull-House remained unlocked twenty-four hours a day.

Like Toynbee Hall on which it was modelled, Hull-House's charter, as Addams conceived it, was "To provide a center for a higher civic and social life; to institute and maintain educational and philanthropic enterprises, and to investigate and improve the conditions in the industrial districts of Chicago." During the next four decades, Addams more than fulfilled these objectives. The house quickly became the focal point of the neighbourhood, and Addams's reputation as a social worker and reformer spread across the country and around the world. In 1891, there were six settlement houses in the United States; by 1900, there were more than a hundred – and Addams's success was largely responsible. Hull-House offered care for infants and young mothers, clubs for youth, meeting groups for labourers to discuss their problems, and reading and citizenship classes – "a whole range of programs to help the poor find hope, self-respect, and more decent lives."

Addams and Starr were soon joined by a group of dedicated and loyal women and men, many of whom volunteered their time or were paid a small amount of money.* Addams's father had left her an income of three thousand dollars a year, a considerable sum. She also raised money to run the house through numerous speaking engagements and obtained donations from a crowd of wealthy admirers. Despite her kind heart and gentle demeanour, Addams was resourceful, shrewd, and determined when it came to soliciting funds for any cause she deemed worthy. In one case, Chicago businessman William Kent initially offered Addams some land near Hull-House. By the time she was done with him, he had not only donated the land but also financed the construction of the first public playground in the city.

Journalists referred to Hull-House as "Jane Addams's salon of democracy," because everyone, no matter what their nationality or socio-economic status, was treated with dignity and respect. Into Hull-House, one writer observed, "passes a Greek fruit vendor, university professors, mayors, aldermen, club-women, factory inspectors, novelists, reporters, policemen, Italian washerwomen, socialists, big businessmen, English members of Parliament, German scientists, and

---

* The residents at Hull-House who came to train with Addams were a diverse group. "She attracted brilliant, aggressive, and talented men and women," writes biographer Allen Davis. They included Gerard Swope, who was later the president of General Electric, historian Charles Beard, and William Lyon Mackenzie King, who in 1921 became the prime minister of Canada.

all sorts and conditions of men." Following a visit to the city in 1893, the British journalist William Stead declared that "If Christ came to Chicago, what would he discover? Vice, criminality, corruption, and above all, neglect such as no other late nineteenth century city would tolerate." The "best hope for Chicago," he added, "is the multiplication of Hull-House into all the slum districts of the city."

Of the many hardships experienced by her immigrant neighbours, none tugged at Addams's heart as much as the pathetic sight of young children labouring in factories and sweatshops ten to twelve hours each day. "I remember a little girl of four," she wrote in her best-selling memoir, *Twenty Years at Hull-House* (1910), "who pulled out basting threads hour after hour, sitting on a stool at the feet of her Bohemian mother, a little bunch of human misery." She encountered a thirteen-year-old Russian Jewish girl who was forced to toil in a laundry, "at a heavy task beyond her strength." The youngster committed suicide because she could not repay a three-dollar loan and was too frightened to ask her parents to give up a week's wages to help her. Such tales pushed Addams to campaign for laws governing child employment, which led to the Illinois Factory Act of 1893, regulating conditions in sweatshops and setting fourteen years as the age when a child could be employed. It was one of the country's first real efforts to control labour conditions for minors.

A year later, she turned her attention to the mounds of garbage and filth that accumulated daily in the area around Hull-House and was largely ignored by Chicago's municipal officials. She exposed their incompetence and corruption and then forced them to appoint her "ward garbage inspector." Paid an annual salary of one thousand dollars, she finally got some of the trash off the streets. "The image of the brave little woman battling the establishment and following the garbage carts to make her neighbourhood safer and cleaner," writes historian Allen Davis, "established her reputation as a practical and determined reformer."

In an age when it was widely believed that nature (race and genetics) rather than nurture (environment and educational opportunities) determined a person's life, Addams was a committed environmentalist. She constantly bemoaned the industrialized city with its vice and sweatshops. If immigrant children turned into juvenile delinquents it was not, she argued, a product of their race but rather of their destitution. This set her apart from most of her contemporaries. Although, as sociologist Mary Jo Deegan points out, "condescending passages" about the immigrants with whom she worked can be found in Addams's books and articles, "her overwhelmingly more frequent and articulate stance against such attitudes outweighs these other portions of her writings."

Before Horace Kallen had conceived any notions about "cultural pluralism" – and decades before Canada adopted an official policy of multiculturalism – Jane Addams preached respect for cultural diversity to anyone who would listen to her. She thought of the newcomers who came to Hull-House "as citizens or citizens-in-the-making" rather than as ignorant or inferior. Nor was she paternalistic. After several years of working with immigrants, she came to understand that they had much to offer America if given the opportunity. And, more importantly, that they brought with them a "cultural baggage" worth preserving. She understood, writes John Farrell, another of her biographers, "that many Italian and German immigrants knew and loved Dante, Schiller and Goethe. . . . She found her immigrant neighbours equal to many and superior to some Americans in their love of and respect for learning, and in their enthusiasm for drama, art, literature and music. Her initial assumption that young college women possess cultural superiority gave way."

Ahead of her time, Addams did not subscribe to the "Anglo-Saxon temptation of governing all peoples by one standard," as she put it. Hence, she promoted and supported adaptation rather than assimilation. She accepted that immigrants had to learn the English language in order to survive and praised the significant work done by the public schools in the area of civic instruction. But unlike other commentators of the period, she did not believe that immigrants had to be transformed into Anglo-Saxons to be worthy Americans. On the contrary, Americanization was a two-way process. "In our assertive Americanism we fail to understand and respect the family life, the many customs, the inherited skill [immigrants] bring with them," declared Addams in a lecture she delivered in 1911.

To make her point, she created, with input from educational expert John Dewey, the Hull-House Labor Museum. Its objective, she explained, was to show the immigrants and the wider community, through exhibits, artifacts, displays, and lectures, the continuity between old and new worlds and, as she said, to "build a bridge between European and American experiences."* She also helped create a League for the Protection of Immigrants, so that the newcomers' legal rights would be recognized.

In the spring of 1908, Addams defended the integrity of a nineteen-year-old Russian Jew named Lazarus Averbuch, a survivor of the 1903 Kishinev pogrom (in Bessarabia). He had recently arrived in Chicago and lived in the West Side, in the Jewish quarter off Maxwell Street, with his sister Olga. For reasons still undetermined, Averbuch, in the early morning of March 2, went to the house of Chief of Police George Shippy, located in the fashionable North Side. Anarchism was on the rise, and the atmosphere of paranoia that followed the assassination of President William McKinley by Leon Czolgosz (the son of Polish immigrants) in Buffalo on September 6, 1901, had not subsided.

Chief Shippy met Averbuch in the front entrance of his home, perhaps, as his sister Olga Averbuch later claimed, to discuss her

---

* Although in the early 1900s Chicago's black population was still small, Addams extended this pluralistic philosophy to African-Americans and was an early advocate for the National Association for the Advancement of Colored People, established in 1909.

brother's request for a "certificate of good behaviour," as was common in Russia, a document he thought he required to seek work outside of Chicago. An altercation ensued that left Averbuch dead. Shippy claimed he thought Averbuch, whom he described as "a dark young man," was an Italian anarchist who had come to kill him. Averbuch was shot six times – at least twice in the back after he had turned to run.

Shippy testified that Averbuch had pulled a gun from his overcoat pocket and shot him. Also involved and injured were Shippy's son Harry and his driver and bodyguard, James Foley. Whether or not Averbuch – who, according to his sister, did not own a gun and was not involved with anarchists – had any weapons on him is unknown. The official investigation by the police and coroner confirmed Shippy's version of the events. (The Chicago *Jewish Courier*, on the other hand, speculated that the wounds received by Shippy, his son, and bodyguard were caused by errant gunfire from the chief and James Foley.) Whatever transpired that morning, police discovered some printed material of "anarchistic tendencies" in Averbuch's apartment. His sister was arrested and browbeaten by police into confessing her anarchist connections, although she was later released. More so-called anarchists living near Hull-House were also rounded up and their apartments and businesses ransacked.

Addams came to the defence of Olga Averbuch and the others arrested, demanding that they were entitled to "equality before the law." With financial assistance from Julius Rosenwald, the head of Sears Roebuck, Addams hired Chicago lawyer Harold Ickes (later the Secretary of the Interior in Franklin D. Roosevelt's cabinet) to investigate the case. He uncovered several inconsistencies in Shippy's story, although the official version remained unchanged and the chief unrepentant.

The story made front-page news across the United States. Editors and reporters assumed Lazarus Averbuch was indeed an anarchist and guilty as the Chicago police claimed. They then accused Addams of encouraging anarchist behaviour by permitting the immigrants (as well as guest speakers like Russian anarchist Peter Kropotkin) to express their political views openly at Hull-House gatherings. This was the first time Addams had been publicly criticized in such a disparaging manner, yet she (showing a certain degree of naivety) was more concerned with the way the press and public so easily believed the worst about Averbuch and the other newcomers. "The more excited and irrational public opinion is," she reflected, "the more recklessly newspapers state mere surmises as facts, and upon these surmises arouse unsubstantiated prejudices against certain immigrants, the more necessary it is that some body of people be ready to put forward the spiritual and intellectual conditions of the foreign colony which is thus being made the subject of inaccurate surmises and unjust suspicion."

Regardless of Addams's sympathies, the Averbuch affair signalled the rise of even more hostile nativist attitudes that reached a climax during the First World War and the early twenties. Addams herself was taken aback by the sometimes hysterical fear of foreigners and their depiction as agitators and socialists. If she had a fault, it was that she underestimated the power of nationalism, the hate it engendered, and the numerous obstacles her cosmopolitan and tolerant multicultural environment faced. She condemned the federal government's restrictive immigration act of 1924 and the racism that motivated it, comparing it to the treatment accorded to Muslims and Jews in fifteenth-century Spain. Yet by then, her outspoken pacifism and opposition to American participation in the First World War had caused her a great deal of trouble. When comments she made about American soldiers drinking liquor to steady them for battle were misinterpreted to mean that she implied they were cowards, she was vilified in the press. Even her former friend and ally Theodore Roosevelt, whom she had supported in the 1912 presidential election when he ran under the Progressive Party ticket, castigated her as "poor bleeding Jane." A decade would pass before she regained the public's support. The high point came in 1931 when she was awarded the Nobel Peace Prize, four years before she died. Only then was she praised, in the words of the *New York Times*, as a "bold crusader for peace," whose lifelong work at Hull-House was "an ultimate expression of an essentially American democracy of spirit."

The Kingdom of God on Earth

It was Jane Addams's compassion for her fellow human beings that ultimately enabled her to triumph over the adversity she confronted during her lifetime. Another group of reformers similarly moved by the plight of the newcomers was inspired more by their deep religious convictions than the secular spirit that guided Addams. Mainly Methodists and Baptists, they put their faith in the tenets of "social gospel," believing that Christianity was at its roots a "social religion" which had to have as its priority the "quality of human relations on earth." It was a clarion call, as the historian Richard Allen says, "for men to find the meaning of their lives in seeking to realize the Kingdom of God in the very fabric of society." The urban slums of late nineteenth and early twentieth century North America, seen as breeding grounds for sin and corruption, and populated with destitute foreigners who needed to be saved, provided an ideal opportunity for believers to put social gospel into action.

In the United States, Walter Rauschenbusch, a Baptist minister from New York, first preached the social gospel. His father was a German Lutheran missionary who had become a Baptist. Born in Rochester, New York, in 1861, "Rauschy," as his friends called him, was ordained in 1886 and worked for eleven years, until 1897, at the Second German Baptist Church. The church was located on the edge of the rough and impoverished New York City neighbourhood on the west side known as Hell's Kitchen – dominated by saloons, brothels, and tenements and ruled by ruthless gangs. Rauschenbusch later studied theology and economics at the University of Berlin and industrial relations in England. He was appointed a professor of church history at Rochester Theological Seminary (now Colgate Rochester Divinity School) in 1902 – by which time he had become partially deaf – and remained there until his death at the age of fifty-six in 1918.

His experience in Hell's Kitchen convinced him that a new approach to "Christ's work" was required, and that the daily social problems confronting his congregants resulted from the inherent weaknesses in capitalism, which was, in his view, an economic system based on greed, fear, and injustice. "Competitive commerce exalts selfishness to the dignity of a moral principle," he wrote in 1907. "It pits men against one another in a gladiatorial game in which there is no mercy and in which ninety per cent of the combatants finally strew the arena. . . . It makes men who are the gentlest and kindliest friends and neighbors, relentless taskmasters in their shops and stores, who will drain the strength of their men and pay their female employees wages on which no girl can live without supplementing them in some way."

Influenced by the British Fabians, who advocated significant changes in capitalist society through moderate action, Rauschenbusch, a devoted and moral individual, envisaged the church as a universal remedy for poverty. As he explained, "The Kingdom of God is the first and most essential dogma of the Christian faith. It is also the lost social ideal of Christendom. No man is a Christian in the full sense of the original discipleship until he has made the Kingdom of God the controlling purpose of his life."

In 1892, Rauschenbusch established the non-denominational Brotherhood of the Kingdom so that both religious and secular social reformers could work together to improve the lives of America's working classes. In the social gospel, he found new meaning and a purpose for his religious life. "The saving of the lost, the teaching of the young, the pastoral care of the poor and the frail, the quickening of the starved intellects, the study of the Bible . . . it was all covered by the one aim of the reign of God on earth," he explained. His philosophy and stature as America's best-known social prophet spread through his various writings, in particular *Christianity and the Social Crisis* (1907), which was reprinted six times in two years, and *A Theology of Social Gospel* (1917). His beliefs had the greatest impact on other preachers and reformers throughout North America – including Martin Luther King, Jr., who said in 1960 that *Christianity and the Social Crisis* "left an indelible imprint on my thinking." Rauschenbusch, added King, "gave to American Protestantism a sense of social responsibility that it should never lose."

Social gospel theory, with its emphasis on saving souls in the here and now, was one thing; putting it into practice in the city slums was quite another. Rauschenbusch's followers were, in fact, less concerned with old-style charity work and approached the social ills in their midst from a scientific, sociological perspective. As the Methodist *Christian Guardian* of Toronto put it, "the gospel of the toothbrush, soap and water and flyscreens has a place in life." Yet, this meant confronting immigration head-on, as well as the attendant immorality, drunkenness, and squalor church leaders associated with foreigners.

Methodists in Canada created a Department of Temperance and Moral Reform to promote civics education for children and to fight the good fight against gambling, obscene literature, and abortion. Reverend Samuel Chown led the department. Like his religious counterparts in the United States, Chown campaigned for a more restrictive immigration policy. "If from this North American continent is to come a superior race, a race to be specially used of God in the carrying on of His work, what is our duty toward those who are now our fellow-citizens?" asked an article published in 1908 in *Missionary Outlook*. "Many of them come to us nominal Christians, that is, they owe allegiance to the Greek or Roman Catholic Churches, but their moral standards and ideals are far below those of the Christian citizens of the Dominion.

These people have come to this young, free country to make homes for themselves and their children. It is our duty to meet them with the open Bible, and to instil into their minds the principles and ideals of Anglo-Saxon civilization."

One prominent social gospeller who wrestled with this issue was James Shaver Woodsworth. He was tall and thin, and with his goatee-style beard he resembled Walter Rauschenbusch, whose teachings he followed. Woodsworth, who valued his "British ancestry," developed, like Rauschenbusch, both an affinity for the working-class foreigners he preached to and taught, as well as resentment for the inequities of capitalism. He was a serious and sober individual – as one reporter said, "he has no sense of humour, he really hasn't" – constantly reflecting on the problems caused by industrialization and city life and searching for solutions to remedy them.

Woodsworth was born in 1874 on a farm not far from Toronto. When he was still a boy, his father, also named James and a Methodist preacher, moved the family west to the small town of Portage la Prairie, Manitoba, fifty miles west of Winnipeg, and then further west to the city of Brandon. Woodsworth followed in his father's footsteps. After finishing high school in Brandon, he entered Wesley College in Winnipeg, where the social gospel was being debated and refined, and studied in the Department of Mental and Moral Science.

Though he had some doubts, he had decided to become a Methodist minister. In 1898, he relocated to Toronto to take theology courses at Victoria College (now part of the University of Toronto) yet learned more about the realities of the social gospel by visiting the city's Fred Victor Mission, sponsored by the Methodist Church. A year later, he took advantage of an opportunity to study at Oxford University in England. Beyond the confines of Oxford's Mansfield College, he found inspiration and a purpose, as Jane Addams had, in the slums of east London. This exposure to dreadful poverty, alcoholism, and hungry children led him to dwell on the application of "Christian ethics" to the modern world. "Surely," he wrote, "there must be one great system of morality. Nor need this exclude Christianity. Rather, if Christianity is as universal as it claims to be it must combine in itself all morality – must allow for its highest development and be an essential factor in that development."

Upon returning to Canada, he received his degree in divinity from Victoria College in the summer of 1900 and was ordained as a Methodist minister in Brandon later that year. He spent a brief time in the rural community of Keewatin, Ontario, in the Lake of the Woods region, before moving to Winnipeg, where he was to make his mark.

At the turn of the century, the city was teeming with optimism, but its burgeoning immigrant population concerned the Anglo-Saxon business elite. While the city's leaders welcomed the newcomers, they, like their counterparts everywhere else in North America, also feared the long-term effect these foreigners would have on Winnipeg's development. Already, Ukrainians, Galicians, Poles, and East European Jews had congregated in the North End, living in overcrowded tenement houses, cut off from the rest of the city by the massive Canadian Pacific Railway yards. Although many of the British working-class also lived in the North End, the area around Selkirk Avenue – "The Foreign Quarter" or "New Jerusalem," as it was often called – was a world set apart. Selkirk Avenue emerged as the main business district, a smaller version of Hester Street in the Lower East Side, where Jewish merchants sold their goods, often on credit, as they had in the old country.

Almost the moment he arrived and was appointed to Grace Church, Woodsworth upset members of the city's powerful elite with his negative comments about capitalism and his evident disdain for materialism of any kind. "I fear that in our own city we have not yet learned the vulgarity of a lavish expenditure of newly acquired wealth," he declared in one sermon. "Costly dresses, magnificent house, expensive entertainments – those are the things we seek after. And the snobbishness that goes with such vulgarity!" Seeing for himself the destitution in the North End, he preached the message of the social gospel: "If it is right to help the sick it is right to do away with the filth and overcrowding and to provide sunlight and good air and good food. We have tried to provide for the poor. Yet, have we tried to alter the social conditions that lead to poverty?"

He found a just cause and real purpose in 1907 when he was chosen to head the Methodist-supported All People's Mission on Stella Avenue in the heart of the North End. Once Woodsworth was in charge, All People's reflected both his social gospel beliefs and the settlement-house approach successfully implemented by Jane Addams. He expanded its various education programs, social clubs, language classes, a kindergarten, summer camp, and help for young mothers, and in general reached out to the immigrant community. He and his family also moved into the neighbourhood so that he could experience and truly understand first-hand the problems they faced.

Woodsworth took a more pragmatic approach than did Addams. He insisted that Canada was a British Protestant nation now and forever, and that the only way to deal with the foreigners was to force them to assimilate. His views were most clearly articulated in his bestselling book *Strangers Within Our Gates* (1909). Assisted by journalist Arthur Ford of the conservative *Winnipeg Telegram* (who wrote several chapters), and based almost entirely on American and British sources – such as the work of Prescott Hall, Jacob Riis, Josiah Strong, and James Whelpley – the book reflected not only Woodsworth's thinking on the immigration issue, but also the feelings of most liberal-minded middle-class Canadians.[*]

In the book, Woodsworth ranked each different nationality and ethnic group according to how easily they would assimilate and adapt to "Canadian" values, as he defined them. Thus, sections on

---

[*] He followed this with *My Neighbour* (1911), about the various problems in the city. Cataloguing the many urban ills and miseries, he argued for new thinking and a new approach in reforming the city. This book, too, while popular, was based largely on American and British sources.

Britons, Americans, Scandinavians, and Germans portrayed them as assimilable and desirable, while chapters on Italians, Slavs, Galicians, and "Hebrews" were far less positive. "Negroes" and "Orientals" were deemed unwelcome and unwanted. "It is true that they may be able to do much of the rough work for which it is difficult to secure sufficient white labor; but where they enter, the whites are out, and out permanently," he noted in one passage about Chinese immigrants. "They constitute an entirely distinct class or caste. They have their own virtues and vices; their own moral standards, and religious beliefs. The Orientals cannot be assimilated." On "the Negro," Woodsworth quoted a 1903 magazine article by the U.S. writer John Commons about Africans' "love of rhythm, excitability . . . lack of reserve . . . strong sexual passion and lack of will power."

Like Prescott Hall, one of the founders of the Immigration Restriction League in the United States, Woodsworth argued that cheap immigrant labour was detrimental to the economy and that its social effects – pauperism, degeneration, and increased crime – were severe. Yet, while he included Winnipeg police statistics that showed immigrants were "fairly prominent in police court," he ignored the fact that it was life in the North End ghetto, rather than racial factors, which bred these problems.

In the decades ahead, Woodsworth rose to national stature as a labour leader and politician, who, as one of the founders of the socialist party the Co-operative Commonwealth Federation in 1932, laid the groundwork for Canada's social programs of the present day. By the time he left Winnipeg in 1913, his views on the moral threat posed by the onslaught of foreigners had eased, but only slightly. "The coming of the immigrant has intensified and complicated the serious problems that would in any case have had to be solved in a young and developing country," he wrote in 1917. "The presence of the alien and unassimilated elements has aggravated the difficulty and tended to retard the development of a sense of community fellowship, or corporate responsibility, and of devotion to a social ideal. . . . Undoubtedly the immigrant has . . . helped to create our problems – as it should not be forgotten, he has helped to create our wealth. . . . The immigrants bring greater assets than we sometimes realize. Many of them have small financial resources but they are endowed with a capacity for patient industry. Not a few of them have skill in various crafts and show boundless ambition. The members of each nationality bring with them a rich and varied culture. Many a peasant, clad in sheepskins, possesses artistic abilities of no mean order. . . . [But] we must stand guard at our gates. In the past numbers of undesirable immigrants have been permitted to enter Canada. We have every right to rigidly exclude those who would lower our standards."

However concerned reformers like Woodsworth were about immigration, there was no denying that the newcomers, wherever they came from, dramatically changed their new environments, just as their new environments changed them. The list of immigrants or children of first-generation newcomers who contributed and shaped North American society, both positively and negatively – some of whose achievements and exploits are described in this book – is impressive. Among the celebrated, as well as the notorious, there were: Irving Berlin, Samuel Goldwyn, Adolph Zukor, Louis B. Mayer, Charlie Chaplin, Abraham Cahan, Al Jolson, Samuel Bronfman, Emma Goldman, Samuel Gompers, Max Factor, Marcus Garvey, Al Capone, Meyer Lansky, Nicola Sacco, and Bartolomeo Vanzetti – to name only a handful. Each of them, and many more, challenged the status quo, questioned middle-class concepts of morality, and were a constant reminder that for better or worse North American society, struggling with the complexities of rapid urbanization, was forever changing.

CHAPTER TWO

Suffragettes

Previous page: U.S. suffragist Alice Paul sewing a flag, c. 1916. Paul embarked on one of the first effective non-violent campaigns of the twentieth century.

Another mistake that people make is to suppose that we want the vote only or chiefly because of its political value. We want [it] far more because of its symbolic value – the recognition of our human equality that it will involve.

— Christabel Pankhurst, 1913

The Price of Liberty

Wednesday, June 4, 1913, was Derby Day, and Emily Wilding Davison had a plan. Early in the morning, she left the flat in Kensington where she was staying with a friend and made her way to Victoria Station. There, having worked their way through the jostling crowd, she and her companion, Mary Richardson, purchased third-class tickets to Epsom Downs, south-east of London. King Edward VII's horse Anmer was running in the third race, and the Royal family would be in attendance, seated in their private box. That always brought out a lot of spectators, even in the middle of the week. In her pocket, Davison had stuffed two purple-white-and-green flags, the colours of the suffragettes.

During the past seven years, few women in Britain matched Davison for their devotion to the cause. With a Bachelor of Arts degree from London University and first-class honours at Oxford in English, French, and German, Davison, who had been born in a village on the outskirts of London, had embarked on a promising career as a teacher – one of the few professions then open to a middle-class single woman. But by 1906, like many women who joined Emmeline Pankhurst and her daughters Christabel and Sylvia in the newly formed Women's Social and Political Union (WSPU), Davison, then thirty-four years old, could no longer tolerate the injustice of British law. Women had a right to the vote, to be citizens equal to men, to have a voice in civic affairs – it was that simple. And if the government of the day – whether Tory or Whig – was not prepared to acquiesce to the women's demands, a more militant approach would be required.

Always a woman of "high spirit," Davison, thin and lanky with a bob of brown curly hair, could be impulsive and rebellious, even for a "suffragette," as the *Daily Mail* labelled the Pankhursts' group to distinguish them from the more genteel and established constitutional "suffragists" of the National Union of Women's Suffrage Societies (NUWSS), led by the refined Millicent Fawcett. Davison was one of the first suffragettes to smash a government-building window as an act of protest and to set a mailbox on fire. Arrested and sent to prison, she had gone on a hunger strike, because prison officials refused to treat her (and suffragettes in general) as a political prisoner, and then endured the torture of forcible feeding. On one occasion, she used the wooden planks from her bed to bar entry to her prison cell, compelling her jailers to use a powerful jet of water from a hose in order to force their way in. She nearly drowned in the ensuing battle. "The thought in my mind was that the moment for the sacrifice, which we all agreed will probably be demanded, was at hand," she later recalled, "and strange to say, I had no fear."

Later, during another stay in prison, she threw herself over a staircase and fell thirty feet to a concrete floor, seriously injuring herself. "The idea in my mind," she said, "was some desperate protest must be made to put a stop to the hideous torture, and the one great tragedy might save others." These words were more prophetic than she likely realized.

That June day in 1913, her latest plan, ill-conceived and foolish in retrospect, would again draw attention to the cause. Whether she truly wanted to commit suicide is doubtful, since the ticket she had bought was a return. The King's horse, ridden by a jockey named Herbert Jones, was trailing as the horses rounded Tattenham Corner and headed for the finish line in front of the Royal box. Davison stood quietly next to the white railing. Her mood was serene, as Mary Richardson later testified. "I was watching her hand. It did not shake," her companion said. "Even when I heard the pounding of the horses' hoofs moving closer I saw she was still smiling."

Without a word, Davison slipped under the railing and onto the track as the horses bore down on her. The first group thundered past, but she stood firm as Anmer came toward her. Witnesses said it appeared as if Davison reached for the horse's rein. Anmer was running too hard. The horse and jockey crashed into Davison. She fell to the ground, rolling over several times before her body came to rest in a bloody heap. The crowd was stunned. It was later reported that many spectators, accustomed to the various protests of the suffragettes, shouted with concern for Anmer rather than Davison.

Herbert Jones fractured a rib, but otherwise was not harmed. Likewise, Anmer did not suffer any serious injury. Davison, however, was badly hurt. She was taken to the Epsom Cottage Hospital where she never regained consciousness. She died four days later from the blows to her head and heart.

The militancy of the suffragettes had already attracted much comment and criticism, and several of the letters sent to Davison were not supportive. "I hope you suffer torture until you die," one man wrote. "You idiot." Another wrote to ask her what the horse had to do with the present system of government.

Had she been able, Davison might have answered her critics with words she had written in an unpublished essay found among her papers. Entitled "The Price of Liberty," it was her defence that martyrdom and sacrifice were the price to be paid if women were to win justice. "The glorious and inscrutable Spirit of Liberty has but one further penalty within its power," she concluded, "the surrender of Life itself. It is the supreme consummation of sacrifice, than which none can be higher or greater. To lay down life for friends, that is glorious, selfless, inspiring! But to re-enact the tragedy of Calvary for generations yet unborn, that is the last consummate sacrifice of the Militant!"

By her death, Emily Davison became the great martyr for the cause she aspired to be. Her body was brought back to London on June 14. The coffin, draped in purple, white, and green, was placed on a horse-drawn hearse. Accompanying it were more than two thousand suffragettes. Wearing white dresses and hats and black arm bands, they solemnly marched from Victoria Station to St. George's Church in Bloomsbury. Some carried banners proclaiming "Give me Liberty or Give me Death!" and "Fight On & God Will Give the Victory!" Thousands more men and women lined the streets to witness this stirring procession.

Before the funeral service began, an outstanding warrant was served for the arrest of Mrs. Emmeline Pankhurst, the guiding spirit of the WSPU. A statement was later read in church in which Mrs. Pankhurst urged her supporters to "carry on our Holy War for the emancipation of our sex." The women listened and resumed their militant campaign of arson, property destruction, and terrorism with a vengeance. Emily Davison's death, they decided, would count for something.

The Proper Sphere

The tragic tale of Emily Davison may be the most extreme example of martyrdom for the suffrage cause, yet for nearly a century a determined group of women in Britain, the United States, and Canada fought for the right to be citizens – a right denied to few men by 1900. The battle in Britain may have been the most violent, but in

North America, too, women were tormented, harassed, and imprisoned for simply demanding the vote.

The fight in all three countries reached its peak in the two decades after 1900. More women were finding employment as factory workers, domestics, and seamstresses, and many were receiving a college education and graduating as teachers, lawyers, doctors, and nurses as well. And with the growth of business and the retail trade, women were being hired in unprecedented numbers as stenographers, office clerks, and salesladies. Most of them were underpaid, yet if they were single they were able to support themselves. In the United States, for example, approximately four million women were employed outside the home, and by 1910 this figure had jumped to nearly 7.5 million. Similarly in Canada, the women in the workforce rose by 25 per cent between 1901 and 1911, with the largest increases in nursing and teaching.

Some women continued to work even after they were married. Those who left the labour force, on the other hand, became members of a female middle-class with enough leisure time to participate (often with their husbands' blessings) in an assortment of important causes – combating the evils of liquor, educating non-English-speaking immigrants, fighting for better health care and schools, and most notably, joining in the crusade to win women the vote.[*]

By 1920 the "suffragists" and the "suffragettes" of the movement, participants in the first true political pressure group of the modern age, could claim a victory of sorts. Still, their battle against (what we would call today) the established order and the traditionalists – men

---

[*] Late nineteenth and early twentieth century technology went some way toward freeing these middle-class women (those who could not afford domestic help) from the tedious and time-consuming chores of daily housework. As the U.S. women's historian Eleanor Flexner points out, "The development of gas lighting, municipal water systems, domestic plumbing, canning, the commercial production of ice, the improvement of furnaces, stoves, and washtubs, and the popularization of the sewing-machine aided growing numbers of women to escape from the domestic treadmill."

and women who feared the new modern woman and everything she represented – was not easy. First they had to confront the well-entrenched perception of a woman's "proper sphere."

In Britain, the Liberal government led by Prime Minister Herbert H. Asquith, a stubborn adversary of the suffragettes, felt no undue pressure by Emily Davison's act of martyrdom. In Asquith's view, it was futile and tragically pointless. Asquith might have believed in free trade, Home Rule for Ireland, and social reform, but he would not be stampeded into altering his basic philosophy on women's proper place in society – and that place was not in the political arena. In one of the first major speeches he gave on the suffrage issue, in April 1892, more than a decade before he became prime minister, Asquith insisted that most women did not really want or need the vote. It was not a question "of whether the average woman is fit for the franchise," he said, but "whether the franchise is fit for her. . . . Their natural sphere is not the turmoil and dust of politics, but the circle of social and domestic life."

Asquith, like his counterparts in North America, had no doubt that it was a man's world and that the Pankhursts and the other suffragettes were tampering with the laws of nature and God. This long-held belief maintained that society was divided in two, between the public sphere, ruled by men, and the private, where it fell to women to supervise the home as wife and mother, as well as serve their husbands in the kitchen and bedroom. As the nineteenth-century adage had it, "the woman, the cat, and the chimney should never leave the house." The opponents of women's suffrage, the "antis," as their friends and foes referred to them, ignored the fact that thousands of women were employed in the workforce. Women, after all, were "delicate" creatures, who according to mid-Victorian perceptions, were "supposed to remain forever dependent upon a man – first as a daughter and then as a wife."

Even with changes to British property acts passed in the 1880s and 1890s – which gave married women limited control over their own estates – women had few legal rights over their "person, property or income." The law regarded "man and wife" as one person, and a woman's "existence [was] entirely absorbed in that of her husband." It was not until 1891, for instance, that a judge ruled that a husband could no longer treat his wife "as he would a recalcitrant animal." Likewise in the United States, women had no legal rights to speak of and were expected to be obedient.

In 1900 in Pennsylvania, a married woman could still not sign a commercial or business contract without her husband's consent. And in many states and Canadian provinces, a woman who committed adultery lost everything, including property she possessed before she married, while the law took no notice of a man who cheated on his wife. A Canadian mother at the turn of the century had, in the eyes of the law, "no more legal relationship to her children than a stranger." Furthermore, in Manitoba in 1913, a person who stole a post letter bag or a cow received a much stiffer prison sentence than someone who seduced a girl of fourteen or committed an act of indecent assault on a woman.

Influenced by Social Darwinist thinking, the antis (several prominent women among them) maintained that there was a "natural order." The thought that a hard-working man would arrive home at the end of the day only to find his wife had gone out to attend a political meeting was unacceptable. Intellectual as well as physical distinctions between men and woman could not be erased, nor was it desirable to do so. "There is much more difference both physically and morally, between an educated European man and woman," pronounced the Earl of Cromer in 1911, "than there is between a Negro and negress belonging to some savage Central African tribe."

By their actions, regarded as "hysterical" by the conservative *Times* of London and others, so-called modern women like the suffragettes in the eyes of the antis not only reaffirmed their inadequacy for dealing intelligently with political issues, but also contributed to the decline of society. Sigmund Freud's learned view that hysteria was "essentially a 'feminine' neurosis" was more or less accepted as the sacred truth of the day, and depictions of the suffragettes as members of the "shrieking sisterhood" were common. And what could be more hysterical and unstable than sacrificing oneself on a racetrack? Emily Davison's behaviour, in the opinion of the antis, was immoral and contravened women's rightful role as wives and mothers. If anything, it strengthened their position that women were far too unstable to vote.

They did not, claimed Lord Curzon, the president of the British Anti-Suffrage League (formed in 1908 to counter the women's suffrage groups), have "the calmness of temperament or the balance of mind, [nor] the training necessary to qualify them to exercise the weighty judgment in political affairs." As Violet Markham, an outspoken anti put it, giving the vote to women was a "gamble with the future of womanhood."

Besides, numerous critics pointed out, women's desire for the vote was based on a false premise. The *New York Times* editorialized in early May 1912 that "the ballot will secure to woman no right that she needs and does not now possess." Or, put another way by Manitoba premier Rodmond Roblin, one of Canadian suffragists' great nemeses, "nice women don't want the vote." In short, the antis insisted that women had all of the rights and legal protections they required. What was not said, but felt deeply nonetheless, was that extending the franchise would give yet one more class of individuals power in a volatile world already threatened by urban blight, trade unionism, socialism, and anarchism. Where would it end? the traditionalists wondered.

When it came to the subject of women, Curzon, Markham, Roblin, and many others feared the unknown and maintained that drastic change would result in a new order of "manly or mannish women" who possessed no maternal instincts and who would upset the status quo between the sexes. "I think that I am perfectly safe in asserting," American physician James Weir, Jr., commented in a September 1895 article in *American Naturalist*, "that every woman who has been at all prominent in advancing the cause of equal rights in its entirety, has either given evidences of masculo-femininity or has shown conclusively that she was the victim of psycho-sexual aberrancy." Time and again, this theme was raised in popular magazines like *Vanity Fair* and *Life* and in scholarly studies. There was even a strong suggestion that active participation in the suffrage movement was a major cause, or at least symptom, of "sexual inversion," as homosexuality was then called.

The suffragettes and more moderate suffragists saw things slightly differently. Interestingly enough, they did not dispute the general consensus that women were the moral guardians of society. In the great debate between those who believed that nature and heredity defined a person's potential – as opposed to the environmentalists who put their stock in the nurture side of the equation – many (but not all) women seeking the vote argued that society's multitude of ills and sins could be cured by adopting a more maternal approach. Carrie Chapman Catt, one of the leaders of the suffragists in the United States, always maintained that a woman was above all "the mother, the wife," a role even more important than being a "loyal American." The line here between the traditionalists and the modernists was hazy indeed. The women argued that with the power of the vote their overall contributions to improving civilization could only be enhanced, but their status as daughters, sisters, mothers, and wives would never be sacrificed. As British historian Lisa Tickner notes, "if politics was too dirty for women, then the women must clean it up."

Near the end of the British militants' campaign in the spring of 1913, for example, Christabel Pankhurst wrote a widely read and contentious book entitled *The Great Scourge and How to End It*, a moralistic attack with Victorian overtones on sexuality, prostitution, and venereal disease. Men, she argued, were morally corrupt and were to blame for the depravity inflicting the city and modern life. "One is forced to the conclusion," she wrote, "if one accepts men's account of themselves, that women's human nature is something very much cleaner, stronger, and higher than the human nature of men." (She also claimed incorrectly that "between 75 and 80 per cent of men contracted venereal disease and warned women against the hazards of marriage.") Almost immediately the WSPU renewed its militant actions and embarked on a "Moral Crusade," as its members called it, to "purge" sin and cure "social evils." Whether or not all of them actually believed in the sanctity of this crusade was not the issue. Most of them would have followed Christabel anywhere she led.

Deeds Not Words

Christabel Pankhurst well may be the most interesting personality in the emotional drama of the British women's suffrage movement. She was clearly her mother's daughter (as well as her favourite, according to her sister Sylvia) in her lovely appearance, firm demeanour, and single-minded – even ruthless – dedication to the cause. "Christabel is not like other women," her mother once commented. "She will never be led away by her affections." Her radiant beauty attracted a lot of men, but her domineering personality intimidated nearly all them. Often lonely, she found companionship with several close female friends.

Christabel was born in Manchester in 1880, the first child of Dr. Richard and Emmeline Pankhurst. He was a lawyer with socialist leanings and an early advocate of women's suffrage. At the age of forty-four, he fell in love with Emmeline Goulden, the beautiful twenty-year-old daughter of a Manchester businessman. Besides Christabel, they had four other children, including Sylvia, born in 1882, who would also become a leading suffragette.

The family relocated to London in 1885, and Emmeline – known far and wide as "Mrs. Pankhurst" – took an active interest in her husband's political work, especially anything to do with extending the rights of women – a fight that had been ongoing since the Reform Act of 1832 had made the franchise the preserve of propertied upper- and middle-class males. (By 1914 approximately 60 per cent of adult men could vote under British law.) Mrs. Pankhurst was a "born rebel," in the words of Frederick Pethick-Lawrence, who worked closely with her and Christabel in the WSPU. Another contemporary remembered her beauty as a "living flame," while Harriot Stanton Blatch, the American suffragette, thought that with her slender and willowy features she belonged in a nineteenth-century Impressionist painting.

Dr. Pankhurst's death in 1898 propelled his wife's career as an activist. Back again in Manchester, she supported her family with a job as the city's Registrar of Births and Deaths. But with her daughters Christabel and Sylvia (who was to uphold and cherish her father's socialist principles throughout her life), she also carried on Dr. Pankhurst's work with the labour movement and trade unions. It seemed obvious to the Pankhursts that granting both working-class men as well as women the vote would give these disenfranchised groups the influence in labour issues they desired as well as the necessary power to reform society.

The Pankhursts might have become more involved in the NUWSS, born in 1897 through the diligent work of its president Millicent Fawcett, but it was too moderate and middle-class for their tastes. Or as Sylvia Pankhurst characterized the organization, it involved nothing more than "brief utterances in nervous high-pitched voices; suffrage ladies were not accustomed to speaking at big meetings in those days. It was all very polite and very tame." Besides, the Pankhursts' socialist connections would not have fit the NUWSS mould under any circumstances. In mid-October 1903, Mrs. Pankhurst invited some like-minded women to join her in the WSPU. The name of the group was deliberate, she later recalled, "partly to emphasize its democracy, and partly to define its object as political rather than propagandist." Only women were allowed to be members, and though the WSPU clearly followed the lead of the Independent Labour Party, they were not officially aligned with it. "Deeds, not words, was to be our permanent motto," as Mrs. Pankhurst affirmed.

At first the WSPU was little more than a weekly gathering of a few dozen Manchester women who supported working-class rights and aimed to raise money and hold lectures for a variety of causes. While Mrs. Pankhurst was the leader of the nascent organization, it was Christabel who soon pushed the WSPU toward more militant action, expanding its membership and living up to her mother's motto more than either of them could have ever imagined.

Early in 1904 at a packed meeting of the Free Trade League, Christabel publicly challenged Winston Churchill, then a thirty-year-old member of Parliament, over his lack of support for women's suffrage. Although the two would tangle on several more occasions during the next few years, that moment left a lasting impression on Christabel. It was her initiation to a life as an activist. "This was the first militant step – the hardest to me," she remembered, "because it was the first. To move from my place on the platform to the speaker's table in the teeth of the astonishment and opposition of will of that immense throng, those civic and country leaders and those Members of Parliament, was the most difficult thing I have ever done."

More than a year later, she had another confrontation with British politicians and authorities at a public gathering that led to her arrest for disorderly conduct and obstructing justice. She was also charged with assault. According to the testimony of the police, Christabel spat at some constables and then hit one of them in the face. In her memoirs, she recollected that she only lightly spat – or as she writes, "shall we call it a 'pout,' a perfectly dry purse of the mouth."

In Police Court, Christabel was found guilty and given the option of paying a small fine or spending ten days in jail – three days for obstructing justice and a week for assaulting the police officer.

Mrs. Pankhurst suggested her daughter pay the fine, but she would not consent. Even Churchill offered to provide the funds to cover the fine; Christabel refused his offer as well. She and a friend who had been arrested with her were taken to Strangeways Gaol and were proud to be there. The morning Christabel was released, two hundred women (and a few of their husbands) were on hand to greet her and a packed meeting was held that evening in her honour. The *Manchester Evening Chronicle* gave the story prominent attention and she was hailed as a "heroine."

The suffragettes' war with the Liberals had begun.

Christabel's determination to confront the Liberals and the police in 1905 was typical of her stubborn resolve and unbending spirit. However one felt about her, and she surely generated a wide range of opinions, it was difficult to dispute her strength of character. With her striking good looks and astute intelligence – she had been educated as a lawyer at Owens College in Manchester, but as a woman was not permitted to practise – she possessed what today is referred to as "charisma." When she entered a room or hall, people noticed. "In her prime Christabel had political flair which was a match for the most subtle of male minds," recalled Frederick Pethick-Lawrence, who, along with his wife, Emmeline, worked closely with the Pankhursts until a dispute over tactics led to a bitter break in 1912. "She had a passion to free women from the stigma of inferiority and saw clearly that the essential pre-requisite was the Parliamentary vote. She had a genius for leadership, which inspired her followers to acts of unbelievable courage. She understood in a high degree the importance of publicity and had an uncanny instinct for evoking it."

But in her dogged pursuit of justice for women, Christabel, with the full support of her mother, became authoritarian and tolerated no criticism of her leadership. More than one suffragette and historian of the movement has pointed out the irony that an organization intent on "winning democratic rights should deny freedom of debate to its own members." Mary Richardson, who was with Emily Davison at Epsom Downs the day she died, recalled that the WSPU "had no argumentative committees in our organization. Everyone knew her job and did it. There were not round-table conferences, which referred back and deferred decisions until the plans they discussed were lost amid the piles of paper. Christabel was our planner; and we placed our lives in her hands."

The Pankhursts purposely ran the WSPU with military precision and strategy as if it were a guerilla operation. Orders were to be followed no questions asked; at least, that was the theory. And nothing, not friendship or personal needs, was placed before the cause.

The military command structure worked only to a point. It was, in fact, often difficult to control the behaviour and spontaneity of some of the women in the group, especially after Christabel was forced to flee to Paris in order to avoid arrest. Mary Leigh was the first suffragette to break a window after an altercation in front of Prime Minister Asquith's home on Downing Street; Marion Wallace Dunlop did not seek permission before she embarked on a hunger strike in prison in July 1909; and Emily Davison, as we have seen, had a mind of her own.

The Pankhursts had not intended to turn the WSPU into a terrorist organization. Their goal from the beginning was to get the men in the government to pay attention to their fight and to accord them respect. During the six years leading up to the First World War, however, the Liberals were faced with more pressing issues, such as the problems in Ireland.

The point of the WSPU was to gain publicity for the cause; to "create an impression upon the public throughout the country, to set everyone talking about votes for women, to keep the subject in the press, to leave the government no peace from it," as Mrs. Pankhurst described it. Hence, the more the government ignored the women, the bolder, more daring, and more violent they became. In a matter of a few years, the core supporters of the group, likely about one thousand women or less, progressed from heckling members of Parliament at political meetings and parading through the streets of London to breaking windows on government property, cutting telegraph wires, and setting mailboxes and homes and office buildings on fire. One suffragette even smashed the crown jewels case at the Tower of London.

At first, before the Pankhursts and their followers resorted to these more violent and destructive tactics, the WSPU's approach seemed to be working. In many ways, the women pioneered modern political interest-group strategy with their demonstrations and high profile in the press. They courted editors, submitted countless letters and articles, and ensured that the newspapers were kept up to date on their various daily activities. They quickly discovered that they were good copy. Even the WSPU's chief rival, Millicent Fawcett of the NUWSS, an organization that represented far more women than the WSPU ever did, conceded that the protests and subsequent arrests of the suffragettes seemed to be making a difference. "I feel that the action of the [suffragette] prisoners has touched the imagination of the country in a manner which quieter methods did not succeed in doing," Mrs. Fawcett wrote in 1909. She was, not surprisingly, much less impressed with the arson.

For their part, the Pankhursts were blinded by their belief in the virtue of their cause and failed to see, like most modern-day terrorists, that the violence had a disastrous effect on their organization. Public opinion, which had been somewhat positive, turned sharply against the women during the worst bout of violence in 1912. Hostile crowds pelted them with eggs and rotten fruits and vegetables and disrupted their public meetings. No matter, they remained firm in their position.

"I want to say here and now that the only justification for violence, the only justification for damage to property, the only justification for risk to the comfort of other human beings is the fact that you have tried all other available means and have failed to secure justice," Mrs. Pankhurst declared in a speech in New York City in October 1913 on one of several North American lecture tours she made. "I tell you that in Great Britain there is no other way." Likewise, from her hideaway in Paris (where she lived for a time as "Miss Amy Johnson") Christabel issued her "Broken Windows" manifesto in 1912: "Our very definite purpose is to create an intolerable situation for the Government, and, if need be, for the public as a whole."

It is essential to point out that as brazen as others believed the Pankhursts to be, and as radical as they saw themselves, they were fairly tame for so-called revolutionaries. "Though the suffragettes attacked and disparaged the parliamentary politicians," as historian Martin Pugh explains, "they desired to join the system rather than to overthrow the status quo. This is scarcely surprising because both their social class and their political connections placed many suffragettes comfortably with the British Establishment." Moreover, the militancy may have generated a lot of publicity and comment in the press and made the Pankhursts into celebrities, but the politicians could not be budged. They were, however, distracted from other official business.

Getting arrested and sent to prison was thought to be a sign of a woman's fortitude and commitment. Unaccustomed to dealing with middle-class ladies, the government was often uncertain how to handle this rather shocking situation. On most occasions, the police showed restraint, yet not always. In one of the more infamous confrontations on November 18, 1910, known in the annals of the suffragettes as "Black Friday," the police got carried away. The Pankhursts had high hopes that the Conciliation Bill, which would have extended the vote to women, would pass. When it did not, the women gathered to protest in front of the Parliament Buildings. Almost immediately the protest erupted into chaos.

The police treated the women no differently than they would a bunch of rowdy pickpockets and thieves. Many of the women were beaten and grabbed around their breasts and legs. Several suffragettes later testified at an official police inquiry into the conflict that police had twisted and pinched their breasts "in the most public way as to inflict the utmost humiliation." Mary Frances Earl accused the police of deliberately tearing her "under-garments, using the most foul language" and seizing her by the hair. Dozens of women were arrested that day.

From the start, the suffragettes demanded to be treated as political prisoners. But the government adamantly refused. In turn, the women went on dangerous hunger strikes, and the government, in its wisdom, responded with forcible feeding. Few official Liberal policies in dealing with the women backfired more. No matter how safe the prison physicians declared the practice to be, the women who experienced this horrific treatment compared it to medieval torture. The *Times* published this personal account by Laura Ainsworth on October 7, 1909, two days after she had been released from prison: "I was raised into a sitting position, and the tube about two foot long was produced. My mouth was pried open with what felt like a steel instrument, and then I felt them feeling for the proper passage. All this time, I was held down by four or five wardresses. I felt a choking sensation, and what I judged to be a cork gag was placed between my teeth to keep my mouth open. It was a horrible feeling altogether. I experienced great sickness, especially when the tube was withdrawn." Numerous other women also decried the agony of the feedings and more than one hundred doctors signed a petition to end the practice.[*]

---

[*] The most memorable case and one that embarrassed the government the most involved Lady Constance Lytton, one of the more prominent upper-class members of the WSPU. In October 1909, "Lady Con," as she was called was arrested with Mrs. Jane Brailsford for throwing stones at an automobile in which Sir Walter Runciman, a cabinet minister, was a passenger. They were convicted and sentenced to one month in the Second Division, rather than the Third, which was for common criminals and where all of the other arrested suffragettes were sent. The two women received preferential treatment and were released on medical grounds

Eventually the government halted the forcible feedings and passed the Prisoners' Temporary Discharge Act, more popularly known as the "Cat and Mouse Act." Under this clever law, suffragettes weak from hunger strikes could be released from prison so they could recuperate and then be re-arrested to finish their prison sentences. This happened to Mrs. Pankhurst several times.

The Great War

The war changed everything. Within weeks of Britain's declaration of war on Germany on August 4, 1914, moderate and militant suffragettes suspended their political activity as a sign of their patriotism. Their country needed them and this was no time for challenging the established order. As an act of good faith, the government, in turn, stopped hounding women under the Cat and Mouse Act and declared an amnesty for any suffragette still in prison as a result of her protest activities. No longer facing arrest, Christabel Pankhurst was able to return to London from Paris and her mother declared that the members of the WSPU would now do whatever was necessary to win the war. As Christabel explained in a report in the *Daily Telegraph* in early September, "the success of the Germans would be disastrous for the civilization of the world, let alone for the British Empire. Everything that we women have been fighting for

---

a short time after. Lady Lytton, the daughter of a peer, did in fact have a heart condition, but a less well-born inmate would not have received the same consideration. Determined to expose the government's transparent bias, Lady Lytton chopped her hair off and disguised herself as a working-class seamstress by the name of Jane Wharton. At a protest in Liverpool, she was again arrested for stone throwing and sentenced to fourteen days in the Third Division. She refused to eat and was forcibly fed. The doctors who examined her failed to detect her heart problems. She was force-fed eight more times. Finally, in a state of exhaustion, she was released and her real identity was revealed. As Christabel Pankhurst later noted, Lady Lytton "had proved her point: that the Liberal Government had . . . a different standard of treatment for working women and for other women."

and treasure would disappear in the event of a German victory."

A few days later, she spoke at a WSPU war rally at the London Opera House about the threat of the "German Peril." In her impassioned speech, she urged the women to support the government's military efforts and encouraged men to enlist. Any suggestion of her previous role as a militant had vanished. The Pankhursts, it turned out, were far less radical than they thought themselves to be. Indeed, by 1915 the WSPU had changed the name of its weekly newspaper, *The Suffragette*, to *Britannia*. Then, in a complete about-face, Lloyd George, the Minister of Munitions in 1915, provided the WSPU with £2,000 so that they could organize a parade in support of women's "right to serve."[*]

Women of every class and background did answer the call and contributed in a hundred different ways to the British war effort. They filled jobs in munitions factories and were exposed daily to deadly chemicals and toxins; they drove trucks, acted as railway conductors, and worked as labourers at the docks. By 1918, close to five million British women were employed. This enormous contribution, plus a general change in attitude by the government, led to renewed efforts to alter suffrage legislation. Even an ardent anti like Herbert Asquith (who remained prime minister until the end of 1916) changed his mind to a degree and conceded that women's participation in the war economy entitled them to the vote – though he still remained noncommittal. Finally, the elevation of Lloyd George, a long-time suffrage supporter, to the head of the government in December 1916 paved the way for reform legislation enacted in February 1918.

Millicent Fawcett, then seventy-one years old, who had been involved with the women's movement since the age of eighteen,

---

[*] Sylvia Pankhurst, on the other hand, remained a pacifist during the war and a committed socialist, even going so far as to support the communist revolution in Russia – a position that neither her sister or mother could accept.

sat in the visitor's gallery the day the bill was passed in the Commons. The government's new bill did not grant the equal suffrage that some women had wanted; it had age and property qualifications attached to it – women thirty years and older could vote provided they met certain property rights. But the suffragettes regarded it as victory nonetheless. "Women at last," wrote Christabel, "were citizens and voters."

Another decade would pass before Britain lowered the voting age to twenty-one and women could vote on the same terms granted to men. Winning the vote, of course, was one thing, altering perceptions about women was quite another.[*] Women, as historian Lisa Tickner suggests, "were enfranchised but they were not emancipated, nor was the vote to that emancipation or to the social regeneration for which so many feminists had hoped for." That struggle belonged to another era in the future.

By 1918, the WSPU's transformation from a militant to moderate group was complete. Now called the Women's Party, and still led by Emmeline and Christabel Pankhurst, its members reaffirmed their support for a victory in the war along with a call for social reform in the areas of women's employment opportunities, education, and family life. In the general election held in December 1918, a month after the war had ended, Christabel ran as a Women's Party candidate (though she called herself the "Patriotic Candidate" and was supported by the wartime coalition of Liberals and Conservatives led by Lloyd George) in a Birmingham constituency and repeatedly attacked her chief rival from the Labour Party as a "Bolshevik and

---

[*] As late as 1960, for instance, as historian Martin Pugh relates, "it was still common for Conservative [Party] selection committees to ask married women [intending to run for a seat in the House of Commons] why they were prepared to neglect their husbands and children, while also interrogating single women on their marriage plans."

pacifist." Despite her plea that voters support the Union Jack rather than the "Red Flag," she lost the election albeit by a slim margin of less than eight hundred votes. Women had not automatically voted en masse for the female candidate, as the suffragettes had always maintained they would.

Within a year, the Women's Party was disbanded and Christabel and her mother left the political arena. Mrs. Pankhurst lived for a time in Toronto during the 1920s and lectured for the National Council for Combating Venereal Disease, carrying on the moral crusade of the pre-war years. She returned to London in 1926 and ran for the Conservative Party but lost the election. She died at the age of sixty-nine in 1928.

Christabel's later years were more curious. She soon discovered religion and became a prominent member of the Second Adventist Movement. As she waited for Christ's Second Coming, she lectured in Britain and North America and between 1923 and 1940 wrote five books on her new-found faith. In one, *Pressing Problems of the Closing Age* (1924), she expressed her disappointment at women's failure to grasp the vote and change the world. "Some of us hoped more from women's suffrage than is ever going to be accomplished," she wrote. "My own large anticipations were based partly upon ignorance (which the late war dispelled) of the magnitude of the task which we women reformers so confidently wished to undertake when the vote should be ours."

As a representative of the modern era, she remained committed to positive change, but had lost her earlier faith in men or women's ability to cleanse and heal the world of its "terrible ills." In 1936, she was made a Dame Commander of the Order of the British Empire in recognition of her work on behalf of women. The radical had become a member of the Establishment, or perhaps she always had been one. She left England for the United States in 1940 and lived alone in Los Angeles until her death in 1958.

A Winning Plan

The Pankhursts' dogged determination set the example for women in the United States and Canada. Although most militant suffragists in North America never resorted to the violence of the WSPU, the British women inspired and motivated a new generation to take action – Harriot Stanton Blatch, Carrie Chapman Catt, and Alice Paul in the United States, and Nellie McClung, Flora Macdonald Denison, and Augusta Stowe-Gullen in Canada.

The initial combatants and heroines of the American suffrage story were Elizabeth Cady Stanton (Blatch's mother) and the indomitable Susan B. Anthony. In 1848, Stanton convened a two-day meeting for women to discuss their social and civil rights in her home-town of Seneca Falls, New York, where she lived with her husband, Henry, and their large family. In an era when few women spoke in public and fewer still met in groups to talk of anything but charity and education, the Seneca convention was nothing less than radical. That gathering produced a "Declaration of Sentiments," modelled after the American Declaration of Independence and essentially a blueprint for the women's movement for the next half-century. Impressed by Stanton's dedication and passion, Susan B. Anthony, a thirty-year-old teacher from Massachusetts, joined the cause. She continued to fight for women's rights until her death, in 1906.

As determined as Stanton and Anthony were, however, their tireless campaigning achieved only limited success.[*] They were

---

[*] As Carrie Chapman Catt later put it, after women had achieved the vote in 1920: "To get the word 'male' in effect out of the Constitution cost the women of the country fifty-two years of pauseless campaign. . . . During that time they were forced to conduct fifty-six campaigns of referenda to male voters; 480 campaigns to get Legislatures to submit suffrage amendments to voters; 47 campaigns to get State constitutional conventions to write woman suffrage into State constitutions; 277 campaigns to get State party conventions to include woman suffrage planks; 30 campaigns to get presidential party conventions to adopt woman suffrage planks in party platforms, and 19 campaigns with 19 successive Congresses."

more than a little disillusioned after the passage of the Fourteenth and Fifteenth Amendments to the U.S. Constitution in 1868 and 1870 guaranteed suffrage and civil rights for black men yet denied the same rights to white women. In the years ahead, they would feel the same way as they watched male "foreigners" and "aliens" – immigrants who had arrived in the United States from every corner of Europe and Asia – vote on election day. From their point of view, it was not only a question of justice and equality, but one also rooted in the same Social Darwinist beliefs about white supremacy and entitlement used by their upper- and middle-class anti-suffrage opponents.

While a handful of states – mainly in the West, where a pioneer spirit promoted a unique brand of American equality – had granted women the right to vote in state elections by 1900, the situation in the rest of the country was no different than it had been back when Stanton and Anthony had begun their campaign. At the turn of the century, the National American Woman Suffrage Association (NAWSA), formed from a merger of suffrage associations in 1890 and led briefly by Stanton and Anthony, was still pressing for the federal government to adopt an equality and suffrage amendment first introduced by a friend of Susan Anthony's (and known thereafter as the "Anthony Amendment") in Congress in 1868. It was no closer to being adopted than it had been at the time.

The movement was indeed "in a rut," as Stanton's daughter Harriot Stanton Blatch later remembered. A graduate of Vassar Women's College and one of the first women of her generation to hold a bachelor's degree, Blatch had left the United States in 1882 for England after she married William Blatch, a British businessman. She spent twenty years in England and became involved in the suffragette cause in London as an associate of the Pankhursts. It was Blatch, in fact, who helped Emmeline Pankhurst organize her first popular North American lecture tour in 1909.

She had returned to the United States in 1902. Based in New York City, she was active in the NAWSA, but also established her own state organization, the Equality League of Self-Supporting Women, which later became the Women's Political Union. While Blatch used the purple, green, and white of the Pankhursts' WSPU in banners and parades she led down Fifth Avenue, the similarity stopped there. Blatch was a true democrat, not a militant, and maintained that the vote for women must come through peaceful and diplomatic methods. Putting a suffragist on a soapbox at a New York City street corner was about as radical as she got. And even that was a strategy that did not prove popular with many men: Blatch's women who attempted to spread the suffragist message were pelted with rotten eggs, apple cores, and wet sponges, while people in the crowd beat drums to drown out their speeches. The police intervened as best they could to protect the women, although the antagonism persisted.[*]

If Blatch replaced her mother in the movement, then the role of Susan Anthony was taken over by Carrie Chapman Catt. Born in Wisconsin in 1859, Carrie Lane also attended college and became a teacher in Iowa. She taught briefly before being appointed superintendent of schools, a highly unusual position for a single woman to hold but typical of Catt's determination to succeed. In 1885, she married her first husband, Leo Chapman, the editor of a newspaper in Mason City, Iowa. She left education and transformed herself into a columnist covering women's issues. Financial problems led Chapman to relocate to California. But before Catt could join him

---

[*] Harriot Stanton Blatch also used the motion-picture industry to promote her cause. The antis had created a variety of anti-suffrage satires and comedies available at thousands of nickelodeons designed to ridicule the women. To counter this, Blatch arranged for several positive films to be produced. These included a romantic comedy called *The Suffragette and the Man*, in which the "beautiful young heroine, forced to choose between her suffrage principles and her fiancé, first picks principles and then overcomes an anti-suffrage competitor and wins back her lover."

he had died from typhoid. She was a widow at twenty-seven years old with few prospects.

Undaunted, she worked for a time selling newspaper advertising in San Francisco. She also took a greater interest in equality for women (especially after she was sexually harassed by a male employee) before returning to Iowa as a committed public speaker for the suffrage cause, a calling in which it was then possible to earn a living. In 1890 she married George Catt, an engineer and an old friend. Unlike most husbands of the era, he accepted and supported his wife's suffrage and public-speaking career.

Catt soon worked her way up the ladder of the NAWSA, making a name for herself as an efficient organizer and popular speaker. Most significantly, she began to slowly transform the organization into a more effective pressure group focused on one goal: the passage of a federal amendment to the U.S. Constitution. In later years, this would become a key part of her "winning plan." While some suffragists found her too blunt and authoritarian – one of the women she worked with aptly described her as "an aristocrat with democratic tendencies" – Susan Anthony, then near retirement, immediately recognized Catt's potential for leadership. "I know of no other woman with leisure, with no children, with a husband who backs her morally and financially, with the brains and disposition to do for the sake of the cause, and seemingly no personal ambition, but Mrs. Catt," Anthony confided to a friend.

Anthony's support helped Catt become president of the NAWSA in 1900. While that year alone she delivered fifty-one lectures in twenty-one states and travelled more than three thousand miles, there were no state victories, nor was she able to raise enough money for her campaign. Despite her persistent efforts, she achieved little progress in her first term in office, and when her husband became ill she opted to relinquish her position. He died in 1905, and for the next decade Catt involved herself in international women's issues as the first (and only) president of the International Woman Suffrage

Alliance, leaving the NAWSA in the hands of Anna Howard Shaw – "a champion of universal suffrage but an inefficient administrator," according to U.S. women's historian Sara Hunter Graham.

Catt returned to the NAWSA in 1912 to join the heated three-year campaign to win women the vote in New York State. When the results went against the women in a New York referendum as well as in four other states, Catt was urged to return to the helm of the NAWSA. She did so in 1916, launching her "winning plan," which was to lobby aggressively in Washington for a federal amendment and to focus even more pressure at the state level. Women throughout the country pledged close to $1 million for the coming battle.

Authoritarian as ever during her second term, Catt was prepared to do whatever it took, except resort to militancy. While she believed that all women, regardless of race, colour, or creed, had the right to vote, she was not shy about demanding in 1919 that several black women's clubs withdraw their applications for admission to NAWSA because she feared that this would work against support for the amendment in the South where there was tremendous hostility to extending the vote to African-Americans. That problem was easily solved. Dealing with the unpredictable Alice Paul proved more difficult.

How Long Must Women Wait for Liberty?

Alice Paul was a petite woman with blue eyes and auburn hair. A Quaker from New Jersey, she was a social worker by profession. Yet her small size, pacifist religion, or career did not stop her from becoming the firebrand of the U.S. suffragist movement. Like Harriot Stanton Blatch, Paul, born in 1884, had also spent time in England studying for a doctoral degree at the London School of Economics. She was more active than Blatch, however, in the Pankhursts' WSPU. Arrested and imprisoned with the British suffragettes, she joined in the prison hunger strike and was subjected to force-feeding. "I didn't give in," she used to say about that experience, and it became her motto.

Back in the United States, she joined the women's fight of the NAWSA in 1910, while still working on her Ph.D. dissertation at the University of Pennsylvania. Anxious for change, Paul had little patience for the NAWSA's plodding tactics. With her friend and fellow suffragist Lucy Burns (who had also been in England with her) she received approval from the NAWSA's executive to organize a women's parade in Washington, D.C., for early March 1913. She chose the day before Woodrow Wilson was to be inaugurated as U.S. president.

As the suffragists proudly marched down Pennsylvania Avenue, the men in the crowd turned hostile. "There was no division between the parade and the crowd," recalled suffragist Suzanne LaFollete nearly six decades later, "and the crowd was a seething mob of men who surged around the struggling marchers, shouting obscenities. There were few police in sight, and those who were in sight were making no effort to control the crowd. It was an obscene spectacle, and it lasted from one end of the avenue to the other; that is, it lasted four hours." The men spat at the women, threw cigar stubs at them, even physically attacked them. According to later newspaper reports, the police "stood by and did nothing."

The *New York Times*, a long-time critic of the suffragists' ostentatious public displays – parades were regarded by the newspaper as "distinctly unfeminine" – deplored the "abominable ill-treatment" accorded the women. With the support of the NAWSA executive, Paul established the Congressional Union, the organization's Washington, D.C., lobby group. Yet like Christabel Pankhurst, Paul was in a rush. She advocated an all-out campaign to win Congressional approval of a constitutional amendment. Within a few years, and particularly following the return of Carrie Chapman Catt, a serious rift developed and Paul split her group – soon to be known as the Woman's Party – from the NAWSA.

Paul's chief strategy, however, was not Pankhurst-style militancy; rather, she embarked on one of the first effective non-violent campaigns of the twentieth century, employing tactics later adopted by Mohandas Gandhi in his fight with the British in India and by Martin Luther King, Jr., in the U.S. civil-rights clashes of the 1950s and 1960s. In mid-January 1917, the "silent sentinels" made their first appearance at the gates of the White House. Solemnly the women stood day and night, clutching purple-white-and-gold banners bearing the slogans, printed in large block letters: "MR. PRESIDENT, WHAT WILL YOU DO FOR WOMAN SUFFRAGE?" and "HOW LONG MUST WOMEN WAIT FOR LIBERTY?"[*]

For the most part, President Wilson, not entirely opposed to granting women the vote, ignored the suffragists, while the press castigated the silent sentinels for making an unnecessary spectacle of themselves. They were "silent, silly, and offensive," in the words of the *New York Times*.

The U.S. declaration of war against Germany on April 6, 1917, altered the situation for the worse. Now Paul, who advocated that "Democracy should begin at home," was regarded in the heightened tension of the First World War as a potential subversive. Repeatedly, she and the other silent sentinels were warned by the police that they would be arrested – although it was never quite clear what law they were breaking by standing outside the White House. Nonetheless, in June the arrests started. The police hauled the women away for such offences as "blocking the sidewalk" and "picketing." It is hard to dispute Eleanor Flexner's observation that

---

[*] Inez Milholland, a suffragist of uncompromising beauty and a popular participant in suffragist parades, supposedly uttered the latter slogan. In October 1916, Milholland, who was thirty years old, collapsed at a suffragist gathering in Los Angeles. Before she passed out, she was said to have declared the words, "Mr. President, how long must women wait for liberty?" It became the rallying cry of Paul's group. Milholland, who was anaemic, was rushed to a hospital where she died a month later.

Paul and her suffragist group were the "first victims [in the U.S.] of the abrogation of civil liberties in wartime."

Clearly, the women did not receive the benefit of American justice (yet as we will see in Chapter Four they were treated far better than thousands of dissidents convicted under the federal espionage and sedition laws of the Second World War period). The courts quickly sentenced them to terms of a few days to six months at the Occoquan Workhouse in nearby Virginia. This was, by all accounts, a dreadful penal facility with a cruel and "sinister" warden, who meted out beatings and forced these middle-class white women to clean the toilets used by the black inmates, regarded by them as a degrading humiliation. The food was terrible, often filled with maggots, and the women were forced to wear coarse uniforms and sleep in a rat-infested cell "side by side with negro [sic] prostitutes."

Advised of the situation after the first series of arrests and court hearings, Wilson pardoned the women. He considered the suffrage issue a legitimate matter that required his attention, although he put it at the bottom of a long list of more pressing problems. More than a little conservative on social concerns, he considered the women's so-called militant actions "unstable" as well as "unfeminine" – an attitude, interestingly enough, also shared by Carrie Chapman Catt and other NAWSA officials astonished by the behaviour of Paul and her Woman's Party. In the months ahead, more women were arrested and sent back to Occoquan as well as the District Jail in Washington.[*] Determined to stand their ground, the suffragists demanded to be treated as political prisoners and then went on hunger strikes. Predictably, this was dealt with harshly by force-feeding.

---

[*] On August 14, 1917, a riot broke out near the White House after the women picketing unfurled a banner calling the president "Kaiser Wilson." Soldiers in the crowd took offence and threw stones and eggs at the women and assaulted them. When the women attempted to retreat, the men trailed them back to their headquarters and did not allow them to leave. Again, the police did little to intervene.

Paul received the brunt of it. She was sentenced to seven months in jail for "obstructing traffic." When she went on a hunger strike, prison officials sent her to a psychiatric ward, force-fed her, prevented her from sleeping, and had a psychiatrist (called then an "alienist") determine if she was insane. Eventually, the Wilson administration intervened, and she and the other women were released. The federal appeals court soon ruled that the arrests had indeed violated the suffragists' Sixth Amendment rights under the U.S. Constitution.

By this time, the behind-the-scenes political manoeuvrings had been set in motion to pass a suffrage constitutional amendment, and as Catt later stated with more than a hint of sarcasm, President Wilson supported the measure "in spite of" Paul and the militants. Yet by their actions (coupled with the NAWSA's persistent and effective lobbying), they had raised awareness of the issue to a new height, gained it even more newspaper attention – the press generally denounced the government's heavy-handed treatment of the women – and were at least partially responsible for the enactment of the Nineteenth Amendment, which was passed by the House of Representatives and Senate in 1919 and ratified by thirty-six states (meeting the necessary three-quarters requirement) in August 1920.

As in Britain, women in the United States, it turned out, did not vote as a bloc as the antis feared, but instead followed the socio-economic voting preferences of their fathers, brothers, and sons. Some of the women of the NAWSA felt that their work was finished, while others like Alice Paul continued to fight on behalf of equal rights. In 1922, Alice Paul and the Woman's Party launched a campaign for the passage of an Equal Rights Amendment, the ERA. Five years before she died at the age of ninety-two in 1977, Congress passed the controversial amendment, but it has still not been ratified.[*]

---

[*] The U.S. House of Representatives and Senate passed the Equal Rights Amendment on March 22, 1972, yet it was not ratified by the required thirty-eight

Maternal Feminism

Winnipeg, located in the middle of Canada, has never been a pleasant place to be in the middle of winter, and the evening of January 28, 1914, was no exception. A blizzard the previous day had left deep snowdrifts. Still, that did not stop the crowds of people in this growing prairie metropolis from filling up the Walker Theatre. Usually home to the premier vaudeville acts touring across North America, the Walker, an Edwardian palace with rosetted lights, crystal chandeliers, and crimson plush seats, was hosting a special fundraising event organized by Winnipeg suffragists, the women of the recently formed Winnipeg Equality League.

Only twenty-four hours earlier, the women of the League, led by their leader Nellie McClung – along with women from the Icelandic Women's Suffrage Association, the Grain Growers' Association, the Woman's Christian Temperance Union (WCTU), the Trades and Labour Council, and the Canadian Women's Press Club – had met with Manitoba premier Rodmond Roblin to discuss extending the franchise to women. Roblin, who had been in office since 1900, was a loyal member of the Conservative Party, a staunch advocate and practitioner of political patronage, a successful grain merchant, and a classic anti-suffragist. He saw no need for women to have the vote. Like Asquith in Britain, he did not believe the majority of women wanted it and arrogantly dismissed any arguments the suffragists advanced to the contrary.

After McClung had demanded "justice" for Manitoba women, Roblin, at his pompous best, stood before the delegation of women to deliver his verdict on their appeal. Referring to the violence of the suffragettes in England, he declared, "As you know, we all draw our

---

states. A seven-year deadline was imposed, but it was extended until 1982. It made no difference, since outspoken opposition by conservative groups found support in enough states to prevent its ratification. It is still being debated in 2005.

inspiration in legislation, theology, art and science and other subjects from the Motherland. Now, that being a fact that none will dispute can you, can anyone, in confidence say that the manifestations that have been made by the women there constitute a guarantee that if the franchise is extended, what we have today will be preserved and not destroyed?" He went on in this vein for some time, touching on the usual anti points of contention: hysterical women, the downfall of the British Empire, and the destruction of the family, home, and motherhood. Throughout the premier's speech, McClung sat back and noted his every gesture and the inflection in his voice. She paid such particular attention because at the Walker on January 28 she was to play the part of premier in the women's "Mock Parliament," in which roles and situations were to be reversed. It was one of the wittiest satires ever delivered on a Canadian stage, then or since.

The Assiniboine Quartet opened the festivities with several catchy suffragette songs and then the curtain rose for "How They Won the Vote," a short play originally performed by suffragettes in London, but adapted by the Manitoba women for a local audience. The premise of the skit was for a group of women, all related to one Horace Cole, a clerk, to convert their male family member into a rabid suffragist. For thirty hilarious minutes, Horace Cole's wife, sister, and cousin bombarded him with such unerring certitude that by the end of the indoctrination he was ready to enlist in the movement.

After an intermission, the curtain opened again, and Nellie McClung and her cadre appeared gathered like a legislative assembly. The female members of the House wore simple black robes. McClung, who at forty-one was a handsome dark-haired woman with deep, penetrating eyes, told the audience as the show got underway, "Remember, life on the stage here is reversed. Women have the vote while men do not." The concept of the Mock Parliament was brilliant: the women staged a parliamentary debate about men's demands for the franchise and used the male politicians' own words against them.

Petitions were the first order of House business, and one by the Society for the Prevention of Ugliness prayed "that men wearing scarlet neckties, six-inch collars and squeaky shoes be not allowed to enter any public building." Other discussions revolved around why women leave men. "Because they do not keep the house attractive," was one answer given and the crowd roared with laughter. The climax of the evening came when a delegation of men led by Robert Skinner arrived at the legislature with a petition for male suffrage. Their slogan was: "We have the brains. Why not let us vote?" In the same way that Premier Roblin had addressed the women a day earlier, Premier McClung now addressed the gaggle of men before her in a voice dripping with sarcasm: "We like delegations," McClung began, "we have seen a great many and we pride ourselves on treating these delegations with the greatest courtesy and candour. We wish to compliment this delegation on their splendid gentle-manly appearance." The audience snickered loudly. "If, without exercising the vote such splendid specimens of manhood can be pro-duced, such a system of affairs should not be interfered with. Any system of civilization that can produce such splendid specimens of manhood as Mr. Skinner is good enough for me, and if it is good enough for me, it is good enough for anybody."

McClung was hardly done, but she had to wait until the applause and laughter subsided before she could continue. She played the crowd like a vaudeville performer. As the debate went back and forth between the government and the male delegation, McClung finally added to the utter delight of the audience, "Another trouble is that if men start to vote they will vote too much. Politics unsettles men and unsettled men mean unsettled bills, broken furniture, broken vows and divorce."

The Mock Parliament was about as militant as Canadian women got during their fight for the vote. When Emmeline and Sylvia Pankhurst visited Canadian cities in 1909 and later, they were cheered and even revered for their work on behalf of British women, but the Canadians would never have hurled a cobblestone or gone on hunger strike. It was not done; it was that simple. Even more than the Americans, suffragists in Canada were conservative modernists who desired to slow down the pace of social change and reinstate Christian values into Canadian society. They witnessed the poverty industrialization had produced in the cities, the high concentration of "foreigners" in the slums, along with an increase in crime, prostitution, and the abuse of alcohol, and they were alarmed for themselves, their families, and their future. With the vote, these middle-class educated white Anglo-Saxon Protestant (and often professional career) women, by far the majority of Canadian suffragists, could save and reform the world they inhabited.

The origins of the movement in Canada began in 1877. Inspired by the American Society for the Advancement of Women, Dr. Emily Stowe, the first practising female physician in the country, organized the Toronto Women's Literary Club. The aim of the club was to "secure a free interchange of thought and feeling upon every subject that pertains to women's higher education, including her moral and physical welfare." Within six years, the Literary Club had reorganized itself as the Toronto Woman's Suffrage Association, but its success was limited.* Meanwhile, in 1893, a contingent of upper-class ladies led by the wife of the Governor-General of Canada, Lady Ishbel Aberdeen, formed the National Council of Women (NCW), yet this organization did not officially endorse suffrage for women until 1910. The NCW was mainly concerned with protecting a woman's role as guardian of the family.

In 1906, Emily Stowe's daughter, Augusta Stowe-Gullen, with assistance from businesswoman (a rarity in Canada) Flora Macdonald

---

* As historian Carol Lee Bacchi points out, "at its height in 1914, the [Canadian suffragist] movement probably had a total membership of ten thousand men and women, only 0.2 per cent of the adult population at that time."

Denison and Dr. Margaret Blair Gordon, attempted to revive the suffragist cause by establishing the Canadian Suffrage Association (CSA). All three women had been influenced by the American writer Charlotte Perkins Gilman (1860–1935). A fairly radical feminist of her day, Gilman wrote such books as *Woman and Economics* (1898) and *The Home* (1903), advocating that women should be equal, politically active, and economically independent of men.

The CSA attracted more professional women to its ranks, but it remained moderate and committed to the ideals of what has been called in Canada "maternal feminism." As wives, sisters, and mothers, women were to maintain their traditional role in the household and cure the world's many ills. Flora Macdonald Denison, one of the more outspoken members of the CSA, conceded in a newspaper interview in 1913 that "the primal mission of woman is to get married and have children." Ironically, some of the social reform-minded suffragists regarded Denison as too outspoken and split away from the CSA in 1914 to create the Toronto Equal Franchise League.

In the west, where husbands and their wives worked side by side on the farm, the issue of equality for women was more popular. From the first day it was in print, for instance, the *Grain Growers' Guide*, the organ of the Manitoba Grain Growers' Association, portrayed prairie women's role in the public realm in a positive light. "Without doubt the democracy of the twentieth century demands the wisdom, sympathy and insight of women for its development," wrote George Chipman, the newspaper's enlightened editor, in a 1914 editorial. "Most men are free to confess that they have made more or less of a botch of trying to run the Government by themselves. We look for a new moral impetus, a saner outlook and wider human sympathy to enter into the settlement of our public questions with the advent of women into public affairs." Chipman had in mind women like journalist Lillian Beynon Thomas, her sister Francis Marion Beynon, E. Cora Hind, the agricultural editor of the *Manitoba Free Press* (and the only woman ever allowed on the floor of the Winnipeg Grain Exchange until 1945), and Nellie McClung.

Of all of them, McClung is best remembered today and epitomizes the typical Canadian suffragist – good-natured, moderate, sensible, and devoted to her family and church. "A woman's place is in the home," McClung once wrote, "and out of it whenever she is called to guard those she loves and to improve conditions for them." On another occasion, after the vote had been won, McClung argued that "reformation does not need to be revolution. We women have in our hands that weapon which gain for us our desires, if we use it intelligently and unitedly." At the same time, she never accepted the notion of women's "proper sphere," nor their subservience to men.

Never Retract, Never Explain, Never Apologize

McClung was born Nellie Letitia Mooney in 1873 near Owen Sound, Ontario. Before she was ten years old, she and her family moved west, to a farm close to Brandon, Manitoba. Until she married pharmacist Wes McClung in 1896 and then with their three children relocated to Winnipeg in 1911 (their youngest child was born soon after they arrived in the city), Nellie McClung was very much defined by her rural roots.

She was trained as a teacher and taught for a number of years in the Manitoba town of Manitou, but it was first as a writer that she made a name for herself. In such novels as *Sowing Seeds in Danny* (1908), a Canadian bestseller, and its sequel, *The Second Chance*, McClung glorified the sanctity of pioneer life and disparaged the many evils of the city. The books were melodramatic, somewhat predictable, and contained a stern Christian message that one should not enjoy life too much. That aspect of her character she inherited from her mother, Letitia, a serious-minded and hard-working Calvinist. Yet the novels also displayed McClung's soon-to-be famous wit and humour, which she acquired from her more fun-loving father, John.

Before she discovered the suffrage cause, McClung's true passion was the prohibition of alcohol. She became a member of the WCTU and fought against the evils of liquor for most of her life. "The drink" was, in her view, the cause of all family hardship and a menace that had to be obliterated. "No one can deny that women and children were the sufferers from the liquor traffic," she concluded. "Any fun that came from drinking belonged to men exclusively, and the men themselves would be the first to admit that."

It was her work in the temperance movement that transformed this somewhat reserved prairie wife into a brilliant orator. Her son Mark later recalled that on a stage she spoke like "an evangelical preacher. She wanted to move people's hearts rather than their reason. . . . She would raise and lower her voice and lower her eyes and then she'd raise her arms. . . . She would gesture to one side of the auditorium and gesture to the other. She was a dramatist." During the height of the suffrage campaign, few individuals could fill up a hall (with ticketed admission) like McClung – or "Calamity Nell," as her opponents labelled her. They burned her in effigy in Brandon and told her to go home and darn her husband's socks. She retorted to great applause that her husband's socks were always well darned. In Manitoba's Premier Rodmond Roblin, a stuffy and old-style politician, she found her perfect antagonist, and no one who witnessed her spot-on mimicry of the politician that January evening at the Walker Theatre ever forgot it.

"Never retract, never explain, never apologize – get the thing done and let them howl," was her motto, and she lived up to those words in every respect. Still, for McClung, winning the vote for women, a cause she dedicated herself to from about 1911 onwards, was part of her larger plan to save the world. Like many middle-class men and women, she feared many aspects of the industrialized twentieth-century city. As she walked the streets of Winnipeg and crossed the Canadian Pacific Railway tracks into the North End, she could not help but be appalled at the slums and disease, the endless bars on Main Street, the brothels in Point Douglas (semi-legal in Winnipeg during the years before the First World War), and the multitude of immigrants from seemingly every corner of the globe.

McClung had become acquainted with J.S. Woodsworth, who was then operating the All People's Mission on Stella Avenue in the heart of the North End foreign quarter. She shared Woodsworth's belief that the "foreigners" not only had to be given welfare, but also more importantly transformed into "Canadians" – as she and another middle-class citizens defined it. Conformity and assimilation, not multiculturalism, was the policy of social reformers like McClung, although she did admire the "foreigners'" determination and their "burning enthusiasm" for Canada, "a land of liberty and freedom," as she put it. Like her contemporaries in the United States, she wondered how men who could barely speak English were given the right to vote when white Anglo-Saxon women born in the country were not. The injustice rankled her.

The First World War gave Canadian women the impetus they needed and convinced more reform-minded male politicians to grant women the vote. Manitoba was first, in 1916 (a scandal had forced Roblin to resign in 1915, and he was replaced by Liberal Tobias C. Norris, a suffragist supporter), followed during the next several years by the rest of the provinces except Quebec, which did not give women the right to vote in provincial elections until 1940.

The federal government, recognizing the hard work of Canadian women in the factories and wartime industries, and taking advantage of wartime patriotism, first extended the vote to women whose husbands were serving in the military and ensured "enemy aliens" would not be enfranchised. Nellie McClung, for one, had already suggested to Prime Minister Robert Borden that only "British-born women" obtain the vote "to offset the lower moral tone of the electorate caused by the 'going away of so many of our best and most public-spirited men.'" It took another decade, however, until McClung and four other women leaders – Emily Murphy, Irene

Parlby, Louise McKinney, and Henrietta Muir Edwards, the so-called Famous Five – challenged a clause in the British North America Act and had the Judicial Committee of the Privy Council determine that women were indeed "persons" under the law and therefore eligible for appointment to the Canadian Senate and had the right to hold public office.

McClung spent the remainder of her life (she died in 1951) as active as ever. After moving with her family to Edmonton, she served as Liberal member of the Alberta legislature and continued writing and commenting on the position of Canadian women.

Despite her religious convictions, her campaign for Prohibition, and her fears of modern life, she was, like Christabel Pankhurst and Alice Paul, more a modernist than a traditionalist. Writing about the extension of the franchise in 1919, she commented, "Women have won as great a victory as the battle of Verdun! But the day of settlement is upon us and that is the time of danger. . . . Women must claim the place they have won. They must take it. . . . Now is our time! We must claim our place in this new world that has been bought with such a price. It is ours. It always was ours, but we had not taken out our papers. . . . But today the World Titles Office is open, it is Ladies Day, and we must go in and file our claim. . . . This is the new citizenship."

CHAPTER THREE

Survival of the Fittest

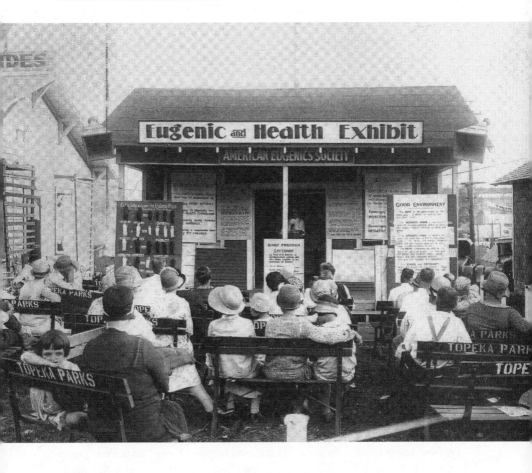

Previous page: The Eugenic and Health exhibit at the Kansas State Free Fair in 1929. "Science knows no way to make good breeding stock out of bad, and the future of the race is determined by the kind of children which are born and survive to become parents in each generation," declared Dr. Paul Popenoe, a specialist in heredity and eugenics.

To be a good animal is the first requisite to success in life, and to be a Nation of good animals is the first condition of national prosperity.

— Herbert Spencer, 1914

Origin of the Species

A letter he received in 1858 from a friend and fellow naturalist Alfred Russell Wallace prompted Charles Darwin finally to complete his study of evolution. It had been his life's work for nearly twenty years, ever since as a young man of twenty-two he had spent five years aboard the H.M.S. *Beagle* surveying the flora and fauna of, among other places, the Galapagos Islands off the coast of South America. While scrutinizing the islands' giant tortoises and other unique animals and plants, Darwin's theories on species variation and evolutionary natural selection were first triggered.

Darwin had returned to England in 1836 with a mysterious illness he likely contracted in Chile. For decades after, it sapped his strength and frequently gave him painful headaches and insomnia. Yet as the son of Robert Darwin, a wealthy physician, and the grandson of the well-known scientist Erasmus Darwin, Charles did not have to worry about earning a living. Wise investments and an inheritance permitted him the luxury of spending his time enjoying his family – he and his wife, Emma, a cousin whom he married in

1839, had ten children (three of whom died at young ages) – and contemplated the beginnings and evolution of life on earth. Although he was a member of the Royal Geological Society and respected as a naturalist, he led a reclusive life at his home near the village of Downe, in southeast England.

That changed in 1858. After reading Wallace's letter, Darwin immediately noted the similarities of their theories (this was unknown to Wallace at the time). Fearful that Wallace would ultimately steal credit Darwin believed he deserved, he rushed to finish a scientific paper on natural selection. He then transformed it over the next year into a book with the unwieldy title: *On the Origin of Species by Means of Natural Selection: Or the Preservation of Favoured Races in the Struggle for Life*. The London publisher, John Murray, was hardly optimistic about the book's sales potential and printed only 1,250 copies. Had a publisher ever so underestimated an author's impact? Priced at fifteen shillings, *The Origin of Species* sold out of London bookshops the first day it was stocked. During the next thirteen years, six more editions were printed. In time, the book would be read and debated in Europe, North America, and beyond, transform its shy author into an icon, both revered and hated, and help alter human perception of science, religion, and the beginning of civilization.

All of this was far from Darwin's mind in 1859. His interest in determining how and why different species evolved, coupled with his reading of English clergyman Thomas Malthus's famous 1798 essay on population control and survival – including the notion that human misery is inevitable and the weak will always perish – led him to theorize about the struggle for existence, adaptation, and natural selection. In Darwin's model, the perpetuation of different species through the ages was based on possessing particular characteristics, obtained through natural selection or chance. This permitted these species to adapt to their environment and survive, thereby altering the composition of the species over the course of many generations.

(An example might be an animal with spots. Those possessing spots were provided with camouflage against predators, as opposed to those of its species without spots who perished and did not procreate.)

What precisely this meant for understanding human evolution and purpose was not immediately clear. From the start, however, the natural and seemingly haphazard universal laws that governed "Darwinism," as the theory was quickly labelled, challenged the basic Judeo-Christian premise that nature was the expression of a divine purpose. Natural selection, American scholar Cynthia Eagle Russett has observed, "offered a convincing alternative to Divine Providence." God did not determine life, as the Bible had it; instead it was the result of a fierce competition in nature. Or, explained more aptly at the time by Thomas Henry Huxley, who was such an ardent defender of Darwin that he earned the nickname "Darwin's Bulldog": "Far from imagining that cats exist *in order* to catch mice well, Darwinism supposes that cats exist *because* they catch mice well – mousing being not the end, but the condition of the existence."

Hence, while many scientists and laymen accepted some aspects of Darwin's theory, his work and that of others of his era sparked a great and controversial debate about the meaning of God and human existence – a debate that in many ways continues to this day. Darwin himself complicated matters further in 1871 when he suggested in his two-volume work, *The Descent of Man*, that men and apes evolved from a common ancestor – "a hairy quadruped, of arboreal habits, furnished with a tail and pointed ears," as he described it.

Decades later, anti-evolutionists like the colourful American politician and evangelist William Jennings Bryan attacked and mocked this theory. For him, it was tantamount to devil worshipping. Where were the so-called missing links, Bryan and other skeptics asked, that bridged our evolution from primate to human being? Important archaeological fossil discoveries in England, France, and Germany in the early twentieth century did little to convince these empiricists and religious advocates. "I do not carry the doctrine of evolution as truth as some do," declared Bryan in a speech he delivered across the U.S. in 1900. "I do not mean to find fault with you if you want to accept the theory; all I mean to say is that while you may trace your ancestry back to the monkey if you find pleasure or pride in doing so, you shall not connect me with your family tree without more evidence than has yet been provided." Such strongly held convictions culminated with Bryan's participation in the 1925 Scopes "Monkey Trial," when traditionalists and modernists clashed over Darwinism and evolution in a Tennessee courtroom.

Bryan also objected to the concept of the "struggle for existence" at the core of Darwin's model, as he understood it. Applied to the history of human civilization, it conceived of a world, said Bryan, in which man reached "his present perfection by the operations of the law of hate – the merciless law by which the strong crowd out and kill off the weak." Later Bryan argued that such thinking was behind the German militarism that instigated the First World War.

There may have been truth in his assessment of European attitudes, except blaming Darwin for this state of affairs was hardly fair. Indeed, of the many ideas associated with Darwinism, "survival of the fittest" and its implied notion that strength or ferocity conquers all was by far the most popular and widely cited. The problem was, Darwin did not coin the phrase. That honour goes to Herbert Spencer.

Trained as a civil engineer, Spencer could be more aptly described as a political philosopher. Nearly a decade or so before Darwin published *The Origin of Species*, Spencer had already contemplated notions about human survival and adaptation. Unlike Darwin, he did not offer abstract scientific models of evolution, rather he offered a reasonable view on the world he lived in and theorized about the future. And while Darwin's theories included room for co-operation and community, Spencer maintained that human evolution thrived more on competition. He believed that progress, which was inevitable, was achieved through unimpeded struggle, free of government interference or other restrictions.[*]

During the latter part of the nineteenth century, Spencer wrote several important popular works on biology, psychology, and sociology, a field he helped develop. His *Study of Sociology* (1873) was used as a textbook in introductory sociology courses in the United States, and his other books sold more than three hundred thousand copies in that country alone. Thus, while Spencer craved respect from Britain's elitist academic community, he instead got it from the upper and middle classes in England and North America attempting to bring order to the chaotic world around them.

In particular, Spencer's vision of liberty, individualism, and laissez-faire capitalism made him a hero to such late nineteenth and early twentieth century U.S. magnates as James J. Hill, John D. Rockefeller, and Andrew Carnegie and made popular what soon became known (somewhat inaccurately) as "Social Darwinism." Spencer, more than anyone else, assured American business and industry that socialist experiments, minimum-wage laws, government charity, even asylums for the physically and mentally handicapped went against the laws of nature. Social Darwinism defended class divisions, the acquisition of wealth, and "the virtues of civility and civilization."

As Rockefeller stated, echoing Spencer's philosophy, "The growth of a large business is merely a survival of the fittest. . . . The American beauty rose can be produced in the splendor and fragrance which bring cheer to its beholder by sacrificing the early buds which grow around it. This is not an evil tendency in business. It is merely the

---

[*] While Darwin included the term "survival of the fittest" in later editions of *The Origin of Species*, he was somewhat indifferent to Spencer as a scientist and social philosopher. "I am quite delighted with what you say about Herbert Spencer's book," he wrote to his fellow naturalist and friend Joseph Hooker on November 3, 1864. "When I finish each number I say to myself what an awfully clever fellow he is, but when I ask myself what I have learnt, it is just nothing."

working-out of a law of nature and a law of God." In short, the suffering of the lower classes and the elimination of the weak were not desirable or gratifying, but it was a harsh and inevitable feature of the modern world. Nature, asserted another of Spencer's disciples, the Yale University sociologist William Sumner, was a "hard mistress against whom we are maintaining the struggle for existence."

At the other end of the spectrum, many, although not all, religious leaders objected to Darwin (and Spencer) because they presented a world in which God seemingly played no part. That, too, would spur on the post–First World War anti-evolution movement in the U.S. in which William Jennings Bryan and Billy Sunday – the bombastic evangelical preacher and former baseball player, who regularly damned Darwin as an "infidel" – among others, would play such a pivotal role. Bryan enjoyed entertaining his legion of supporters by ridiculing the Darwinian theory that the eye evolved from a light-sensitive freckle. "The increased heat irritated the skin – so the evolutionists guess, and a nerve came there and out of the nerve came the eye!" he declared at every stop on his lecture circuit. "Can you beat it? Is it not easier to believe in a God who can make an eye?"

Bryan's colleague, Thomas Martin, the Secretary of the Anti-Evolution League, was more succinct about the threat Darwinism posed to Christianity. "Every honest man knows that accepting evolution means giving up the inspiration of Genesis," he wrote in a 1920 newspaper article, "and if the inspiration of Genesis is given up, the testimony of Jesus to the inspiration of his scripture goes with it; and if his testimony to the scriptures is given up, his deity goes with it, and with that goes his being a real Redeemer and we are left without a Savior and in the darkness of our sins."

Countering these traditionalists were those who revelled in Darwinism, archaeological discoveries, new inventions, and the hope that science would deliver the decisive truth into their everyday secular lives. For them evolution signified only one thing – inescapable and unavoidable progress. Science, they argued, should not be shunned, but rather embraced and utilized to create a society in which rationalism would take precedence over superstition. This would be a modern world in which civilization reached its true potential.

In his later years, Darwin tried to escape the conflicts he had unwittingly unleashed. Yet by the time he died, from a heart attack at the age of seventy-three in 1882, he had already become, says historian Peter Bowler, "a multi-faceted symbol used by different people for their own purposes. To rationalists he epitomized the scientists' ability to penetrate areas of knowledge once obscured by religious dogma. For liberals his theory underpinned an optimistic philosophy of progress, providing a conceptual guarantee that things would continue to improve if only nature and society were left to develop on their own. Conservative theologians protested that his theory undermined moral values and the social order by reducing the human race to the level of animals. Extremists on both sides saw the debate over *The Origin of Species* as a battle in the ongoing war between science and religion for control of the human mind."

Each interest group, too, at one time or another, was guilty of distorting Darwin's ideas beyond all recognition. As the twentieth century began, supporters used his writings to justify imperialism, racism, and eugenics not only on moral grounds, but also on scientific. Detractors, meanwhile, blamed him for every problem of the modern world, including the decline of religion, Bolshevism, sexual immorality, and the disintegration of the family. "In their vocabulary," historian Willard Gatewood observes, "evolution became a catchall, scare word meaning modern evils in general. One zealot even insisted upon spelling it 'devilution.'"

The Science of Improving Stock

Herbert Spencer argued that the march of progress was best left to nature's design and that, given the right opportunity, most individuals, no matter who their parents were, might be able to overcome inherited weaknesses and other obstacles on the road to a fulfilling life. But Francis Galton disagreed, and within a brief time so, too, did a diverse group of scientists, academics, intellectuals, and politicians – everyone from George Bernard Shaw and H.G. Wells to Emma Goldman, Margaret Sanger, and Theodore Roosevelt.

Galton was Charles Darwin's first cousin – his mother, Violetta, and Darwin's father, Robert, were sister and brother. He had Quaker roots and was brought up in a prosperous middle-class family in Birmingham, England. Not certain what he wanted to do with his life, Galton studied medicine and mathematics, went on an extended exploration of Africa, and later became something of an expert on meteorology. He was devoted to science and disdained religion. A large and powerfully built man, he also suffered from frequent emotional breakdowns.

Inspired by *The Origin of Species* and desiring to make a name for himself, Galton, by now in his early forties, turned his attention to the issue of heredity. Unwilling to leave the future of civilization to chance or natural selection, and maintaining that it was heredity rather than environment that was the key determinant in the history of mankind, Galton proposed a type of "artificial selection." The wealthy and educated, those with "natural ability," had to be encouraged to have more children, while those of the "inferior classes," the poor, illiterate, unfit, and criminal, had to be prevented from "breeding" altogether.

His cousin Charles did not entirely disagree with this view. "With savages, the weak in body or mind are soon eliminated," Darwin wrote in *The Descent of Man*, "and those that survive commonly exhibit a vigorous state of health. We civilized men, on the other hand, do our utmost to check the process of elimination; we build asylums for the imbecile, the maimed, and the sick; we institute poor-laws; and our medical men exert their utmost skill to save the life of everyone to the last moment. . . . Thus, the weak members of civilized societies propagate their kind. No one who has attended to the breeding of domestic animals will doubt that this must be highly injurious to the race of man."

Galton first explained his position in a two-part article in *Macmillan's Magazine* in 1865 and then developed his thesis at greater length in his book *Hereditary Genius* (1869). He soon coined the word *eugenics*, derived from the Greek root meaning "good in birth" or "noble in heredity," to describe his utopian scheme. Eugenics was, he said, "a brief word to express the science of improving stock, which is by no means confined to questions of judicious mating, but which, especially in the case of man, takes cognizance of all influences that tend in however remote a degree to give to the more suitable races or strains of blood a better chance of prevailing speedily over the less suitable than they otherwise would have had." So convinced was he of the flawlessness of his theory, he believed "its principles ought to become one of the dominant motives in a civilized nation, much as if they were one of its religious tenets."

The scientific and intellectual communities did not immediately embrace Galton's plan for a better and fitter world. Many later did. Their faith in the paramount significance of heredity was not really confirmed until the turn of the century. In 1900, scientists showed renewed interest in and acceptance of the work of an Austrian monk and botanist named Gregor Mendel, who had extensively studied the breeding of pea plants in the 1860s. From his experiments, Mendel had been able to draw reasonable conclusions about what he called "elements" – dominant and recessive genes – which were passed on from one generation to the next. Mendel's Law of Segregation and Law of Independent Assortment, as they became known, laid the foundation of modern genetics (the term was first used in 1906). It only made sense to early eugenicists that human traits – not just physical, but also, intellectual and moral character-istics – were transmitted in the same way.

That was Karl Pearson's view at any rate. Like Galton, Pearson came from a middle-class Quaker background and grew up in London. Educated in mathematics at Cambridge and at universities in Germany, Pearson, who fancied himself a socialist (intellectually, at least), began teaching at University College in London in 1884. Working with zoologist Walter Weldon, a keen student of Galton's work, Pearson soon was undertaking statistical research on heredity. His scientific endeavours eventually brought him into contact with Galton. Thereafter Pearson was devoted to promoting eugenic prin-ciples, insisting, "the only way to keep a nation strong mentally and physically is to see that each new generation is derived chiefly from the fitter members of the generation before." When Galton died in 1911, he left in his will £45,000 to University College to establish the Galton Eugenics Professorship. Pearson received the first appointment, influencing and popularizing eugenics in England and the United States.

Two classic heredity studies contributed further to the growing appeal of eugenics and to the sense of urgency that real action had to be taken. In 1877, Richard Dugdale, a New York merchant and prison reformer, attempting to prove that pauperism was a heredi-tary trait, published the results of an examination he had conducted on the bloodlines of a family named Juke. According to Dugdale's findings, a frontiersman named Max Juke and his "degenerate" wife, who had lived in upstate New York in the 1730s, were respon-sible for seven generations of misfits and criminals. Among their 709 descendants, Dugdale discovered, 181 were prostitutes, 106 were illegitimate, 142 were beggars, and 70 were convicted of crimes – seven of them murders. In all, Dugdale estimated that between 1730 and 1874 the Jukes had cost taxpayers about $1.3 million. Interestingly, he did not completely discount environmental factors, yet "hereditarians" ignored that aspect of his study and focused exclusively on biological factors. A follow-up study on the Jukes in 1915 by Arthur Estabrook, a young American eugenicist, confirmed that four decades later the family remained plagued with "feeble-mindedness, indolence, licentiousness, and dishonesty."

Dugdale's pioneering work inspired Henry Goddard, a psychologist and director of research at a school for mentally handicapped children in Vineland, New Jersey. Committed to measuring intelligence, utilizing tests similar to those developed by the French psychologists Alfred Binet and Théodore Simon, Goddard established categories to differentiate degrees of feeble-mindedness. At the bottom of the scale were "idiots," who had a mental age of one or two; "imbeciles" came next, followed by "morons," a term Goddard created from the Greek word *moronia*, meaning "dull" or "stupid." In 1911, Goddard followed in Dugdale's footsteps with a study of his own of a family he creatively called the Kallikaks – from the Greek *kalos*, or "good," and *kakos*, or "bad."

The Kallikaks saga began in 1776, when Martin "Kallikak," a soldier in the American War of Independence, impregnated a feeble-minded tavern girl named Deborah. From this one encounter came several generations of bastards, sexual deviants, alcoholics, epileptics, criminals, and mentally handicapped individuals. What convinced Goddard that his study was truly significant – and what made his book *The Kallikak Family* so well known and admired outside of academic circles – was the fact that Martin Kallikak had produced another long line of healthy and fit descendants when he had married a "respectable" young woman. Feeble-mindedness, Goddard concluded, surely was hereditary.

A Trustee of Germ Plasm

In the years leading up to the First World War, and again in the early 1920s, middle-class Americans could not hear or read enough about eugenics. Countless articles appeared in the *New York Times* and other newspapers espousing its virtues, and the best magazines – *Harper's Weekly*, *The Atlantic Monthly*, *Saturday Evening Post*, and the *New Republic* – profiled the movement's proponents and analyzed their apparently scientifically sound findings. According to one estimate, popular magazines and periodicals in the United States between 1910 and 1914 published "more articles on eugenics than on the three questions of slums, tenements, and living standards combined."

Writers J.F. Bobbitt, Granville Stanley Hall (a prolific American educator), and particularly journalist Albert E. Wiggam – author of the 1923 bestseller *The New Decalogue of Science* – spread the gospel of eugenics across the United States. Wiggam's book appeared the same year the American Eugenics Society (AES) was founded. The AES provided a national forum for academics, scholars, physicians, lawyers, university officials, and other experts in the field, and with financial assistance from such business tycoons as John D. Rockefeller, Jr., and George Eastman, it soon had local groups in twenty-eight states, from New York to California. One of its early pamphlets likened the eugenics movement to the "founding and development of Christianity, something to be handed on from age to age." Eugenics had become a "secular religion," as Francis Galton had envisioned.

At Harvard, Columbia, Cornell, and other North American colleges and universities, eugenics found its way into the science curriculum. "We know enough about agriculture so that the agricultural production of the country could be doubled if the knowledge were applied," claimed Charles Van Hise, a geologist and president of the University of Wisconsin, "we know enough about disease so that if the knowledge were utilized, infectious and contagious diseases would be substantially destroyed in the United States within a score of years; we know enough about eugenics so that if the knowledge were applied, the defective classes would disappear within a generation."

The tremendous appeal of the eugenics movement was partly based on hope and partly on fear – hope for building a stronger and more intelligent populace, and the fear that the trend was in the opposite direction. Progressive-minded Americans watched in trepidation as their country was swamped by foreigners, who not only challenged the supremacy of the Nordic or Anglo-Saxon race, but also brought to their cities nothing but poverty, slums, crime, prostitution, and corruption. "National deterioration," was what pro-eugenics academics and propagandists called it in Britain. Then the First World War began, and they saw their best and brightest march off to die in the battlefields of Belgium and France, while the unfit, degenerate, and feeble-minded, remained at home to reproduce more of their own kind. (It was not lost on eugenics supporters that improvements in modern medicine and the quality of life generally also permitted the weak and feeble-minded to survive and have children when in an earlier era they might have perished.)

Most eugenicists dwelled incessantly on controlling the birth rate of the unfit, but for some, ridding society entirely of the mentally subnormal was the obvious next step. In London, George Bernard Shaw, the Fabian Socialist and dramatist, who preached positive eugenics, which emphasized the importance of "good breeding quality," also argued that "extermination must be put on a scientific basis if it is ever to be carried out humanely." Adding, "If we desire a certain type of civilization and culture, we must exterminate the sort of people who do not fit it."

The popular novelist H.G. Wells, Shaw's colleague at the Fabian Society, likewise worried about the impact of "vicious, helpless and pauper masses" in his non-fiction book *Anticipations of the Reaction of Mechanical and Scientific Progress upon Human Life and Thought* (1901). "Their characteristic weaknesses are contagious and detrimental in the civilizing fabric," he wrote, "and . . . their range of incapacity tempts and demoralizes the strong. To give them equality is to sink to their level, to protect and cherish them is to be swamped in their fecundity."

Novelist D.H. Lawrence was more direct and eerily prophetic. In a letter to a friend in 1908 he explained his plan to save the world: "If I had my way, I would build a lethal chamber as big as the Crystal Palace, with a military band playing softly, and a Cinematograph working brightly; then I'd go out in the back streets and main streets and bring them in, all the sick, the halt, and the maimed; I would lead them gently, and they would smile me a weary thanks." Lawrence died in the south of France in 1930, not knowing that the Nazis would indeed implement such a devastating policy ten years later.

These ideas were shared and widely promoted in the United States by Charles Davenport, the best known and likely most influential American proponent of eugenics. Born in Brooklyn Heights, New York, in 1866, Davenport came from a large family. His father, Amzi, a one-time teacher who had made his money as a real-estate broker, could trace his roots back to America's first Puritan settlers. The senior Davenport, who disdained alcohol, was a harsh and demanding parent, and Charles's childhood was filled with prayers, education, and little fun. Such an upbringing left its mark. Davenport was serious, sombre, somewhat arrogant, and "bridled at the merest hint of sexual indulgence." He had a high forehead with a receding hairline, penetrating dark eyes, and sported a thick moustache and goatee beard that had turned a salt and pepper colour by the time he was forty years old.

At college, Davenport studied biology and engineering and in 1891 obtained his doctorate in natural history from Harvard. Three years later, he married Gertrude Crotty of Kansas, who had received an undergraduate degree in zoology from the Society for Collegiate Instruction of Women (which later became Harvard's Radcliffe College) and she became his devoted supporter. The Davenports had two daughters: Jane, who obeyed her parents' directives, and Millia (called "Billy"), who was much more trouble and likely regarded as sexually immoral by her puritanical father. Not only did she disagree and argue with him about eugenics, she was also a divorcée, lived an avant-garde life in Greenwich Village during the roaring 1920s, and worked as a costume designer for a drama company.

During the latter part of the 1890s, Davenport taught at Harvard, but in 1899 moved to Chicago after he was offered a position in biometry (the study and analysis of biological statistics) at the newly established University of Chicago. In the years that followed, Davenport visited England and met with Francis Galton and geneticist Karl Pearson. He returned to the U.S. believing more than ever in the salvation of eugenics. Substantial research funds from the Carnegie Institute in Washington, D.C., and later from a private benefactor, Mrs. E.H. Harriman, the wealthy widow of the railway magnate (between 1909 and 1918, she reportedly gave Davenport more than $500,000), permitted Davenport to leave teaching and establish a centre and laboratory for evolution and eugenics study at Cold Spring Harbor on Long Island.

At the Cold Spring Harbor station and adjacent Eugenics Records Office, located thirty miles from New York City on a large rural property next to the palatial estates of the American elite, Davenport and his staff conducted genetic research and began amassing data from prisons, mental hospitals, and similar public institutions. Hundreds of physicians across the U.S. also aided his work either by supplying him with heredity data or encouraging their patients to complete a "Record of Family Traits." He participated in international eugenics conferences in Germany (organized by the International Society for Racial Hygiene), sharing his thoughts with such participants as Leonard Darwin, son of Charles and in 1912 head of the British Eugenics Society, Alexander Graham Bell, and Charles Eliot, the president of Harvard University, among many other notables.

Back home, Davenport involved himself in national conferences on "Race Betterment" and how to improve "American stock." The second such gathering took place in 1915 in San Francisco in conjunction with the Panama Pacific Exposition being held in the city at the time. It included an exhibit at the Palace of Education, complete with graphs, photographs, and portraits displaying the impact of heredity on the American population. For the thousands of people visiting the exhibit it was a lesson in "the rapid increase of race degeneracy." In the years ahead, eugenics societies sponsored "fitter family" contests at state fairs, in which each member of a family submitted him- or herself to physical medical exams and intelligence tests. At the Kansas State Fair in 1924, the winners received a "Governor's Fitter Family" trophy from Governor Jonathan Davis.[*] In San Francisco, Dr. Paul Popenoe, a specialist in heredity and eugenics, and the founder, in 1923, of the AES's southern California branch, gave one of the keynote addresses of the five-day conference. For him, as for Davenport, environmental factors were fairly irrelevant.

"Science knows no way to make good breeding stock out of bad, and the future of the race is determined by the kind of children which are born and survive to become parents in each generation," Popenoe told the attendees. "There are only two ways to improve the germinal character of the race, to better it in a fundamental and enduring manner. One is to kill off weaklings born in each generation. This is Nature's way. . . . When we abandon that, we have but one conceivable alternative, and this is to adopt some means by which fewer weaklings will be born in each generation. The only hope for permanent race betterment under social control is to substitute a selective birth-rate for Nature's selective death-rate. That means – eugenics." Within three years, such concepts reached a wide audience across the United States in Popenoe's popular college textbook

---

[*] More hard-hitting was another travelling exhibit called "Some People Are Born to be a Burden to the Rest." It consisted of a large board on which lights flashed at different intervals. It indicated that every sixteen seconds a person was born in the United States; that every fifteen seconds "a person with bad heredity costs the citizenry $100"; and that every seven and a half minutes, a person of "high grade" heredity was born.

Applied Eugenics, a work he co-authored with Roswell Johnson.

Davenport used research conducted at his Cold Spring Harbor station in his book *Heredity in Relation to Eugenics*, published in 1911. It was a classic declaration of his faith that environment counted for little in determining an individual's life path. The only thing that mattered, he argued, was blood: "Man is an animal and the laws of improvement of corn and race horses hold true for him also. Unless people accept this simple truth and let it influence marriage selection, human progress will cease."

That progress, in his view, was dependent upon segregating and sterilizing the feeble-minded in order to stop the spread of insanity, epilepsy, criminal behaviour, alcoholism, sexual immorality, "shiftlessness," and pauperism, which he regarded as inherited traits. Maintaining a ban on marriage between "races," – by 1914, thirty states, including those in the south where pro-segregation "Jim Crow Laws" were enforced, had already outlawed interracial marriage – and keeping lower-order nationalities out of the country were just as important. These were the key components of what became known as "negative eugenics" – curtailing the numbers of feeble-minded, insane, and degenerates in the country. "Positive eugenics," on the other hand, meant encouraging white middle-class women to have more children and campaigning for the right type of immigrants.

Davenport was a product of his era, a white Protestant who was deeply troubled by the declining birth rate of upper- and middle-class white Americans and concerned for the future survival of his race. President Theodore Roosevelt (borrowing the phrase from scientist Edward A. Ross) had likened the situation to "race suicide," a sentiment shared by the most liberal northerner to the most committed member of the reborn Ku Klux Klan. Roosevelt established a commission to investigate implementing a more restrictive immigration policy. Davenport, like others of his generation, accepted as fact the racist and anti-Semitic stereotypes of the day, which treated American "Negroes" as second-class citizens; they had, he wrote, a "strong sex instinct, without corresponding self-control." Jews, or "Hebrews," showed "the greatest proportion of crimes against chastity," and their "intense individualism and ideals of gain at the cost of any interest" were inimical to "American" interests. Poles were "independent and self-reliant though clannish," and Italians tended to commit "crimes of personal violence."

In a lecture he gave to the American Philosophical Society about the effects of "race intermingling," Davenport issued dire warnings about the birth of "hybrids" and their negative impact on the American population. In particular, interracial marriages would create a breed of mulattoes, "with intellectual inadequacy which makes the unhappy hybrid dissatisfied with his lot and a nuisance to others." These and other dubious conclusions about "mongrelization" confirmed the worst fears of many white Americans and inspired racist tracts, state sterilization laws, and the U.S. restrictive immigration legislation of 1924.

Despite occasional criticism from scientists and physicians who questioned Davenport's inconsistent research methods and oversimplified inferences – "our friend Davenport is not a clear strong thinker," Karl Pearson told Francis Galton as early as 1906 – Davenport remained firmly committed to his eugenic creed.[*] "I believe

---

[*] In his brilliant study of the eugenics movement, historian Daniel Kevles explains Davenport's shortcomings as follows: "He combined Mendelian theory with incautious speculation. He knew that certain traits expressed combinations of elements – that is, were polygenic in origin – and had advanced the notion in his own research on skin color, yet his analysis of mental and behavioural traits usually neglected polygenic complexities. Davenport thought in terms of single Mendelian characters, grossly oversimplified matters, and ignored the forces of environment. Sometimes he was just ludicrous, particularly in various post-1911 studies on the inheritance of 'nomadism,' 'shiftlessness,' and 'thalassophila' – the love of the sea he discerned in naval officers and concluded must be a sex-linked recessive trait because, like color blindness, it was almost always expressed in males. His eugenic analyses rested on pedigrees gathered without rigorous rules of evidence concerning the traits they purported to show. His analytical concepts drew uncritically on vague, unproven notions – notably the neuropathic basis of mental illness."

in striving to raise the human race and more particularly our nation and community to the highest place of social organization, of cooperative work, and of effective endeavor," he explained. "I believe that I am a trustee of the germ plasm I carry . . . and that I betray the trust (if the germ plasm being good) if I so act as to jeopardize it. . . . I believe that, having made our choice in marriage carefully, we the married pair, should seek to have 4 to 6 children. . . . I believe in such a selection of immigrants as shall not tend to adulterate our national germ plasm with socially unfit traits. . . . I believe in doing it for the race."

The Passing of the Great Race

Charles Davenport was by no means the first scientist to make the connection between evolutionary theory, Social Darwinism, and race. In Germany, for instance, biologist Ernest Haeckel (1834–1919), stirred by *The Origin of Species*, devoted himself to promoting Aryan superiority and the notion of "polygenesis" – that each race somehow appeared separately as a result of multiple creations (this was contrary to Darwin's "monogenetic" view).

Similarly, Houston Stewart Chamberlain (1855–1927), a British writer with a university degree in science, who married composer Richard Wagner's daughter Eva and shared his father-in-law's anti-Jewish attitudes, gained wide notoriety with his book *The Foundations of the Nineteenth Century* published in 1899 in German and in 1913 in English.[*]

Like Haeckel, Chamberlain's version of human history focused on the moral and cultural supremacy of Aryanism – in all its glory.

------

[*] It was Count Joseph Arthur de Gobineau (1816–1882), a French diplomat and the author in 1855 of *Essai sur l'inégalité des races humaines* ("Essay on the Inequality of the Human Races") who influenced a generation of Europeans. He maintained that "the history of mankind proves that the destinies of people are governed by racial law," and that "all civilization flowed back to the Aryan race . . . the purest and most creative of the historic races of the world."

"Nothing is so convincing as the consciousness of the possession of Race," he argued. "The man who belongs to a distinct, pure Race never loses the sense of it." Despite the condescending, hate-filled, and anti-Semitic tone of the book, Chamberlain (who even tried to show that Jesus was not Jewish) received accolades from the likes of Theodore Roosevelt and George Bernard Shaw, who called it "the greatest Protestant Manifesto ever written." Both Haeckel and Chamberlain played a pivotal role in the spread of anti-Semitism (which declared Jews were a race rather than a religion) and racist ideology that was eventually embraced by the Nazis. Indeed, Julius Streicher, the rabid anti-Semitic publisher of the Nazi organ *Der Stuermer*, praised *The Foundations of the Nineteenth Century* as "the greatest book since the gospel." Chamberlain met with Hitler in early 1923 and was a major inspiration.

In North America, the term "Aryan" became "Nordic" (or Teutonic), but the implication of white Anglo-Saxon superiority was the same. Darwinism and eugenics provided racism with the scientific credibility it was lacking. "Negroes" now became a separate species, and an evolutionary inferior one at that. When Frederick Douglass, the African-American leader and former slave, died in February 1895, the *New York Times* explained Douglass's brilliance and success like this: "It might not be unreasonable, perhaps, to intimate that his white blood may have had something to do with the remarkable energy he displayed and the superior intelligence he manifested." With more white blood in him, he would have been "an even better and greater man than he was." Yet, as historian John Higham has pointed out, Darwinism also "suggested a warning: the daily peril of destruction confronts every species. Thus the evolutionary theory, when fully adopted by race thinkers, not only impelled them to anchor their national claims to a biological basis; it also provoked anxiety by denying assurance that the basis would endure."

With the possible exception of Charles Davenport, no one popularized these views, and spread the fear that the white race was under attack, more effectively than Madison Grant. In many ways he personified the accepted intolerance of the age. A staunch advocate of Nordic supremacy, eugenics, and anti-immigration, the anti-Semitic Grant became the toast of the town. He was invited to the best social events of the season, congressmen sought his opinions on immigration, and he was asked to be a director of several prominent boards, including the American Museum of Natural History in New York.

Grant was born in Newark, N.J., in 1865, and later relocated to New York City with his family. His father, Gabriel Grant, was a physician, a Civil War hero, and wealthy. Little is known about his early years, as Grant himself refused to discuss it. He attended a private school in Dresden, Germany, and Yale and Columbia universities. He graduated in 1890 with a law degree, although does not seem to have practised. Once he discovered eugenics, he referred to himself as a scientist.

A distinguished and handsome man, Grant achieved notoriety with his book *The Passing of the Great Race*, published in 1916 by Charles Scribner after his good friend Henry Fairfield Osborn, head of the Museum of Natural History, lobbied the publisher on his behalf. Even with a glowing introduction from Osborn, the book did not immediately sell well. Once the First World War had ended, however, and the anti-immigration movement continued to gain momentum, Grant suddenly became the author that everyone wanted to read. He was active in the Galton Society, formed in 1918 in New York by a who's who of eugenicists, including Osborn, Davenport, Princeton biologist E.G. Conklin, and Carnegie Institution president John Merriam. And in 1921 Grant was a keynote speaker on race at the Second International Congress of Eugenics, also convened in New York. Between 1920 and 1939, his book was reprinted seven times, and it was translated into German, French, and Norwegian. Grant later sent Hitler a copy and received a note from the Führer thanking him and indicating that the book "was his Bible."

Echoing Houston Stewart Chamberlain and imperialists every-where, Grant chronicled the story of the Nordic race, complete with its pure blood, blue eyes, fair skin, and wavy brown or blond hair. "The Nordics are, all over the world, a race of soldiers, sailors, adventurers, and explorers, but above all, of rulers, organizers, and aristocrats," he wrote. "The Nordic race is domineering, individu-alistic, self-reliant, and jealous of their personal freedom both in political and religious systems, and as a result they are usually Protestants." But the part of the book that attracted most attention was where Grant set out his belief that the "Great Race" was under attack from "Mediterraneans," Negroes, and Jews (or, as he described them, "hordes of the wretched submerged populations of the Polish ghettos").

Like Davenport and others, he warned that racial mixing could lead only to disaster, because the lower race always dominated. "The cross between a white man and an Indian is an Indian," he asserted. "The cross between a white man and a Negro is a Negro; the cross between a white man and a Hindu is a Hindu; and the cross between any of the three European races [which he designated as Nordic, Alpine, and Mediterranean] and a Jew is a Jew." The only way to stop this racial calamity was to declare intermarriage a "social and racial crime of the first magnitude."

It is not surprising that Grant's book – as well as that of his friend, lawyer and historian Lothrop Stoddard, author of another bestseller, entitled *The Rising Tide of Color Against White World Supremacy* (1920) – made a positive impression on members of the Invisible Empire of the Knights of the Ku Klux Klan. Inspired by D.W. Griffith's sensational film *The Birth of a Nation* (1915) – which glorified the inaugural Klan that terrorized the south in the years immediately after the Civil War – William J. Simmons, a travelling salesman and former Methodist preacher, had helped re-establish the organization. Now, it was not only African-Americans who were a target of the group's hatred, but also Jews, Catholics, and foreigners.

By the mid-twenties it boasted a membership of more than two million people in forty-five states. Klansmen resorted to violence to cleanse the country, but their concerns about the apparent threats to white Protestants were the same ones articulated by Grant, Stoddard, and Davenport, among others.

More telling was the enthusiastic reception that Grant received from politicians, scientists, and mainstream readers. Emphasizing that Grant's work was based on "recent advances in the study of heredity and life sciences," the editors of the *Saturday Evening Post* recommended *The Passing of the Great Race* as one of the "books every American should read if he wished to understand the full gravity of our present immigration problem."

Grant's success was based on his brilliant exploitation of white Americans' fear of their changing society. Today the eugenics movement is regarded as a conservative, even fascist, pseudo-science. In the 1920s, however, it was seen in a much more positive light, as a progressive movement to improve modern life.

In his review, former president Theodore Roosevelt extolled it as a "capital book; in purpose, in vision, in grasp of the facts." It showed, he said, a "fine fearlessness in assailing the popular and mischievous sentimentalities and corroding falsehoods which few men dare assail." Parroting Grant, Vice-President Calvin Coolidge, in a February 1921 article for the magazine *Good Housekeeping*, wrote that "America must be kept American. . . . Biological laws tell us that certain divergent people will not mix or blend. The Nordics propagate themselves successfully. With other races the outcome shows deterioration on both sides." (On the other hand in a review for the *New Republic*, anthropologist Franz Boas, who was Jewish and an outspoken critic of eugenics, castigated Grant's book as "a modern edition of Gobineau.")

This made a lot of sense to Albert Johnson, a Republican congressman and chairman of the Immigration and Naturalization Committee, who was then wrestling with recommending a more restrictive immigration policy. Rough around the edges and a high-school dropout, Johnson was from the state of Washington and wary of Communist radicals and Asian immigrants, who in his view were flooding the west coast. In 1923, he was recruited by the AES to head its "committee on Selective Immigration."

Johnson heeded the words of Grant, with whom he regularly corresponded, and met with biologist Harry Laughlin, one of Davenport's disciples and the superintendent of the Eugenics Records Office. As devoted and fanatical as his mentor, Laughlin so impressed Johnson that he was appointed the Immigration and Naturalization Committee's "expert eugenics agent." After visiting Ellis Island and conducting a two-year study on U.S. immigration, Laughlin returned to Washington, D.C., with his predictably disturbing (and distorted) findings on the over-representation of immigrants in U.S. mental asylums. The future "germ plasm" of the country was endangered, he warned, and unless Congress took some preventive action, the "blood of the nation" would be weakened.

Laughlin needn't have worried. Many years of intensive lobbying from the Immigration Restriction League (of which Madison Grant was then vice-president), the American Federation of Labor, the American Legion, and most major urban newspapers, had pushed immigration restriction to the top of Congress's agenda. Only a select group of businessmen, who were concerned over the decline in unskilled labour, voiced some reservations. The election of Republican Calvin Coolidge as president in 1924 – a politician who had never hidden his desire to keep America American – ended the debate with the passage of a restrictive immigration act which imposed more limited quotas for Europeans and added Japanese immigrants to the list of Asian groups already banned by existing legislation. Nordics and eugenicists cheered the news. But while the alien issue had now been effectively dealt with, the ever-increasing birth rates of the feeble-minded still loomed as a grave threat.

Three Generations of Imbeciles Are Enough

Hoyt Pilcher, the superintendent of the Kansas State Home for the Feeble-minded, wanted to do something positive for his nation. So in 1894, without possessing a legal warrant or proper authorization from his board of directors, he ordered the castration of forty-four boys in his care. Many Kansas physicians approved of his actions, and most people in the region were equally supportive of the idea of sterilizing the feeble-minded, although they believed Pilcher had gone too far. The State Home's directors agreed and he was fired.

What was required was to find a more humane method of accomplishing Pilcher's "noble" objectives. It did not take long. Within a few years, physicians like Harry Sharp, a surgeon at the Indiana Reformatory in Jeffersonville, had perfected the vasectomy for males and the salpingectomy, or the tying of the Fallopian tubes, for females, making castration only necessary in the most radical and serious cases. Dr. Sharp immediately went to work, and during a ten-year period ending in 1907 he had performed 465 vasectomies. Approximately one-third of his patients had reportedly asked to have the procedure. Owing in large part to Sharp's efforts, Indiana was the first state to enact a sterilization law, in 1907, making the procedure mandatory for confirmed criminals, "idiots," "imbeciles," and rapists as determined by a board of experts.

During the next decade, another fifteen states followed Indiana's lead. California passed legislation in 1909 (with revisions in 1913 and 1917) and soon led the U.S. in sterilizations; by 1921, almost 80 per cent of the 3,223 sterilizations conducted in the country had been done in that state. More states passed similar legislation during the twenties, so that by 1941 approximately forty thousand Americans had been sterilized (the exact total may have been substantially higher, as not all procedures were officially reported).*

But it was hardly enough, according to such experts as Henry Goddard and Edward M. East, a talented researcher and a pioneer of multiple-gene theory. America was not yet winning the war against the feeble-minded. In 1914, Goddard had estimated that there were between three hundred thousand and four hundred thousand feeble-minded persons in the United States. Writing at the end of the twenties, East suggested that there were "more than twenty million 'morons' genetically incapable of simple literacy, and yet another twenty million 'dullards,' who did not justify the effort necessary to prod them through grammar school." Sterilization legislation could deal effectively with approximately one million of these individuals, and "the effect would be excellent," declared East. Yet that still left millions more who were free to reproduce.

With the health of the nation at stake, few of the supportive physicians and eugenicists concerned themselves with the civil rights of the feeble-minded. In this matter, they insisted that the ends clearly justified the means. That was the opinion of Charles Davenport, who argued that society had the inherent right to safeguard itself by "annihilating the hideous serpent of hopelessly vicious protoplasm." Besides, the doctors who performed the operation claimed that those who were sterilized always felt healthier afterwards. But not everyone agreed with them, and sterilization laws came under attack from civil libertarians, lawyers, and religious officials. Eugenicists were determined to settle the matter once and for all in court. They got their opportunity in 1924 in Virginia.

That spring, Virginia passed its own sterilization law. About the same time, seventeen-year-old Carrie Buck was deemed to be a

---

* It is significant that once Hitler came to power in Germany, he and his underlings modelled their own eugenic and sterilization laws after those developed in the United States.

"moral imbecile" and committed by the state to the Colony for Epileptics and Feeble-minded in Lynchburg, Virginia. A male relative of Carrie's foster family had raped her, and Carrie had become pregnant and given birth to a daughter. To protect the rapist, the family commenced commitment proceedings against her. Carrie's mother, Emma, a prostitute, was also feeble-minded. She had been an inmate at the Colony for four years. Her mental age was said to be that of an eight-year-old; similar tests on Carrie showed that her intelligence level was only slightly higher, although the results were later shown to be suspect.

The Colony's superintendent, Dr. Albert Priddy, was a strong proponent of sterilization. Even before the state had passed its law, he had ordered patients sterilized when he deemed it medically necessary. He regarded Carrie as the perfect candidate for such an operation: She was the child of a feeble-minded woman and had likely given birth to a feeble-minded daughter (who remained in the custody of the foster family). Carrie arrived at the Colony in June 1924, and by September Priddy and the board of directors, invoking the new state act, had instructed that she be sterilized. To test the act's validity, they opted to put the matter before the courts by having Carrie's state-appointed legal guardian challenge the order.

The outcome of the case was never in doubt. A local Red Cross social worker named Caroline Wilhelm examined Carrie's seven-month-old daughter, Vivian, and testified that "she has a look about [her] that is not quite normal." Eugenicist Arthur Estabrook, an associate of Charles Davenport from the Eugenics Records Office, conducted an intelligence test on Vivian and agreed with that diagnosis. Several years later, Vivian's performance at school showed that she was, in fact, quite normal for her age, as her mother, Carrie, may have been too. It hardly mattered. After a cursory study of the facts, eugenicist Harry Laughlin gave his expert opinion to the court, declaring that Emma, Carrie, and Vivian "belong to the shiftless, ignorant, and worthless class of anti-social whites of the South."

Carrie's lawyer did not dispute the testimony given by the opposing counsel's witnesses, and the judge ruled that the sterilization could proceed. But the Colony's plan was to have the decision appealed in order to obtain a Supreme Court decision on Virginia's law.

That legal process took three more years, by which time Dr. Priddy had died. Dr. John H. Bell was hired to replace him at the Colony, and thus the case was thereafter known as *Buck v. Bell*. In early May of 1927, Chief Justice Oliver Wendell Holmes delivered the majority verdict upholding Virginia's statute by an eight-to-one decision (Justice Pierce Butler was the lone dissenter). Much to the satisfaction of eugenicists everywhere, the courts not only accepted that feeble-mindedness was an inherited trait, but also that the overall needs of society sometimes outweighed those of individuals.

"We have seen more than once, that the public welfare may call upon its best citizens for their lives," Holmes stated. "It would seem strange if it could not call upon those who already sap the strength of the State for their lesser sacrifices . . . in order to prevent our being swamped with incompetence. It is better for all the world, if instead of waiting to execute offspring for crime . . . society can prevent those who are manifestly unfit from continuing their own kind. . . . Three generations of imbeciles are enough."

Every Mental Defective Is a Potential Criminal

The victory in *Buck v. Bell* gave new impetus to the eugenics movement. Another sixteen states enacted sterilization legislation, mainly for patients already committed to state institutions. It also influenced the eugenics movement in Canada. As in the United States, many Canadian physicians, public health officials, and social reformers regarded eugenics and sterilization of the feeble-minded as a positive and progressive step. Many doubted, and even dismissed, the notion that government social welfare legislation would solve the growing degenerates problem – a situation made worse, they argued, by the flood of illiterate immigrants from eastern Europe and Asia. (Canada tightened its immigration regulations in 1928, but the new rules were not as restrictive as those implemented in the U.S.)

One of the first organizations in the country to launch a campaign to segregate the feeble-minded was the National Council of Women (NCW). As early as 1901, its message to the feeble-minded was: "You are an uncurable [sic] degenerate, a being unfit for free, social life. Henceforth I shall care for you, I will feed and clothe you. . . . In return you will do the work I set for you . . . [and] you will no longer pro-create your kind; you must be the last member of your feeble and degenerate family." The NCW campaigned for segregation, sterilization, and restrictions on immigration for the next three decades.

It was a woman, too, who was the most outspoken and ardent advocate for sterilizing Canada's feeble-minded. Helen MacMurchy is remembered as one of the country's pioneers of public health, although she often sounded like Charles Davenport in her passionate conviction that feeble-mindedness – clearly linked, she argued, to crime, prostitution, and juvenile delinquency – and an open-door immigration policy posed a real threat to Canadian survival.[*] Influenced by the work of Henry Goddard, Richard Dugdale, and others, she accepted that "individual inadequacy," rather than environment factors, had caused a crisis and required a bold solution. "Poverty, of course, is not a simple, but a complex condition," she wrote in a 1912 report. "It probably means poor health, inefficiency, lack of energy, less than average intelligence or force in some way, not enough imagination to see the importance of details."

---

[*] These fears were realized when W.G. Smith, a psychology professor at the University of Toronto, published his book *A Study in Canadian Immigration* in 1920. Among other "disturbing" facts, Smith's calculations showed that while at New York's Ellis Island, "the Americans' rate of rejection of mental defectives was one to every 1,590 immigrants . . . Canada's was only one to every 10,127 as evidence of leniency of the latter country's screening process."

Born in Ontario in 1862, MacMurchy, seemingly prim and proper from a young age, was also unorthodox; she opted to become a doctor, which was not a usual career choice for a Canadian woman at the turn of the century. She graduated from Women's Medical College in Toronto in 1901 and then furthered her studies at Johns Hopkins University in Baltimore. Returning to Canada, she was the first woman offered a position in the Toronto General Hospital's Department of Obstetrics and Gynaecology. She gradually became more active in public health and starting in 1906 submitted reports on the feeble-minded to the Ontario government. She was appointed the province's first Inspector of the Feeble-Minded in 1914 and briefly worked for the Ontario education department supervising special-education classes. Recognized for her expertise in the area, the federal government recruited her for its newly established Department of Health in 1920. She ran its Division of Maternal and Child Welfare for the next fourteen years, taking a special interest in reducing infant mortality – a problem she typically blamed on "ignorant mothers."

The same year she became an Ottawa civil servant, she also published her bestselling book *The Almosts: A Study of the Feeble-Minded*. Using research she had conducted during her work as Ontario's Inspector of the Feeble-Minded, MacMurchy educated Canadians (as well as Americans, since the book was published in Boston) beyond the medical and political communities on the unfit and degenerate menace afflicting the country – yet always with a feeling of empathy. One had to treat the feeble-minded with care, she noted, yet never lose sight of the fact that they were abnormal and had to be treated as such. "It is the age of true democracy," she wrote, "that will not only give every one justice, but will redeem the waste products of humanity and give the mental defective all the chance he needs to develop his gifts and all the protection he needs to keep away from evils and temptations that he never will be grown-up enough to resist, and that society cannot afford to let him fall a victim to."

Hester Street near Essex, Lower East Side, New York, 1899. In this ramshackle
neighbourhood, newcomers found affordable housing in tenements and wood shanties.
They also found friends and family from the old country who spoke the same language,
shops and stores where they could buy familiar food on credit, churches, synagogues,
and social clubs, and a plentiful supply of work in garment factories and sweatshops and
on road gangs.

Jacob Riis in 1904. Riis was a journalist, photographer, and chronicler of the Lower East Side in New York. Day after day, he reported on the immigrants' various struggles in short, gritty depictions of their lives.

Jacob Riis took this photograph of "street arabs" sleeping on the streets of New York in 1890.

Social worker Jane Addams in October 1912. Newspapers hailed her as the country's "only American saint." Addams established Hull-House in Chicago to work and educate the city's immigrants and impoverished. Motivated more by a good heart than by faith in the Almighty, she spent her life as a social worker in pursuit of the highest ideals of humanity.

James S. Woodsworth (back row, second from right) at the All People's Mission, Winnipeg, in 1912. A Methodist minister and writer, Woodsworth promoted the social gospel and worked diligently to "Canadianize" the multitude of immigrants arriving in Canada during the first decade of the twentieth century. He was later involved in the Winnipeg General Strike of 1919.

Left: Mrs. Emmeline Pankhurst in 1913. She led the fight for the suffragettes in Britain. Mrs. Pankhurst was a "born rebel," according to one of her colleagues in the movement.
Right: Christabel Pankhurst in January 1925. The daughter of Emmeline Pankhurst, Christabel was equally active in the suffragette movement. "Christabel is not like other women," her mother once commented. "She will never be led away by her affections." Her radiant beauty attracted many men, but her domineering personality intimidated nearly all of them.

Nellie McClung in the 1920s. McClung, a best-selling author and passionate advocate of temperance, led the fight for the women's vote in Manitoba between 1909 and 1916.

Left: Charles Davenport in 1927. Davenport was the best known and likely the most influential personality of the American eugenics movement.
Right: Madison Grant in 1921. Grant was the author of the 1916 best-seller *The Passing of the Great Race*, in which he chronicled the story of the Nordic race, complete with its pure blood, blue eyes, fair skin, and wavy brown or blond hair. He also personified the accepted intolerance of the age. A bigot and anti-Semite, he was a staunch advocate of Nordic supremacy and eugenics.

Carrie (left) and Emma Buck in 1924. Seventeen-year-old Carrie Buck was deemed a "moral imbecile" and committed by the State of Virginia to the Colony for Epileptics and Feebleminded in Lynchburg. She was the focus of a major legal case that tested the validity of Virginia's sterilization laws.

Helen MacMurchy in the early 1920s in Toronto. MacMurchy is remembered as one of Canada's pioneers of public health, although she often sounded like American eugenicists in her passionate conviction that feeble-mindedness and an open-door immigration policy threatened Canadian survival.

Clarence Darrow (leaning on the table) at the Scopes Monkey Trial in Dayton, Tennessee, in July 1925. Teacher John Scopes was being tried for disseminating Darwin's evolutionary theories in his high-school biology class. "Scopes is not on trial," Darrow told reporters prior to his departure for Dayton. "Civilization is on trial."

United States attorney general Alexander Mitchell Palmer (pictured in inset) in 1913. Following a botched terrorist attack on his Washington home in June 1919, Palmer led a crusade against anarchists and terrorists that initiated the Red Scare. The background photo shows the aftermath of the explosion at Palmer's home.

Bartolomeo Vanzetti (wearing bow tie) and Nicola Sacco, manacled together and surrounded by a heavy guard and onlookers in 1927. The two suspected anarchists are about to enter the courthouse at Dedham, Massachusetts, where they will receive the death sentence for a murder they allegedly committed in 1921. To this day there is great doubt as to their guilt.

J. Edgar Hoover in December 1924. Hoover was the first director of the Federal Bureau of Investigation. He was one of the fiercest opponents of communism in American history and led the arrests of hundreds of alleged anarchists and Communists during the Red Scare of 1919.

Emma Goldman in 1910. Goldman was vilified for more than a decade as "Red Emma," "Queen of the Anarchists," and "the most dangerous woman in America." She was eventually deported to the Soviet Union in December 1919 for her anarchist activities.

Should society, in fact, have failed these hopeless and helpless people, then the consequences would be severe. The feeble-minded might have been a small percentage of the total population, but as she maintained in a 1916 report – "with dubious statistical precision," as Canadian eugenics historian Angus McLaren has put it – they accounted for the vast majority of alcoholics, juvenile delinquents, unmarried mothers, and prostitutes. Quoting from the work of an American physician, Dr. Walter Fernald, she expressed the sentiment shared by eugenicists across North America that "every mental defective is a potential criminal."

Beyond education and a more efficient immigration inspection system, MacMurchy campaigned for segregation and sterilization. Birth control, in her opinion, was not a practical solution – she later referred to it in another book on the subject as "unnatural" and "contrary to one's higher instincts." Still, Canadians were more reticent than were the Americans to introduce sterilization legislation. Following the precedent set in Indiana in 1907, Dr. John Godfrey attempted five years later to introduce a sterilization bill for asylum patients in the Ontario Legislature. Despite support from such esteemed medical experts as psychiatrist Charles Clarke of the Toronto General Hospital, a staunch proponent of eugenics, the politicians took a more cautious approach. Canadians were perhaps less certain that an aggressive eugenics program would result in a glorious future. Sensing that the public was uncertain how to proceed, Ontario politicians let the matter drop for the moment.

Throughout the twenties, women's groups in particular continued to push for legalized sterilization. In British Columbia and Alberta, Nellie McClung, Judge Emily Murphy, Henrietta Edwards, among others, believed sterilization was a panacea for society's ills. In her memoirs published in 1945, McClung recalled visiting one prairie family who had sterilized their feeble-minded daughter, named Katie. The effect was apparently soothing, almost magical.

"Katie was well and neatly dressed," wrote McClung. "Her mother told me that she was taking full charge of the chickens now, and in the evenings was doing Norwegian knitting which had a ready sale in the neighbourhood. The home was happy again." Always more pragmatic than McClung, Emily Murphy, an Alberta police magistrate (the first female judge in Canada as well as the British Empire), was also more direct. "We protect the public against diseased and distempered cattle," she declared. "We should similarly protect them against the offal of humanity."

Sterilization bills were introduced into the B.C. and Alberta legislatures. In B.C., the government decided to appoint a Royal Commission on Mental Hygiene in 1925. It took more than two years to study the issue, although the commissioners – who were influenced by developments in the United States and by American experts like Paul Popenoe – recommended the sterilization of individuals in mental institutions. The editors of the *Vancouver Sun* added their support in an editorial on the U.S. Supreme Court's decision in the *Buck v. Bell* case. Sterilization, they wrote, was "the only reasonable way of protecting the strains from which the world must draw its leaders." By the time the commissioners submitted their final report in 1928, however, there had been a change in government in B.C. and the matter was not resolved for another five years.

Events were more decisive in Alberta. Support for a sterilization law had been voiced in the provincial legislature since the early 1920s. Lectures, presentations, and articles had convinced many Albertans of the pressing need to deal decisively with this issue. Asked Margaret Gunn, the president of the United Farm Women of Alberta in 1924: "Shall we continue our present system of merely taking charge of the very lowest physical and mental types, those who cause a menace to the state, the feeble-minded who in large measure fill our jails and penitentiaries and make up the great sub-stratum of humanity – social derelicts, doomed because of congenital inferiority to lead lives that are crass and unlovely, and to lower the vitality of our civilization?"

She advised the government to adopt a policy of "racial betterment through the weeding out of undesirable strains." Adding that, "democracy was never intended for degenerates."

George Hoadley, the health minister in John Brownlee's United Farmers of Alberta government, concurred with such sentiments. Arguing that the continuing increase in the province's feeble-minded population – a majority of whom, he pointed out, were foreigners – was an undue burden on taxpayers, he introduced a sexual sterilization bill in February 1928. Still, not everyone approved. Soon Alberta newspapers were filled with letters to the editor from concerned citizens who questioned what they regarded as the government's heavy-handed actions. "Are we animals and soon to be classed as Tomworths, Holsteins or Clydes?" asked one writer in the *Edmonton Journal*. "Possibly Mr. Hoadley in his desire for physical perfection will bring in a bill next year that all children, such as those suffering from infantile paralysis or any deformity, be taken to the high level bridge and thrown into the Saskatchewan." A group of prominent Edmonton residents organized the People's Protective League to fight the proposed legislation, which it declared was "interfering with the rights of people."

It was to no avail. The government passed Canada's first sterilization act on March 6 along with provision for the establishment of a "Eugenics Board" (consisting of two medical practitioners and two lay people) whose job it was to evaluate each case on its own merits. According to the act, parents or guardians were to be consulted before any medical procedure was to occur, a stipulation that was eliminated by the Social Credit government of William Aberhart in 1937. Alberta's sterilization act remained untouched until it was finally repealed in 1972. By then, 2,822 Albertans had been sterilized.

British Columbia instituted a similar bill in 1933, yet other provinces, including Ontario, where there always had been substantial support for such a law, felt that it was too drastic a measure. The

Eugenics Society of Canada, organized by a group of committed academics and doctors in late 1930 to promote "race betterment" and sterilization, never stopped hoping that the situation would change.

During the thirties, Canadian and American physicians and scientists watched almost with envy as Hitler and the Nazis imposed their own eugenics program. In their view, it was something to behold. According to a January 1936 article in the magazine *Canadian Doctor*, the Nazis' policy had ensured that two hundred thousand unfit German citizens would not have children. The financial saving to Hitler's government was supposedly enormous. That same year, Harry Laughlin was awarded an honorary doctorate of medicine by the University of Heidelberg for his eugenics work at Cold Spring Harbor. He was unable to attend the ceremony but wrote to thank the university's officials. It was, he noted, "evidence of a common understanding of German and American scientists of the nature of eugenics."

Historians estimate that by the end of the Second World War, the Nazis, who had transformed their forced sterilization program of more than 400,000 individuals into a massive killing machine, had likely murdered 140,000 physically handicapped and mentally ill people. At one mental institution in Nazi Germany, the staff toasted with beer the cremation of the ten-thousandth patient – a child gassed to death. In 1946, at the trial of Nazi doctors held at Nuremberg, one physician after another stated that they had modelled their system after the one in the United States.

Civilization Is on Trial

Charles Darwin may have changed the world. The science of eugenics may have been equated with progress. But the ambitious changes the eugenicists promised for their biologically engineered society of the future were also slightly alarming. Would there still be a place in the modern world for traditional Christian values? Many Americans, including those who promoted and supported eugenics, believed that faith in science did not necessarily negate faith in God. People still looked to the Almighty for true salvation. A national poll undertaken by two hundred newspapers in early 1927 indicated that 91 per cent of those interviewed (approximately 125,000 people) expressed "a belief in God"; 77 per cent said they were "active church members"; and 85 per cent regarded "the Bible as being inspired as no other book is inspired."

A few months later, a storm of controversy erupted over the publication of Sinclair Lewis's new novel *Elmer Gantry*. Lewis, best known for his 1922 biting satire *Babbitt* about a small-town businessman, had now decided to turn his pen on the Church. In *Gantry*, his main character, as described in the press, was "a moral leper who achieves excess as a seducer and eminence as a minister of the gospel." The book was banned in Kansas City, where Lewis had conducted much of his research at the local Episcopal church. Its congregation felt betrayed. The evangelical preacher Reverend Billy Sunday was so angry that had he been the Lord, he claimed, he would have "soaked Mr. Lewis so hard that there would have been nothing left for the devil to levy on." Not surprisingly, the commotion was great for book sales and the publisher could not keep up with demand.

The clash over *Elmer Gantry* pointed to a more heated fight that had been brewing between fundamentalists and modernists since before the First World War. It was a battle that started over differences between Protestants about interpreting the Bible and Christian doctrine – that is, symbolically, as the modernists wanted, or literally, according to the fundamentalists – and escalated into a larger dispute about morality, the role of women and marriage, the abuse of alcohol, attitudes towards sex, and, above all, the teaching of evolution in schools. Neither side, it should be added, was homogeneous – there were moderate fundamentalists and conservative modernists – nor were the fundamentalists, as they were often portrayed, uniformly anti-intellectual, anti-liberal, rural, and southern.

Few fundamentalist leaders, for example, could match John Roach Straton of the Calvary Baptist Church in New York. "The moral decline of the present day started two generations ago when the dark and sinister shadow of Darwinism fell across the field of human life," he declared. "America's educational system ultimately will be wrecked if the teaching of evolution is allowed to continue. . . . Better wipe out all the schools than undermine belief in the Bible by permitting the teaching of evolution."

In 1924, Straton carried on a running feud with Henry Fairfield Osborn, head of the Museum of Natural History and a eugenicist, over the museum's "Hall of the Age of Man," which used fossils to present the Darwinian version of human creation. In his sermons, Straton proclaimed that Osborn was misusing tax-payers' dollars and was guilty of "treason against God." Popular, too, was anti-evolutionist William Bell Riley of the First Baptist Church in Minneapolis, who ministered an ever-increasing congregation of three-thousand-plus worshippers. And Albert S. Johnson in Charlotte, North Carolina, who said with less hesitation that teaching evolution led to "sensuality, carnality, Bolshevism and the Red Flag."

It was William Jennings Bryan, however, who transformed the anti-evolution movement into a crusade. By 1925, Bryan was sixty-five years old, heavy-set, but as feisty as ever.[*] From the moment he arrived in Washington, D.C., as a thirty-year-old congressman from Nebraska in 1890, he was a larger-than-life figure. Trained as a lawyer, he ran three times for the presidency, in 1896, 1900, and

---

[*] Bryan was also wealthier than ever. He and his wife, Mary, had relocated to Florida four years earlier, because of Mary's arthritis, and he had made some smart and lucrative investments during Florida's land boom. "Although publicly he played down his profits," writes historian Edward Larson, "the spectacular rise in land prices made Bryan into a millionaire almost overnight."

1908, and lost each time. Yet it hardly mattered. He was a brilliant campaigner and an even more brilliant orator, certainly the greatest of his generation. In a clear, booming voice – the first time he used a microphone with a sound system was in 1920 at the Democratic National Convention – he ruminated about the major social and economic issues of his day. He wrote many books, contributed to newspapers, and regularly criss-crossed the country lecturing in every town and city that would listen to him. Woodrow Wilson had made him his secretary of state in 1914, but he was devoted to peace and resigned when it appeared the United States' entry into the First World War was imminent. His legion of supporters called him "the Peerless Leader" or "the Great Commoner"; while his legion of detractors referred to him as "the Beerless Leader" (he fought for Prohibition) or "the Great Windbag."

In 1916, Bryan had read a book entitled *The Belief in God and Immortality*, written by psychologist James Leuba. He became profoundly distressed by Leuba's conclusion that a growing number of young adults had entered college with a firm belief in God but had changed their minds by the time they graduated. The chief culprits for this state of affairs, Bryan decided, were Darwinism and the teaching of evolution in high schools. "What shall it profit a man if he shall gain all the learning of the schools," he asked, "and lose his faith in God?"

From then on, he made the fight over evolution the focus of his life and career. The idea that man and apes had the same ancestor was, he argued, merely "a guess." He filled halls and auditoriums from New York to Los Angeles delivering a lecture he called "The Menace of Darwin," and was invited in February 1922 to debate the topic in the *New York Times*, with Henry Fairfield Osborn making the case for evolution. Although Osborn marshalled an intelligent and scientifically sound argument, Bryan was at his best castigating Osborn and his colleagues as "three men," who "weaken faith in God, discourage prayer, raise doubt as to a future life, reduce Christ to the stature of man, and make the Bible a 'scrap of paper.'" If nothing else, Bryan got Americans' attention. He had, as the *Chicago Tribune* put it, "half the country debating whether the universe was created in six days."

Owning in part to the efforts of Bryan, Straton, Riley, and other fundamentalist spokesmen, anti-evolution legislation was introduced in more than a dozen states. The success rate, however, was not tremendous. By 1925, only three states had actually passed anti-evolution statutes – Oklahoma, Florida, and Tennessee. In Kentucky, where Bryan was personally involved, the bill was defeated by a single vote. Later, Mississippi and Arkansas would join the small group. At the same time, it would be fair to say that there was a large and vocal mass of anti-evolutionists across the United States.

In Tennessee, a state that could claim that nearly all of its adult population of 1.2 million were church members (half of whom were Baptists), John Butler, a Democratic farmer and Baptist lay leader, had spearheaded the campaign in the legislature. It took only six days to have the "Butler Bill" passed in the state's lower house. Then, following intense discussions in the state senate and press, Governor Austin Peay, who considered his actions and the act a symbolic gesture, approved it. The governor ignored the fact that many of the science textbooks then being used in Tennessee high schools – among them *A Civic Biology: Presented in Problems* by George W. Hunter – contained sections about Darwin's theory and evolution. Nevertheless, as of the end of March 1925, it was illegal for any teacher in Tennessee's schools or universities "to teach any theory that denies the story of the Divine Creation of man as taught in the Bible, and to teach instead that man has descended from a lower order of animals." Any educator violating the act could be found guilty of a misdemeanour and fined a maximum of five hundred dollars and not less than one hundred.

There matters stood for about a month until a series of related events triggered a momentous legal battle and courtroom drama like few others. First, the American Civil Liberties Union (ACLU), believing that Tennessee's anti-evolution act violated the Fourteenth Amendment of the U.S. Constitution – that prevented states from depriving "any person of life, liberty or property, without due process of law" – issued a press release offering to pay the legal costs of any educator who was willing to challenge the act in court.

Next, the *Chattanooga Times* reprinted the ACLU's announcement, which caught the eye of George Rappleyea, a thirty-one-year-old New York chemical and mining engineer working as the manager of Cumberland Coal and Iron Company in the sleepy town of Dayton, Tennessee (Dayton was halfway between Chattanooga and Knoxville with a population in 1925 of 1,800). Rappleyea, more liberal and religiously modern than most of his neighbours, resented the anti-evolution law. The ACLU's offer got him to thinking about how he could not only protest the act, but also boost the town's economic prospects by putting "Dayton on the map."

With his plan jelling, he paid a visit to the drugstore operated by Fred Robinson, who also happened to be the chairman of the Rhea County school board. Robinson listened intently and within a few hours a scheme was hatched. Robinson, who likely thought more about the public relations angle than the legal and moral ones, brought in other education officials and lawyers. It was agreed that Rappleyea was to sign the complaint and that brothers and lawyers Herbert and Sue Hicks (named for his mother) would prosecute the case under the anti-evolution law. All the group needed now was someone who would consent to play the role of the defendant.

They quickly decided on the ideal candidate and sent for John Scopes – a twenty-four-year-old, single, tall, shy, bespectacled, chain-smoking physics and algebra teacher, a popular figure who also coached the football team at the Rhea County high school.

Scopes objected to the state's anti-evolution law, and during the last semester before the summer break, he had filled in for the regular biology teacher, who was off sick, and assigned his students readings from the state-approved textbook: Hunter's *A Civic Biology*.

Scopes later recalled the fateful meeting at Robinson's drugstore as follows: "'John, we've been arguing,'" Rappleyea told him, "and I said nobody could teach biology without teaching evolution. 'That's right,' I said, not sure what he was leading up to." Rappleyea, showed him a copy of the Hunter biology textbook. "'You've been teaching 'em this book?' Rappleyea said. 'Yes,' I said. I explained that I had got the book out of storage and had used it for review purposes," Scopes remembered. "'Then you've been violating the law,' Robinson said." Robinson finally posed the question they had wanted to ask from the start: "John, would you be willing to stand for a test case?"

More discussion ensued, and after being assured by his friend Sue Hicks that the group's plan was legitimate, Scopes accepted the offer. Two days later, he was "arrested" and charged with violating Tennessee's anti-evolution law. Little could he have guessed that his life was about to be permanently altered. Upon being notified of what had transpired in Dayton, the ACLU, as per its original offer, agreed to support and finance the legal proceedings. It was anticipated – indeed, hoped by all concerned – that Scopes would be found guilty and the case would eventually wind its way to the U.S. Supreme Court.

If it was the intention of Rappleyea, Robinson, and the others to gain some notoriety for their town, they certainly got more publicity and interest than they had ever imagined. In hindsight, the involvement of the ACLU and a team of brilliant, dedicated, and eccentric lawyers – including John Neal, a law professor from Knoxville, Arthur Garfield Hayes, a prominent civil liberties advocate, and Dudley Field Malone, a well-connected New York attorney – ensured that Scopes's trial for a misdemeanour crime would attract some attention outside of Dayton. Yet what propelled the case to be immortalized as the "Monkey Trial" and "the greatest since that held before Pilate," in the words of the celebrated and witty journalist H.L. Mencken, who covered every fascinating moment of it, was the participation of William Jennings Bryan for the prosecution and Clarence Darrow for the defence.

Bryan had not practised law in more than three decades, but that mattered little. Apart from the religious and moral issues of the case, which he felt deeply about, as a lifelong populist he also maintained that the tax-paying citizens of a state had the right to control the curriculum in their own schools. And, of course, he knew that the trial would offer him a marvellous pulpit to espouse his various views. When Sue Hicks heard that Bryan was interested in joining the prosecution, he immediately invited him, and Bryan packed his bags for Dayton. He soon transformed himself, as Mencken described, into "a sort of Fundamentalist Pope."

In the spring of 1925, Clarence Darrow was sixty-eight years old and still going strong. He was, by all accounts, the most renowned criminal lawyer in the country. Only months earlier, he had single-handedly saved the lives of Richard Loeb and Nathan Leopold, his two young and wealthy clients found guilty of murdering a fourteen-year-old acquaintance (for no apparent reason other than to see if they could pull off the perfect crime). His twelve-hour summation, in which he quoted Omar Khayyam and blamed the murder on a variety of psychological factors and external influences, kept Loeb and Leopold from being executed. Darrow had been fighting for the underdog for decades. As an agnostic, he had little use for organized religion and did not want to be told what to believe by the likes of Bryan and his misguided fundamentalist followers.

ACLU officials were not overly enthusiastic about Darrow's offer to work for the defence, even if it was with no fee attached, but he had represented them on other legal matters and he was not easily dismissed. They wanted to keep the case focused on Scopes's constitutional rights; Darrow, who enjoyed the limelight as much as Bryan, saw the issue slightly differently. "Scopes is not on trial," he told reporters prior to his departure for Dayton. "Civilization is on trial." It was not long after the proceedings began that Darrow was referred to in Tennessee as the "infidel" and in one Memphis political cartoon as the "anti-Christ."

At the end of May, Scopes was formally indicted by a grand jury for violating the Butler Act and Judge John T. Raulston, who made no attempt to display his favourable opinion about the anti-evolution law, set a trial date for July 10. Dayton became the focus of worldwide newspaper coverage. Led by Mencken, hundreds of journalists from every corner of the country flocked to the town.[*] With only three small hotels available, many reporters rented rooms in private homes. Once the trial started, Chicago radio station WGN set up the first remote broadcast to keep Americans informed, as its announcers put it, of "the strange happenings in the Tennessee hills."

By then, Dayton had been transformed into a circus, a permanent Fourth of July celebration. Around the courthouse, journalists competed with preachers and hucksters hawking Bibles, ice cream, and hot dogs. The town's local merchants took advantage of the situation and decorated their windows with monkeys and apes. At Robinson's drugstore, where the plan had been hatched, customers could sip on "simian" sodas.

Even before the jury was selected on the first day, the end result of the trial was not at issue; everyone, including Scopes, who did not testify and was almost irrelevant to the proceedings, understood that he was guilty of violating the state's law. These were the questions that required answers: How far could Darrow and the defence push

---

* As an easterner and a bit of a snob, Mencken did not expect much from Dayton, but he confessed that the town surprised him. "I expected to find a squalid Southern village," he wrote on the eve of the trial, "with darkies snoozing on the houseblocks, pigs rooting under the houses and the inhabitants full of hookworm and malaria. What I found was a country town full of charm and even beauty."

Judge Raulston into transforming the case into a great debate about constitutional rights and the role of religion in society? And, how would Bryan respond to this challenge? The "Great Commoner" intended for the case to be about the control of public education, yet if Darrow wanted to dissect Darwin's theory of evolution, that was fine by him. As he liked to tell his audiences: "How can teachers tell students that they came from monkeys and not expect them to act like monkeys?"[*]

The courtroom was stifling. Judge Raulston, who allowed each day of the trial (against Darrow's vehement objections) to start with a prayer, also permitted the lawyers to dispense with their ties and jackets. As the two sides contested the constitutionality of the Butler Act, the moral implications of the law, the bigoted nature of fundamentalism, and the meaning of Darwinism, reporters and spectators were treated to some of the greatest oratory ever heard in the United States. While Darrow was superb in the preliminary hearing, and Bryan played the crowd like the evangelical preacher he was, it was Dudley Field Malone's brilliant argument – during the debate about whether expert testimony on evolution should be permitted – that was judged to be the finest speech delivered. "We feel we stand with science," he concluded. "We feel we stand with intelligence. We feel we stand with fundamental freedom in America. We are not afraid." When he had finished, the crowd in the courtroom cheered and applauded.

In the end, Judge Raulston ruled against the jury hearing testimony from biologists and other experts about evolutionary theory (instead, written submission of their testimonies were placed in the

---

[*] Defence lawyer Dudley Field Malone saw the case in yet another light. "The issue is not between science and religion, as some of us believe," he remarked to reporters. "The issue is between science and Bryanism. I believe that the scientists we have called to act as witnesses in the trial really know more about science than Mr. Bryan; and I also believe that the ministers we have called know more about religion than he does."

official record), yet he did allow Darrow to pull off the biggest stunt of the trial by calling Bryan as a defence witness to testify about the validity of the Holy Scriptures. Concerned that the floor of the courtroom would collapse from the large crowd assembled each day, the judge took the unprecedented step of moving the trial outside to the front lawn. On the day Darrow cross-examined Bryan, upwards of five thousand people gathered in the heat to watch this historic match of wits. For two hours, Bryan was questioned about Adam and Eve, Cain and Abel, and Noah and the Flood, finally conceding that some stories in the Bible were open to interpretation.

By the time Raulston halted the often testy inquisition (the following day he had it struck from the record), Darrow had succeeded, at least in his opinion, as he later told Mencken, in showing "what an ignoramus [Bryan] was." Yet Bryan had won the hearts of the spectators by his defiant tone and spirited defence of the Scriptures. "Darrow succeeded in showing that Bryan knows little about the science of the world," reported the Memphis *Commercial Appeal*, but "Bryan succeeded in bearing witness bravely to the faith which he believes transcends all the learning of men."

Having made its point and prepared for the next step in the Appeal Court, the defence team asked Raulston to direct the jury to find Scopes guilty. This clever tactic prevented Bryan from delivering what was certain to be a rousing summation. The judge did so, and the jury complied. Scopes was found guilty of violating the state law and Raulston fined him $100. The "trial of the century," as the reporters were apt to call it, was over.

Bryan was satisfied with the outcome; Darrow was slightly bitter. "I think this case will be remembered because it is the first case of this sort since we stopped trying people in America for witchcraft," he declared at the conclusion. "We have done our best to turn the tide . . . of testing every fact in science by a religious doctrine." Bryan had plans to use the case to bolster the fundamentalist cause throughout the country. But less than a week later, after consuming a large lunch, he lay down for a nap and died.

The fundamentalist struggle did not die with him. Mississippi and Arkansas soon passed their own versions of the Butler Act, and state regulations prevented teachers from discussing evolution in classrooms in Louisiana and Texas. Indeed, Tennessee's state legislature did not repeal the Butler Act until 1967, and it took another year after that for the U.S. Supreme Court finally to rule that anti-evolution laws were a violation of the Constitution.

Still, the debate over Darwin and *The Origin of Species* persists to the present day. On the seventy-fifth anniversary of the Scopes trial, in July 2000, Doug Linder, a professor at the University of Missouri–Kansas City Law School, pointed out in a speech commemorating the event that recent public opinion polls "show an overwhelming majority of Americans believe that evolution accounts for the nature and characteristic of non-human species, only a bare plurality of Americans believe that humans are the product of evolution."*

---

* In a 1991 Gallup poll, 47 per cent of Americans who were asked, claimed that "God created man pretty much in his present form at one time within the last 10,000 years." Only a mere 9 per cent believed that God had no part in this process. Similar results were recorded in another Gallup poll done in 1999, and as recently as November 2004 the American Civil Liberties Union launched a lawsuit against school officials in Cobb County, Georgia, for promoting creationism. The officials, with the tacit support of more than two thousand people in the school community, inserted a sticker in science textbooks warning students that "evolution is a theory, not a fact, regarding the origin of living things. This material should be approached with an open mind, studied carefully and critically considered." And opening in the spring of 2005 near the Ohio-Kentucky border (close to Cincinnati) will be the Museum of Creation. At a cost of twenty-five million U.S. dollars, the museum is the brainchild of evangelist Ken Ham, the head of Answers in Genesis, an influential American creationist organization. Needless to say, the museum, which will have exhibits on Adam and Eve and Noah's Ark, will contain no mention of Charles Darwin or the theory of evolution.

CHAPTER FOUR

The Red Scare

Previous page: "Bloody Saturday," June 21, 1919. Strikers and their supporters overturn a streetcar in Winnipeg and set it on fire. Opponents of the General Strike feared that the city was "under the sway of Bolshevism."

The "Red" movement is not a righteous or honest protest against alleged defects in our present political and economic organization of society. It does not represent radicalism of progress. It is not a movement of liberty-loving persons. It is a distinctly criminal and dishonest movement in the desire to obtain possession of other people's property by violence and robbery. A justification of such a course necessarily means the destruction of government and the destruction of religion.

– A. Mitchell Palmer, 1920

Palmer, Do Not Let This Country See Red

It was a few minutes after eleven o'clock on the evening of June 2, 1919. United States Attorney General Alexander Mitchell Palmer – known to his friends and associates as Mitchell – and his wife, Roberta, were in their bedroom on the second floor of their home in a quiet neighbourhood of northwestern Washington, D.C. Suddenly, they were startled by a loud noise downstairs near their front door. A booming explosion followed and shattered glass flew in every direction. A large elk's head mounted on the bedroom wall crashed to the floor.

Directly across the street, Franklin D. Roosevelt, then assistant secretary of the Navy, and his wife, Eleanor, had just walked into their home after returning early from a dinner party. The explosion at the Palmers' was so intense that it blew out the Roosevelts' front windows as well. "The world has come to an end!" shouted their cook. Immediately, Roosevelt rushed upstairs to check on his young son, James, who was gawking wide-eyed out his bedroom window at the smoke and debris at the Palmers' residence. Satisfied that his family was unharmed, Roosevelt called the police and then ran to check on the attorney general and his wife. He discovered Palmer already downstairs surveying the damage. A pungent, acid smell hung in the air. A devout Quaker, Palmer was not a man quick to anger, but that night, as Roosevelt later told Eleanor, "he was 'theeing' and 'thouing' me all over the place."

It seemed certain that a bomb had either exploded on the Palmers' front steps or been hurled through one of the front windows. The two politicians' suspicions were confirmed when the police discovered a man's leg and other parts of a body scattered on the front lawn and the street. Officers at the scene speculated that the attacker had lit a fuse and then likely stumbled on a ledge as he tried to throw the bomb, blowing himself up.

Beside the remains, the police found strewn about dozens of copies of an anarchist pamphlet entitled *Plain Words*. "A time has come when the social question's solution can be delayed no longer," declared the manifesto, "class war is on and cannot cease but with a complete victory for the international proletariat. . . . We have aspired to a better world and you jailed us, you clubbed us, you deported us, you murdered us whenever you could. . . . We know the proletariat has the . . . right to protect itself. Since their press has been suffocated, their mouths muzzled, we mean to speak for them through the voice of dynamite, through the mouths of guns." The declaration was signed "The Anarchist Fighters."

That night, bombs went off at approximately the same hour in seven other cities – New York, Boston, Philadelphia, Pittsburgh, Cleveland, Paterson, N.J., and Newtonville, Mass. – killing one night watchman in New York City at the home of Judge Charles Cooper and causing much property damage. Copies of *Plain Words* were found at several of the bomb sites, leading Palmer to conclude that a terrorist conspiracy had been launched against the government and citizens of the United States.

This was not the first bombing incident of the year. In April explosives in small brown packages had been mailed to Seattle mayor Ole Hanson, a well-known opponent of radicalism who had ruthlessly combated a brief general strike in his city in February, and to a former senator, Thomas W. Hardwick of Atlanta, a moderate who had spoken out against "alien agitators." The package in Seattle had leaked acid, alerting people in Hanson's office – the mayor was out of town at the time – to the bomb before it did any damage. In Atlanta, Hardwick's maid was not as fortunate. She opened the small box and it exploded, blowing off her hands.

When news of these events was reported in the newspapers, a New York mail clerk by the name of Charles Kaplan remembered that he had set aside sixteen other small brown packages for insufficient postage. If this was an operation launched by a large-scale terrorist organization, it seemed it was also the work of amateurs. Kaplan notified the police, and they discovered that all sixteen parcels, plus another eighteen found at other post offices or intercepted en route, contained bombs intended for a list of notable American government officials and businessmen, among them Anthony J. Caminetti, the commissioner general of immigration, Senator Lee S. Overman, chairman of the Senate Bolshevik Investigation Committee, Oliver W. Holmes, Jr., associate justice of the Supreme Court, and business tycoons John D. Rockefeller and J.P. Morgan. Justice Department officials deduced that the mail bombs were likely the beginning of an insurrection planned for the first of May. Police and vigilante mobs in New York, Boston, Chicago, and other cities did battle with hundreds of May Day labour marchers. Rioting, violence, including several deaths and many arrests, marked the annual celebration that year.

Still, Palmer, described as a "progressive reformer" and a friend of labour before the First World War, was not yet convinced of the coming revolution, nor was he prepared to suspend civil liberties.

A lawyer, former congressman, and devoted Democrat, he was, however, as suspicious of and hostile to foreigners as any "patriotic" American in 1919. After serving in several administrative offices during the war, President Woodrow Wilson had finally appointed Palmer as his attorney general in the spring (following the retirement of Thomas Gregory). Palmer was forty-seven years old and had presidential aspirations. His biographer, historian Stanley Coben, labelled him a paradox and a "liberal demagogue."

At any rate, everything changed for Palmer on the night of June 2. The bombing of his house convinced him that the radicals responsible posed a serious threat to U.S. security. They should be dealt with decisively and harshly. "The morning after my house was blown up," he later stated in testimony before a Senate Committee, "I stood in the middle of the wreckage of my library with Congressmen and Senators, and without a dissenting voice they called upon me in strong terms to exercise all the power that was possible . . . to run to earth the criminals who were behind that kind of outrage."

Almost immediately, fingers were pointed by the *New York Times* and other newspapers at "Bolsheviks," still thought to be secretly working for the Germans, and members of the militant Industrial Workers of the World (IWW), or the "Wobblies," as the union was nicknamed.[*] Indeed, Palmer, like many Washington officials, did not draw a distinction between the various labour and radical groups. Whether they were Communists, Socialists, Wobblies, or anarchists, it hardly mattered. They were equally culpable and dangerous.

Prominent Communists like journalist John Reed (author of the eyewitness account of the Russian Revolution *Ten Days that Shook the World*) and Max Eastman, the editor of the socialist magazines *The Masses* and *The Liberator*, among numerous others,

---

[*] The term "Wobbly" was derived from a mocking of Chinese immigrants' pronunciation of IWW as "Eye, Wobbly, Wobbly."

denied any communist involvement in the bombing campaign. And they were right.

Evidence found by the police at the scene of the crime – including a hat purchased at a store in Philadelphia and a tattered and partially burned copy of an Italian-English dictionary – strongly suggested that the bomber was an Italian anarchist. The Justice Department later concluded that the bomber was likely Carlo Valdinoci, publisher of *Cronaca Sovversiva*, the influential and recently suppressed Italian-American periodical edited by Luigi Galleani, the most notable Italian anarchist of the era. In all probability, it was Galleani's followers – including Nicola Sacco and Bartolomeo Vanzetti, soon to be involved in a sensational murder trial – who were responsible for the bombing attempts that spring, as revenge for the arrest and deportation of several of their members during the war. Galleani, himself, was already in custody on charges of "obstructing the war effort," and was deported to Italy at the end of June.[*]

None of this made a difference to Palmer. He asked Congress for an additional five hundred thousand to expand the fight against radicals, and the sum was immediately approved. Next, he appointed William J. Flynn, formerly head of the Secret Service, as head of the Justice Department's Bureau of Investigation (it would become the Federal Bureau of Investigation in 1935). Flynn,

---

[*] Luigi Galleani (1861–1931) was born to middle-class parents in Vercelli, Italy, not far from Turin. During his university years as a law student, he became a committed and active anarchist, keeping one step ahead of the police in a number of European countries. He arrived in the United States in 1901 from London and quickly attracted a devoted following among the growing Italian anarchist community. He became the editor of the popular anarchist newspaper *La Questione Sociale* and later was instrumental in founding the periodical *Cronaca Sovversiva*, published by Carlo Valdinoci. Galleani wrote dozens of pamphlets, none more important than *La Fine dell'anarchismo?* ("The End of Anarchism?"), in which he declared that anarchism "lives, it develops, it goes forward." He was deported from the United States in 1919, and once back in Italy faced the wrath of Mussolini and the Fascists, who put him in jail. Released, he was under the surveillance of the police for the rest of his life. He died from a heart attack in early November 1931.

whom Palmer called the "greatest anarchist expert in the U.S.," subscribed to the attorney general's view that the bombings were the work of "foreigners within the ranks of organized labour." In early July, Flynn told a convention of police chiefs that the bombers were "connected to Russian Bolshevism, aided by Hun [German] money and are operating and spreading their propaganda under the guise of labour agitation."

Two more key members were added to Palmer's team. Detective and lawyer Francis P. Garvan became assistant attorney general and was to work on all prosecutions of radicals. And an ambitious twenty-four-year-old lawyer named John Edgar Hoover, who was already working for the Justice Department in their Enemy Alien Registration unit, was picked to head the General Intelligence Division. His task was to collect as much information as possible on radical activities.

Within five years, Hoover would be director of the Bureau of Investigation, a job he moulded in his own dictatorial image and held on to until the day he died in 1972. Hoover is remembered not only as the fiercest opponent of communism in U.S. history, but also as a law-enforcement official who was prepared to use any tool at his disposal, including violating rights and civil liberties guaranteed in the U.S. Constitution, to ensure the future of a free and secure America.[*]

It was Hoover's mother, Annie, who instilled in him the "righteous-Christian sensibility" he was famous for. Hoover never married and lived with his mother until she died in 1938. He was as complex a personality as ever worked in Washington. Hoover was insecure, talked fast, and tried to dominate any conversation. A self-professed

---

[*] A comparison to current United States policy, following the terrorist attacks of September 11, 2001, is clear. The implementation of the U.S.A. Patriot Act in October 2001, giving the government sweeping powers and the subsequent arrest of thousands of innocent people, many of whom remain in custody without legal recourse, is a chilling reminder that the leap between a democracy and a dictatorship is not as wide as most Americans believe.

"avid student of human weakness," he liked to exploit his opponents' foibles if he could – and he always could. His conservative attitudes to God, country, duty, women, "coloreds," and "Negroes" – as he referred to black Americans well into the 1940s – never changed. As he studied communism in 1919, Hoover came to see it as a tremendous threat to American liberty and the American way of life. In this he never wavered. His goal was a peacetime seditious law that would give the Justice Department the same dictatorial powers it had possessed during wartime. And he nearly got it.

Within months, Hoover's Radical Division had collected information on 200,000 "various subjects and individuals," all neatly recorded in a card catalogue. Within two years, there would be more than 450,000 entries. His staff regularly scanned 625 newspapers and journals for radical and seditious material. As U.S. writer Richard Powers notes in his history of American anticommunism, Hoover "had turned himself into the government's first resident authority on communism, a reputation he jealously guarded for the rest of his long life."

The days and weeks that followed the attack on Palmer's house were filled with labour strife and terrorist threats. President Wilson implored his attorney general on several occasions, "Palmer, do not let this country see red." Palmer heeded that advice. He, too, was distressed by the peril to the country. "Like a prairie fire, the blaze of revolution was sweeping over every institution of law and order," Palmer later wrote. "It was eating its way into the homes of the American workmen, its sharp tongues of revolutionary heat were licking the altars of the churches, leaping into the belfry of the school bell, crawling into the sacred corners of American homes, seeking to replace marriage vows with libertine laws, burning up the foundations of society." Along with his team of Flynn, Garvan, and Hoover, he set out to drive Bolshevik agitators and anarchists from the country one way or the other. The threat was genuine, Palmer maintained. Repression was required. The police and other authorities had to use whatever power was at their disposal, and if that meant trampling on civil liberties – so be it.

The Red Scare had begun.

The Glorious Red Dawn

Perhaps it was inevitable that 1919 should be the year this all occurred. It was not merely an American phenomenon. Throughout the western world there was a decisive showdown between capital and labour, manager and worker. It was a clash between the unregulated world of the nineteenth century, in which labour was a commodity to be exploited, and the more modern complex world of the early twentieth century, when workers not only questioned their place in society, but also demanded change. The end of the First World War, with its severe economic dislocation and social upheaval, as soldiers came home to find their jobs taken by women and foreigners, further exacerbated the situation.

Added to this was the Bolshevik-led revolution in Russia in October 1917 with its initial promise for a glorious communist future. Lenin's success in eliminating capitalism and establishing a so-called dictatorship of the proletariat, loomed large. Everywhere there was fear that the revolution would spread. Indeed, few events in the twentieth century frightened the ruling classes in Western Europe and North America as much as the Russian Revolution. Bolsheviks were atheists and free thinkers. They had "wild eyes," "long, bushy hair," and wore "tattered clothes." They denied God and held a bomb in one hand and a dagger or gun in the other. They advocated "free love" and were intent on destroying everything sacred in western society. Their every move occupied the "peace-makers" at the treaty talks in Paris. Winston Churchill, Britain's secretary of state for war in early 1919, reaffirmed in a speech in London what everyone else was thinking. "Of all the tyrannies in history," he declared, "the Bolshevik tyranny is the worst, the most destructive, the most degrading." It was a view he would hold for the rest of his days.

Already, communists in Germany, Austria, and Hungary had attempted, with limited success, to emulate Lenin and Trotsky in a revolutionary takeover. Radicals in France and Italy, too, were vocal.[*] In an open letter Lenin wrote to American workers in August 1918, he urged them "to revolt against your rulers." Then, at the Third International (also called the Comintern) convened by Lenin in March 1919, it was declared in a manifesto that, "the aim of the International Communist Party is to overthrow [capitalism] and raise in its place the structure of the socialist order."

Throughout the previous decade, the Socialist Party of America (SPA) (founded by Eugene Debs and Morris Hillquit in 1901) had been growing. In 1918 it had reached a membership of about 110,000. It was a party that appealed to both native-born Americans as well as immigrant workers (approximately 35 per cent of its membership in 1917). Ironically, success in Russia hurt the movement in the United States as a great debate erupted over strategy and tactics. In September 1919, the right and left wings of the party split apart. The right remained in the SPA, denouncing the use of violence, while the left, still embroiled in dispute, divided further. The English-speaking group, led by journalist John Reed and Benjamin Gitlow, formed the Communist Labor Party, and the foreign section, organized by Louis Faraina, Nicholas Hourwich, and Charles Ruthenberg, created the Communist Party of America. Both organizations promised to save the country with the overthrow of capitalism and the rise of the working class.

---

* In January 1919 in Berlin, the Spartacists (later the German Communist Party) led by Karl Liebknecht and Rosa Luxemburg, a Polish-born Jew who rejected her heritage in her fight for social justice, tried to start a proletariat revolution. They failed and were both murdered by right-wing army officers. In Hungary, Béla Kun, a committed Marxist, successfully established a Soviet-style government in Hungary for several months.

THE DEVIL IN BABYLON

Socialists, communists, and anarchists from New York's Lower East Side to Winnipeg's North End, had cheered the events in Russia. They cheered because, as one Canadian immigrant put it, the Bolsheviks' success meant "equal rights for men and women, no child labour, no poverty, misery and degradation, no prostitution, no mortgages on farms, no revolting bills for machinery to keep peasants poor till the grave, no sweatshops, no long hours of heavy toil for a meagre existence but an equal opportunity for all."

The events in Russia caused Emma Goldman, vilified for more than a decade as "Red Emma," "Queen of the Anarchists," and "the most dangerous woman in America," to think about returning there, where she was born in 1869. The lecture she presented on her tour in 1917 was appropriately entitled "The Bolsheviki Revolution: Its Promise and Fulfillment." And, from a jail cell, where he was awaiting a trial for "interfering with the war effort," William "Big Bill" Haywood, one of founders of the IWW, wrote, "We have lived to see the breaking of the glorious Red Dawn . . . the world revolution is born, the change is here."

The First World War and the Russian Revolution were only the catalysts. The roots of the 1919 struggle and its aftermath in North America started half a century earlier, when the nascent working class began to challenge its position in the capitalist system. In time, workers across the continent demanded fairer wages, better working conditions, shorter hours, and, most of all, recognition for their unions. The battle, however, was not easily won. At every step of the way, employers – the members of the wealthy elite like the Rockefellers, Carnegies, Vanderbilts, Morgans, and Huntingtons – stubbornly resisted change. Unions were evil, they argued, collective bargaining destructive, and it was their God-given right to make as much money as they could.

The workers would not surrender and created large trade associations such as the American Federation of Labor (AFL) to reform the system from within. Others, like the members of the IWW, imbued with the spirit of the new radical "isms" – socialism, communism, and anarchism – wanted an immediate transformation and were prepared to use violence, if necessary, to achieve their goals. As a result the United States experienced, in the words of labour historian Thomas Emerson, "the bloodiest and most violent labor history of any industrial nation in the world." The fact that many workers were immigrants, willing to take the lowest-paying jobs to survive, merely compounded the problem, often alienating them from employers as well as their fellow American-born comrades in the factories. Between 1873 and 1937, when the U.S. Supreme Court upheld the constitutionality of the National Labor Relations Act (the Wagner Act) guaranteeing workers the right to form unions, more than seven hundred Americans died and thousands were wounded – all in the name of workers' rights.

From the first day it was organized in 1886, the AFL adhered to the British model of craft unions, and skilled workers preferred it that way. The various unions in the AFL were generally moderate in their demands, but the response of business was harsh and inflexible. If a strike was called – and they were not as frequent as is thought, at least until after 1900 – employers routinely brought in strike-breakers and Pinkerton detectives to protect them and punish the strikers. If that did not work, then calling in the federal and state militia to help keep order, as was done during the Pullman Rail Strike of 1894, the first national strike in U.S. history, was another popular option.

Still, the AFL persisted. By 1900, its membership was five hundred thousand, and by 1919 it exceeded four million. From its inception, the organization's driving force was Samuel Gompers – "short-legged, stocky, [with a] large bald head, wide mouth, [and] piercing gray eyes," was how socialist and union leader Morris Hillquit once described him. "The superiority of Samuel Gompers," observed Hillquit, "sprang from a moral rather than intellectual source. . . . What he lacked in book learning he amply made up in personal character, integrity, will power and single-minded devotion to the cause of labor." (Lenin, on the other hand, called him an "agent of the bourgeoisie.")

Born in London in 1850 of Dutch-Sephardi Jewish descent, Gompers began working at the age of ten. He became a cigarmaker and immigrated to New York in 1863 with his family. Within a decade or so, he was running the Cigarmakers International Union, then the Federation of Organized Trades and Labor Union of the United States and Canada, and finally became the president of the AFL, a job he held (except for one year, 1895) for the rest of his life. Gompers was a highly talented union organizer. He travelled across the country, establishing union locals, and then turned his attention to Canada. By 1902, thanks to Gompers's efforts, AFL affiliates had taken control of the Trades and Labour Congress of Canada.

In his youth, Gompers was slightly more radical than the conservative labour leader he became. But the violence of such events as the Pullman Strike convinced him that a radical approach would not work. In January 1874, he had been involved in an altercation at New York's Tompkins Square where the police attacked protesting unemployed workers. It left a lasting impression on him. "I saw how professions of radicalism and sensationalism concentrated all the forces of organized society against a labor movement and nullified in advance normal, necessary activity," he later recalled. "I saw the danger of entangling alliances with intellectuals who did not understand that to experiment with the labor movement was to experiment with human life."

He rejected the dramatic societal solutions advanced by socialists and anarchists and tended to ignore the needs of immigrant and unskilled workers. He dismissed the idea of the revolutionary "One Big Union" as an attempt to subvert the capitalist order and, sounding much like a tycoon, declared that the IWW was "never more than a radical fungus on the labor movement." In 1919, he thought the general strikes in Seattle and Winnipeg were, "evil," "ill-advised," and "a complete fiasco." He welcomed the Justice Department's assistance to "purge" the AFL of Reds.

During the late nineteenth century, unskilled (and largely immigrant) workers who had been shunted aside by the AFL and those skilled labourers who demanded a faster pace of change than Gompers advocated, began to take matters into their own hands. Their pursuit of industrial unionism – in which workers in one industry, regardless of skill, joined together – led to the beginning of violent conflict that would last for more than two decades. The riot in Haymarket Square in Chicago in May 1886 ignited the fuse. Workers led by the radical International Working People's Association had gathered in the square to demonstrate their support for striking employees of the McCormick Harvester Company, who had been attacked by private detectives and police. Speakers at the protest rally included well-known socialists Albert Parsons, Augustus Spies, and Samuel Fielden.

The gathering was peaceful until a large contingent of Chicago police showed up. Then all hell broke loose. A bomb exploded, killing seven police officers. A riot broke out, and many foreigners and anarchists were beaten and arrested. While the bomb-thrower's identity remained a mystery, eight men were tried for inciting the riot and, in what was certainly a miscarriage of justice, four of these men – Parsons, Spies, Adolph Fischer, and George Engel – were hanged on November 11, 1887.*

---

* As the noose was placed around Spies's neck, his last words to the assembled witnesses and authorities were, "The time will come today when our silence will be more powerful than the voice you strangle today!" Fischer and Engel both shouted, "Hurrah for Anarchy!" while Parsons said through his hood, "Will I be allowed to talk, O men of America? Let me speak, Sheriff Matson! Let the voice of the people be heard! O –" The trap door fell open before he could finish. The *Chicago Tribune* echoed the sentiment of most Americans that day, "Law has triumphed over Anarchy."

The executions had a profound impact in two distinct ways. Workers throughout the world forever after commemorated November 11 as a day for sombre reflection, but the American public now regarded anarchism and terrorism as one and the same. "For years, the memory of Haymarket and the dread of imported anarchy haunted the American consciousness," writes historian John Higham. "No nativist image prevailed more widely than that of the immigrant as a lawless creature, given over to violence and disorder."

For young Emma Goldman, a Russian-Jewish immigrant living in Rochester, New York, in 1887, the Haymarket affair was a pivotal moment. It transformed her into an anarchist. "I read about their heroic stand while on trial and their marvellous defence. I saw a new world opening before me," she later remembered. "The next morning [after the hangings] I woke as from a long illness, but free from the numbness and the depression [of] those harrowing weeks of waiting, ending with the final shock. I had a distinct sensation that something new and wonderful had been born in my soul. A great ideal, a burning faith, a determination to dedicate myself to the memory of my martyred comrades, to make their cause my own, to make known to the world their beautiful lives and heroic deaths."

And dedicate herself she did. Goldman became a journal editor, publishing the anarchist periodical *Mother Earth* for twelve years. She was a captivating orator, who could fill up labour halls across North America, challenging authority at every turn, an outspoken advocate for birth control and "free sex," and a symbol to many of everything frightening about the modern world.

Goldman's lifelong companion (and one-time lover) Alexander Berkman – Sasha to his friends and colleagues – also a Russian-Jewish immigrant, was similarly influenced by the Haymarket affair. He had still been in Europe when it happened, yet he arrived in the United States in 1888 at the age of seventeen a committed anarchist ready to change the world. Four years later, Berkman decided to take decisive action. He was angered by the ruthless and anti-union Henry

Clay Frick, manager of the Carnegie Steel Mill in Homestead, Pennsylvania, where striking workers had been treated roughly by Frick and his band of Pinkerton men. Berkman planned to kill Frick and then blow himself up as a martyr for the cause. In early July 1892, he managed to gain entry to Frick's office, shoot him, and then stab him. But Frick did not die and Berkman was not able to commit suicide. He was arrested, tried, and given a fourteen-year prison sentence, which he served under brutal conditions.

The authorities had tried to implicate Goldman in this murder plot – in fact, while Berkman protected her, she later admitted that she had known about it – yet were unable to do so. Nine years later, she was linked to the sensational assassination of President William McKinley, another event that clouded the legitimate demands of labour with the acts of terrorism committed by anarchists. McKinley's assailant was Leon Czolgosz, the twenty-nine-year-old son of Polish immigrants (and likely mentally ill). He had shot the president while he chatted with visitors at the Pan-American Exposition in Buffalo on September 6, 1901. Later, when the police interrogated him, Czolgosz stated that he had killed McKinley after attending one of Goldman's lectures. Goldman was arrested, yet again there was insufficient evidence to link her to the murder. The assassination, however, led to tougher anti-anarchist immigration laws in 1903 and set off another wave of panic about aliens and anarchists.

When a Wobbly Comes to Town

Among the numerous radical groups and organizations operating in North America, few frightened authorities and middle-class civilians as much as the IWW. Founded in Chicago in 1905, its style was epitomized by William "Big Bill" Haywood, its most dominant personality until after the First World War. Born in Utah in 1869, Haywood led a rough life. A miner at the age of fifteen, he lost an eye in an accident. He was a powerfully built man more than six feet tall with a thunderous voice. It was rumoured he had once "crushed" the heads of two men together at an altercation on a picket line; his friends, however, in the Western Federation of Miners thought him "gentle."

The decision to create the IWW was a backlash against the AFL and an attempt to bring unskilled labourers – migrant farmhands, lumberjacks, sweatshop immigrants, women, and non-whites – into one industrial union. From the start, the IWW was "part union [and] part revolutionary," says Pittsburgh historian Charles McCormick. The IWW, he adds, "combined elements of homespun radicalism traceable to populists, Knights of Labor, single-taxers, and the like with a belief in the labor theory of value, European syndicalism, and Marxist class struggle." Haywood and other IWW leaders talked tough about using violence to alter society through revolution. Yet it never happened.

At its peak in 1917, the IWW had close to one hundred thousand members in the United States, another ten thousand in Canada, mainly in Alberta and British Columbia, and affiliates in Mexico and Australia. Its officials proclaimed the dawn of a new age and advocated the "One Big Union," general strikes, and revolutionary tactics. But in fact the IWW's real impact was that it provided its members with hope for a utopian future. The AFL was responsible for far more actual strikes than the IWW, although it was the IWW, owing to its rabid anti-capitalist rhetoric, that was targeted by police, government, and vigilantes.

"When a Wobbly comes to town, I just knock him over the head with a nightstick and throw him in the River," claimed one small-town sheriff. "When he comes up, he beats it out of town." A San Diego *Tribune* editor did not mince words either. "Hanging is none too good for them," one editorial put it. "They would be much better dead for they are absolutely useless in the human economy. They are the waste matter of creation and should be drained off into the sewer of oblivion, there to rot in cold obstruction like any excrement."

Before the war, one of the worst incidents of violence against the IWW occurred in Lawrence, Massachusetts. In 1912, more than twenty thousand mill-workers went out on strike and many were loyal IWW supporters. When the strikers tried to hold a peaceful march, they were met by thousands of police and state militiamen. During the melee that followed, men, women, and children were killed and martial law was declared. Two IWW leaders were wrongfully accused for a murder they did not commit – neither of the men was even in Lawrence when the killing took place – and police attacked the striking mill-workers' wives and children, who were trying to get out of town by train. It was later revealed that one of the Lawrence mill executives had paid a man posing as a striker to set explosives in several locations so that the IWW would be held responsible. The man was fined five hundred dollars and the executive not even charged. But there was enough public outrage that the mills settled the strike and the IWW was able to claim a victory of sorts. In Washington, President William Taft ordered a full-scale investigation into the IWW's activities. It would not be the last.

A Clear and Present Danger

The threat posed by the IWW and other radicals took on a more ominous tone from 1914 to 1918, the years of the First World War. Patriotism became not merely desirable but mandatory. The logic was as follows: If there was a threat to the civilized world from the "Hun," then anyone who spoke out against the war effort, opposed conscription and military service, disrupted the economy, or was an obstacle in any way to victory was a menace to mankind. To protect the North American way of life, Canada and the United States adopted laws intended to preserve liberty. Yet in the name of freedom, governments in both countries felt compelled to curtail, even trample on, the rights of minorities and dissenters. Here was the real moral dilemma and contradiction of the era.

Canada entered the war as soon as the conflict began in early August 1914. The federal government immediately passed the War Measures Act (WMA), which gave it virtually unlimited power to do anything in the name of the "security, defence, peace, order and good government" of Canada. The WMA allowed officials in Ottawa to censor newspapers and magazines, and arrest, detain, incarcerate, and deport "enemy aliens." By 1918, nearly 9,300 men, women, and children had been interned at camps in Northern Ontario and British Columbia, while the Wartime Election Act of 1917 stripped former citizens of enemy countries who had become naturalized Canadians of their right to vote. Many British-born socialist and labour leaders, including Frederick Dixon, John Queen, and Abraham Heaps, denounced the war and opposed conscription. All three would be caught up in the Winnipeg General Strike of 1919. Meanwhile the authorities braced themselves for an IWW-led Soviet-style revolution.

The United States finally declared war on Germany on April 6, 1917. This was followed by a presidential proclamation authorizing the detention of enemy aliens. Within two months the government had passed the Espionage Act, making it a crime, among other infractions, "to interfere with the operations or success" of the U.S. war effort, "to cause insubordination [and] disloyalty," or to obstruct recruiting or enlistment services. Less than a year later, Congress added the Sedition Act. Now it was against the law to utter, print, write, or publish anything about the U.S. government or Constitution that might be considered disloyal or profane. Both laws carried with them harsh penalties: a ten-thousand-dollar fine and a twenty-year jail sentence.

Socialists, anarchists, and Wobblies ignored the government's new legal restrictions, defiantly speaking out against the war and profiteers, who were making millions of dollars from the conflict. "Don't be a Soldier," one IWW pamphlet declared, "Be a Man." Another urged workers not to become "hired murderers" or make themselves "a target in order to fatten Rockefeller, Morgan, Carnegie . . . and the other industrial pirates."

The reaction to these "unpatriotic" actions was loud and hostile. IWW meetings were raided, its books and literature seized, and its members arrested and beaten. In July 1917, IWW organizer Frank Little was lynched by a mob in Butte, Montana. "Big Bill" Haywood was arrested under the Espionage and Sedition acts for his anti-war activities and given a twenty-year jail sentence in Leavenworth Penitentiary (he served only a year before he was out on appeal and then escaped to Russia before his case was decided). Other Wobblies were tarred and feathered. The organization's literature was banned from the mails. Patriotic societies like the American Protective League (with 350,000 loyal members by 1918) denounced IWW members and socialists as "traitors" and "agents of Germany." Newspaper editors referred to the IWW as "America's canker sore" and described the typical Wobbly as "a sort of half-wild animal." Former president Theodore Roosevelt thought they were on "a homicidal march," and Senator Henry F. Ashurst of Arizona suggested the Wobblies had turned murder into a "science." In private, President Wilson, who believed that German agents had infiltrated the country, regarded the Socialist Party of America's opposition to the war as "almost treasonable." Almost on cue, one state after another began passing laws making it illegal to fly a red flag.

More than 2,100 people were indicted under the U.S. Espionage and Sedition acts and more than one thousand were convicted – often for merely declaring in public (and private) their negative view about the war.[*] Among them were Emma Goldman and Alexander Berkman,

---

[*] On one occasion, a person was sent to jail for saying, "Men conscripted to Europe are virtually condemned to death and everyone knows it." Another got a sentence of twenty years for claiming that the war was "a rich man's war and the U.S. is simply fighting for money" and that he hoped the "government goes to hell so it will be of no value." In what historian Robert Justin Goldstein calls the "single most incredible case," Walter Matthey of Iowa received one year in jail for, in the words of Attorney General Thomas Gregory, "attending a meeting, listening to an address in which disloyal utterances were made, applauding some of the statements made

who had organized the No Conscription League. They were both arrested in mid-June 1917 for opposing the war and the draft in what the government referred to as a "conspiracy." Both were eventually sentenced to two years in prison, received fines of ten thousand dollars each, and faced possible deportation when they got out.[**] The *New York Times* called their convictions "a public service that honors the jury. . . . Deportation, if any country will consent to receive them, is the proper punishment of such alien demonstrators of anarchy."

Their legal struggles were typical of the way the courts supported the government's dictatorial and often repressive rule. The outcome in two cases involving the SPA was especially revealing of the era. Charles Schenck, the SPA's general secretary, was arrested for printing and distributing fifteen thousand pamphlets in which enlisting in the military was strongly discouraged. "Do Not Submit To Intimidation," urged the leaflet. He was convicted under the Espionage Act and appealed the outcome all the way to the U.S. Supreme Court, arguing that his First Amendment rights to free speech had been violated. In March 1919, in a unanimous decision, Justice Oliver Wendell Holmes deemed that the "yardstick" in this case was whether Schenck's actions had created "a clear and present danger." The justices ruled that it had and upheld the guilty verdict.

Similarly, SPA leader Eugene Debs was arrested after delivering a controversial speech in Canton, Ohio, in which he denounced the government and urged those in the audience not to support the war effort. "Do not worry over the charge of treason to your masters," he declared. "This year we are going to sweep into power and in this

---

by the speaker claimed to be disloyal, their exact nature not being known, and contributing 25 cents."

[**] Berkman had never bothered to take out American citizenship and therefore was still an alien. Goldman's naturalization, which she obtained from a brief marriage to Jacob Kersner, was declared void on a technicality. The Justice Department ruled that Kersner had lied when he applied for his papers.

nation we are going to destroy capitalistic institutions." He was also charged with violating the Espionage Act and was sentenced to ten years in prison. Like Schenck, Debs appealed to the Supreme Court. And once again, Justice Holmes upheld the conviction under the "clear and present danger" principle. Interestingly, most newspapers editors applauded the decision, which established defined limits on freedom of speech in the United States. Debs was not released from prison until 1921, by which time the tense atmosphere in the country had died down.

Every Strike Is a Small Revolution

The war had ended in November 1918, but the real trouble with the labour movement was only beginning. The year 1919 soon saw a bitter confrontation between dissatisfied workers and business leaders unwilling to accept a new labour-management relationship. Before the year was done, there would be 3,600 strikes in the United States involving four million workers and 428 in Canada with nearly 150,000 workers on the picket lines. These massive labour disruptions may have been about inflation, low wages, and poor working conditions, but to upper- and middle-class North Americans they seemed nothing less than a left-wing attempt to take over the world. And who could blame them for thinking that? "Every strike is a small revolution and a dress rehearsal for the big one," the IWW proclaimed early in the year.

The opening offensive was launched in Seattle. On January 21, 1919, thirty-five thousand shipyard workers struck for higher wages and better working conditions. Within days, the Seattle Central Labor Council, without quite realizing the consequences of its actions, voted in favour of a general strike in support of the shipyard men. Mayor Ole Hanson did everything he could to change the Council's mind and the city's major newspapers cried that a revolution was imminent. Two days before the General Strike was to begin, the *Seattle Star* warned workers, "You are being urged to use a dangerous weapon, the general strike. . . . These false Bolsheviks haven't a chance on earth to win anything for you in this country because this country is America – not Russia."

The appeals went unanswered. Determined to proceed, workers echoed with enthusiasm the sentiments expressed by reporter Anna Louis Strong in the *Seattle Union Record*. "There will be many cheering and there will be some who fear," she wrote in an editorial. "Both of these emotions are useful, but not too much of either. We are undertaking the most tremendous move ever made by Labor in this country, a move which will lead – No One Knows Where!"

On February 6, more than sixty thousand Seattle workers walked off their jobs, nearly shutting down the city. The strike committee had made exemptions for such essential services as the police and hospitals to keep operating. But this strategy led, as it would in Winnipeg several months later, to accusations that the workers had taken over the city. And, indeed, across the U.S., the Seattle strike was portrayed as a "Bolshevik coup."

Mayor Hanson, who detested the IWW, was enough of a political opportunist to take advantage of the situation. He later maintained that the strike was an act of class war by radicals who "want to take possession of our American government and try to duplicate the anarchy of Russia." He added 600 more men to the police force, swore in another 2,400 deputies, and prepared for the worst. "The time has come," he stated in a public proclamation soon after the strike began, "for the people in Seattle to show their Americanism. . . . The anarchists in this community shall not rule its affairs."

The next day, Hanson, riding in a car draped in an American flag, led federal troops into the city from nearby Camp Lewis. He warned that unless the strike was called off within twenty-four hours, he would declare martial law. A few more days passed before the strikers accepted the hopelessness of the situation and ended the action. The shipyard workers remained off the job. Proclaimed the *Seattle Star* on February 10: "Today this Bolshevik-sired nightmare is over."

The Seattle General Strike lasted only five days and was by all accounts a failure for the city's labour organizations. Hanson, however, made the most of the occasion, became a national hero for stopping the spread of Bolshevism, and contemplated running for president as a Republican candidate. Six months later, he resigned as mayor and went on a speaking tour. Unable to charge the strike leaders with any crime, the authorities targeted the remaining members of the IWW still residing in the state and wiped out the organization.

Seattle was hardly the end of the labour disputes and troubles. A two-day police strike in Boston in the first week of September 1919 led to looting and violence. Then came the national steel strike, in which twenty-four AFL-affiliated steel unions representing between 250,000 and 300,000 workers walked off their jobs. Again, newspapers portrayed the strikers, whose main demands were higher wages and an eight-hour day, as "Un-American," and "Bolsheviks." The attention of the press and the Bureau of Investigation was focused mainly on one strike leader, William Z. Foster, who earlier in his career was connected to the IWW. J. Edgar Hoover considered his radical activities "subtle and pernicious." A Senate Committee later investigating the strike wrongly concluded that it was a plot by "a considerable element of IWW's, anarchists, revolutionists, and Russian Soviets" who manipulated the strike "as a means of elevating themselves to power." In truth, any violence during the four-month labour action usually was caused by private detectives hired to protect strikebreakers brought in to reopen mills and factories.

Before the steel strike was settled, workers in the coal industry, four hundred thousand miners who were prepared to leave Americans with no fuel for the winter, also demanded better working conditions and pay. Attorney General Palmer used a federal injunction to break the strike, although it took longer than he expected to end an action that he regarded as dangerous and revolutionary.

It was not in the United States, however, where the most serious labour disruption of 1919 took place, but north, on the Canadian prairies. Earlier in the year, Palmer's attention, like that of most North Americans, was riveted by the dramatic events in Winnipeg.

We Are Under the Sway of Bolshevism

The "hello girls" who worked as operators for the Manitoba Telephone Systems were the first to take action. On May 15, 1919, at seven o'clock in the morning as the women on the night shift left their stations, no one replaced them. Four hours later, at the designated hour of eleven, approximately thirty thousand workers in Winnipeg walked off their jobs, setting the stage for one of the great labour-management confrontations in North American history.

For the next six weeks, the Winnipeg General Strike paralyzed this prairie city of 175,000 people and had a far greater impact than the general strike in Seattle. The police, the majority of whom were sympathetic with the strikers' demands, agreed to remain on duty; otherwise, Winnipeg would have been put under military or martial law. The business elite, who had dominated Winnipeg's government and who ran the city as if it were their own personal fiefdom, feared, with some justification, that a Bolshevik-style revolution had descended upon them. They quickly formed themselves into the Citizens' Committee of One Thousand to keep Winnipeg operating. At the local army barracks, the military commander, Brigadier-General Herbert D.B. Ketchen, was asked by the mayor of Winnipeg, Charles Gray, to put his men on alert.

The strike leaders, on the other hand – mainly British-born working-class men influenced more by moderate Socialist Fabianism than revolutionary Marxism – saw in the General Strike an unprecedented opportunity. They wanted collective bargaining (as they defined it) to be recognized as legitimate and demanded higher wages and better working conditions for their members. Yet they were also intent on challenging the capitalist world view that placed them at the bottom of the social hierarchy. They were determined to be heard – one way or another. It was not a violent Bolshevik revolution they wanted; they did not seek to topple the government, despite what the business community and press so vehemently argued. But they did advocate radical change, nonetheless. "What they did not see in their enthusiasm," observes historian David Bercuson, "was that a general strike must create social chaos and by itself brings society crashing down unless special measures are taken."

Within the first week of the strike, the leaders of the strike committee – a fifteen-man group including Robert Russell, Reverend William Ivens, Ernest Robinson, Harry Veitch, and James Winning – agreed to allow the Winnipeg General Hospital to keep its essential operations running. Then, as in Seattle, milk and bread wagons appeared on the streets with signs announcing, "Permitted by Authority of Strike Committee"; the strikers had realized that the city could not do without these staples, but the men delivering them did not want anyone to think that they were scabs. Next the strike committee permitted theatre and picture-show owners to open up again, with the requisite sign posted, so that idle strikers would have something to do. The decision to allow the hospital, theatres, and milk and bread delivery to proceed, while understandable under the circumstances, may have been one of the strike leaders' biggest miscalculations, since it led authorities to believe that a Soviet-style government had been established. At the order of the mayor and city council, the signs on the wagons and theatres were eventually removed, yet the damage had been done.

From New York City came this assessment of the tense situation. Under the heading, "Utopia in Winnipeg," the editors of the *New York Times* suggested, "There is a beautiful demonstration going on in Winnipeg of essential Bolshevism. If a Winnipegian is allowed to eat, if he takes a drink of milk or water, if he doesn't go to bed in the dark, he enjoys the favour by the clemency and august permission of the Strike Committee." Closer to home, sixty-eight-year-old Methodist minister Reverend John MacLean, no fan of the strike despite his social gospel leanings, wrote in his diary on May 20, "We are under the sway of Bolshevism in the city. Everything is quiet, but there are some ugly rumours floating around, and the Home Defence Guards are all ready for action at a given signal."

Winnipeg in the spring of 1919 was a city under tremendous pressure. It had long been divided between the wealthy commercial elite – the men of the Grain Exchange and financial sectors – who resided in the south sections of the city, and the working-class and foreign immigrants who lived in the western section and more impoverished North End. A downturn in the economy in 1913 followed by the First World War, which tended to inflate prices far more than wages, had led to further charges that the owners were making "fat profits" on the backs of their workers. It was difficult for many workers to make ends meet.[*]

Misconceptions about the Russian Revolution, the threat of foreign agitation, and the strike in Seattle simply added fuel to a growing fire. An editorial in the *Winnipeg Telegram* at the end of January 1919 – the most conservative of the city's three daily newspapers – likely echoed a sentiment shared by many members of the elite: "Let every hostile alien be deported from the country, the privileges of which . . . he does not appreciate."

Trade unions, organized by crafts, had made some progress in Winnipeg and Canada. Yet many businessmen, including the employers in the city's volatile metal industry, so-called ironmasters

---

* According to the *Western Labour News* of May 2, 1919, wages had risen by 18 per cent since 1914, so that a bricklayer, for example, was making eighty cents per hour, a janitor who cleaned the floor of the factory much less. But prices had risen nearly 80 per cent. Bacon, bread, shoes, and clothing had all jumped in price. The newspaper figured out that the average family of five had an income of about $136 a month, when it actually needed $196 just to survive.

like Tom Deacon and L.R. Barrett, were skeptical, if not outright hostile, to the idea of collective bargaining and loath to accept orders from any union. "God gave me this plant, and by God I'll run it the way I want to!" Barrett once declared.

Challenging Deacon, Barrett, and the other chieftains of capitalism was a new breed of labour leader – more vocal, political, ideological, and militant than those who had preceded them. Yet they also came in all varieties, from ardent Marxists, to middle-of-the road socialists, to God-fearing Utopian social gospellers. They could agree that society needed to be saved, but they could not decide among themselves (not even during the strike) how to achieve their lofty goals.* The vast majority had arrived in Canada from Britain and Scotland, where many had been trained as youngsters in factories and been exposed to the new socialist ideas that demanded more from a union than a membership card.

That was the experience of Robert B. Russell. He was born in Glasgow in 1888, attended school until he was twelve years old, and then went to work as a young apprentice in the shipyards. He arrived in Canada in 1911 as a master mechanic, married Margaret (Peggy) Hampton, the sister of a friend who had accompanied him on his journey to North America, and found a job in the metal industry in Winnipeg. But Russell, who referred to his friends as "comrade," had read the writings of Karl Marx and had been influenced by the Spartacists in Germany and the IWW in the United States. By the time he settled in Winnipeg, he had resolved that

---

* "Years later when the passions of the moment had subsided," as Harry and Mildred Gutkin relate, "Bill Pritchard [one of those later arrested on charges of seditious conspiracy near the end of strike] could repeat with amusement the comment of a young newly arrived Scottish guard at the prison farm where he and the others convicted with him served their sentences. 'Conspiracy?' the guard exclaimed, as they all enjoyed a forbidden smoke together, with Pritchard, John Queen, Dick Johns, and some of the others vehemently arguing politics, 'Seditious conspiracy? My god, you fellows can't agree on any one point!'"

"the interests of all working people were the same, and in conflict with the designs of capital." He was drawn to the Socialist Party of Canada (SPC) – where he became acquainted with John Queen, Frederick Dixon, and Dick Johns, all later prominent in the General Strike – and began making his voice heard at union meetings. He argued against Canadian participation in the First World War – "a capitalists' war," in his view – and by 1918 had played a key role in the formation of the Metal Trades Council (a labour organization representing six of the city's metal-craft unions) and emerged as one of the more radical labour leaders in the city.

In December 1918, at a momentous labour rally held at a downtown theatre at which the seeds of the General Strike were sown, Russell predicted the demise of capitalism, adding, "the red flag is flying in every civilized country in the world, and it will fly here." With spies of the Royal North-West Mounted Police (RNWMP) in the audience that afternoon, those words would later be used against him as proof that he was one of the masterminds behind a seditious conspiracy.

In the spring, Russell attended a labour conference in Calgary and gave his full support to the radical concept of the One Big Union, or OBU, a body strong enough to challenge the power of employers and conceivably the state as well. It was further evidence of his supposedly revolutionary scheme. Indeed, the OBU convention passed a resolution declaring the delegates were in favour of "the principle of 'Proletariat Dictatorship' as being absolute and efficient for the transformation of capitalistic private property to communal wealth." Organizers made little progress on the OBU plan until after the Winnipeg General Strike had ended, but its dangerous prophecy for a Soviet-style future hung over the city throughout the conflict. Some months earlier James B. Coyne, a prominent Winnipeg lawyer and later a member of the Citizens' Committee (his son James E. Coyne, only nine years old in 1919, would become the Governor of the Bank of Canada), suggested with more than a little trepidation that the Winnipeg Trades and Labour Council, with which Russell was affiliated, was "largely dominated by labour leaders who are acknowledged Bolsheviki and whose desire I believe is to substitute a workmen's council with the Russian motto as the governing force in the municipality instead of the representative bodies now constituted by law."

Further adding to the tension in Winnipeg were hundreds, if not thousands, of discontented veterans who had only recently returned from the trenches in Europe. They were the General Strike's random element, so to speak. As a group the soldiers were disillusioned. They had marched off to war full of idealism, believing in the cause of freedom and having faith in those who led them. But the bloodshed at places like the Somme, Verdun, and Vimy Ridge, had showed them another side of war – its futility, waste, and destruction. They had watched their friends die in vain as foolish British and Canadian generals insisted on sending the men "over the top" into a no man's land of treacherous barbed wire and enemy machine-gun fire that picked them off with ease. Their Russian allies had deserted them when the Bolsheviks finally took power in October 1917, a clear indication that Reds and revolutionaries were not to be trusted – not ever. And when the survivors had returned to Canada they found that foreigners and women had replaced them in the factories.

During the past few months, several confrontations had flared between the returned soldiers and anyone they felt was disloyal. That included most unions, Socialist Party members, and certainly anyone connected to Ukrainian, Jewish, or "alien" organizations, no matter what their political affiliation. In January 1919, for example, a horde of angry soldiers had converged on Sam Blumenberg's dry-cleaning shop. Blumenberg was a member of the SPC. The veterans forced his wife to kiss the flag and then vandalized the store.

There were scuffles at Market Square behind City Hall when labour leaders attempted to speak in public. And in one incident a group of soldiers invaded the Socialist Party headquarters, ransacked the second-floor office, and threw files and papers onto the street along with a piano, all of which was then set on fire. Men paid unannounced visits to factories or companies employing "alien" workers and threatened to destroy the premises if the foreigners were not fired. In fact, the RNWMP worried that soldiers would "fall easy prey to Bolsheviks." Late in January 1919, RNWMP commissioner A.B. Perry was warned that all efforts must be made to get returned men "on the right track" and away from radicals and agitators, if not "it would be hard to tell what would happen." As it turned out, the soldiers, like everyone else in the city, were split. Many did support the strikers, following labour leader Roger Bray, a Methodist preacher and veteran, while others organized the Loyalist Veterans Association, allying themselves with the Citizens' Committee and swearing an oath to stop the spread of Bolshevism at all costs.

The Winnipeg Strike started as a confrontation between workers in the metal and building trades. The ironmasters refused to accept the Metal Trades Council as the legitimate collective-bargaining agent of their employees and the building contractors could not meet the workers' wage demands (they wanted twenty cents more an hour than they were being paid). Soon, however, nearly every other union in the city declared their solidarity with the metal-workers and builders and a localized battle escalated into a massive sympathetic strike, as it had in Seattle. On May 13, 1919, the night the strike vote was taken at a gathering of the Winnipeg Trades and Labour Council, the *Western Labour News* reported that the mood in the hall "was tense, electric and determined, yet seized with a wonderful gravity. Every inch was jammed with a seething mass of trade union-ists, men and women."

Two days later, once these men and women had walked off their jobs, the authorities prepared themselves for a siege. The Citizens' Committee of One Thousand organized an army of volunteers, women included, to staff firehouses and steam plants, service gasoline pumps, work the telephone lines, and, since the streetcars also stopped running, taxi people around the city. Meanwhile, at the headquarters of the Trades and Labour Council, the Central Strike Committee determinedly, yet with a feeling of exuberance, made some critical decisions about which services and businesses could remain open. "It is a fine spectacle," Russell wrote to Victor Midgley, a comrade in Vancouver, "to see employers coming to the Labour Temple, asking for permission to operate their various industries."[*] But to John W. Dafoe, the editor of the *Manitoba Free Press* (stereotypers and pressmen joined the strike on May 16, shutting down the newspaper for nearly a week until Dafoe and his managers began putting out a smaller strike edition), such attitudes and actions were nothing more than, as he wrote in an editorial entitled "The Great Dream of the Winnipeg Soviet," the work of "either madmen bent upon destruction or desperate schemers who plan to make a general strike the starting point for adventurous experiment in government." The strikers countered these and similar assertions in the pages of the *Western Labour News* and the *Daily Strike Bulletin*, both edited by William Ivens, yet the perception that official authority was being usurped lingered.

Anticipating the worst, General Ketchen had quietly arranged for a shipment of portable Lewis machine guns, and the federal government, urged by lawyer Alfred A. Andrews, a former Winnipeg mayor, amended the Immigration Act so that it would be possible to deport the British-born leaders of the strike. Ketchen did not have to wait too long. Several events in early June brought the strike to a violent climax.

---

[*] Russell also liked to tell the story of how he supposedly witnessed two North End women on a Winnipeg street, "pulling each other's hair, screaming and kicking." Sure that labour would be victorious and wealth would be redistributed in short order, they had rushed down to Wellington Crescent, where the city's elite lived, to choose which mansions they desired – except both had selected the same one.

First was Winnipeg City Council's imprudent decision to attempt to force the members of its police department to sign a loyalty oath and renounce their right to strike. Most of the men refused to sign the oath, leaving the city without a proper police force. The council then recruited 1,800 "special constables," mostly veterans (with some characters best described as "thugs" among them), who were given wagon yokes and clubs and instructed to "exercise good judgment and restraint" in keeping the peace.

On June 10, when the "specials" on foot and horseback attempted to disperse a crowd of strikers listening to a speech a block from Portage Avenue and Main Street, a riot broke out. The pro-strike mob began throwing stones and bricks at the mounted men. One of the specials, a veteran and recipient of the Victoria Cross, Sgt. Frederick Coppins, was pulled from his horse and beaten. The Citizens' Committee later blamed "three Austrians" for the attack, but Coppins claimed he had been assaulted by a group of returned soldiers. No matter, the riot pushed the government to the edge.

A week later, and with no sign of the strike ending, RNWMP constables swept through the city in the early hours of June 17 and arrested as many of the strike leaders as they could find. The authorities planned to use a newly enacted clause in the federal Immigration Act that would allow them to deport all "anarchists and Bolsheviks" from the country. Eleven men, Robert Russell among them, were arrested that night, incarcerated at Stony Mountain Penitentiary (twenty miles north of the city), and charged with seditious conspiracy. More arrests would follow.

This unprecedented legal action left the workers stunned. Even such opponents of the strike as *Free Press* editor John Dafoe and Canadian Trades and Labour Congress president Tom Moore (in Toronto) believed that the government had gone too far. Three days after the arrests, the government, perhaps sensing that it had overstepped the rules of "British justice," released the Canadian and British-born leaders on bail (five foreigners who had also been arrested were kept in custody). Russell and his colleagues agreed not to participate any further in the strike. As talks were underway between the metal-industry owners and the metal unions, the city announced that the streetcars would start running again. At the same time, pro-strike veterans declared that despite Mayor Gray's ban on parades they would hold a "silent march" in support of the arrested leaders on Saturday, June 21.

That morning, the soldiers met with the mayor and demanded that the streetcars not run until the strike was officially over. The mayor refused and, fearing more violence, called on the RNWMP and the military to keep order. He then read the Riot Act. But his voice, as one witness recalled, was "drowned in bedlam." By early afternoon there were thousands of people in the downtown area. One group converged on a streetcar that had started its run, tipped it on its side, and set it on fire.[*]

While this was taking place, the Mounties on horseback, dressed in both red and khaki uniforms (the khaki was worn by men who had recently returned from duty in Russia) arrived on Main Street. They charged into the crowd several times, swinging clubs and firing their guns. Several people were killed. Next on the scene was General Ketchen accompanied by cavalry and trucks mounted with Lewis machine guns. Specials on foot also joined the melee and started swinging their clubs in an attempt to clear the streets. They attacked people in alleys, causing numerous casualties. Dozens of bystanders and veterans were injured, and close to one hundred individuals were arrested.

In his report in the Monday edition of the *Western Labour News*, Frederick Dixon, who, along with J.S. Woodsworth, had taken over writing the newspaper following the arrest of William Ivens,

---

[*] The photograph of this incident taken by local photographer Lewis Foote is today one of the most famous images of the strike.

compared the events of June 21 to the "Bloody Sunday" assault on Russians perpetrated by Czarist soldiers in St. Petersburg in January 1905. In the annals of Winnipeg history, this day became known as "Bloody Saturday."

When the violence had run its course it had taken a toll on the strikers. They informed the premier of Manitoba, Tobias Norris, that they would call off the strike if he would create a Royal Commission to investigate labour conditions in the province. Over the objections of the Citizens' Committee, he agreed. The Winnipeg General Strike officially ended at 11:00 a.m. on June 26.

After more than six weeks of labour strife, what had the strikers accomplished? In the short term, the answer was very little. Several of the leaders, including Russell, were found guilty of seditious conspiracy and sentenced to two years in prison. The metal-workers, who had initiated the action, won only minor concessions, while the building tradesmen received slightly higher wage rates. Labour relations in Winnipeg and throughout Canada were set back by the failure of the strike. Workers would have their say eventually, but many more battles would first have to be fought. For the moment at least, the parameters of progress, capitalism, and the modern world, as well as the relationship between workers and managers, remained firmly in the purview of traditional politicians and businessmen.

All Aboard for the Next Soviet Ark

Throughout 1919, the various strikes had left many Americans on edge. And any issue or comment perceived as a threat, no matter how minor, triggered reactions that today can only be described as paranoid and hysterical. In early May in Washington, D.C., the "Star-Spangled Banner" was sung at a victory-loan parade, except one of the spectators did not stand. When the anthem had ended, an enraged sailor shot the man in the back, and the crowd, it was later reported, "burst into cheering and hand clapping." In

Hammond, Indiana, a jury required only two minutes to deliberate in a case involving the murder of an individual who had shouted, "To hell with the United States." Despite the strong evidence against the assailant, the jury acquitted him. During the steel strike, an angry mob in a town in West Virginia forced a group of "aliens" on the picket line to kiss the American flag, while a riot broke out in the Waldorf-Astoria Hotel in New York City after someone cried, "to hell with the flag." And schoolteachers and university professors put their jobs at risk if they even discussed the events in Russia.

The worst incident of vigilantism during the entire Red Scare took place on November 11, 1919, in Centralia, Washington, south of Tacoma. The American Legion had organized a parade commemorating the first anniversary of the end of the war. A troop of Boy Scouts and members of the Elk Lodge were also invited to participate. As the marchers passed by the IWW headquarters (one of only two then still operating in Washington), they decided to go inside. Anticipating trouble, the Wobblies had posted armed guards. As the Legionnaires moved towards the office, shots were fired, killing three of them. Several IWW members were immediately arrested, but one, Wesley Everest, eluded capture. A posse eventually tracked him to a hiding spot by a river, but before he could be apprehended, he shot another Legionnaire. He was arrested and badly beaten.

The town could not wait for justice to take its course. That evening, a mob broke into the jail cell and took Everest. He was castrated, beaten again, and then hanged on a nearby bridge. For good measure, he was also shot. His body was not cut down for days and no one was ever charged with his murder. The Centralia coroner summed up his report as follows: "Everest broke out of jail, went to the Chehalis River bridge, and committed suicide. He jumped off with a rope around his neck and then shot himself full of holes." The press bemoaned the killing of the Legionnaires rather than the lynching. Washington senator Wesley L. Jones was applauded when he stated that "the shots that killed these boys [the Legionnaires] were really aimed at the heart of this Nation by those who oppose law and seek the overthrow of Government."

There was no turning back now for Palmer and Hoover. The "Red Menace" had to be stopped at all costs, no matter how many civil liberties had to be violated. As they worked to have a peacetime sedition law passed, Palmer and Hoover decided their next target was to be the Union of Russian Workers (URW), a small anarchist group with approximately four thousand mainly "alien" members based in New York.

On November 7 – the date deliberately chosen by Hoover because it was the second anniversary of the Bolshevik takeover in Moscow – Bureau of Investigation agents and local police raided URW offices in twelve cities. Many of those who were arrested were severely beaten before being incarcerated at Ellis Island. Not to be outdone, the following day, on orders from the state, New York police rounded up another 700 anarchists and delivered them to Ellis Island as well. Some were later released, but as a result of the two raids the government had in custody 240 known radicals it could now deport.[*]

In the early hours of December 21, 249 radicals being held at Ellis Island were loaded onto the U.S.S. *Buford*, an aging transport ship that had been used during the Spanish-American War of 1898. On board, headed for the Soviet Union via Finland, were fifty-one anarchists, 184 members of the URW, and fourteen aliens. The two most famous deportees were Alexander Berkman and Emma Goldman. Berkman had been arrested soon after his release from

---

[*] When attorney Isaac Schorr of the National Civil Liberties Bureau wrote complaining about violations that had occurred in the New York raid, Hoover ignored the letter and opened a file on Schorr. The attorney is "the first person known to have made J. Edgar Hoover's enemies list," according to Curt Gentry, one of Hoover's many biographers.

prison; Goldman had turned herself in on December 5, after she decided not to fight the order to expel her.

Flynn and Hoover arrived in New York in time to see the "Soviet Ark," as the *Buford* had been dubbed, leave port. Hoover later remembered that seeing Goldman, he shouted "Merry Christmas, Emma" and "she responded with a thumb to her nose." Goldman, on the other hand, recalled the sadness of her fellow passengers as the ship sailed past the Statue of Liberty.[*]

Before the ship had reached its final destination, Hoover, with approval from Palmer, had struck again. On the evening of January 2, 1920, hundreds of agents from the Bureau of Investigation, assisted by local police and volunteers from the American Legion, swarmed across much of the United States – thirty-three cities in twenty-three states – to arrest close to four thousand suspected radicals, Bolsheviks, anarchists, and aliens. Hoover had cleverly instructed his agents inside the two American communist parties to try to schedule meetings that night. Without proper arrest or search warrants in their possession for all of those apprehended, the agents invaded political party headquarters, private homes, and pool halls – even bowling alleys. Many of those arrested were beaten, herded into crowded, unsanitary detention centres, and permitted no contact with their families or

---

[*] Emma Goldman remained in Russia only two years. Disillusioned by Soviet repression, she and Berkman relocated to Germany and published many pamphlets and articles denouncing the Soviet regime. Later, she spent time in London, Paris, and the south of France, where she worked on her autobiography, *Living My Life* (1931). She returned only once to the United States, in 1934, on special permission to conduct a ninety-day lecture tour. After Berkman committed suicide in 1936, Goldman helped the fight against Franco in Spain and visited Toronto in 1940, where she suffered a stroke. She died there on May 14, 1940, at the age of seventy. As historian Paul Avrich points out, "For a quarter century after her death, Goldman was a largely forgotten figure. Since the 1960s, however, she has had a remarkable revival. . . . She appeared as a character in E.L. Doctorow's novel *Ragtime* and in Warren Beatty's movie *Reds*, for which the actress who played her, Maureen Stapleton, won an Academy Award. Her story, moreover, has inspired a spate of plays, poems, and songs."

lawyers for weeks. Hoover had argued against granting bail since it would enable those detained to contact their lawyers. It "defeats the ends of justice," as he put it.

Those infamous raids, known as the Palmer Raids, turned out to be the Red Scare's climax. At first, the public cheered. "Revolution Smashed" was the headline on the front page of the *New York Times*, and an editorial inside applauded the "alacrity, resolute will, and fruitful intelligent vigor of the Department of Justice in hunting down those enemies of the United States." The *Chicago Tribune* was more succinct: "All Aboard for the Next Soviet Ark," its headline blared on January 3.

The actual results of the raids were less dramatic. In all, the Bureau of Investigation agents found about four guns – and three of them were rusty. No dynamite was discovered, although agents in Newark believed they had found four bombs. They turned out to be boccie balls. "Undoubtedly these raids are the most stupid thing yet done by the administration," said Pittsburgh socialist leader Jacob Margolis. "To hold the belief that 2,000 people can ever overthrow this country is seeing spooks in the worst form."

Margolis's logic may have made sense, but this hardly mattered to the Attorney General. Palmer and Hoover continued dispatching propaganda – articles, editorials, and cartoons – to newspaper editors in an effort to keep the scare alive. "My one desire is to acquaint people like you," wrote Palmer in a cover letter accompanying a stack of material, "with the real menace of evil-thinking which is the foundation of the Red movement."

And, for a brief time, it had the desired effect. Newspapers continued to berate Bolshevism and equate labour strife with revolution. Moreover, the January raids had crushed the two communist parties, leaving them, by 1920, with fewer than six thousand members. Yet within a few months, civil libertarians and lawyers began to criticize publicly the Justice Department's tactics. The ensuing uproar eventually killed Palmer's proposal for a peacetime sedition act.

Then, when nothing out of the ordinary happened on May 1, 1920, despite dire warnings by Palmer and Hoover that there would be assassinations and bombings, public enthusiasm for the Red Scare started to wane, and with it went Palmer's presidential bid. The final blow was a stinging report by the National Popular Government League and the (recently reorganized) American Civil Liberties Union detailing the many abuses committed by the Justice Department in carrying out their anti-Communist operations. Hoover opened a file on each of the lawyers involved in preparing the report, including Felix Frankfurter and Zechariah Chafee, Jr., but it was the end of the Red Scare, nonetheless. A decision by federal court judge George Anderson in June ruled at last that membership in a communist party was not sufficient grounds to deport an alien. The detention centres were soon emptied and any planned deportations were halted.[*] Still, Hoover maintained for years after that he had played a key role in destroying the communist movement in the United States. And rightly so. The great radical dream of transforming modern society had suffered a serious setback – not to mention the battle of the working class to evoke their rights to unions and collective bargaining. That victory would come, yet in the future and at a steep price.

The Red Scare did have an aftershock. On September 16, 1920, a bomb filled with heavy cast-iron slugs hidden in a wagon on the

---

[*] During the period from April 1917 to November 1918, when the U.S. was involved in the First World War, the government deported 4,125 aliens. From November 1918 to September 30, 1919, another 3,205 were added to the deportation list. But by October, officials had deported only 4,067 of the approximate 7,400 on the list. It was much easier to order someone back to "Bolshevik Russia," than to actually transport them there.

corner of Wall and Broad streets in Lower Manhattan exploded. Thirty-three people were killed and many more were wounded. Property damage was extensive, and "blood was everywhere." Despite amassing a seven-thousand-page dossier, the Bureau of Investigation never determined who had planted the bomb.

More than likely, the culprit in question was Mario Buda, an Italian anarchist who wanted to protest the indictment on murder charges of his friends and fellow anarchists Nicola Sacco and Bartolomeo Vanzetti. Five months earlier there had been a robbery and fatal shooting in the town of South Braintree, Massachusetts, south of Boston. In the afternoon of April 15, four men confronted two employees of the Slater & Morrill Shoe Company, paymaster Frederick Parmenter and his guard, Alessandro Berardelli. Parmenter had in his possession two boxes of cash totalling $15,776.51. Two men were in the getaway car, and two men grabbed the money. Shots were fired. Berardelli was killed instantly; Parmenter died the following day.

Three weeks later, the police arrested two well-known anarchists, Sacco, a shoe peddler, and Vanzetti, a fish peddler. Despite the fact that both men had reasonable alibis, they were apprehended carrying guns. Both also foolishly lied to the police. By September, they had been indicted for murder.

The state's case against them was never that strong. Key prosecution witnesses changed their stories, yet the Red Scare hovered over the courtroom. According to historian Paul Avrich, the district attorney, Frederick G. Katzman, "conducted a highly unscrupulous prosecution, coaching and badgering witnesses, withholding exculpatory evidence from the defence, and perhaps even tampering with physical evidence." He played on the jury's fears of immigrants and anarchists. Judge Webster Thayer, too, was biased and did not try to hide his disdain for the accused, whom he was heard referring to as "sons of bitches" and "dagos." Sacco and Vanzetti's own lawyer, Frank Moore, was brought in from outside the state and did not perform well. The verdict was never in doubt.

On July 14, 1921, the two men were found guilty. They immediately appealed, and for the next five years various courts considered their fate. New evidence revealed that the Morelli gang of Providence, who were known to be operating in the region, might have committed the robbery and murder.[*]

Almost immediately, the case became the most celebrated of the day. There were demonstrations in Europe and South America, and back in the U.S. lawyers and intellectuals like Felix Frankfurter took up the cause, arguing that Sacco and Vanzetti were victims of a great miscarriage of justice. The two anarchists became symbols, says Richard Gid Powers, "of the wretched earth ground down by the wealthy concealed behind the law. . . . The case dramatized in the starkest terms the confrontation between the powerless and the powerful, the poor and the rich, [and] the obscure and the famous."

Massachusetts governor Alvin T. Fuller had no choice but to order an investigation. Assisting him was a distinguished team: A. Lawrence Lowell, the president of Harvard University; Samuel Stratton, the president of the Massachusetts Institute of Technology; and Robert Grant, a former justice of the Massachusetts Probate Court. The trio concluded that Judge Thayer was indeed guilty of a "grave breach of decorum," but that justice had been done. Fuller decided that the guilty verdict would stand. By this time, Sacco and Vanzetti had been given death sentences.

Amid great outcry, and in defiance of worldwide opinion, the two anarchists were executed by electrocution on August 23, 1927. Millions were convinced that they had been wrongfully convicted. Sacco's last words were "Long live Anarchy!" Vanzetti went to his

---

[*] According to Curt Gentry, "In 1973, the Mafia informant Vincent Teresa claimed in his book, *My Life in the Mafia*, that the South Braintree crimes had actually been committed by the Morelli gang and that one of its members, Butsey Morelli, had admitted this to him." Other writers and investigators have concluded that Sacco may have been involved; Vanzetti probably was not.

death maintaining his innocence. Fifty thousand marchers wearing red arm bands joined a funeral procession in their honour – a sure sign that class struggle would continue.[*]

---

[*] In 1977, on the fiftieth anniversary of the executions, Massachusetts governor Michael Dukakis stated, "I do hereby . . . declare . . . further that any stigma and disgrace should forever be removed from the names of Nicola Sacco and Bartolomeo Vanzetti, from the names of their families and descendants, and so from the name of the Commonwealth of Massachusetts; and I hereby call upon all people of Massachusetts to pause in their daily endeavors to reflect upon the tragic events, and draw from the historic lessons to prevent the forces of intolerance, fear, and hatred from ever again uniting to overcome the rationality, wisdom, and fairness to which our legal system aspires."

CHAPTER FIVE

Booze

Previous page: Enforcing the "Noble Experiment." Prohibition officers raid the lunchroom of 922 Pennsylvania Avenue, in Washington, D.C., in April 1923, four years after prohibition of alcohol was instituted in the United States.

I make my money by supplying a public demand. If I break the law, my customers, who number hundreds of the best people in Chicago, are as guilty as I am. The only difference between us is that I sell and they buy. Everybody calls me a racketeer. I call myself a businessman. When I sell liquor, it's bootlegging. When my patrons serve it on a silver tray on Lake Shore Drive, it's hospitality.

– Al Capone, c. 1928

The Reign of Tears Is Over

In the minds of many, there were only two kinds of people in the world. Either you were a "wet" and tolerated or even supported the drinking of spirits – liquor, beer, and wine – or you were a "dry" and regarded alcohol abuse as a threat to mankind. For the former, the issue was one of personal taste and individual choice; a progressive society allowed its members the right to choose whether or not to drink. For the latter, the only answer was total prohibition. To add a twist to this conflict, each side believed it was championing progress and modernity. History has remembered the teetotallers as the traditionalists, yet this story was not so black and white. On the eve of Prohibition in Manitoba, one journalist wrote, "Undoubtedly the historian of the future will describe the body blow to the drink traffic . . . as a social revolution. It is nothing less. For it is a far-reaching change in our habits as a people – one might almost say as a race. It is a drastic break with the past in popular behaviour. It is a drastic revision of our social economy . . . it is an inevitable revolution."

In the United States, only slavery divided Americans more than liquor. In Canada, it was just as contentious. The dry side appeared victorious in Canada in 1916, when for about six years most provinces had adopted some form of Prohibition. And then, more significantly, in 1919, when the Eighteenth Amendment to the U.S. Constitution instituted Prohibition, along with the Volstead Act that regulated and enforced it.

The amendment would abolish "half the misery of half the people," wrote newspaper magnate William Randolph Hearst in a signed editorial. Liquor, he added, "had destroyed more [people] each year than the World War had destroyed. . . . [T]he suppression of the drink traffic is an expression of the higher morality upon which we are now entering." More moderate reformers such as New York City missionary Charles Stelzle, who maintained, "poverty causes alcoholism as much as alcoholism causes poverty," were ignored. Stelzle repeatedly argued that workers who were well paid did not spend all of their leisure hours in saloons drinking away their wages. "The answer," he suggested, "is to shorten working hours and pay employees a living wage."

Stelzle's voice and others like it were lost in the din of jubilation. Prohibition would be a panacea. Dry advocates from Oregon to Florida believed Americans would change their ways overnight; that money normally spent on whisky and beer would now be used for food, life insurance, and education. "The reign of tears is over," declared the outspoken revivalist preacher Reverend Billy Sunday. "The slums will soon be memory. We will turn our prisons into factories and our jails into storehouses and corncribs. Men will walk upright now, women will smile and children will laugh. Hell will be forever for rent."

He was wrong on all counts. Prohibition did not work. At best, it was a "partial failure" (in the words of historian Norman Clark). It did not cure poverty, halt crime, or change the drinking habits of North Americans.

On the contrary, until its repeal in the United States in 1933, Prohibition presented Al Capone, Meyer Lansky, and Charles "Lucky" Luciano, among other notorious mobsters, with the opportunity to make millions. It led to violent clashes – according to one estimate, Chicago, where Capone was king, was the scene of 530 gangland murders during the twenties – contributed to police and political corruption, and encouraged thousands, if not millions, of Americans to break the law. As the great vaudeville and film star Groucho Marx so aptly put it, "I was a teetotal until Prohibition."

The disrespect for the law went right to the top. During his term in office, from 1920 to 1923, President Warren Harding and the members of his Cabinet always had easy access to liquor. Similarly, historian Charles Merz – who in 1931 wrote one of the first books about Prohibition's many problems – noted that to fill the 3,060 agent positions at the Bureau of Prohibition required ten thousand men between 1920 and 1926 – since one in twelve was dismissed for corruption.

For the dry side, Prohibition was the culmination of decades of campaigning and struggling against what often seemed overwhelming forces. Indeed, there does not appear to be a moment in North American history when concerns over alcohol were not raised. Thomas Jefferson, who enjoyed a glass of wine with his dinner, "came to see alcohol not as a blessing but as a curse, and [regarded] liquor as a national disease." By 1873, there were about one hundred thousand saloons in the United States, or about one for every four hundred Americans. That number had risen to three hundred thousand, or one for every 250 Americans, by the turn of the century. The annual per-capita consumption of brewery beer had been 2.7 gallons in 1850; thirty years later it had increased to 17.9 gallons – a natural development with the arrival of thousands of European immigrants who often preferred beer to other beverages.[*]

North American saloons were nasty places. Usually located near the railway or the "bad" part of town and often adjacent to a hotel, they were rowdy and not for the faint of heart. In 1914 in Winnipeg, for instance, when the population of the city was about 136,000, there were ninety-six hotels each with a saloon, within walking distance from the Canadian Pacific Railway station. David Murray, who had served as the city's police chief before the turn of the century, had declared that, "many hotels are resorts for thieves and blackguards and are hotbeds for drunkenness. They would be better described as cesspools operating under the guise of hotels." He was not far wrong.

Saloons probably were the hellish dens of iniquity that their opponents said they were. After all, the main point of visiting a bar was to socialize and to get drunk. As Albert Kennedy, a settlement worker in New York, discovered after he conducted a national survey of slum areas between 1908 and 1920, saloons were everywhere: "There were in many neighbourhoods," he stated, "a heavy proportion of men and a great many women, who from one year's end to the other, were never for a single hour completely sober."

Bar floors were covered in sawdust to soak up the spills. There was a stench of stale liquor and tobacco juice that rarely vanished. Bartenders offered their generally male-only customers free lunches of salted pretzels, pickles, sausages, oysters, and dried herring to ensure that they would keep on drinking. There was usually a pool table, gambling in the backroom, and if the saloonkeeper did not operate a brothel inside his establishment, he probably knew where his clientele could seek the services of prostitutes.

Most saloons were open twenty-four hours, seven days a week, until many jurisdictions passed Sunday laws. In the 1890s, when five dollars a week was a decent wage for a working man, a

---

* In about 1860, a creative New Jersey businessman by the name of Edmund C. Booze sold whisky in bottles shaped like small log cabins. The "booze" bottle became very popular and the term was soon used for all liquor.

twenty-six-ounce bottle of whisky cost about three dollars in a bar, but only one dollar in a liquor store. And yet saloons were likely the only place where a working man could relax, enjoy himself, gossip, find out the latest news, and, most importantly, cash his paycheque after the banks had closed in the early afternoon. Later it was charged that the atmosphere in saloons encouraged not only excessive drunkenness – the most frequent crime by far in most North American cities – but also the promotion of subversive ideas. "The names of Karl Marx and leaders of social and political thought," it was said, "are often heard [in saloons]."

The hotelmen and brewery owners, who operated the saloons, were well aware of the negative image of their businesses, yet for the most part they ignored the depravity as well as the moralists who complained about it. It was, in hindsight, a foolish error in judgment. "There was never a moment in the history of these years (1890s–1914)," noted Charles Merz, "when the brewers could not have reformed the [saloons] which was the chief point of attack in the campaign against their vested interests made by the Prohibition movement."

Reformers targeted the saloons early. Lyman Beecher of New England organized the American Society for the Promotion of Temperance in 1826. Further north, in British North America, preachers delivered sermons about the evils of "demon rum." There were soon approximately a hundred temperance societies with more than ten thousand members gathering weekly across the continent to pray for the sins of their fellow men and promote the virtues of a life of "industry, sobriety and thrift."

U.S. temperance advocates took a step forward in 1869 with the National Prohibition Party. While the party never achieved much success at the polls, it did push for a number of social reforms (including votes for women) and began campaigning for a Prohibition amendment to the Constitution.

In Canada, Parliament passed the Scott Act (1878), which permitted any city or municipality to vote itself dry – the so-called local option. Within ten years, sixty-two communities, mainly in eastern Canada, had opted to ban liquor. Yet enforcement was nearly impossible, a recurring theme in the history of Prohibition, and by the early 1890s more than half had surrendered to the wets. A federal referendum on national Prohibition followed in 1898. With a majority in every province except Quebec, the drys claimed victory. Prime Minister Wilfrid Laurier, ever conscious of his support in Quebec, was not convinced and pointed out that only 23 per cent of eligible male voters had bothered to cast a ballot. Prohibition legislation remained on the shelf for the time being.

Temperance was never entirely a rural backlash against the evils of the city. In the early years, it did have this component, but it was the movement's urban middle-class leadership – teachers, journalists, businessmen, and women – that succeeded in pushing through Prohibition in both Canada and the United States. As historian John Rumbarger has shown, the U.S. business elite, in particular, felt it was in their best interests, and the interests of the country, that workers went to church rather than the saloon. A healthy America was a dry America. D.C. Beamon of the Colorado Fuel and Iron Company, for example, told the U.S. Industrial Commission investigating the liquor issue in 1900, that his company paid its employees monthly, and paid them in scrip, to halt the negative influence of the saloon. "It is within the knowledge of all," he stated, "and cannot be denied that 'payday' at coal mines and in some other occupations means 1, 2, or 3 days of idleness and often . . . many days of dissipation. . . . If the state legislatures would prohibit sales [of intoxicants] at or near the mines, it would do more to promote the general welfare of the mines than any other law that could be enacted."

Women who witnessed first-hand the physical and psychological abuse that alcohol engendered were among the earliest advocates of Prohibition. Frequently they dedicated themselves to the cause with a conviction bordering on religious fervour. Only their battle for the right to vote was more intense. The Woman's Christian Temperance Union (WCTU) was established in Ohio in 1874. For two decades, until 1899, Frances Willard, an educator and the former dean of Evanston College for Ladies in Illinois, was the leading figure in the organization. With her wavy hair tied back in a tight bun and her wire-rimmed glasses, along with the mandatory white ribbon fastened to her blouse, Willard was the quintessential WCTU member. She epitomized the organization's slogan, "For God, Home and Native Land." Men, who were not permitted to join, liked to joke that WCTU really stood for "Women Constantly Torment Us."[*]

The WCTU was structured like a church. Its meetings began and ended with prayers and hymns. "I hereby promise," the women pledged, "God helping us, to abstain from all distilled, fermented and malt liquors, including beer, wine and cider, as a beverage, and to employ all proper means to discourage the use of and traffic in the same." Willard brought her message north to Canada on a visit in 1886, inspiring women like Nellie McClung, who regarded the WCTU then and later as "the most progressive organization of the time."

McClung and her WCTU sisters found staunch allies in the preachers and reformers of the Methodist Church, advocates of the social gospel. As one leading Methodist spokesman in Ontario declared in 1913, "The only proper attitude of Christians towards

---

[*] One of the more radical members of the WCTU was Carry Nation. A large woman, Nation made a name for herself in the early 1900s by attacking illegal saloons in "dry" Kansas with a hatchet. As Norman Clark related, "she found an anti-saloon, abolitionist following, and the more she chopped and smashed, the more she was praised and cheered by her followers. She did go to jail, but never for long, for city officials found it awkward to prosecute her if they had to admit the existence of illegal saloons. Ministers and businessmen paid her fines. Crowds followed her from town to town. Encouraged by the Prohibition press, she soon saw herself not only as a protestor but as a divinely ordained liberator." In truth, Nation had a miserable life. Her marriage to an alcoholic ended in divorce, her daughter was born "enfeebled," and she herself suffered from anxiety. She died in 1911 at the age of sixty-five.

the unholy traffic [of liquor] is one of relentless hostility, and all members of the Methodist church who possess the elective franchise are urged to use their influence to assure the nomination of municipal and parliamentary candidates known to favour and support Prohibition and to use their votes as a solemn trust to elect such candidates." Such well-known "social gospellers" like J.S. Woodsworth also worked with immigrants, assimilating them to "Canadian" values and ideals, and promoting temperance – all with the good intention, as noted, of establishing the "Kingdom of God on Earth." "No one, of course, knew exactly what the Kingdom of God would be like," writes historian Michael Marrus. "But one thing was certain for all of those who championed it with so much activism and devotion: in the Kingdom of God there would be no alcohol."

Less evangelical, but more influential were the members of the Anti-Saloon League (ASL), a non-partisan group of bankers, businessmen, and merchants who saw in alcohol abuse and public drinking the death of America. One of its more prominent supporters was John D. Rockefeller, Sr., who aimed to stop excessive drinking among his employees and rid his Colorado mining camps of saloons. The distilleries and breweries may have had a lot of money to protect their interests, but the ASL was well funded too. Its members were willing to spend thousands of dollars waging a war against liquor.

From 1896 to 1908, the ASL was instrumental in shutting down saloons in Ohio, Oklahoma, Georgia, and in Washington, D.C. Wayne Wheeler, a lawyer and powerful lobbyist, who was employed by the ASL from 1893 until his death in 1926 – and who was a virulent opponent of the liquor interests, the result of a boyhood accident when he was attacked by drunken neighbour wielding a pitchfork – conceded a few months before he passed away that the League had spent upwards of thirty million dollars on its anti-drinking campaign during the preceding thirty years.

The ASL sponsored sermons and debates where they featured the popular and flamboyant revivalist preacher Billy Sunday. In one of his more celebrated talks, appropriately entitled "Booze," Sunday could whip up even the most skeptical of adherents. "After all is said that can be said upon liquor traffic, its influence is degrading upon the individual, the family, politics and business, and upon everything you touch in this old world," Sunday declared. "The saloon is the sum of all villainies. It is worse than war or pestilence. It is the crime of crimes. It is the parent of crimes and the mother of sins. It is the appalling source of misery and crime in the land. And to license such an incarnate fiend of hell is the dirtiest low-down, damnable business on top of this old earth."

One of the few people willing to take Sunday on was the renowned lawyer Clarence Darrow, who had made a name fighting for the rights of labour before becoming the country's most famous criminal attorney. He regarded the campaign for Prohibition "a fanaticism and intolerance that would hesitate at nothing to force its wishes and way of life upon the world." He linked the battle against liquor with Puritanism and the Salem witch trials.

In June 1909, both Sunday and Darrow were in the lumber town of Everett, Washington, where the citizens were fighting a tenacious battle over liquor. Brought there to support the wets in a local election, Darrow delivered one of his more famous speeches, "Prohibition, a Crime against Society," in which he advocated for the rights of the individual against the tyranny of the majority. The family-oriented people of Everett, however, were not listening to Darrow's appeal, and in the ensuing election (women could not yet vote) the drys won a slim victory.

State-by-state successes and local option referendums were satisfactory, but the ASL set its sights higher. In 1913, on its twentieth anniversary, its executive announced the group's intentions to fight for a constitutional amendment on Prohibition.

The Only Wealthy People Today Are Bootleggers

The catalyst for dramatic change was, once again, the First World War. Victory in Europe meant sacrifice at home, and almost immediately social reformers like Nellie McClung drew the connection between liquor and patriotism. "When we find ourselves wondering at the German people for having tolerated the military system for so long, paying taxes for its maintenance and giving their sons to it," McClung wrote in a collection of essays entitled *In Times Like These* (1915), "we suddenly remember that we have paid taxes and given our children, too, to keep up the liquor traffic, which has less reasons for its existence than the military system of Germany."

How could Canadians continue to spend money on booze or use precious grain for liquor, she and other temperance advocates asked, when soldiers required so much help on the battlefields? (That soldiers were given a shot of whisky before being ordered to go "over the top" was overlooked.) "The dealings of the liquor trade were the dealings of unpatriotic acts of the men behind the trade," added the General Superintendent of the Methodist Church in a speech delivered in Regina. "The liquor traffic was killing off men by the thousands when the country demanded the best of its sons and when every living person was an asset." Prohibitionists implored Canadians to "use ballots for bullets and shoot straight and strong in order that the demon of drink might be driven from the haunts of men."

A few years later, after the United States entered the war, the ASL publicly attacked the beer industry – Pabst, Schlitz, and Anheuser-Busch, among others with European roots – as being "pro-German and treasonable." The charges were groundless, but wartime hysteria deemed anything that could be associated with Germany dangerous and un-American. There was even a campaign to change the name of sauerkraut to "liberty cabbage."

Prohibition, or rather a form of it, came first to Canada. Saskatchewan shut its bars in the summer of 1915. Manitoba,

Ontario, Alberta, and British Columbia followed. By mid-1917, the only province that had not closed its saloons was Quebec. The bartender's union had brought Clarence Darrow to Winnipeg to denounce the proposal. At a meeting on March 12, 1916, he condemned Prohibition as an infringement of personal freedom, arguing that poverty, not liquor, was to blame for the rising crime rate. But it was to no avail. In Manitoba's referendum, the drys outvoted the wets by almost two to one. Had women been allowed to vote (suffrage for the province's women was a few months away), the dry vote would have been twice as strong.

The real problem with Canadian Prohibition was that the federal government was reluctant to impose it on a national basis. The provinces could do nothing to halt the interprovincial trade in liquor and beer until the spring of 1918, when Ottawa finally plugged this loophole by forbidding the manufacture, transportation, and sale of liquor in provinces that had imposed Prohibition. Exceptions existed, however, for the use of liquor for medicinal and religious purposes. To add further confusion, the federal government in its wisdom declared that these regulations would remain in effect for one year after the war had ended. At that time, in November 1919, the government passed the Canada Temperance Act with the same regulations but with the stipulation that another referendum had to take place before it could come into effect. They then set the referendum for October 25, 1920, effectively making any provincial Prohibition law unenforceable until the matter was decided.

For entrepreneurs, the loopholes were a golden opportunity. There was money to be made, and lots of it. Demand for liquor did not vanish with Prohibition. Physicians and pharmacists quickly found themselves besieged by patients and customers requiring whisky to cure coughs and other ailments. According to writer James Gray, one Manitoba pharmacy filled 180 alcohol prescriptions an hour. Doctors, who charged two dollars for each prescription, could not write them fast enough. To acquire a bottle of "medicinal" whisky in Ontario, observed humorist Stephen Leacock, a person had only "to go to a drugstore . . . and lean up against the counter and make a gurgling sound like apoplexy. One often sees these apoplexy cases lined up four deep." Pharmacists required a steady stock of liquor to meet the new demand, and that was how the legendary whisky tycoon Sam Bronfman and his brothers became a part of the Prohibition saga.

The Bronfman family arrived on the Canadian prairies from Bessarabia, Russia, near the end of the 1880s. They spent a few years in a Jewish agricultural colony in Saskatchewan before settling in Brandon, Manitoba, where Sam was born in either 1889 or 1891 (his birthday is a matter of some debate, and he may have been an infant when the family emigrated). By 1906, the Bronfmans had relocated to Winnipeg, where they resided in a house in the city's North End immigrant quarter. Sam was the third son in a family that grew to eight children, but it was Sam and his three brothers, Abe, Harry, and Allan, the youngest, who laid the foundations for one of the world's great whisky empires. Fittingly, in Yiddish, "Bronfman" means "whisky man."

With guidance from their father, Ekiel, the Bronfman boys gradually moved into the hotel business, which also brought them into the liquor trade. Their first establishment was in the border town of Emerson, Manitoba, in 1903. Hotels in Yorkton, Saskatchewan, which Harry ran, were then added to the business. In 1912, when Sam was only about twenty-three years old, the family purchased the Bell Hotel for him on Winnipeg's Main Street, not far from the CPR station. It was soon doing a booming trade. Sam later claimed that in those years his personal annual income was a phenomenal thirty thousand dollars.[*]

---

[*] Naturally enough, there are a great many stories about Sam Bronfman. One from these early days was that the Bell Hotel, as well as the ones in Yorkton, were also

Once Prohibition was passed in Manitoba, Sam tried running the Bell Hotel's bar as a "temperance hotel," serving legal low-alcohol beer, but could not make enough money to cover his expenses. The brothers quickly realized that the legal interprovincial trade was a prospect they could not ignore. Sam visited Montreal and acquired sufficient liquor stock from the big distillers located there. Then the Bronfmans followed the lead of the country's largest liquor company in 1917, the Hudson's Bay Company, and went into the mail-order catalogue business. They set up a warehouse in Montreal and established outlets in Saskatchewan and Ontario to look after the neighbouring provinces. The bush town of Kenora, Ontario, seventy-five miles east of Winnipeg, was almost overnight transformed into a booming outlet for whisky and beer for thirsty Manitobans.

The Bronfmans could not keep up with demand. Certified bank cheques flowed in and the liquor flowed out. Sam, in particular, had an eye for detail, and he ensured that his customers always received their liquor properly packaged in an unbroken bottle. Until the federal government closed down the trade in 1918, it was a tremendous success. Sam later estimated that the whole enterprise required an investment of one hundred thousand dollars and that within two years profits exceeded half a million dollars.

There were now other avenues to explore. To meet the ever-increasing demand of the pharmacies, which were still able to fill prescriptions for medicinal liquor, Harry and Sam set up the Canada Pure Drug Company in 1918. By this time, the Bronfmans had started experimenting with distilling their own whisky. According to testimony at the 1927 Royal Commission on Customs and Excise, the Bronfmans's drug company imported from the United States (which

_____

used as brothels. Sam, who died in 1971, and who never missed an opportunity to make a witty quip, pointed out when confronted with this story: "If they were, they were the best in the West."

still allowed liquor to be exported) approximately three hundred thousand gallons of alcohol, sufficient to produce eight hundred thousand gallons of homemade whisky that was "blended, bottled and fed into a Canada-wide sales operation."[*] In late 1919, when the federal government permitted interprovincial trade in liquor to continue for another year, the Bronfmans's mail-order business was reactivated. It was events in the United States, however, that truly enabled the family to transform its business interests.

With the war over, many Canadians (as opposed to Americans) lost much of their patriotic fervour for Prohibition. The law and its many loopholes was an easy target to lampoon. During a 1922 debate in the Alberta Legislative Assembly on proposed new liquor legislation, MLA Bob Edward, a journalist, satirist, and all-around raconteur, proposed that the sale of beer be legalized not in order to kill Prohibition but to make it work. "The only wealthy people today are bootleggers," he stated. "They drive around in a big 'whiskey six' and are rolling in money. Whiskey is not hard to get hold of because good beer is hard to get hold of. No sane man would drink bad whiskey if he could get good beer, and if the government would allow this, the liquor laws would be obeyed."

Likewise, Stephen Leacock, a supporter of the Liberty League, which supported a more moderate approach to alcohol, declared at a Toronto rally in 1919 that "a fanatical minority has captured the ear of the public and the power of the [Ontario] Legislature. They

---

[*] Harry Bronfman's first attempt to blend his own whisky in 1920 was a famous disaster. After mixing the various ingredients – 382 gallons of water, 318 gallons of 65-overproof raw alcohol, 100 gallons of aged rye whisky, a dash of caramel, and a shot of sulphuric acid – into new one-thousand gallon oak vats, he waited two days and then was shocked to discover that his mixture had turned a dirty blue rather than an appetizing amber. The dismayed Bronfmans refused to pay the $3,200 they owed a Winnipeg company for a vat and bottling supplies, which in turn led to a court case when the company decided to sue. The company won, and it was determined that the discolouration was likely caused by Harry's use of sulphuric acid. His blending talents improved after that.

have contrived to throw around them a false mantle of religion and morality. . . . Prohibition declares it to be a crime to drink beer. The common sense of every honest man tells him that it is not a crime to drink a glass of beer. . . . The attempt to make the consumption of beer criminal is silly and as futile as if you passed a law to send a man to jail for eating cucumber salad."

In truth, and despite the flaws, Prohibition did have a positive effect. Prohibition might be "quite hard on a few men," Nellie McClung retorted to her critics in 1922, "but the women and children are not saying a word about it." Public drunkenness stopped being a major preoccupation of law enforcement. More than 1,700 people were arrested for being drunk in the streets in Calgary in 1914 and a mere 183 three years later. Across Canada, crime rates dropped and provincial jails were closed. In private, though, Canadians continued to make homebrew and skirt the rules of the legislation as much as possible. The solution arrived at in the early twenties did not satisfy the dry side: provincial government sale of liquor and a campaign for moderation. But Canadians had more or less decided that drinking alcohol was indeed part of modern life as long as it was done with some self-control. But to the south, a different and more drastic approach was taken.

The Noble Experiment

Prohibition was not foisted upon an unsuspecting American public. By 1917, twenty-six of forty-eight states had some form of Prohibition in place. Yet it was also true that most of these states were west of the Mississippi and did not include large metropolitan cities. Michigan, for instance, was dry, but in the referendum the wets won handily in Detroit. As Charles Merz noted in 1931, "For every nineteen people who wanted Prohibition, fourteen opposed it. The total vote is very small: so small that all of the state Prohibition laws, which were enacted in this country prior to the war, were enacted by the affirmative votes of less than 4 per cent of the adult population of the country."

None of this stopped politicians in Washington from forging ahead. Dedicated and passionate advocates such as Wayne Wheeler of the ASL lobbied behind the scenes for Prohibition, and the drys won the day in a tense atmosphere given a new sense of urgency by the First World War. The liquor interests did not have a chance. Congress ratified the Eighteenth Amendment to the U.S. Constitution on January 16, 1918. The "manufacture, sale or transportation of intoxicating liquors" was prohibited. People could drink in their own homes, and doctors could prescribe medicinal liquor as in Canada, but all saloons, nightclubs, and hotel bars were to shut down. The states were given seven years to ratify the amendment, but few took more than a couple of months to get the job done.

Within a year, forty-five states – more than the required three-quarters of the states necessary under the Constitution – had voted in support of the amendment (in the end, only Connecticut and Rhode Island did not ratify it). In May 1919, Congress passed the Volstead Act, named after one of its authors, Republican congressman Andrew Volstead of Minnesota (although Wayne Wheeler had actually drafted the bill), to enforce the amendment. In one of his last gasp efforts, President Woodrow Wilson, then suffering from a debilitating stroke, and no fan of the temperance movement, vetoed the Volstead Act at the end of October. Congress immediately overrode his veto with a two-thirds vote in both the House of Representatives and the Senate. Prohibition was slated to take effect in the United States on January 16, 1920.

Drys everywhere proclaimed a victory, and not just against the evil forces of liquor. "Let the church bells ring and let there be great rejoicing," announced the WCTU at a gathering at Hampstead, Long Island, "for an enemy the equal of Prussianism in frightfulness has been overthrown and victory crowns the efforts of the forces of righteousness. Let us see that no Bolshevistic liquor interests shall tear the Eighteenth Amendment from the Constitution of the United States." The *New York Herald* was more concise. "Tonight John Barleycorn makes his last will and testament," the newspaper noted on January 15, 1920. "Now for an era of clear thinking and clean living!" Later, Herbert Hoover, president from 1929 to 1933, in a letter to fellow Republican senator William Borah, characterized Prohibition as "a great social and economic experiment, noble in motive and far-reaching in purpose."

Hoover may have been correct. Yet by the time he wrote his letter to Borah in 1928, the "noble experiment" had proved to be a major debacle. It is likely, as historian Norman Clark has argued, that most Americans, certainly ones who resided outside of the large cities, more or less obeyed the law and did not personally have any dealings with bootleggers.[*] But enforcing Prohibition with the limited and meagre resources allocated to the Prohibition Bureau, the agency of the Bureau of Internal Revenue given the task of keeping the United States free of booze, was impossible. The same congressmen and senators who voted in favour of the Eighteenth Amendment refused to fund its enforcement. Federal appropriations did increase, from $7.1 million in 1921 to $13.3 million by 1927, yet more than ten times that amount was needed for proper border control, coast-guard patrols, and a sufficient army of Prohibition agents. The state governments' contributions were worse, even laughable. By 1926, the forty-eight state legislatures had earmarked a mere $698,855 for Prohibition enforcement, far less than the total amount these governments had allocated to monitor their fishing and hunting regulations.

---

[*] As James Gray explains, "the word 'bootlegging' goes back to the days of smuggling when thigh-length boots were the fashion, and contraband could be hidden in the boot folds. The word was adapted to the illicit liquor trade in the United States as early as the 1830s. Bootleggers were therefore sellers of booze by the drink, or at most by the bottle, rather than the boatload."

In New York, Chicago, Detroit, and other big cities, millions of Americans simply went ahead and broke the law. In his 1926 report to Congress, General Lincoln Andrews, head of the Prohibition Bureau, stated that in the preceding six years, his agents had seized seven hundred thousand stills and estimated that approximately a half-million Americans were connected in some fashion to the production of illegal alcohol. Overnight, private clubs, and speakeasies (also called "blind pigs"), where more well-to-do patrons could quench their thirst, opened up to meet a growing consumer demand. The *Chicago Tribune* estimated that by the end of 1921, nearly two years after Prohibition began, there were four thousand saloons doing business in Chicago alone.

In New York City the drinking never truly stopped for a moment. Reporters from the *New York Telegram* were assigned the task of finding liquor in Manhattan. It was the easiest job they had ever been given. They found it in "dancing academies, drugstores, delicatessens, cigar stores, confectionaries, soda fountains, behind partitions of shoeshine parlors, backrooms of barbershops, from hotel bellhops . . . in paint stores, malt shops . . . boarding houses, Republican clubs, Democratic clubs, laundries, social clubs, newspapermen's associations."[*] The fashionable speakeasies were located in the six blocks between 52nd to 58th streets near Fifth Avenue. Sherman Billingsley's Stork Club was popular, as was the debonair Belle Livingstone's five-storey Country Club on East 58th Street, which had an admission of five dollars. Belle, who met her guests in "Chinese red lounging pyjamas," offered her elite clientele the best in entertainment, food and drink. Under Prohibition, prices naturally rose, so that the same bottle of Scotch whisky that used to cost a few dollars could now run as high as sixteen dollars for a quart.

---

[*] Liquor was abundant, too, in Washington, D.C., and even on Capitol Hill – including in a room in the Capitol Building called the "Library," which was down the corridor from the offices where the Volstead Act had been written. The book-lined room hid the stocks of whisky readily available to congressmen and senators.

Champagne was even pricier, at anywhere from twenty-five to forty dollars a bottle.

Less well off Americans had to settle for homemade rotgut, which sometimes contained deadly doses of methanol or wood alcohol used for industrial purposes. In 1928, in New York City's Bowery area, seven hundred people died from alcohol poisoning. Thousands more died nationwide or, if they survived from drinking the poison, suffered all sorts of debilitating effects, including blindness and "jake foot" which prevented them from walking. As humorist Will Rogers, who was no fan of Prohibition, caustically remarked, "Governments used to murder by the bullet only. Now it's by the quart." ASL executive Wayne Wheeler was far less sympathetic. "People who drink bootleg beverages after the government has warned them of the danger," he said, "are in the same category as the man who goes into a drugstore, buys a bottle of carbolic acid with a label on it marked 'Poison,' and drinks the contents."

The police, for the most part, looked the other way. Most of them drank themselves or were involved in getting around the regulations. "In order to enforce Prohibition," stated Congressman (and later mayor of New York City) Fiorello La Guardia, a confirmed wet, "it will require a police force of 250,000 men and a force of 250,000 men to police the police." In 1926, Chicago mayor William E. Dever conceded that as many as 60 per cent of his police officers were somehow linked to the illegal traffic in and consumption of liquor, and there was little he could do about it. Governor Al Smith of New York, an outspoken critic of Prohibition, passed a bill in 1923 relieving local police from the onerous responsibility of enforcing the Volstead Act. That left the job in New York State to about two hundred federal Prohibition agents. For a time, the entire U.S.–Canadian border was the responsibility of a mere one hundred men. Every one of them – earning a modest $1,980 a year – could potentially be bribed to look the other way.

Several of the federal agents, however, were successful, perhaps none more than Isidor Einstein and Moe Smith. During a five-year period, from 1920 to 1925, Izzy and Moe, as the duo was famously known, arrested close to five thousand people for breaking Prohibition laws and impounded more than five million bottles of booze worth approximately fifteen million dollars. Before Prohibition, Einstein, forty years old and the livelier of the two, had worked as a postal clerk. Seeking better wages, he signed on to become a Prohibition agent. His friend Moe Smith operated a cigar store in the Lower East Side. Einstein talked him into being his partner. They were most famous for their daring actions and assortment of disguises – Izzy was a man of a hundred accents. They dressed as women, waiters, and Bowery bums to foil their prey. On one bust, they used blackface to fool a restaurant in Harlem into serving them liquor. As they travelled across the United States, stories of their exploits grew. Einstein would keep track of how long it took to find a drink after they arrived in a new city. It took eleven minutes in Pittsburgh, seventeen in Atlanta, twenty-nine in St. Louis, and only thirty-five seconds in New Orleans, where the cab driver who picked them up at the railway station offered them a swig in his taxi.[*] Ego, however, cost Izzy and Moe their jobs. Their superiors in the Bureau resented the attention the two agents received in the press and foolishly relieved them of their jobs.

Speakeasies and private saloons were only a minor part of the lawlessness produced by Prohibition. The more serious and enduring crisis was its obvious appeal to organized crime. Millions

---

[*] Detroit was the "scene of Izzy's proudest ploy," relates writer John Kobler. "In a Woodward Avenue dive the bartender refused to serve him because, he apologized, pointing to a picture of Izzy himself draped in black crepe, 'Izzy Epstein's in town.' Izzy corrected him. 'You mean Einstein, don't you?' The bartender insisted it was 'Epstein.' 'I'll bet you,' Izzy ventured. 'What'll you bet?' said the bartender. Izzy suggested the price of a drink. The bartender poured him a shot. After emptying it into his funnel [that led to a flask in his coat pocket in which he collected evidence], Izzy arrested him."

of dollars were at stake, and an army of bootleggers, thugs, and gangsters was ready and willing to take advantage of this unprecedented opportunity.

We Can Make a Fortune

At his core, Arnold Rothstein was a gambler. Born in New York City in 1882 to a middle-class Jewish family, he started his career in gambling as a teenager. By the time he was twenty, and unhappy with the paltry wages he made selling cigars, he had started his own bookmaking operation, taking bets on horse races, baseball games, and boxing matches. Among other nicknames – including "A.R." "Mr. Big," and "The Fixer" – he was known as "The Big Bankroll," since he usually carried in his pocket a wad of one-hundred-dollar bills. He once bet upwards of $240,000 on a horse race and $100,000 on a roll of the dice. He won both times. According to legend, Rothstein – though he later denied it before a government inquiry – was responsible for fixing the 1919 World Series by paying off the members of the Chicago White Sox and made for himself more than $250,000 by wagering on their opponents, the Cincinnati Reds.[*] In

---

[*] According to Eliot Asinof, the author of *Eight Men Out*, the most thorough account of the scandal, several of the discontented Chicago players, led by Chick Gandil, hatched the idea of fixing the series. In part, it was a reaction to the tight-fisted policies of the team's owner, Charles Comiskey. The players – including the immortal "Shoeless" Joe Jackson, who had been coerced into the scheme – initially demanded eighty thousand dollars and then raised the ante to one hundred thousand dollars. The local gamblers they approached did not have this amount of money and contacted Rothstein. At first he was reluctant to become involved. But once he was convinced that the players were prepared to fix the series, he agreed to the terms. Much of the money intended for the players was never given to them, however, even though they threw the first few games of the series. Then, with the series nearly tied, Rothstein sent a thug named Harry Sullivan to intimidate the Sox's starting pitcher in the eighth game, Lefty Williams. In the end, the Cincinnati Reds won the eighth and took the series. Revelations a year later about the fix stunned the sports world. Several of the players were charged with defrauding the public but were acquitted. They were, nonetheless, never permitted to play professional baseball again.

The Great Gatsby (1925), F. Scott Fitzgerald modelled his character Meyer Wolfsheim after Rothstein, a natural choice. He was smooth and likeable and regarded himself as just another businessman – except that was not quite the truth.

Almost from the day Prohibition was implemented, Rothstein understood more than most of his underworld colleagues how much money there was to be made by supplying wealthy Americans with decent whisky. First, he needed some help and gathered around him his protegés, an assortment of the most colourful, ruthless, and conniving figures in the history of U.S. organized crime. Many were, like him, Jewish, the children of immigrants who wanted to get out of the slums of the Lower East Side any way they could.

Meyer Lansky (originally Maier Suchowljansky), again like Rothstein drifted into gambling as a youngster. Born in 1902 in Grodno, Poland, he arrived in the United States in 1911 and settled in the Lower East Side. Though scrawny as a youngster, he was tough and never backed down from a fight, particularly one with a member of the Irish gangs that picked on Jewish boys. Lansky dropped out of school and for a brief time worked as an apprentice toolmaker.

One day, when he was still in his teens, Lansky crossed paths with a Sicilian gang led by one Charlie Lucania (changed later to Luciano). Lansky was told he would have to pay Lucania "protection money." Lansky refused. "He stood there, this little punk," Luciano recalled later. "I was five years or so older than him and could have smashed him to pieces. But he just stood there staring me straight in the face, telling me to stick my protection up my ass. He was ready to fight. His fists were clenched." Impressed by Lansky's spunk, Luciano became his lifelong friend and partner. Lansky, in fact, gave Luciano his famous nickname "Lucky" after Luciano survived a brutal beating and knife attack at the hand of Mafia boss Salvatore Maranzano and his thugs during a gangster war in late 1929.

Lansky was also friends with the tall and handsome, but unpredictable, Benny Siegel, another of the Jewish mob from New York's

East Side. Siegel had a bad temper, which earned him the nickname "Bugsy," a moniker he did not appreciate. Siegel was fearless and did not hesitate to use a gun if necessary. FBI records linked him to at least thirty murders.[*] Other key members of the Lansky-Siegel gang included Arthur Flegenheimer, the son of Galician-Jewish immigrants, who grew up in the slums of the South Bronx and called himself "Dutch Schultz" after a well-known member of the old Frog Hollow Gang; and Abner "Longy" Zwillman, a lanky tough who was involved in gambling and the rackets in Newark, New Jersey.

They all looked up to Rothstein. "Prohibition is going to last a long time and then it'll be abandoned," he told them in early 1920. "But it's going to be with us for quite a while, that's for sure. I can see that more and more people are going to ignore the law, they're going to pay anything you ask to get their hands on good-quality liquor. . . . We can make a fortune meeting this need."

Before too long, Rothstein and his men had set up a highly profitable bootlegging operation. Rothstein personally arranged for distillers in Britain and Scotland to ship him their finest, and he added stock from his Canadian contacts. The Bronfmans did not directly deal with Rothstein, but their whisky ended up in his warehouses, nevertheless. The ships' cargo was unloaded either in Cuba or onto speedboats waiting outside of the American three-mile (later expanded to twelve) jurisdiction area on the east coast in an area between Boston and Atlantic City that soon became known as Rum Row. Canadian liquor was also smuggled in massive quantities across the Great Lakes – the prominence of Bronfman whisky led Lansky and others to refer to Lake Erie as the "Jewish Lake" – and indeed across the entire length of the U.S.–Canada border. The only way

---

[*] In the mid-1940s, as Siegel struggled to make the Flamingo Hotel in Las Vegas a success, he was murdered, possibly on the orders of his former friends Luciano and Lansky.

to stop the shipment of booze from Canada to the United States, it was suggested, was to have "an armed guard every hundred yards from Vancouver to Winnipeg, and fifty feet everywhere else."

Ethically, Canadian entrepreneurs like the Bronfmans, the executives of the Hudson's Bay Company, and Harry Hatch – who built a multi-million-dollar business with the acquisition of several major distilleries, including Hiram Walker – were, perhaps, on shaky ground. But legally, they were doing absolutely nothing wrong, despite the later and futile attempts by the Canadian Customs Department and the RCMP to indict the Bronfmans for a variety of alleged misdemeanours. In 1935, after the RCMP tried to prove that the Bronfmans were part of a vast conspiracy "to defraud the Canadian government of $5 million in customs duties on liquor that was smuggled back into Canada," the courts ruled that the Bronfmans, as well as the other distillers, were not responsible for what the buyers of their whisky did with the product once the sale had been completed. At the same time, notes Michael Marrus, Sam Bronfman's biographer, "the presence of so many Jews in the trade [was] a point hardly overlooked by those for whom the sale of whisky was a moral abomination and an assault upon Christian society."

The statistics alone tell an amazing story: Canadian whisky exports to the U.S. rose from 8,335 gallons, worth $11 million, in 1921 to 1,169,002 gallons, worth $19 million, in 1928. The value of all liquor cleared for the U.S. in 1928 exceeded $26 million, and that year, "approximately one-eighth of all Dominion and all Provincial revenue was derived from the trade in alcoholic beverages." There were in 1926 an estimated one hundred thousand Canadians whose sole task it was to send liquor into the United States. "Rum Running," the *Toronto Financial Post* stated tongue-in-cheek in 1921, "has provided a tidy bit towards Canada's favourable balance of trade."

On the states bordering the Great Lakes a navy of rum-runners, who pocketed about two hundred dollars a trip (at a time when a school principal was earning forty-eight dollars per week), ran their boats across the waters with ease. One particularly successful sailor was Ben Kerr. Dubbed by the press "King of the Rum-Runners," Kerr, who had several scrapes with the U.S. Coast Guard, wound up with fifty thousand dollars in the bank and a beautiful house in Hamilton, Ontario.

As the United States began to crack down on traffic on the Great Lakes and eastern seaboard, the operations moved out to the two small French islands off the coast of Newfoundland, St. Pierre and Miquelon, which overnight experienced an economic boom the likes of which the two fishing colonies have never again witnessed. The Bronfmans set up a large warehouse on St. Pierre using their subsidiary, the Atlas Shipping Company, which in turn entered into a partnership with a local enterprise, called the Northern Export Company. In a matter of months, Northern Export was the island's top seller and the Bronfmans made millions of dollars.

One of the more famous rum-runners who brought the Bronfmans' whisky out of St. Pierre (and operated in the Caribbean area as well) was Captain William McCoy.[*] Starting in 1921, McCoy was responsible for transporting hundreds of thousands of bottles of whisky. So legendary were his exploits that if bootleggers in the U.S. received one of his shipments, they knew "it was the real McCoy."

Meanwhile, on the Canadian prairies, the Bronfmans, among others, serviced their American customers from depots established at sleepy Saskatchewan border towns such as Gainsborough, Estevan, Oxbow, and Bienfait – otherwise known by the locals as "Beanfate," only ten miles from the U.S. border. American bootleggers, a rather tough lot employed by the likes of Rothstein and

---

* According to Michael Marrus, "The Bronfmans maintained a weekly insurance policy on the warehoused stocks at St. Pierre, with a coverage of between $1 million and $1.5 million during several years. To avoid snooping by competitors – not to mention the U.S. Coast Guard – correspondence was often in secret code. . . . Dozens of vessels came and went from the harbour of St. Pierre . . . [including] one vessel, possibly christened by a Bronfman company agent or associate, *Mazel Tov*."

Lansky, arrived in the towns usually driving trucks or Studebaker "whisky-sixes." These were Studebakers that had been refitted with six-cylinder engines and had the back seats taken out so that the liquid cargo could be stored more easily. The gangsters also mounted spotlights on their automobiles, which blinded anyone attempting to chase them in the dark, and long chains that caused dust storms as they drove. Some of the more inventive operators rebuilt their vehicles with false floorboards and gas tanks in which could be stored about twenty quarts of liquor.

Until the Saskatchewan government took action against the export houses in late 1922, the Bronfmans' "boozorium," as it was affectionately called, in Bienfait was bringing in a reported five hundred thousand dollars per month. Locals there still talk about the time Dutch Schultz came to town and stayed at the King Edward Hotel for a week. In 1922, Paul Matoff, Sam and Harry's rather flamboyant and fun-loving brother-in-law (the husband of their sister Jean), managed the Bronfmans' Bienfait operation. On the night of October 4, Matoff completed a cash deal of about six thousand dollars with Lee Dillege, a notorious North Dakota thug involved in prostitution, gambling, and sports promotion. With the money in his pocket, Matoff took a walk over to the town's railway station. As he sat there, someone, according to one witness, poked a twelve-gauge sawed-off shotgun through the station's bay window and fired, instantly killing him. The shooter entered the station, grabbed the six thousand dollars from Matoff along with his ring and diamond tie pin. The police eventually charged Dillege and Jimmy LaCoste, a local garage mechanic, but there was not enough evidence to convict them, and the murder, like so many others during the era, went unsolved.

Scarface

Once the European and Canadian liquor had arrived in the U.S., it was stored in secret warehouses and trucked to thousands of speakeasies and clubs from New York to Chicago. As Arnold Rothstein had predicted, the profits were enormous. A case of twelve bottles of Scotch whisky, for instance, cost the bootleggers twenty-five dollars. This included the price of bribing customs guards, hiring sailors, and paying for help with the loading and unloading of the shipment. But on that one case, with the normal Prohibition markup, Lansky and Luciano could make one thousand dollars, and often much more. They also started supplying physicians and pharmacists and could not keep up with demand. In time, and contrary to Rothstein's initial plan, the gangsters began watering down the whisky, thus turning one bottle of premium Scotch into three or four and making even more money.

The real trouble began when other mobsters attempted to enter the business. Liquor shipments were hijacked, trust betrayed, war was declared, and much blood shed – nowhere more than in Chicago. With links to the Rothstein-Lansky network, Al Capone established one of the most infamous and feared underworld organizations in U.S. history.[*]

Born Alphonse Capone (not Caponi as was commonly believed) in 1899 to Italian immigrants, the famous gangster grew up in Brooklyn in an apartment close by the gambling halls, saloons, and brothels located down by the docks area. Young Al quickly became street savvy. He dropped out of school at age fourteen (after defending himself against a teacher who had hit him), spent much of his time at the neighbourhood pool hall hustling other players, and eventually became associated with Johnny Torrio, the reigning local Italian gang leader. It was under Torrio's tutelage that Capone learned how to be a top-notch racketeer – the ins and outs of gambling, fixing a prizefight, and dealing with prostitutes. A liaison

---

[*] In 1928, Arnold Rothstein was shot in a dispute with a fellow gambler at the Park Central Hotel in New York. He survived for one day, but refused to reveal his assailant's identity before he died.

with a prostitute, in fact, had a profound impact on Capone's life.

Some time between 1914 and 1918, Capone contracted syphilis. In many cases, syphilis was fatal, or it could affect the brain with a form of dementia over a long period of time (today, it is easily treated with penicillin). That was what happened to Capone, and that was why he had such a volatile temper. Ironically, syphilis "made Al Capone larger than life," writes Laurence Bergreen. In 1917, a confrontation between Capone and a drunken patron, a thug by the name of Frank Galluccio – Capone had tried to pick up Galluccio's sister, Lena, by telling her she had "a nice ass" – ended with Capone being slashed across the face with a knife. The scars healed, but they left their mark, and much to Capone's dissatisfaction, the newspapers started calling him "Scarface."

Soon after Prohibition was law, Johnny Torrio left Brooklyn for Chicago to work for mob boss "Big Jim" Colosimo. On May 11, 1920, Colosimo was assassinated by New York gangster Frankie Yale (who was himself murdered two years later). Torrio inherited much of Colosimo's interests in gambling halls and brothels and invited Capone to join his organization. Capone, along with his new bride Mae Coughland, relocated to Chicago in 1921. At first, he managed the Four Deuces Saloon (and brothel) on South Wabash Avenue. Later, he assumed control of Torrio's criminal enterprise when Torrio was nearly killed and then sent to jail for operating a brewery. By then, Capone was living in the Chicago suburb of Cicero, where he ran hundreds of casinos and speakeasies, including the Cotton Club, with little or no interference from the police, whom he paid off in any event.

In his prime in the mid-twenties, Capone owned Chicago. "He was atavistic, flamboyant, impossible to ignore," writes Bergreen. "A big fat man with a cigar and a $50,000 pinkie ring. A jowly smiling Satan nearly six feet tall, with two scars across his left cheek. He weighed over two-fifty, yet despite his bulk and the sloppy grin, he could move with lethal speed and force. Not an articulate man, he was nonetheless charismatic: warm, charming, generous." He gave freely to churches and during the Depression operated a soup kitchen.

Capone did not tolerate disloyalty, nor was he willing to lose any of his territory or lucrative liquor profits to such rivals as George "Bugs" Moran.* When the popular comedian Joe E. Lewis, for example, tried to leave a Capone-operated hotel in 1927 to perform at a venue owned by a competitor, he ran afoul of Capone's main lieutenant and bodyguard "Machine Gun" Jack McGurn. Presumably with Capone's consent, McGurn ordered that Lewis be taught a lesson. He was beaten, a knife inserted in his jaw, and his scalp pulled back. Amazingly, Lewis survived, though refused to name his assailants.

McGurn was also the mastermind behind Capone's near successful attempt to wipe out the Moran gang, the St. Valentine's Day Massacre of February 14, 1929. McGurn and his men, disguised as police officers, gained entry to Moran's headquarters on the pretext of a liquor raid. Seven men were gunned down and died instantly. Moran's chief henchman, Frank Gusenberg, survived for a few hours before succumbing. The assassins had mistaken one of the men they killed for Moran. In fact, Moran was not in the warehouse. Capone was in Miami at the time of the daring killing and despite the best efforts of the authorities he could not be linked to the gangland murders.

It is true that Capone likely would have been involved in crime with or without Prohibition. But the trade in illegal liquor definitely was a boost. Capone probably had links to thousands of speakeasies, clubs, breweries, distilleries, gambling houses,

---

* On one infamous occasion, Capone had invited three Sicilians to a lavish dinner at the Hawthorne Inn, the hotel in Cicero that he used as his headquarters. Everyone was having a wonderful time, when suddenly Capone turned serious, accusing his guests of disloyalty – an offence for which there was only one punishment. His men tied the guests to their chairs and Capone bashed each of them in the head with a baseball bat.

brothels, and horse-racing tracks – the list was seemingly endless. According to the U.S. Attorney General's office, in 1927 Capone's revenue from his crime empire totalled $105 million and broke down as follows: alcohol manufacture and sale produced $60 million; gambling, $25 million; vice and resorts, $10 million; and other rackets, $10 million. In short, he made most of his money from Prohibition. (Capone later complained that it cost him at least $30 million annually in payoffs to politicians and law enforcement officials to look the other way.)

In the end, it was not the "heroic" efforts of Capone's chief nemesis, Department of Justice Special Agent Eliot Ness (in 1928 the Prohibition Bureau was transferred to the Department of Justice) that did Capone in, but a curious U.S. Supreme Court ruling.[*] In 1927, the Court decided in the case of *United States v. Sullivan* that bootleggers were required, like all other citizens, to file income-tax returns – despite the fact that the income they earned was illegal. Justice Oliver Wendell Holmes deemed that the defendant's Fifth Amendment right against self-incrimination did not apply. After this, it was only a matter of time before the Treasury Department built a case against Al Capone, declared by the Bureau of Investigation to be "Public Enemy No. One." Capone was brought to trial for income-tax evasion in late 1931, and in short order he received a ten-year prison sentence and a

---

[*] Near the end of his turbulent life, Ness penned his story in a book entitled *The Untouchables* (1957). Published two years after he died, the book was, says Laurence Bergreen, worthy of a Mickey Spillane novel. Though it was eventually made into a television series (and decades later a movie starring Kevin Costner), Ness's chronicle of his battles with Capone was highly embellished and "often inaccurate." "Although the real Ness was intelligent, well educated, and ambitious," writes Bergreen, "he was also a publicity hound, impenetrably naïve, and insecure – a lonely, melancholy, haunted man who bore scant resemblance to the self-assured character played by Robert Stack [in the television show]. . . . Ness's worst enemy was not Al Capone, who was assuredly the best thing that ever happened to him, but Ness himself, who was plagued throughout his life by his problems with women and with alcohol."

fifty-thousand-dollar fine. He served eight years and died in 1947 suffering from brain dementia caused by syphilis.

A Large Part of the Population Is Sick of Prohibition

On the morning of December 12, 1927, a group of powerful businessmen, including former U.S. senator James Wadsworth, Pierre S. du Pont, the retired chairman of the board of General Motors, and Charles Sabin, the president of the Guarantee Trust Company of New York, gathered together in Washington, D.C., to form the Association Against the Prohibition Amendment (AAPA). They had arrived at the conclusion that Prohibition, rightly or wrongly, was responsible for the lawlessness of Capone, Moran, Lansky, and the other gangsters who had taken over American cities. Moreover, from an economic standpoint, a liquor tax – which du Pont speculated "would be sufficient to pay off the entire debt of the United States" – made perfect sense. The AAPA proved to be as good a pressure group as the ASL had been a decade before when it fought in favour of Prohibition.

A few months earlier, the *New York Times* had been more succinct about the problem facing the country. "Fed by war psychology, mistaken patriotism, by inexhaustible propaganda, by Utopian hope and political cowardice, the torrent of Prohibition swept over the country," the newspaper's editors wrote. "The waters have been receding. A reaction has been gathering strength. A large part of the population is sick of . . . a Prohibition law grounded on absurdity, of an old evil continued in new forms and creating grave social and moral deterioration."

Governor Franklin Roosevelt of New York, soon to be the Democratic candidate and elected president in November 1932, also declared himself in favour of repealing the Eighteenth Amendment. "This convention wants repeal," he told the delegates to the Democratic National Convention after accepting their nomination.

"Your candidate wants repeal. And I am confident that the United States of America wants repeal."

F.D.R. was right. Such attitudes and sustained lobbying eventually paid off with the repeal of Prohibition in 1933. Americans, like Canadians, had arrived at the inevitable conclusion that alcohol, no matter how it could be abused, was an inevitable part of life. The best approach was not to restrict it entirely but to encourage moderation through government regulation. Governments, too, on both sides of the border, learned the hard way that it was far better for them to reap the profits in the form of liquor taxes than to hand it to gangsters on a silver platter. The modernists, in this case, finally had defined one aspect of progress.

CHAPTER SIX

Innovators and Innovations

Previous page: Henry Ford in 1924 in Dearborn, Michigan, standing between the first Ford car, the Ford Quadricycle, and the ten millionth Model-T, then the most popular automobile in the world. "Mr. Ford, it will take a hundred years to tell whether you have helped us or hurt us," wrote the humorist Will Rogers, "but you certainly didn't leave us like you found us."

I will build a motor car for the great multitude. It will be large enough for the family but small enough for the individual to run and care for. It will be constructed of the best materials by the best men to be hired, after the simplest designs that modern engineering can devise. But it will also be so low in price that no man making a good salary will be unable to own one – and enjoy with his family the blessings of hours of pleasure in God's great open spaces.

– Henry Ford, 1908

God Bless Henry Ford

His neighbours on Detroit's Bagley Avenue referred to him as "Crazy Henry." Each evening after a twelve-hour shift at the nearby Edison Illuminating Company, where he worked as an engineer, thirty-three-year-old Henry Ford headed for the shed behind his brownstone home and tinkered with grease, oil, and machine parts until well past midnight. He was not in the least concerned that his neighbours thought he had lost his mind.

Born in nearby rural Dearborn, Michigan, in 1863, he would have made his father happy had he become a farmer. But at an early age, young Henry showed an aptitude for things mechanical. He left the family farm when he was only sixteen to work in a variety of factories until he landed a job at Edison. By then Ford was married to Clara Bryant and they had one child, a son named Edsel born in 1893.

Ford, who for about five years had been experimenting with a design for an internal combustion engine, was determined to construct a horseless carriage – an automobile like no other. After many false starts, the triumphant moment came in the middle of the night on June 4, 1896. The loud sputtering brought the residents of Bagley Avenue to their windows. There he was, Crazy Henry, chugging down the cobblestone road in a four-horse-powered buggy mounted on twenty-eight-inch bicycle wheels. The "car" did not even have brakes.

Few who witnessed that odd sight or other forays in the days ahead would have guessed at its tremendous historical significance. Within the next two decades, the automobile, more than any other modern innovation or invention, transformed the lives of millions of people in North America and Europe. It altered their day-to-day activities, work patterns, social interactions, and fashions, and even challenged notions about proper etiquette and male-female relationships. From a moral standpoint, the automobile was trouble. And the one person above all others linked with the early history of the automobile, the person most responsible for this economic, social, and cultural revolution was Crazy Henry Ford, soon to be one of the most celebrated and wealthiest men in the world. As Will Rogers put it some decades later when Ford's legacy was assured, "Mr. Ford, it will take a hundred years to tell whether you have helped us or hurt us, but you certainly didn't leave us like you found us."

Despite the excitement of that evening in June 1896, Henry Ford was not the first person to build an automobile, nor for that matter did he invent the assembly line, the other innovation for which he is famous. Ransom Olds, Karl Benz (in Germany), John and Horace Dodge, Charles and Frank Duryea, and William "Billy" Durant, the colourful founder of General Motors, among many others, all played important roles in the annals of automobile history. Yet it was Ford whose perseverance ultimately paid off. By 1930, four out of every five American families owned a car, thanks primarily to his genius.

It took Ford several attempts and about six years to find the right combination of investors to found the Ford Motor Company, on June 16, 1903. The first Ford cars, like those of its competitors, were high-priced – the 1904 Model-B sold for $2,000 – far too expensive for the average American content to use a horse and buggy. Even Ransom Olds's 1901 Oldsmobile, at $650, was out of reach for many members of the middle-class, who did not earn that much in a year.

The key event occurred in 1908, when the Ford Motor Company introduced the Model-T, affectionately known as the "Tin Lizzie" by the millions of people who soon owned one. Ford's plan had been to develop a car that would be practical, economical, durable, and affordable, and he accomplished this feat by simplifying and speeding up the pace of production. The answer was an automated assembly line, a highly cost-efficient manufacturing process Ford had first seen while working in a bottling plant. Later he visited an abattoir, where he watched animal carcasses move along a pulley system. By utilizing similar methods, with each worker performing one assigned task at a fixed station, and by reducing supplies to the bare minimum – since black paint dried the fastest, all Model-T's were black – the new mammoth Ford factory in Highland Park, outside Detroit, was soon turning out a Model-T every twenty-four seconds. (As a comparison, in 1914, Ford's 13,000 workers made 260,720 cars, while its various competitors employed 66,350 workers who made 286,770.)

The success of the Model-T was astounding. As the price dropped from $825 in 1909 to $490 in 1913 (in the same year a McLaughlin-Buick in Canada sold for $2,350) the Ford Company could not keep up with demand. Its annual output reached 300,000 vehicles, and Ford controlled the North American market. By the early twenties, close to 60 per cent of all cars sold in the United States were Model-T's. And it was a similar success story in Canada and England, where, between 1908 and 1927, sales reached one million and 250,000 respectively. Whereas in 1905 owning a car was considered a luxury, less than two decades later, thanks in large part to Henry Ford, it had become a necessity.[*]

Despite the nuisance (and frequent danger) of hand-cranking the starter, having the gas tank under the front seat, the lack of a roof, and a poor braking system, the "Tin Lizzie" (also nicknamed the "flivver") became an integral part of North American life. "You know, Henry," wrote the wife of one farmer in Rome, Georgia, to Ford in 1918, "your car lifted us out of the mud. It brought joy into our lives. We love every rattle in its bones." The Model-T changed rural lives the most, emancipating isolated farm families and letting them see the rest of the country – often for the first time. "Until your father provided low-cost transportation," a farmer near Berea, Ohio, pointed out to Edsel Ford in a 1938 letter, "the vast majority of [rural] families had scarcely been five miles from home. I can truthfully say that every time [I saw a family travelling in a Model-T] I would reverently say, 'God bless Henry Ford.'"

Ironically, Ford himself disdained the modern city, where the car was soon king, as a "pesteriferous growth," and idolized the very rural lifestyle that he had almost single-handedly transformed. This was only one of the various quirks of his eccentric personality. As the automobile gradually replaced the horse – in one 1903 poll, only 5 per cent of Americans said they preferred cars to horses – as the regular mode of urban and rural transportation, it also came to symbolize, in the eyes of some critics, everything wrong with the modern age.

---

[*] In 1929, sociologists Robert and Helen Lynd published *Middletown*, a book based on field research done in the town of Muncie, Indiana, in 1924–25. They found that people at every income level considered the automobile a basic requirement. People were willing to sacrifice food, clothing, and their savings in order to own a car. Two of every three families in Muncie owned an automobile. Among the 123 working-class families they interviewed, for example, sixty of them had cars. Yet among these sixty car owners, twenty-one families did not have bathtubs in their homes.

Early automobile advertisements highlighted the superiority of the car over the horse. As one Oldsmobile ad declared, "It never kicks or bites, never tires out on the long runs, and during hot weather you can ride fast enough to make a breeze without sweating the horse. It does not require care in the stable, and only eats while it is on the road, which is no more than at the rate of 1 cent per mile." And the first real generation of public health officials applauded the reduction of horse manure on the streets.[*]

Women's fashions changed next. Traditional wide-brim hats with feathers, bows, and ribbons and ankle-length dresses were unsuitable for a drive on a windy or wet day. Women started cutting their hair shorter and wearing smaller hats, scarves, and skirts with a slit, necessary to get in and out of a car. Women whose slit-skirts fluttered in the wind were soon called "flappers."

Beyond that, automobiles gave women as well as teenagers a feeling of independence. "The automobile was the quintessential expression of individualism," Heather Robertson points out in her social history of the car in Canada. "The driver was in control of a machine that magnified human speed and power to a degree that no one had never experienced. Walking, by comparison, was tedious and laborious; even cycling was too much work."

At the same time, traditionalists argued that this new-found freedom threatened morality. Dating and social activities took on an entirely new form. Now, as *Harper's Magazine* noted in August 1924, when a young man came to "call," his girlfriend was already wearing her hat ready to go out for a ride and an adventure. Liberated from the supervision of their parents, teenagers quickly discovered that anything was possible in the back seat of a car. "Automobiles have become a menace to the morality of boys and girls," the Woman's

---

[*] According to historian Daniel Kyvig, "In 1900 in New York City, 15,000 horses dropped dead on the street while those that lived deposited 2.5 million pounds of manure and 60,000 gallons of urine on the streets every day."

Christian Temperance Union declared in an October 1922 circular. A juvenile court judge in Muncie, Indiana, weary of dealing with young female transgressors apprehended in vehicles, was more succinct, comparing the automobile to a "house of prostitution on wheels."

The more people bought cars, the greater the number of accidents. It took several years before adequate roads were constructed, traffic lights installed, and speed limits imposed. Eighteen people were killed in accidents involving automobiles in Toronto in 1914; twenty-eight died in 1918; and within a decade, in excess of two hundred. On a more positive note, the car also led to family outings, the establishment of resorts and beaches now accessible by a Sunday drive, and adventurous Model-T caravan journeys across the U.S. Midwest and Canadian prairies.

Through it all, Henry Ford, challenged by the likes of William Durant and General Motors, among others, never wavered in his faith that the automobile's potential was unlimited.[*] In 1908, during a court hearing about the ownership of the automobile patent, Ford was accused of creating a "social problem" with his car. "My friend, you're mistaken," he replied. "I'm not creating a social problem at all. I am going to democratize the automobile. When I'm through everybody will be able to afford one, and about everybody will have one. The horse will disappear from our highways, the automobile will be taken for granted and there won't be any problems."

---

[*] Next to Henry Ford, William "Billy" Durant (1861–1947) was one of the most important figures in automobile history. Certainly he was much more of a "character" than Ford. Writes Heather Robertson: "[He] radiated boyish enthusiasm, and his confidence was infectious. He was able to raise millions in an afternoon, and his investors trusted him implicitly. He seemed never to sleep. . . . [Whereas] the Ford company existed to manufacture cars; for Durant, a car was a vehicle to build General Motors." GM was a merger of companies, including Buick, Chevrolet, Cadillac, and Oldsmobile, assembled by Durant beginning in 1908. Durant likely made and lost more than $90 million and was forced out of GM by disgruntled bankers and shareholders in 1920.

The Five-Dollar Day

Money, Ford, once said, meant nothing to him. Yet the huge profits he reaped from the sales of Model-T cars made him not only an American hero – it was said that no American had more written about him in his own lifetime than Ford – it also made him very rich. By 1922, Ford was undoubtedly one of the wealthiest men in the world, surpassing even John D. Rockefeller and J.P. Morgan in annual income. But he would have frowned at the comparison. He was a millionaire in wealth, though not in temperament or spirit – at least, in his opinion. He ignored the fact that he owned a magnificent estate in Dearborn and property in Florida. He scorned the eastern and "speculative capitalists," as he called them, who ruled Wall Street and railed against urbanites – above all, the Jews – who "encouraged the breakdown of the family, of morality, of order."

Ford was ambitious, idealistic, and even sentimental. He was an ardent believer in the "gospel of progress" with its Protestant and moral overtones that hard work was rewarded (hence his stubbornly held notion of rural virtue). His motto was "A man who is living aright will do his work aright." To practise what he preached, Ford announced early in 1914 to his skeptical board of directors that the company's employees would share in its enormous profits. At the time, workers toiled nine hours a day for a grand total of $2.34 (steelworkers received $1.75 per day and coal miners about $2.50). Ford's plan called for an eight-hour day for an unheard-of salary of five dollars. (For the time being, women at the plant continued to be paid $2.07 per day.) As newspapers spread this sensational story across the continent and overseas, businessmen everywhere shuddered. According to *Forbes* magazine, Ford was "hailed as the friend of the worker, an outright socialist, or as a madman bent on bankrupting his company." The *Wall Street Journal* criticized the scheme as immoral. "Biblical or spiritual principles," its editors argued, did not belong in a factory.

Typical of Ford, however, there was a catch. Before a worker was eligible for the five-dollar wage, he would have to prove himself morally worthy of it – "sober, saving, steady, and industrious." According to a company news release, "Mr. Ford" intended "to help the men to a LIFE – not a mere LIVING." The onerous task of making this judgment fell to the company's nascent Sociological Department, created by Ford in 1913.

The department was led by John R. Lee, the head of the Ford employment section and by all accounts a principled and honourable individual. Ford also recruited the Reverend Samuel Simpson Marquis, dean of St. Paul's Episcopal Cathedral in Detroit, first as an unpaid volunteer and then as Lee's successor in November 1915. "I want you, 'Mark,'" Ford had told him, "to put Jesus Christ in my factory!" A dedicated social gospeller, Marquis relished the opportunity to shape and influence the men of the Ford factory according to his precepts. He remained the head of the Sociological Department for six years, until a falling out with Ford and two of his key executives, "Cast-Iron" Charles Sorensen and Ernest Liebold (Ford's powerful personal secretary) forced him to quit.

To ensure that the company's workers walked a straight and narrow path, the department hired a team of social-work investigators essentially to spy on them. They would pay unannounced visits to the employees' apartments, teaching them such life skills as how to maintain a bank account, proper hygiene (spitting on the floor was to be avoided), and how to shop for nutritious food at the neighbourhood grocery store. They were also continually warned against the sins of gambling, drinking, and smoking tobacco (Ford detested cigarettes, referring to them as "little white slavers"). If they could not speak English, then they were encouraged to learn it. If investigators found a man and woman living together who were not married, arrangements were quickly made to make the union legal. In short, they were given a short course on how to become ideal Americans – as defined by Henry Ford. Any apprehended transgressor was given the opportunity to reform and upon doing so was rewarded with the five-dollar-a-day wage. Most willingly complied. Guided by his firm, almost messianic, religious convictions, Ford introduced a paternalistic compassion into North American business. Still, it had to be on his terms, a fact later affirmed in his bitter battle to keep unions out of his factory.

That stubborn, and often irrational, side of Ford was his great weakness. He could be domineering – especially with his son, Edsel, in whom he rarely had faith – opinionated, impulsive, and often rashly judged.[*] "We used to say around Dearborn," recalled Fred Black, one of his business managers, "that if Henry Ford saw three blackbirds in the morning all birds were black that day." His temper was legendary. In 1912, when his executives surprised him with an upgraded design for the Model-T, he exploded. He tore the doors right off the new car, smashing its windshield and doing as much damage as he could with his bare hands – cursing loudly all the while.

As a pacifist, he was determined to stop the First World War, which he blamed on "German-Jewish bankers." He organized a trip to Europe in 1915 for an assortment of peace workers and journalists aboard a chartered Scandinavian ocean liner, only to have the entire expedition turn into a fiasco. Ford planned to convene a conference with European leaders to convince them to halt the conflict. But soon after the ship arrived in Oslo, Norway, Ford, realizing the futility of his mission and weary of the negative press coverage he had received, abandoned his group. His most famous utterance was when he remarked to Charles Wheeler of the *Chicago Tribune* (and

---

[*] Even in the 1930s, when Ford was already in his early seventies, he found it impossible to relinquish control of the company he had founded. Edsel had assumed the presidency of Ford in late 1918, but his father continued to countermand his decisions. A softer, more sensitive individual, Edsel always abided his father's wishes on matters dealing with the company, although he did manage to convince him that the Model-T had to be replaced with the modern Model-A in 1927. Still, ulcers and stress wracked Edsel for many years. He died at age forty-nine in May 1943 from a combination of stomach ulcers and cancer.

repeated during the proceedings of a libel trial he waged against the newspaper in 1919) that "history is more or less bunk." What he meant, he repeatedly explained, was that historians often distorted the true version of the past for their own purposes, but the harm was done. The depiction of Ford by his critics as simple-minded and ignorant spread far and wide.

"He speaks at times with an air of great finality, as a man who has received a revelation or has secret sources of information on the great subjects of the day," noted Reverend Marquis in his memoirs. The well-known writer Hamlin Garland, although conservative himself in outlook, was not as diplomatic on Ford's penchant for extreme views. "He has the way of discoursing on one of his favourite themes," Garland observed, "Wall Street, the Jew, international bankers sitting in a secret conclave somewhere and planning another war – in a way that produces among his listeners a profound and embarrassing silence."

Nothing damaged Ford's reputation or historical legacy as much as his virulent anti-Semitism, a fact he never truly understood. To counter what he felt was overly critical coverage he received in the press, Ford acquired the *Dearborn Independent* in 1919 and immediately transformed it into his mouthpiece. He installed Ernest Liebold as the newspaper's general manager.

As opinionated and domineering as his boss, Liebold was loyal as well as ruthless. One historian has described him as "a squat, heavy-set, bullnecked man with short-cropped hair." Liebold was Prussian in manner and style and shared Ford's disdain for what he perceived to be excessive Jewish economic power strengthened by the wave of Bolshevism emanating from Russia. With William Cameron, a Canadian journalist, as the paper's second editor – Edward Pipp, the celebrated muckraker and the *Independent*'s first editor, resigned in 1920 over the paper's anti-Semitic slant – Liebold, with Ford's full support, launched one of the most devastating anti-Semitic propaganda campaigns in U.S. history. Influenced by such writers as David

Starr Jordan, an ardent Social Darwinist and eugenicist, Ford had long believed that Jews – at least those who were bankers and money-lenders – were the curse of civilization.

Beginning in May 1920, the *Dearborn Independent* ran a series of ninety-one articles on "The International Jew: The World's Problem," which depicted a Jewish conspiracy to rule the world. The basis of the articles was the newspaper's acquisition of the English version of *The Protocols of the Learned Elders of Zion*, a notorious piece of propaganda that can be traced back to Czarist Russia during the first decade of the twentieth century.* Month after month, to the dismay of Detroit's growing Jewish community as well as Jewish communities throughout North America, the newspaper spread one falsehood after another. (Articles about the *Protocols* in the *Times* of London and other newspapers soon confirmed it as a sham.)

Condemned as an anti-Semite of the worst kind, Ford finally defended himself in an interview in the *New York World* on February 16, 1921, with his friend and editor Joseph Jefferson O'Neill. "Henry Ford holds the belief that 'international Jewry with its racial programme of domination' is an evil influence in America and the world," wrote O'Neill. "Those who have profited [from the World War] and are profiting now are the international financiers –

---

* In 1905, a Russian civil servant named Sergei Nilus on orders of the Czar's secret police composed the tract aimed at stirring agitation against the country's Jews. The premise was that at the first Zionist Congress held in Basel, Switzerland, in 1897, the "Wise Men of Zion" had met to plot the overthrow of the Christian world – a conspiracy supposedly contained in twenty-four "protocols." "The instrument of their scheme defined at first as the international banking system," historian Howard Sachar notes, "later was equated with political liberalism and Marxist socialism." After the Russian Revolution of 1917, a group of former Czarist soldiers reissued Nilus's forgery as *The Protocols of the Learned Elders of Zion*. It was brought into the United States in 1919 by a group of White Russian immigrants led by Boris Brasol, the leader of the Romanov restoration movement. Brasol gave it to Harris A. Houghton, a physician employed in army intelligence, who had it translated into English. Eventually a copy was given to Ernest Liebold and the *Dearborn Independent*.

the Jews." Ford insisted that "we do not hate Jews," yet maintained that the *Protocols* "fit with what is going on."

Later, another friend and prominent journalist, Arthur Brisbane of the *New York Evening Journal*, who on several occasions had urged Ford to halt the attacks, remarked that the automobile magnate "did not ever realize the full effect of the articles." Nearly a million people each week read the *Independent* and Ford car dealers were compelled to sell a subscription to every customer who purchased a Model-T. The newspaper then reissued the "International Jew" series as a pamphlet a few months after the articles had concluded in late December 1921. It reached millions more readers in the United States, Canada, and in Europe, where it was translated into several languages and was especially popular in Germany.* Since Ford refused to accept advertising for the *Independent*, it consistently lost money, despite its growing subscription list. But this did not deter him or Liebold from continuing their campaign to expose what they saw as the truth about Jews. In April 1924 a new series of articles about "Jewish Exploitation of Farmers' Organizations" focused on the work of Aaron Sapiro, a successful and influential Jewish lawyer who had organized co-operatives from Saskatchewan to California.

Angered by the *Independent*'s accusations that he had cheated farmers, Sapiro filed a libel suit. It took until April 1927 for the case to come to trial. After the initial proceedings were declared a mistrial – owing to allegations that an unknown individual with pro-Jewish attitudes had corrupted one of the jurors – Ford abruptly agreed to settle with Sapiro and also to call off his seven-year attack

---

* The Nazis, in the early twenties still a fringe group of extremists under Adolf Hitler's leadership, distributed many copies of the "International Jew" pamphlet and worshipped Henry Ford. Hitler had a photograph of Ford hanging on his office wall in Munich and called him a "great man" in his book *Mein Kampf*. More than a decade later, after Hitler had become Chancellor and turned Germany into a dictatorship, he awarded Ford the Supreme Order of the German Eagle, the highest honour a non-German citizen could receive.

on Jews with a public apology. This apology was a complete repudiation of everything the *Independent* had published. It was composed by Sapiro's lawyer, Louis Marshall, and representatives of the American Jewish Congress. Ford signed the document without reading it, and still did not truly comprehend the damage he had done.

So great was Ford's reputation that most American Jews were quick to forgive him and lay most of the blame instead on Liebold, as Ford had done. Within months, the *Independent*, which was in grave debt, ceased publication, and Ford now concerned himself with making his new Model-A a commercial success. It is, however, debatable – as author Neil Baldwin shows in his recent and detailed account *Henry Ford and the Jews* – whether Ford's long-held anti-Semitic beliefs were altered in the least.

A Tremendous Civilizer

David Sarnoff was precisely the kind of Jew that Henry Ford feared. As one of the chief executives with the Radio Corporation of America (RCA), and then with the National Broadcasting Corporation (NBC), he had power, influence, and vision. Sarnoff did not invent the radio, but he was nevertheless, like Ford, an innovator of the modern age. He played a key role in its development and promotion (as he later did for television) and understood more than most people in the early twenties how significant its impact could be. "I have in mind a plan of development which would make radio a 'household utility' in the same sense as the piano or phonograph," he wrote in his famous "Radio Music Box" memo, likely in 1920 and not in 1915 as was later claimed. "The idea is to bring music into the house by wireless. . . . Communication between peoples widely separated in space and thought is undoubtedly the greatest weapon against misunderstanding and jealousy."

Born in a small Russian village near Minsk, Sarnoff immigrated to the United States at the age of nine with his mother, Leah, and two brothers. They joined his father, Abraham, who had arrived four years earlier and settled in New York City's Lower East Side. After finishing the eighth grade, Sarnoff landed a job as an office boy with the American branch of the British Marconi Wireless Telegraph Company. When the founder of the company, Guglielmo Marconi – who in 1901 at the age of twenty-seven had successfully conducted the first wireless transatlantic transmission from Cornwall, England, to St. John's, Newfoundland – visited the New York office, Sarnoff acted as his personal messenger. With Marconi's encouragement, Sarnoff gradually moved up the ranks, becoming first a telegraph operator and then the manager of a station.

In 1919, General Electric purchased Marconi's U.S. business interests and created RCA (along with its partners, Westinghouse and AT&T). Sarnoff remained in a management position, and by the mid-twenties, as the radio craze swept North America, was instrumental in establishing NBC as the first U.S. radio network. He became RCA's president in 1930.

At first, radio – merely crystal sets that could be assembled for two dollars – was a novelty enjoyed by a few thousand amateur ham operators who communicated and bantered with each other. But in 1920 one of those enthusiasts, Frank Conrad, an engineer with Westinghouse based in Pittsburgh, began broadcasting recorded music from a transmitter he had put together in his garage. As word of Conrad's program spread, more and more people wanted receiving equipment and Westinghouse started making lots of money selling it to them. Taking full advantage of the situation, the company obtained the first federal licence for its radio station, KDKA, and with a new and more powerful transmitter now located on its roof, Conrad's music and concerts reached a larger listening audience. The first scheduled broadcast of KDKA, on November 2, 1920, also included a report on the victory of Warren Harding's election as president. The age of radio news had dawned.

It was sports broadcasting, however, that moved radio to the next level. The top sporting event of 1921 was the heavyweight championship boxing match between Jack Dempsey of the United States and Georges Carpentier of France. The bout took place on the evening of July 2 at an arena in Jersey City before a crowd of ninety thousand frantic spectators. Working with Major Andrew White, the president of the National Amateur Wireless Association, Sarnoff and RCA provided a new powerful transmitter for the radio broadcast. Theatres, lecture halls, and clubs in more than sixty cities were rented for the occasion so that boxing fans could gather to enjoy the fight.

From his "station" ringside, White, who went on to become one of the pioneers of sports broadcasting, reported the details of the fight, which were broadcast on the air. Thanks to Sarnoff's efforts, three hundred thousand people from Maine to Florida listened to the fight on the radio. This included close to one hundred thousand in New York's Times Square, who heard the match – which ended when Dempsey knocked out Carpentier in the fourth round – over a loudspeaker system erected for the event.

Having proven itself a tremendous success, "wireless telephony" was used with great fanfare to broadcast World Series baseball games and the celebrated Jack Dempsey–Gene Tunney boxing matches in Philadelphia in 1926 and Chicago in 1927. With the added hype accorded the story in the newspapers, more than forty million people listened to the broadcast of the two fights. The second fight was famous for the "long count." During the seventh round, Tunney was knocked down, and the referee waited several seconds while Dempsey returned to his corner before starting the ten count. This allowed Tunney to recover. Later it was reported that at least five Americans listening to the match on the radio died from heart attacks caused by the suspense.

Meanwhile in Toronto, young Foster Hewitt, a cub reporter with the *Toronto Star*, who had also listened to the Dempsey-Carpentier fight, began writing a newspaper column about the radio. Like other newspapers in Canada the *Star*, anxious to control potential rivals, established its own radio station. On March 22, 1923, the paper dispatched Hewitt to broadcast a local senior league hockey game. Although he had already read news and sports reports on the air, Hewitt was reluctant to accept this assignment. Complying with his editor's wishes, he sat on a small stool and used a telephone to relay the play-by-play back to the station. As the game went into three extra periods of overtime, journalist Knowlton Nash recalled, "listeners heard for the first time the flat, nasal tones of an excited Foster Hewitt shouting what was to become one of Canada's most memorable phrases, 'He shoots! He scores!'" Within a few years, Hewitt would become a staple of Canadian hockey broadcasts, first on radio and later on television.

Accustomed as we are today to computer technology and instantaneous global communication, it is difficult to appreciate the excitement that radio generated. Within a decade of its introduction, radio stations were in business across the U.S. and Canada and sales of radios skyrocketed – in the United States alone, from $60 million in sales in 1922 to $824 million by 1929. In 1925, approximately one hundred thousand Canadians owned a radio; just five years later, this number had increased to half a million and had made the radio the centre of attention in their homes.

Across North America, people in cities and rural areas were linked by the shared experience of listening to the "miracle of the radio," as it was often referred to. A September 1923 story in *Radio Broadcast* magazine, for instance, pointed to the "ability to astound our friends by tuning in a program a thousand miles away," and asserted that there "is something fascinating about hearing a concert from a long way off, and the pleasure does not seem to wane with familiarity." A year earlier in Toronto, more than one thousand people waited in line for two hours for admission to a Masonic

Temple so that they could hear a concert played by musicians in a distant studio. The crowd was mesmerized by the sounds emanating from the black box sitting at the front of the hall. "Men strained forward in their seats with their hands cupped to their ears. . . . Women were rigid as if carved from stone," the *Toronto Star*, which had sponsored the event, reported the next day.

Not everyone welcomed this communications revolution. Concern was raised about radio's negative impact. It would destroy book reading, keep children from completing their schoolwork, and prevent husbands and wives from doing their chores and talking to each other. "The radio is turned on before breakfast and in some homes runs all day long," one journalist noted. "Radio is making our children deaf." There were also references in popular magazines to "radio maniacs" and "radio widows." Religious leaders, with some justification, suggested that the radio would interfere with church attendance. And in fact it did soon put an end to Sunday evening services in Canada. Congregants were more interested in listening to the music and entertainment, mainly American in origin, that filled the airwaves.

Millions of Americans and Canadians tuned in to such shows as *The Happiness Boys*, *Moran and Mack* (the Two Black Crows), and especially *Amos 'n' Andy*, about two black country bumpkins trying to find their way in the big city. Played by two white actors, Freeman Gosden and Charles Correll, Amos and Andy were always trying to get themselves out of some impossible situation – or "sitchiation," as they would have put it. ("Ain't dat sumpin," was another favourite.) In its prime in the early thirties, nearly forty million Americans – one-third of the country's population – and another few hundred thousand in Canada tuned in at seven each night for the fifteen-minute show on NBC. White audiences adored the urban adventures of *Amos 'n' Andy*, while black listeners were more circumspect.

The show's remarkable success drew attention to several other significant effects of the radio. When Pepsodent sponsored *Amos 'n'*

Andy its sales of toothpaste tripled in just a few weeks. By 1931, the American Tobacco Company was spending more than nineteen million dollars annually to advertise Lucky Strike cigarettes on the radio. Large-scale advertising campaigns soon became the norm, as ads on the radio and newspapers competed for space and airtime promoting everything from Kellogg's breakfast cereal to Listerine mouthwash as the number-one cure for bad breath. Vaudeville performers like Eddie Cantor, Jack Benny, George Jessel, and Fred Allen quickly discovered the radio's power to make them even bigger celebrities and were more than willing to host radio variety shows sponsored by whichever company would pay them.

Similarly, politicians such as Franklin Delano Roosevelt took note of radio's marketing might. Indeed, no other politician took to the radio or dominated it as did F.D.R. He was the "first professional of the art," according to David Halberstam. "For most Americans of this generation," he adds, "their first memory of politics would be sitting by a radio and hearing *that* voice, strong, confident, totally at ease." Herbert Hoover, whom Roosevelt succeeded as president in 1933, received about forty letters a day; after F.D.R. went on the air, his daily mail reached four thousand letters. It was not by chance, Halberstam concluded, that F.D.R. was president of the United States for an unprecedented twelve consecutive years.

The enormous popularity of *Amos 'n' Andy* and other American shows worried some Canadian politicians. The radio knew no borders. While the U.S. Congress in the Radio Act of 1927 was content to regulate frequencies and allow private broadcasting companies to take the lead, the Canadian government adopted the model followed by the British government when in 1922 it created the publicly owned British Broadcasting Corporation. In 1928, the Canadian federal government appointed Sir John Aird head of a Royal Commission to study broadcasting problems directly related to U.S. cultural influence. It was the first of forty such inquiries. To counter American radio's overpowering influence, which the Commission felt "has a tendency to mold the minds of young people in the home to ideas and opinions that are not Canadian," it was recommended that a publicly owned and operated broadcasting system be established. This led to the creation of the Canadian Radio Broadcasting Commission – later the CBC – in 1932.

Radio advocates in the two countries may have thus differed on the question of government control or even the benefits of commercial advertising ("sponsoritis," its opponents called it), but they did share similar views on radio's unlimited potential for enlightenment and education. Beyond its novelty, supporters claimed radio would not only change the world, it would improve it as well. *Collier's* magazine suggested that radio would become "a tremendous civilizer," which would bring "mutual understanding to all sections of the country, unifying our thoughts, ideals, and purposes, making us a strong and well-knit people." The editors of the Toronto *Globe* agreed. In 1927, a day after a Canada-wide broadcast from Ottawa of celebrations marking the fiftieth anniversary of Confederation, the *Globe* observed that radio "is a democratic science, ready to instruct, and entertain all manner and conditions of humankind who prepare to receive its blessings." This was a point not lost on church officials, priests, preachers, and evangelicals – many of whom championed a traditional, even anti-urban, morality, but did so, ironically, using the most modern communication invention of its day.

Radio Priests

On Christmas Eve 1906, history was made when Reginald Fessenden – a young radio pioneer from Canada who had been conducting sound experiments at a lab in Brant Rock, Massachusetts – produced a holiday program for ships off the east coast. That memorable night, sailors heard a selection from the Gospel of Luke, a recording of a woman singing Handel's "Largo," and a violin solo played by Fessenden of "O Holy Night."

Fessenden may have been more interested in testing his theories of sound transmission, but his broadcast equally symbolized the radio's remarkable capacity to spread the word of God. One of the first official religious services on the air was broadcast from Pittsburgh's Calvary Episcopal Church in January 1921. Manned (somewhat ironically) by two engineers, one Jewish and the other Roman Catholic, the program on station KDKA was heard by about one thousand people. The church's senior pastor later recalled that he did not have much faith that "the little black box was really going to carry out the service to the outside world. I knew there was such a thing as wireless, but somehow I thought there would be some fluke in the connection, and that the whole thing would be a fizzle!" But it was hardly a fizzle.

It was clear at once that religion and radio were a natural fit. Within a few years, as radio became more fully developed, its rate of adoption as a pulpit was astounding. By 1925, religious organizations or groups operated about sixty radio stations in the United States.

Charles Fuller, for instance, a popular Los Angeles–based Protestant evangelist and radio preacher, could reach in a few thirty-minute segments "more living people on this earth than the greatest evangelist of the nineteenth century, D.L. Moody, was able to reach, with long journeys, fatiguing travels, and sometimes three meetings a day in his entire forty years of Christian service." Likewise, R.R. Brown, an Omaha evangelical who went on the air in 1923 with his "Radio Chapel Service," had built up a following of one hundred thousand listeners within a few years. "We believe," declared Rev. A.A. McIntyre, the editor of the *Canadian Churchman*, "that radio is one of God's most wonderful gifts to man." Dr. H.A. Terry, an evangelist in Winnipeg, claimed that owing to his efforts on the radio he had "at least three conversions in one weekend alone."

Broadcasting from studios and church pulpits, the growing band of radio priests touched on a wide range of topics – from the sanctity of rural life to the evils of immigration and communism. They saw themselves as moral guardians of a simpler and endangered era, shunted aside by urbanization and the sin and depravity of the city. At the same time, the radio brought the very same listeners into the modern world. "The rise of radio and mass culture during [the twenties] increased rural folks' awareness of national trends and tastes," argues American historian Tona Hangen, "a development which paradoxically increased their sense of remoteness and isolation." In those moments, the voice on the radio was also comforting.

One of the earliest and most brilliant practitioners was Paul Rader, a former prizefighter and oil speculator from Chicago. One day in 1912 he "heard the voice of God." He joined the Christian and Missionary Alliance based in New York and transformed himself into an evangelist. Charismatic and determined, his revivalist-style sermons were popular wherever he spoke. He was fascinated with the possibilities that a radio show offered. Beginning in 1922, his message that sinners had to be saved was broadcast from Chicago to points in every direction. Rader made his listening audience feel as if they were part of his family. A farmer in Saskatchewan put it this way in a letter he sent to the preacher: "The Spirit of God was so real that we could feel His very presence, through the air into our room, and my wife, my family, myself and the hired boy all got so blessed that we had a little revival meeting right here in our home. We cannot get out to church very often, but we can feel the Spirit of God moving through your meetings."

Rader's pioneering style influenced the careers of several other popular radio priests. By 1923, William Aberhart, born in a small town in Ontario in 1878, and who had a successful career as a public-school teacher and principal, had developed a sideline as a Sunday-school preacher and leader. He had established the Calgary Prophetic Bible Conference (later the Calgary Prophetic Bible Institute) in 1918 and at its weekly gatherings he disseminated his fundamentalist gospel to a growing group of supportive believers. Aberhart's motto was "The Bible, the whole Bible and nothing but the Bible!" and he maintained that the 1611 King James edition "embodied the literal, unabridged, and undiluted Word of God." It was one of the reasons he was nicknamed "Bible Bill." He vehemently opposed the trend to adopt more modern religious interpretations, and closely followed the debate during the Scopes trial in 1925. His success on the radio (particularly when he became involved in Alberta politics in the 1930s) was based on his zealous convictions, superior intelligence, authoritarian streak, and natural ability to combine preaching with acting.

"He commanded attention the moment he stepped on the platform," write his biographers David Elliott and Iris Miller. "The vitality that radiated from him gave his great bulk an appearance of tremendous power. He was now in his early forties, and obesity had begun to overlay his muscular physique. . . . He paced the platform lightly while he spoke and brought down his fist every now and then on a stout-legged table. He seemed to get great satisfaction from public speaking, beginning his lectures in a quiet voice that gradually became more passionate as he lunged forward at his audience to make his points. His oration developed into a roaring crescendo after which climax his voice became very quiet again, as if he had experienced an emotional release."

In 1925, William Grant, the founder of Calgary radio station CFCN and wily pioneer of early Canadian radio, spoke with Robert Scrimgeour, a friend who was a member of the Bible Conference. Grant proposed that Scrimgeour approach Aberhart with the idea that he broadcast his sermons. At first, Aberhart was reluctant, but after a "Radio Club" with a two-dollar membership was organized to assist with the expenses, he agreed to give it a try. His first "Back-to-the Bible" broadcast from the Palace Theatre before a large crowd aired on a Sunday afternoon in early November 1925 and was an instant success. "He did not then know, but was soon to discover, that in radio he had found his greatest single means of influencing the public," add Elliott and Miller. "It was indeed his own medium. He was to use it to the full, and without it his career might have developed very differently."

As his fame grew, so too did his audience, as well as the number of letters he received and the amount of money sent to him for his radio club. At the height of his career as a radio priest in the late twenties, an estimated 350,000 people on the Canadian prairies and the northwest region of the U.S. tuned into his Sunday afternoon sermons. Within two years, he had raised the fifty-thousand dollars required to build a new institute in downtown Calgary. Another one of his innovations, popular with parents, was a Radio Sunday School, which was a part of his regular broadcasts. His on-air talks were supplemented with fifty-two lessons prepared by the Bible Institute. In time, more than eight thousand children, ages six to sixteen, were enrolled.

With the onset of the Depression in 1929, Aberhart switched directions, embracing the quirky monetary Social Credit theories of Scottish engineer Major Clifford H. Douglas.[*] Utilizing the radio to spread his message of hope and his promise to return money back into the hands of those who earned it, he gradually transformed the Alberta Social Credit organization from a lobby group into a full-fledged political party.

Starting in October 1934, Aberhart inaugurated his *Man from Mars* radio series, in which an actor playing a Martian questioned a group of actors in the role of typical Albertans about the disastrous state of the province's economy. At the end of the show, the Man from Mars would inquire why earthmen were not clever enough to

---

[*] Social Credit was based on what Douglas referred to as the "A plus B Theorem." "A" represented wages paid to workers; "B" was the cost of production; and A plus B equalled the price of consumer goods. Aberhart's solution to the constant disparity in wages was to reform the monetary system. "By issuing social dividends, the government would put money into the hands of consumers and thus keep the economy moving."

recognize that the Social Credit offered them the solution they were seeking. The series ran until February 1935, and in historian John Irving's opinion it was "the most dramatic of all the ingenious devices developed by Aberhart for arousing and maintaining public interest in Social Credit." Amazingly, the Social Credit formed the government of Alberta after the election of August 22, 1935, and a few weeks later William Aberhart agreed to become premier.

Earlier in his career, Aberhart, like other radio preachers in North America, had been in awe of the determination and zeal of Aimee Semple McPherson. How could they not have been? Based in Los Angeles, McPherson was – with her fashionable dresses and her stylishly bobbed hair – the most modern of evangelists, a faith healer who cherished her rural roots and traditional values yet became one of the first North American mass-media sensations. She gave "the old-time religion . . . a new buoyancy, vitality and bounce," according to William McLoughlin, a historian of popular culture. "She remains," adds Tona Hangen, "a fascinating example of the way religion functions as a form of popular culture entertainment in America and how faithful believers – religion's spokespeople – become transformed through their relationship with the media into objects of intense interest ranging from ridicule to reverence."

Her performances on stage and on the radio were choreographed wonders, complete with props, tightly rehearsed script, and magnificent costumes. When she appeared on stage, she usually wore "a flowing gown with a cross sequined on the bosom, or a red gingham dress and a sunbonnet." McPherson never forgot, or let anyone else forget, where she came from. Her rural roots were important – on her birthday she liked to deliver an autobiographical sermon entitled "Milkpail to Pulpit" – and acted as a magnet for others. "How many of you," she would ask her audience, "have ever lived on a farm?" Usually, the entire audience would rise.

She was born Aimee Kennedy in the southwest Ontario farming community of Ingersoll in 1890. Her mother, Minnie, was a loyal member of the Salvation Army who educated her daughter on the Army's evangelical and activist community-oriented mission. As a teenager she was deeply troubled by the evolutionary theories she was taught in geography and science classes – teachings, she argued, that "tend to undermine and destroy . . . faith in God as a Supreme being and Creator."

Her first life-defining moment occurred when she was sixteen years old. She heard the inspiring words of Robert Semple, an Irish Pentecostal revivalist. By the end of the evening, Aimee was speaking in tongues and praising God. The attraction to Semple was powerful and reciprocal. The two were married a year later and travelled together to China to work as missionaries. Soon after they arrived, Semple became ill with malaria and died. Aimee was eight months pregnant. After her daughter, Roberta, was born, she returned to the United States and lived with her mother in New York. She took a series of low-paying jobs, but continued her missionary work as Sister Aimee. In 1912, she married a grocery salesman, Harold McPherson, and had a son, Rolf Kennedy McPherson. With her husband's support, Aimee became even more active in the evangelical community.

Still, she was not content. Searching for a more meaningful life, she took her children and left McPherson (they officially divorced in 1921). Following several years on the road, preaching to whomever would listen about the power of faith and the coming of Judgment Day, she settled in Los Angeles, where her reputation as a faith healer and evangelical grew. By 1923 she had raised enough money to open her Angelus Temple. It had sufficient seating for five thousand people. A Bible College soon followed, along with two steel towers to relay her sermons (as well as a variety of religious-oriented programs) from her own radio station, KFSG, throughout the west and as far away as Hawaii. A popular and electrifying orator, she incorporated her entire religious operation as the International Church of the Four Square Gospel.

Sister Aimee's remarkable success was due partly to her over-arching belief in the Almighty, but also to her brilliant media savvy. She injected entertainment and pageantry into her spectacular revival meetings and broadcasts, and her titillating private life gen-erated a fair amount of juicy, and beneficial, gossip. She used music, choirs, and Hollywood sets choreographed with the assistance of Thompson Eade, a vaudeville stage manager. And she promoted herself whenever and wherever possible. She rode in a float in Pasadena's Tournament of Roses Parade and dropped invitations to her gatherings out of an airplane. Her broadcasts were so moving that thousands of listeners heeded her call to kneel and place their hands on their radios so they could be healed physically as well as spiritually. Letters and money poured in.

"These are the days of invention!" she declared in one early appeal for funds to support her network. "The days when the impos-sible has become possible! Days more favourable than any that have ever been known for the preaching of the blessed Gospel of our Lord and Saviour Jesus Christ! Now, the crowning blessing, the most golden opportunity, the most miraculous conveyance for the Message has come – The Radio!" She was naturally protective of her station and in 1927 dispatched a telegram castigating Secretary of Commerce Herbert Hoover when the federal government tried to introduce regulations to solve an increasing number of radio-frequency prob-lems: "Please order your minions of Satan to leave my station alone STOP You cannot expect the Almighty to abide by your wave length nonsense STOP When I offer my prayer to Him I must fit into his wave reception."

By this time, her fame had spread across the continent. A year earlier, in mid-May 1926, she had disappeared. Newspaper stories claimed that she had drowned. The Los Angeles police searched the beaches but found nothing. Five days later, she was sighted in a town on the Arizona-Mexico border. She claimed that she had been kidnapped. Further investigation exposed inconsistencies in her tale, and it was eventually revealed that she had, in fact, run off for a few days of romance with Kenneth Ormiston, an engineer who worked at her station.

She was compelled to appear before a grand jury, although after several days of well-reported hearings, no charges were forthcoming. And the publicity surrounding the case only confirmed her status as a national celebrity. Within months, she embarked on a cross-country tour, preaching and healing in nearly every major centre in the United States. "Her voice is a full-throated contralto," the *New York Times* wrote after following her sermon at the Glad Tidings Tabernacle on West 33rd Street. "She has an expressive mouth, even teeth and brown eyes that flash or are luminous with tears at will . . ."

Not everyone was as positive about her exploits. The critic H.L. Mencken, for example, no fan of fundamentalists, denounced her and her followers as "poor and wormy folk." But McPherson was resolved to save the world from the moral corruption she insisted was threatening it. That did not mean forsaking modern life or conveniences, but instead trying to control its pace. This she did until the day she died in 1944.

Radio Messiah

As big and influential a celebrity as Aimee Semple McPherson was, Father Charles Coughlin was bigger, more renowned, and certainly more controversial. He portrayed himself as a champion of freedom and democracy and a "solitary fighter" against the bigotry of the Ku Klux Klan. In fact, he used his enormous popularity as the "Radio Messiah" to spread his narrow definition of morality, which came mixed with a healthy dose of anti-Semitism. For more than a decade, he cast a spell over thousands of North Americans, preying on their fears about immigration, communism, and the other complexities and adjustments of modern life. His story, more than any other, epitomized the serious flaw in early radio and the inherent danger of allowing one individual, especially one blessed with a charismatic personality and "golden voice," such a powerful medium to promote malicious personal views. The opportunities for manipulating and distorting the truth were ripe, and Father Coughlin rarely missed a chance to do so.

Like Aberhart and McPherson, Charles Coughlin was also a Canadian. He was born in Hamilton, Ontario, on October 25, 1891. His working-class parents, Tom and Amelia, were devout Roman Catholics and wanted nothing more than for their son to become a priest. When he reached high-school age, he was sent to board at St. Michael's College School in Toronto, forty miles from home. Later he attended the University of Toronto, graduated with a Bachelor of Arts in 1911, and then followed his parents' wishes. In June 1916, Coughlin, then twenty-four years old, was ordained as a Catholic priest. His teachers at the St. Basil's Seminary in Toronto (members of the Basilian Order) had already instilled in him a healthy aversion to modern capitalism, particularly the seemingly immense power of banks.

For several years, Coughlin taught history, literature, and drama at the Basilians' Assumption College, a school for boys in Windsor, Ontario. While his students appreciated his enthusiasm and dramatic flair, his colleagues found him to be self-centred and obstinate. In 1924, Coughlin decided to leave the college to become a diocesan priest in nearby Detroit. With a reputation as a talented lecturer and speaker, he was soon given his own church to preside over in the suburban community of Royal Oak. The church, yet to be built, was to be called the Shrine of the Little Flower after a recently canonized nun, Saint Therese of Lisieux, the Little Flower. Coughlin immediately undertook a fundraising drive, and with assistance from the Catholic diocese, along with help from baseball players from the Detroit Tigers and New York Yankees (including Babe Ruth), the church was on solid financial footing soon after it opened in May 1926.

It was two of his parishioners, automobile tycoons and brothers Fred and Lawrence Fisher, who suggested to Coughlin that he broadcast his sermons from the pulpit. They had contacts with the Detroit radio station WJR and introduced Coughlin to the station's owner, George A. Richardson, who shared their enthusiasm about the priest's potential as a radio star. Coughlin's inaugural broadcast took place on Sunday afternoon, October 17, 1926.

The reaction was more than promising. Indeed, to describe what happened over the next few years as a sensation would be an understatement. Coughlin rapidly became the number-one radio celebrity in North America. At first, his program, the *Golden Hour*, was broadcast in twenty-three states. Then, as his popularity exploded, the CBS national network picked up the show.

"Within three weeks," writes Coughlin's biographer Donald Warren, "so many letters to the radio priest arrived that fifty-five clerks were needed to process the mail. After a year, another forty clerks were hired and a new post office was constructed in Royal Oak solely for coping with the bags of mail arriving almost daily for the Shrine of the Little Flower. In an average week, eighty thousand letters were delivered to Coughlin's church." Many of those letters contained one-dollar donations to the Radio League of the Little Flower, his on-air congregation, from listeners who were thus assured of salvation. So much money was sent in that it had to be "carried in gunnysacks to the bank," as one congregant later remembered. When critics complained to CBS about the anti-Semitic tone of Coughlin's remarks – he commonly referred to the power of "international financiers," his euphemism for Jews – and his office publicized this fact, CBS received close to 350,000 letters supporting him.

What accounted for his astonishing appeal? Coughlin was a brilliant and persuasive orator with as, one contemporary writer called it, "a beautiful baritone" voice. But his almost hypnotic allure owed more to his instincts and the way he constructed his radio talks. Radio, he said, "must not be high hat. It must be human, intensely human. It must be simple."

Coughlin created a unique relationship with his audience by using words and images ordinary people could relate to and understand. "What occurred," explains Warren, "was a special reciprocity between speaker and listener. To an uncanny degree, Charles Coughlin constructed a personal bond between himself and each listener. The result was the transcendence of physical, social, and denominational distance: Coughlin had built an electronic neighbourhood."

As the Depression dawned, this mixture of politics, religion, and entertainment found a large audience growing more desperate, without hope and more than willing to blame any scapegoat he could offer them. First, it was the "Red Menace" of communism, and then it was the communists and the Jews, who were responsible for the stock market crash. In one of his more famous radio sermons, "Prosperity," broadcast in mid-January 1931, the enemy to be feared, he declared, was "Karl Marx, a Hebrew." In time, his virulent anti-Semitism proved his downfall as he later supported the Nazis, viewing their persecution of Jews as a necessary "defence mechanism against Communism."

Yet in a radio career that spanned seventeen years, Coughlin's ideas had prejudiced millions of people. The real culprit, argued journalist Malcolm Bingay of the *Detroit Free Press*, among other critics, was the radio. "One of the great problems before our Civilization today is the sinister insidiousness of the radio," he wrote in a column in 1933. "Long after Coughlin has passed out of the picture . . . the insidious radio will still be before the people. . . . It steals into the home with its whispered words, coming from no man knows where. It is a voice and it is gone. There is no record. There is no permanent printed word. The poison of the demagogue, of the atheist, the communist, and the lecherous fills the air of the home and is gone, leaving its stain."

Bingay's harsh critique of the radio was more accurately an indictment of the way in which the mass media had changed day-to-day life. The car had made North Americans increasingly mobile. More creative and slicker advertising – a billion-dollar industry in the U.S. by 1927 – had sold them on a wide array of products they now believed they could not live without. They had been linked through the intimacy and shared experience of the radio, and it made them more curious and more demanding. Newspapers, too, were forced to respond to this new medium with more gossip, sensationalism, stories about crime – the more shocking and bloodier the better – and celebrity profiles with as much sex and mayhem as reporters could uncover or invent. These all came together in the tabloid press of the 1920s.

The Public Is Even More Fond of Entertainment

Early on the morning of May 20, 1927, a shy and skinny pilot, who grew up in Little Falls, Minnesota, took off from a field near New York City in a small plane called *The Spirit of St. Louis*. Thirty-four hours later, Charles Lindbergh reached his destination: Le Bourget Field in Paris. He had become the first person successfully to fly solo non-stop across the Atlantic. Not only was he entitled to the twenty-five thousand dollars in prize money offered by New York hotel owner Raymond Orteig to the first person to accomplish this difficult feat, but he became, too, an instant hero and celebrity – the original media-created superstar.

In Paris, a frenzied crowd of more than one hundred thousand greeted him. Journalists and radio broadcasters everywhere hailed him as a courageous adventurer, a man who had conquered the elements and embodied goodness in an era that many considered sinful.

"What is the greatest story of all time?" the *New York Times* editors asked in one of their numerous articles on Lindbergh's exploits. "Adam eating the apple? The landing of the Ark on Arat? The discovery of Moses in the bulrushes? . . . But Lindbergh's flight, the suspense of it, the daring of it, the triumph of the glory of it . . . these are the stuff that makes immortal news."

In the days that followed, Lindbergh was the number-one story in the western world. More than 250,000 newspaper stories were written about him, and he was acclaimed in hundreds of radio broadcasts.

Thereafter, his life was altered. He merely tolerated the adulation at first. But later, especially after his infant son, Charles Jr., was kidnapped and killed in 1932 – a German immigrant Bruno Hauptmann was executed for the child's murder in 1936, despite his insistence that he was innocent – Lindbergh detested his celebrity status. Publishers, editors, reporters, and columnists, particularly those who toiled in New York City, had no choice but to cover his every move they claimed. The competition for business and advertising was intense, and Charles Lindbergh, whether he liked it or not, sold a lot of newspapers.

By the early 1920s, there were close to two thousand daily newspapers in the United States, all vying for more and more readers. How to attract them and keep them loyal became the greatest challenge for the press barons of the era. There was no one more successful at this than William Randolph Hearst.

Privately, he was shy and aloof – a "lonely soul," as journalist Lincoln Steffens described him in a 1906 profile – but in public there was no greater self-promoter. He had served two terms in Congress in the first years of the twentieth century and had sought the Democratic Party's presidential nomination in 1904, which he desperately desired. He had, however, too many enemies. Instead, he governed a vast empire of twenty-two newspapers from San Francisco to Boston and a stable of the most popular magazines in the country, including *Cosmopolitan*, *Good Housekeeping*, and *Harper's Bazaar*. His publicists declared that one out of every four families in the United States read a Hearst publication. It cost an estimated $90 million annually to produce these papers, which generated profits in excess of $12 million. For Hearst, this was not nearly enough money. He was extravagant, spending millions of dollars on prime real estate and expensive art. He lived in a spectacular Spanish-colonial-style castle outside of San Francisco called San Simeon. It came with its own movie theatre with seating for fifty and a private zoo, where he kept giraffes, zebras, and ostriches, among other animals.

Hearst had married his wife, Millicent, a former Brooklyn chorus girl, in 1903, and together they had five sons. He considered himself a devoted husband and father. Yet from about 1919 onward, when he was fifty-two years old, he carried on a very public affair with Marion Davies, a stunning *Ziegfeld Follies* singer and dancer. She was eighteen when they met and remained Hearst's mistress until he died in 1951. It was mainly due to his affection for Davies that Hearst bought a Hollywood film studio in 1919. He wanted to make her a movie star, and he nearly succeeded.[*]

From the moment his father, George, a self-made millionaire, had permitted him to take charge of the *San Francisco Examiner* in 1887 when he was only twenty-four years old, Hearst had understood that newspaper readers wanted to be informed, amused, and, perhaps most importantly, surprised. "The public," he said in 1896, "is even more fond of entertainment than it is of information." As the proprietor of the *Examiner* and then the *New York Journal*, his most

---

[*] Millicent Hearst learned of the affair in the early 1920s. She and Hearst never divorced, but after 1925 they did lead separate lives. When Hearst and Marion entertained at San Simeon, he insisted that his guests, usually moguls and stars from Hollywood, follow certain cardinal rules. As actor David Niven later recalled, for those guests staying overnight there were three important ones: "'No drunkenness,' 'No bad language or off-colour jokes,' and above all 'No sexual intercourse between unmarried couples.'" Adds Niven, "This last was a strange piece of Puritanism from a man living openly with his mistress, but it was rigorously enforced."

important newspaper, which he acquired in 1895, he insisted that his reporters be as creative as possible. If that meant stretching the truth a little or altering a photograph, so be it. Headlines were always in large type, and long before tabloids were on the scene, Hearst newspapers played up crime, scandal, and celebrity personalities.

"An ideal morning edition to [Hearst]," one critic suggested in a *Collier's* magazine article of September 1906, "would have been one in which the Prince of Wales had gone into vaudeville, Queen Victoria had married her cook, the Pope had issued an encyclical favouring free love . . . France had declared war on Germany, the President of the United States had secured a divorce in order to marry the Dowager Empress of China . . . and the Sultan of Turkey had been converted to Christianity – all of these being 'scoops' in the form of 'signed statements.'"

Another source of amusement was the Sunday "funnies." Hearst's newspapers were pioneers in innovative colour comics – especially after he lured away cartoonist Richard Outcault, the creator of the enormously popular comic strip the "Yellow Kid" from his chief rival, Joseph Pulitzer, publisher of the *New York World*. Not to be outdone, Pulitzer hired another cartoonist, George Luks, to draw the same comic so that each Sunday New York newspaper reader got a double dose of the "Yellow Kid." In the circulation war that ensued, the epithet "yellow journalism" (mocking the comic strip) soon came to describe newspaper sensationalism and cutthroat-style competition in general.

"Yellow journalism" soon reached new heights with Hearst's coverage of the Spanish-American War in 1898, perhaps his most famous (or infamous) journalistic exploit. He had decided some time before the conflict that Spain was guilty of committing atrocities in its rule of Cuba. The facts were beside the point. "Everything is quiet. There is no trouble here. There will be no war. I wish to return," cabled *New York Journal* reporter Frederick Remington from Cuba in early 1897. "Please remain," Hearst replied. "You furnish the pictures and I'll furnish the war." A year later, when the U.S. battleship *Maine* mysteriously blew up in Havana Harbor – likely triggered by an accident or a mine – Hearst's headlines raged against the evil Spanish enemy and contributed to President William McKinley's declaration of war. "Hearst's coverage of the *Maine* disaster," argued one of his biographers, W.A. Swanberg, "still stands as the orgasmic acme of ruthless, truthless, newspaper jingoism."

Hearst always fancied himself more of a muckraker in search of corruption and exploitation than a mere purveyor of sensational and gossipy news. Perhaps that was one of the reasons he initially refused to create his own tabloid. This smaller-format newspaper, filled with stories about murder, sex, and scandal, was imported from Britain. By 1909, the most popular tabloid in London was Alfred Harmsworth's (later Lord Northcliff) halfpenny *Daily Mirror*, which boasted a daily circulation of close to one million. A decade later, cousins Joseph Medill Patterson and Robert McCormick, the publishers of the *Chicago Tribune*, introduced the tabloid to New York City with their *Daily News*, an instant hit with readers. Unlike many newspapers, the *News* featured photographs to enthrall their readers – most of whom were women.

"Think in terms of pictures," Patterson had instructed his editors. And it worked. As the *News'* daily circulation hovered near half a million copies, Hearst reluctantly conceded that this style of paper was not, in fact, a "passing fad," as he had argued. In 1924, after nearly a year of planning, he launched his own tabloid, the *Mirror*. Yet despite a concerted effort, as well as plenty of hype, the *Mirror's* circulation trailed that of the *News*.[*] Three months later, both tabloids were

---

[*] In 1925, the *Mirror* sponsored a contest for the "homeliest girl" in New York City. Many women sent in photographs and readers chose the winner: An "Italian seamstress who aspired to be an opera diva. Her prize was free plastic surgery and an audition."

challenged by a third and even more racy and *outré* paper, the *Evening Graphic*.

Owned by Bernarr Macfadden, who had made millions with his women's magazine *True Story*, the *Graphic* was in a class by itself. "Don't tell my mother I'm working on the *Graphic*," went the joke told by New York reporters. "She thinks I'm a piano player in a whorehouse." Often referred to as the "porno-*Graphic*," its stories of sex and crime – along with provocative and usually faked photos (or "composographs," as they were called) of bodybuilders and under-dressed women – were too much for some newsstand owners, who would not stock the tabloid, as well as the city's librarians, who refused to display it on the New York Library's newspaper racks. Many businesses (apart from its mainstay, used-furniture salesmen) were reluctant to purchase advertising space in it.

Macfadden, a bodybuilder himself, was not troubled by the critical reaction or the loss of money (his magazine profits sustained him). "Sensationalism is nothing more than a clear, definitive, attractive presentation of the news," he said, "and is perfectly proper as long as one adheres to the truth."[*] Nevertheless, it was at the *Graphic* where the entertainment columnist Walter Winchell first learned the gossip trade – before Hearst convinced him to jump to the *Mirror* in 1930 – and became a household name with his vivid and often lurid tales about "mistresses, 'secret' rendezvous, lavish weddings, spectacular funerals, society events . . . sports and entertainment." (Later the television host Ed Sullivan also wrote for the *Graphic*.)

Here, for example, was how, Winchell depicted the "Real Broadway" in a piece he wrote for the journal *Bookman* in 1927: "As a standard of moral comparison [Broadway] is at once an enticement and a hell, a Circe's caravan of lascivious and soul destroying delights,

---

[*] In 1927, the New York Society for the Suppression of Vice, as historian John Stevens notes, "charged Macfadden with publishing pictures of 'bloodshed, lust and crime.' . . . The judge called the paper 'disgusting' but eventually dismissed the charges."

an unholy place where producers are the seducers of women, where stars without talent are made meretriciously overnight, where pure girls succumb to rich admirers for diamond brooches, furs, imported automobiles, apartments and other luxuries – a Babylon, a Sodom and Gomorrah all within the confines of a garish district extending from just below Forty-second Street to Columbus Circle at Fifty-ninth."

The tabloids tried to outdo each other in sensationalism, stunts, lotteries, contests, and chronicles of crime. "Slain, Beheaded, Left Nude, In Woods," blared the *Daily News* on August 27, 1927. "Drown Boy for $140,000," ran another headline a few days later. And so on. With a daily readership of more than one million by the fall of 1926, the *News* paid a minimum of fifty cents for each tip it received, regardless of the information. By 1927, the paper was spending one thousand dollars a week for leads.

In some quarters the tabloids were denounced as the "black plague" of American journalism. The blatant distortion of news – in which everything was "all murder, divorce, crime, passion, and chicanery" – preyed upon the exploitable, and contributed to the erosion of morals. Even for a generally hard-nosed business tycoon like Hearst, the stories of his Hollywood friends in the *Mirror* became a problem. After one especially gossipy piece about Gloria Swanson, he wrote to his editor Phillip Payne, "Please Phil be more kindly to people and try to make friends with them. Nearly everybody I know is weeping on my shoulder because of the way the *Mirror* roasts them. Can you not get some good natured reporters on staff?"[*]

---

[*] During the time of Charles Lindbergh's flight, Hearst had sponsored his own contest to fly the Atlantic non-stop from New York to Rome. Phil Payne decided that he would join an aircrew and attempt the journey in Hearst's own plane, *Old Glory*. Hearst opposed the plan since he did not believe his plane could handle such a flight. But Payne insisted. Tragically, the plane, with Payne on board, crashed into the Atlantic Ocean, killing all the passengers. As David Nasaw notes in his biography, "Hearst, deeply embarrassed and ashamed that the life of his editor had been lost in so obvious a circulation stunt published his correspondence with Payne (in which he tried to stop him from taking the trip) in the [New York] *American*."

Yet Hearst's readers – workers, housewives, and young single women – could not get enough of the smut, dirt, and sexual shenanigans of the rich and famous. One fan of the tabloids, a New York department store publicist, explained the abiding fascination like this: "These people (95 per cent of the population) are intensely human. . . . They tread the daily grind in the home, the office, the workshop; but they are potential adventurers. . . . And the tabloids dish up to them, every day, food which keeps alive an unexpressed part of their nature, makes them feel they belong in the human chorus, though not in the spotlight." A sure sign, moreover, of the power and influence of the tabloids was when such newspapers as the *New York Times* began covering some of the same crime stories, which in earlier years its editors would have ignored.

Three trials, in particular, during the twenties received excessive and gratuitous coverage in the tabloids and the mainstream press, capturing the attention of millions of North Americans. In many ways, this fascination epitomized the moral tone of the decade and anticipated the future.

In mid-September 1922, the bloody bodies of forty-one-year-old Reverend Edward Hall, a pastor of the Episcopal Church of St. John, and thirty-four-year-old Mrs. Eleanor Mills, his choir director, were discovered in a country lane near New Brunswick, N.J. The two had been shot to death. Around Mrs. Mills's throat was a blood-soaked brown silk scarf. A white Panama hat covered Rev. Hall's face. Both victims were married. There were pieces of shredded paper beside them, later determined to be love letters. In one, as the tabloids reported, Mrs. Mills was claimed to have written, "Oh honey, I am fiery today. Burning, flaming love." In another, she implored the reverend to call her "Babykins."

While evidence of their four-year tryst emerged, no one was initially charged with the crime, although suspicion fell on their jealous spouses. Not satisfied and sensing a dramatic story of love, betrayal, and murder, reporters from the *Mirror* and the *Daily News* probed the case for four years until they finally succeeded in discovering evidence of a murder plot. Rev. Hall's wife, Frances, her brothers, Henry and Willie Stevens, and their cousin, broker Henry Carpender, were brought to trial. The legal proceedings provided the tabloids – as well as the *New York Times*, which reported the case in great detail – with melodramatic fodder for weeks. As one of the *Graphic*'s bold headlines put it, so aptly capturing the mood of the day, "Hall Tragedy Shows Judgement Awaits All Who Sin."

There were accusations of payoffs, rumours that the reverend intended to divorce his wife and run off with Mrs. Mills, and stories about conspiracies. By far the most bizarre moment in the trial was the testimony of Mrs. Jane Gibson, a pig farmer, who was referred to in the press as the "pig woman." Supposedly near death (in fact, she lived for another three years), she was brought into the courtroom on a stretcher and questioned while she lay on a bed supervised by nurses. She claimed she had seen Willie and Henry Stevens and Henry Carpender kill the couple. Then she had watched Mrs. Hall cry over her husband's body. "I have told the truth, so help me God, and you know I've told the truth!" she shouted to the jury as she was carried from the room. But the jury did not believe her and the defendants were acquitted. The murders remained unsolved.[*]

The second case was less gruesome, but more salacious. It revolved around the escapades of Edward Browning, a fifty-two-year-old millionaire real estate magnate who was obsessed with teenage girls. In March 1926, Browning, later nicknamed "Daddy," in the papers, met Frances Belle "Peaches" Heenan, a fifteen-year-old

---

[*] After extensive research, the attorney William Kunstler believed that the murders had been carried out by local members of the Ku Klux Klan. Another theory has been advanced by Mary Hartman, a crime historian, who "is persuaded by the confession of a dying man in 1970 that on the day after the murders he delivered $6,000 from Mrs. Hall to two local hoodlums. While the man claimed he knew nothing about the arrangements, he said Willie Stevens had tried earlier to recruit him in a plan to get rid of the minister."

beauty. And thus began the Daddy Browning and Peaches saga. Browning was not sure if he wanted to adopt Heenan or wed her. He opted for the latter. Several weeks after their first encounter, and with the full support of Heenan's mother, who wanted only the best for her daughter, a Justice of the Peace in Cold Spring, New York, married them.

As soon as the tabloids learned of the relationship, it was front-page news. The situation only got more delicious when six months later Heenan filed for separation on grounds of mental and emotional abuse – including "sexual perversion." "Peaches' Shame!" read the headline on Hearst's *Mirror*, followed by "Oh!-Oh!-Oh! Daddy Browning." The *Graphic* topped this with a series of controversial composographs picturing Heenan scantily clad and Browning in his pyjamas with the caption, "Woof! Woof! Don't Be A Goof!" In another, Browning, dressed like a sheik, says to Heenan, cowering on the floor in her nightgown, "You'll have to be satisfied with this, Baby Doll!"

There were stories, too, that Heenan had refused Browning's order "to parade nude." Remarkably, the editors of the *Daily Express* thought the situation had gone too far and worried that such sordid tales would leave the public "drenched in obscenity." The saga finally ended in March 1927, when a judge ruled that Browning had been "taken in" by the mother-daughter duo. The two had been attempting essentially to extort Browning's millions.

The last case received even more coverage. More, it was said, than the sinking of the *Titanic*. Indeed, it may have been the most written-about incident of the decade, creating a media frenzy like no other. On the first day of the trial, "fifteen Western Union operators transmitted 62,711 words from two press rooms." And on one occasion, the *Daily News* devoted the first fourteen pages of its edition to the story.

It began on March 19, 1927, in Long Island, New York, when Albert Snyder, the editor of *Motor Boating* magazine, was murdered.

He had been bashed on the head with a window-sash weight. His wife, Ruth, was found tied up beside the body. She claimed they had been robbed and that the burglars had killed her husband. The problem was that Ruth's jewellery, which had been supposedly stolen, was soon discovered tucked under a mattress. It did not take the police much time to uncover the truth: Ruth Snyder, thirty-two, "a chilly-looking blonde with frosty eyes and one of those marble, you-bet-you-will chins" – in the words of the flamboyant journalist Damon Runyon – and determined to enjoy the "good life," had carried out the killing with her accomplice and lover, Judd Gray, a dull-witted thirty-three-year-old corset salesman. Gray was a man who did what he was told (at Ruth's insistence he called her "Mommie"). He had hidden in the closet and attacked Snyder. Then Ruth had finished the job, strangling her husband with picture wire. The police also learned that a month or so before the murder, Ruth had taken out a forty-eight-thousand-dollar life-insurance policy on Albert, which had a double-indemnity clause. (The case later inspired the popular films *Double Indemnity* as well as *The Postman Always Rings Twice*, both based on novels by James Cain.)

Once they were apprehended, each confessed but blamed the other. Gray, a meek man, claimed he had been manipulated by the domineering Ruth with "drink, veiled threats, and intensive love." Needless to say, when the case finally came to trial, hundreds of reporters descended on the courthouse in Long Island City. For days there was literally nothing else to read in the tabloids other than the details of Ruth Snyder and Judd Gray's machinations – and the countless mistakes they had made (Gray's tie clip was found at the crime scene) which left a trail a child could have figured out. Runyon and others called their nefarious deed the "Dumbbell Murder." Such notable public figures as Rev. John Roach Straton, evangelist Billy Sunday, historian W.E. Woodward, and philosopher Will Durant all commented on the case and offered their theories on Ruth Snyder's motives.

Both Snyder and Gray were found guilty and sentenced to die by the electric chair on January 12, 1928, at Sing Sing Prison. The tabloids, however, were not to be denied. The *Daily News* gave Tom Howard, a *Chicago Tribune* photographer not known to New York prison authorities, the assignment of obtaining a picture of Snyder's execution. She was to be the first woman put to death in this manner. Showing a lot of guile, Howard attached a miniature camera to his ankle with a long shutter release that went up his pant leg into his pocket. He gained access to the execution and then just as the executioner pulled the switch, he snapped a photograph. The next day, to an outcry of horror mixed with fascination, the grisly shot ran on the front page of the *Daily News* with the large bold-faced headline: "DEAD!"

The *News* could not keep up with demand for the paper. It was a sure sign that modern journalistic practices would never be the same. For better or worse, acceptable ethics and standards of morality were changing. As future generations would learn, the public's craving for scandalous, sensational, and sordid stories would rarely be satisfied.

CHAPTER SEVEN

Sex, Flappers, and a Shimmy

Previous page: The cover illustration of *LIFE* magazine, February 18, 1926. It was the age of the flapper. Many young women were not content merely to dance – although they soon made the Charleston their trademark jive. They also began wearing looser and shorter dresses, using cosmetics, smoking in public, driving alone in their automobiles, attending hops, proms, and ball games, and talking openly about sex.

Babbitt had heard stories of . . . "goings-on" at young parties; of girls "parking" their corsets in the dressing-room, of "cuddling" and "petting" and a presumable increase in what was known as Immorality.

– Sinclair Lewis, Babbitt (1922)

The Suppression of Vice

In early April 1895, New Yorkers, like everyone else in North America, were shocked to read in the papers that the popular British playwright Oscar Wilde had been charged with "gross indecency" for corrupting young Alfred Douglas, the son of the influential Marquess of Queensberry. After discovering "love" letters Wilde had written to his son, the Marquess had publicly declared Wilde a "sodomite." At the New York theatre where Wilde's play *An Ideal Husband* was then being performed, his name was deleted from all programmes and advertisements. In St. Louis, the city's chief librarian ordered that Wilde's literary works be removed from the stacks. Six weeks later, the "disgrace" and "depravity," as the *New York Times* called it, was confirmed when Wilde was found guilty and sentenced to two years of imprisonment with hard labour.[*]

---

[*] Wilde died in poverty in London at the age of forty-six on December 1, 1900. Alfred Douglas was by his side.

The reaction to the Wilde case was hardly surprising. Many North Americans may not have subscribed to moral crusader Anthony Comstock's view that lust was evil and "the boon companion of all other crimes," yet most would have shared his strongly held belief that homosexuality or "inversion," as it was called, was vile and perverted.[*]

Sexual inversion was considered by many physicians, including the influential German sexual psychologist Richard von Krafft-Ebing (1840–1902), to be an abnormality possibly linked to young girls' sharing the same bed and excessive masturbation or autoerotism in boys. Even Sigmund Freud, who had gained some critical notoriety with the publication of several significant works on hysteria, dream analysis, and psychotherapy and sex, suggested that male homosexuality was an acquired condition, the result of an "unsuccessful resolution of the Oedipus complex."

Early twentieth century North Americans may not have been entirely Victorian in their outlook about sexual issues, but most husbands and wives refrained from speaking openly about what went on in their bedrooms. The typical middle-class marriage tended to be chaste; sexual intercourse was for conceiving children, nothing more. In short, pleasure for either partner had little to do with it, but especially for the woman. If a husband craved something more

---

* In some parts of the United States, this view has remained firm for more than a century, despite the general acceptance of gay rights in North America and Europe. It was not until June 2003 that the U.S. Supreme Court in a 6-3 decision struck down a Texas law banning sodomy between same-sex couples, in effect ending all anti-sodomy laws in the thirteen states in which they still existed. Still, as Justice Antonin Scalia wrote for the minority: "Many Americans do not want persons who openly engage in homosexual conduct as partners in their business, as scoutmasters for their children, as teachers in their children's schools. . . . They view this as protecting themselves and their families from a lifestyle that they believe to be immoral and destructive." In Canada, on the other hand, federal anti-sodomy laws were revoked in 1969 and provincial governments passed laws prohibiting discrimination based on sexuality in the 1970s and 1980s. In June 2003, the federal government gave legal sanction to same-sex marriages, setting off protests in some conservative quarters.

exciting, he could sneak away to a burlesque show or visit a brothel. He knew full well that his wife, dutiful and obedient, perhaps educated but content to stay home, would be there to serve his needs.

This was, after all, an era when many people still considered the display of nude statues in museums or paintings and posters depicting nudes outrageous. Anthony Comstock had been fighting such vulgarity for much of his illustrious career. At his peak, in the late nineteenth and early years of the twentieth centuries, Comstock looked the part of a man with a serious mission. Square, stocky, and bald with reddish whiskers, he is remembered today for his puritanical fanaticism, pro-censorship mentality, and his battle with birth-control advocate Margaret Sanger.

In his own lifetime, however, Comstock was seen in a much more positive light, as a dedicated, even progressive, reformer who devoted decades to protecting children and society from the evils of obscenity – as he and others defined it. His career points to the difficulties in determining precisely who was a traditionalist and who was a modernist.

Comstock was born in 1844 in the town of New Canaan, Connecticut. For a time his father operated a profitable farm, but he encountered business problems during the Civil War and lost the property. Comstock's mother died when he was still a young boy. In the last part of the war, he enlisted in the Union Army, but did not see much military action. He had by then adopted a religious demeanour and did not drink alcohol. He also refused to pass on his ration of whisky to his fellow soldiers, a decision that did not endear him to them. When the war ended in 1865, he journeyed to New York City, got married, and found a job as a clerk in a dry-goods store.

Comstock found his true calling in the late 1860s. One of his friends, after purchasing an obscene book, visited a brothel where he contracted a venereal disease. Comstock had the bookseller arrested, and the link between obscenity, lust, disease, and sin were forever cemented in his mind. It was classic cause and effect: The obscene material excited the passions, which led to a visit to a saloon, gambling house, or "house of ill-fame." Disease or abortions (illegal at the time) were the result of this wicked behaviour. As he explained in an article he wrote in 1892, if one "combine[s] intemperance with evil reading, it is an influence more to be dreaded than the microbes of smallpox, scarlet fever or Asiatic cholera."

In the early 1870s, Comstock became associated with the New York branch of the Young Men's Christian Association (YMCA), which was undertaking a campaign against obscenity. He detested the city for its perpetuation of sexual immorality. Through his involvement with the YMCA, Comstock met Morris Jessup, a wealthy merchant and financier who helped him organize a YMCA Committee for the Suppression of Vice. Two years later, this group declared its independence, becoming the influential and powerful New York Society for the Suppression of Vice. Comstock would be its leader and main promoter for the next forty years.

Next, he lobbied politicians in Washington who shared his concern about obscenity and passed what became known as the Comstock Law. The act, which became section 211 of the U.S. Penal Code, banned the sale and distribution of "lewd" and "lascivious" and "indecent" books, pamphlets, and literature, including information "or any article or thing designed or intended for the prevention of contraception or the procuring of abortion." Twenty-two states followed the federal government's lead and instituted their own Comstock-like laws.

As a reward, Congress made Comstock a special agent for the U.S. post office. He was relentless in his new position and boasted that in nine years, between 1873 and 1882, he "confiscated fourteen tons of books and sheet stock and a million and a half obscene circulars, poems and pictures." In the same period, he had nearly one hundred people arrested for advertising or selling contraceptives ("indecent rubber articles") and for providing advice on obtaining abortions.

Ole Hanson, the mayor of Seattle, in 1919. A well-known opponent of radicalism, Hanson ruthlessly combated the brief general strike in Seattle in February 1919.

A group of deputies receiving weapons on February 6, 1919, during the Seattle General Strike. When the strike ended four days later, the Seattle *Star* declared, "Today this Bolshevik-sired nightmare is over."

The Winnipeg General Strike on "Bloody Saturday," June 21, 1919. Deputized "specials" wait at the corner of Market Avenue and Main Street. Note the wooden clubs in their hands as they prepare to meet the strikers and their supporters.

The North-West Mounted Police in action during the Winnipeg General Strike. They rode into the crowd several times on "Bloody Saturday," swinging clubs and firing their guns. Several people were hit and killed in the ensuing melee.

Samuel Bronfman at age thirty. Canada's greatest whisky merchant, he made a fortune during the Prohibition era.

Al Capone, in May 1932, smoking a cigar on the train carrying him to the federal penitentiary in Atlanta, where he will start serving a ten-year jail sentence for tax evasion. Capone established one of the most infamous and feared underworld organizations in U.S. history and made millions of dollars during Prohibition. "I make my money by supplying a public demand," he declared in 1928. "If I break the law, my customers, who number hundreds of the best people in Chicago, are as guilty as I am."

By the miracle of radio, an "anxious wife" receives a reassuring personal message about her husband's whereabouts. Within a matter of years, listening to the radio had become the most popular pastime in North America and altered work and leisure habits forever.

William Aberhart, Calgary preacher and politician and the founder of the Social Credit Party in Canada. Aberhart (shown here behind a radio microphone in the early 1930s) discovered the power of the radio for broadcasting his religious and political messages.

Radio evangelist and faith-healer Aimee Semple McPherson, in London, c. 1930. With her fashionable dresses and stylishly bobbed hair, she was the most modern of evangelists. McPherson cherished her rural roots and traditional values, while also seizing the opportunity to become one of North America's first media sensations.

Radio evangelist Father Charles Coughlin. For a time, Father Coughlin was the most popular personality in North America. He portrayed himself as a champion of freedom and democracy and a "solitary fighter" against the bigotry of the Ku Klux Klan. In fact, he used his enormous popularity as the "Radio Messiah" to spread his narrow definition of morality, which came mixed with a healthy dose of anti-Semitism.

Aviator Charles Lindbergh in his airplane at Lambert–St. Louis Field in April 1923. When Lindbergh flew alone from New York to Paris in 1927, he became the number-one news story in the Western world. More than 250,000 newspaper stories were written about him and he was acclaimed in hundreds of radio broadcasts.

The front page of the *New York Daily News* on January 13, 1928, devoted entirely to a photograph of Ruth Snyder's execution by electric chair at Sing Sing prison. Tom Howard got the photograph for the *News*. He used a miniature camera attached to his ankle with a long shutter release that went up his pant leg into his pocket.

Margaret Sanger, the U.S. birth-control advocate, c. 1920. "I was resolved to seek out the root of evil, to do something to change the destiny of mothers whose miseries were as vast as the sky," she wrote in her autobiography. She later claimed dramatically that she intended to "awaken the womanhood of America to free the motherhood of the world!"

The comedic actor Fatty Arbuckle. The San Francisco Police took this mug shot after Arbuckle's arrest in 1921 on charges that he was criminally responsible for the death of chorus girl Virginia Rappé.

Will Hays in the 1920s. The former postmaster general in the Republican administration of Warren Harding, Hays was chosen by the Hollywood movie moguls to head the Motion Picture Producers and Distributors Association. He had the next-to-impossible job of ensuring that motion pictures conformed to community standards.

The actress Claudette Colbert, playing a Roman empress, bathing in milk on the film set of *The Sign of the Cross* in 1932. Director Cecil B. De Mille used 500 gallons of real milk for the bath. The hot studio lights curdled the milk, but despite the stench Colbert persevered.

Crowds gather outside the New York Stock Exchange following the Crash of October 1929. Franklin Delano Roosevelt tried to reassure Americans in his presidential inaugural address in January 1933 that the "only thing we have to fear is fear itself." His words had little effect.

He remained vigilant until the day he died, in 1915, and claimed he was responsible for the convictions "of enough persons to fill a passenger train of sixty-one coaches, sixty of which contained sixty passengers each with the sixty-first half full." But his main failing, as Arthur Schlesinger noted many years ago, was that Comstock would not "distinguish between pornography on the one hand and literary classics and medical treatises on the other." He also engineered the arrest of many physicians who were legitimately assisting needy women with information about contraception. In one case, Comstock went after a doctor for helping two women in this manner, one of whom had a husband who infected her with syphilis. Thanks in large part to Comstock's influence and testimony, the doctor was sentenced to six years at Leavenworth Penitentiary.

Upper and middle-class Americans cheered Comstock's efforts; they sent his organization money. Merchants, judges, clergymen, publishers, bankers, skilled workers, and representatives from such women's groups as the Woman's Christian Temperance Union (WCTU) and the League of American Mothers were among his supporters and benefactors. It was a broad cross-section of the population, mainly based in New York, but from other cities and towns as well. These individuals had come to the same conclusion as Comstock: that saving American youth from the corruption and immorality of the city was of paramount importance. Progress, in this case, did not mean tolerance and free speech, but rather censorship and repression.

Often working side by side with Comstock, the WCTU's Department for the Promotion of Purity in Literature and Art also led a vigorous pro-censorship campaign against the proliferation of vice, pornographic books, lewdness in novels, Sunday newspaper comic strips, suggestive dancing, and nudity in theatre and motion pictures. "This Department of Purity . . . means much, because it touches directly the home, and the life connected with it," one member explained in 1908. "Our American home is the heart of our great country, and we must see to it, by our influence, that it is kept clean." Immorality in art or literature, as the women defined it, could mean everything from "suggestive and objectionable" to "vile," "salacious," and "pernicious." Hence reading a "trashy" novel was dangerous, said Mary West, the editor of the WCTU's journal, *Union Signal*, because "it engenders a dreamy sentimentalism which makes real work distasteful, thus leading to discontent with one's surroundings." Was there anything worse, West and other WCTU members asked, than allowing a young boy to get his hands on the racy *National Police Gazette*, filled with lurid stories and sketches of opium dens and burlesque houses?

In 1912, Comstock went after a prominent art dealer in New York City for showing a copy of Frenchman Paul Chabas's painting *September Morn*, because it had a nude woman in it.[*]

Until the 1920s, sex education in schools was non-existent. One New York City school superintendent, for example, commented that such instruction would bring about "spiritual havoc and physical ruin." As for masturbation, "the secret vice," as Comstock labelled it: the common view was it produced insanity, immorality, and deviant behaviour. Arthur Beall, who worked as a "purity agent" for the Ontario branch of the Woman's Christian Temperance Union and later as a morality lecturer for the provincial department of education for more than two decades starting in 1911, took special care to

---

[*] The public relations pioneer Harry Reichenbach later claimed in his memoirs that he brought the painting to Comstock's attention as a marketing gimmick. He was working for the art store, which had two thousand copies of the picture in stock. "It occurred to me," he wrote, "to introduce the immodest young maiden to Anthony Comstock. . . . At first he refused to jump at the opportunity to be shocked. I telephoned him several times, protesting against a large display of the picture, which I myself had installed in the window of the artshop. Then I arranged for other people to protest and at last I visited him personally." Comstock eventually took the bait. Once he brought the owner of the shop to court, demand for the reproduction soared and the art store sold all of its copies.

warn young boys on the evils of masturbation. A eugenics advocate, he admonished his charges to protect their "life fluid" since the consequences were severe – "mental bankruptcy" and the insane asylum.[*] At the end of each lecture, he would have the boys stand and declare, "The more you use the penis muscle, the weaker it becomes; but the less you use the penis muscle, the stronger it becomes!"

The Chief and Central Function of Life

Ask most people today which historical personality is most responsible for altering attitudes about sex and women and the odds are they would point to Sigmund Freud. In his own lifetime – he was born in Vienna in 1856 and died in 1939 in London after fleeing Nazi rule – his theories on sexuality were not without controversy and criticism. Still, as U.S. writer Ann Douglas points out, "the case studies he wrote of his early women patients, are, despite their shortcomings, the first vivid accounts of female sexuality in the modern era; indeed they could almost be said to have initiated the modern era."

It was not until 1908, at the first International Psychoanalytical Congress in Salzburg, that the medical and scientific community as a whole acknowledged Freud's significance. His one and only visit to the United States occurred a year later, when he spoke about psychoanalysis at Clark University in Worcester, Massachusetts. His lectures generated a fair degree of excitement among intellectuals, and soon his revolutionary theories about sexuality filtered down to the masses. But the process was gradual.

---

* One of Beall's favourite stories involved a boy from Perth County, Ontario, who was committed to an insane asylum. According to Beall, this boy "couldn't keep his hands off the MALE PART of his body – a half dozen times a day he was playing with it, and bleeding away the precious life fluid, until one day the doctors came along and cut off the two life glands, just to keep the miserable dregs of a miserable existence from all being frittered away. And there [in the asylum], after all these years, useless to God or man, he still exists as a bit of mental punk, a scrap of rotting refuse on life's highway."

It took until the mid- to late-twenties before popular writers and playwrights began to incorporate Freudian themes into their work and acknowledge that the desire for sex was a significant aspect of human existence. Freud was very evident, for example, in three of Eugene O'Neill's successful dramas of this period – *Desire Under the Elms* (1924), *Strange Interlude* (1928), and *Mourning Becomes Electra* (1931) – plays in which he explored such controversial sexual themes as incest and the relationship between mothers and sons. Soon, too, the middle-class ladies who read *Good Housekeeping* learned that their sexual natures demanded "every kind of sensory gratification. . . . If it gets its yearning it is as contented as a nursing infant. If it does not, beware! It will never be stopped except with satisfactions."

Freud was, however, not solely responsible for this intellectual and literary transformation. The British sexual theorist Havelock Ellis is barely spoken of today, but in many ways his contributions to shaping our attitudes about sex were more profound and lasting. Through his writings, Ellis was the catalyst for the twentieth century's sexual revolution. (Six of the seven volumes of his monumental *Studies in the Psychology of Sex* were completed between 1897 and 1910; the seventh was published in 1928.) More than anyone else, he grasped that, as he put it, "sex penetrates the whole person" and that a "man's sexual constitution is part of his general constitution." Sex was not immoral or a sin, Ellis argued; it was to be savoured and enjoyed by both men and women. Eroticism and passion were human emotions to be embraced, not restrained. What did women want? His answer was, "A more fulfilled sensual life." In his first book, *The New Spirit* (1890), he referred to sex as "the chief and central function of life . . . ever wonderful, ever lovely." It was a view from which he never wavered.

Ellis was born in Croydon, Surrey, in 1859, but grew up in South London. His father was a sea captain. The first real adventure of his life occurred at age sixteen, when he embarked on a trip that took him to Australia, where he remained for four years working as a teacher. When he returned to England, he studied medicine and in 1889 obtained a Licentiate in Medicine, Surgery and Midwifery from the Society of Apothecaries, "a somewhat inferior medical degree which always rather embarrassed him," according to his biographer Phyllis Grosskurth.

He was too much an intellectual to spend his life as a physician, and during the next decade established a writing career, publishing articles on philosophy, science, spiritualism, and literature. In 1891 he married the feminist Edith Lees, whom he probably knew was a lesbian. They were colleagues and companions, and had the most open marriage in London. They often lived apart and each had several affairs with women. He later documented Edith's homosexuality (anonymously) in *Sexual Inversion*, the first volume of his sexuality study published in 1897. Their relationship was not free of jealousy, yet they remained loyal to each other until Edith's death in 1916.

No one had ever approached the topic of sex in all of its many dimensions like Ellis did. He was the first to treat homosexuality as a congenital rather than pathological condition. He was a voice of common sense on the subject of masturbation for men and women – it was Ellis who coined the term "autoerotism" – examined sadism and masochism, questioned monogamy, and accepted that men visited prostitutes for "erotic adventure." Above all, he viewed women as sexual creatures with their own wants and needs separate from those of men.[*] In a Victorian world where the ideal woman took no pleasure from sex, this was a truly radical notion. Women, suggested Ellis,

---

[*] Ellis could not entirely escape his Victorian background. "He continued to believe," notes Paul Robinson, "that masturbation might result in slight nervous disorders. However, his essential objection to masturbation was not medical but moral: masturbation entailed in a particularly extreme form the divorce of the physical and psychological dimensions of sexual expression. Consequently, Ellis argued, extensive masturbation in childhood and adolescence might leave the masturbator incapable of associating sexuality with affection."

"have the law of their own nature; their development must be along their own lines, and not along masculine lines." (At the same time, he did regard women's prime function to be child-bearers and mothers, adding that, "in a certain sense, their brains are in their wombs.")

His volumes on sex were rarely bestsellers – in 1897, one of the few London booksellers brave enough to sell *Sexual Inversion* was arrested – and for many years his studies were marketed in Britain and North America only to physicians, lawyers, and other interested professionals. Still, he always considered himself a pioneer of the field (which may explain his jealousy of Freud's fame).

Margaret Sanger, the birth-control advocate, first met him in 1914 after she fled to England to escape her legal problems in the United States. "He seemed a giant in stature, a lovely, simple man in loose-fitting clothes, with powerful head and wonderful smile," she later recalled. "He was fifty-five then, but that head will never change – the shock of white hair, the venerable beard, shaggy though well-kept, the wide, expressive mouth and deep-set eyes, sad even in spite of the humorous twinkle always latent. I was conscious immediately that I was in the presence of a great man." Despite the age difference – she was then thirty-one years old – the attraction was instantaneous and within a few months they began an affair.

The Torrent of an Elemental Passion

Sanger's friends and supporters in the United States were also influenced and inspired by Freud and Ellis. Among them were Emma Goldman, Henrietta Rodman, Mabel Dodge Luhan, Floyd Dell, Neith Boyce, and Hutchins Hapgood. They made New York's Greenwich Village their own in the years before the First World War and lived like bohemians. The women preached free love, fought for birth control, "smoked in public, drank with men, discussed their dreams and 'complexes' and bobbed their hair. They were 'flappers' before the term was coined," writes historian Carolyn

Johnston. Even more than the suffragists, they saw themselves as the equal of men on the streets and in the bedroom. "Feminism," declared Henrietta Rodman, who helped establish the Feminist Alliance in 1914, "is a movement which demands the removal of all social, political, economic and other discriminations which are based on sex, and the ward of all rights and duties in all fields on the basis of individual capacity alone."

Both the men and the women subscribed to the British socialist dictum that "marriage shall mean friendship as well as passion." Yet there was no denying that "free love" and extramarital affairs caused jealousy and resentment. It was not always easy being a new woman or a modern man.

Mabel Dodge Luhan was one such new woman. Born in Buffalo in 1879, she grew up surrounded by wealth and privilege. By the time she was thirty-three years old, she had been married twice, lived in Florence, and become enamoured with Renaissance history and culture. When she separated from her second husband, Edwin Dodge, in 1912, she relocated to Greenwich Village and eventually convened the city's most famous salon at her Fifth Avenue apartment, where artists, philosophers, writers, and radicals debated and socialized.[*]

For three years, she carried on a torrid love affair with the socialist journalist John Reed. Despite her convictions about sexual freedom, she expected him to be faithful to her. When he was not, it deeply troubled her. "Reed & I love each other as much as any people can – that's why we torment each other so – but one of us has to give in on this," she confided to her friend the novelist Neith

---

[*] Mabel married two more times. Her third marriage was to post-Impressionist painter Maurice Sterne, whom she left in 1918 for Tony Luhan, a Pueblo Indian she met while on a trip to Taos, New Mexico. She envisioned Taos as a new Eden and created an artist and writers' colony at her home, where in later years D.H. Lawrence, Andrew Dasburg, Georgia O'Keeffe, and Leon Gaspard would visit. She died in Taos in 1962.

Boyce. "Yet if I didn't feel this & feel this important it would be because I would have him as I would a whore – indifferent to what he did so long as he doesn't deprive me of himself. . . . To him the sexual gesture has no importance, but infringing on his right to act freely has the first importance. Are we both right & both wrong – and how do such things end? Either way it kills love – it seems to me. This is so fundamental – is it what feminism is all about?"

Boyce was sympathetic. She, too, had an open marriage with journalist Hutchins Hapgood. "Both Hutch and I feel that we are free to love other people," she had told Dodge, "but that nothing can break or even touch the deep, vital, passionate bond between us that exists now as it always has." Her heart, however, often clashed with her intellectual principles. The so-called new morality that she and her husband had chosen to live their lives by caused her pain. "I have an abiding love for you – the deepest thing in me," she wrote to Hapgood. "But in a way I hate your interest in sex, because I have suffered from it. I assure you that I can never think of your physical passions for other women without pain – even though my reason doesn't find fault with you. But it's instinct and it hurts. The whole thing is sad and terrible, yet we all joke about it every day."

The elder of the group was Emma Goldman. She was more radical, wiser, and far less tolerant of middle-class aspirations than were many of her peers, but she suffered similar anxiety over the "great passion" of her life, Ben Reitman, as she later referred to him. Goldman epitomized the new attitudes about sex – or so she thought. She had several lovers and condemned marriage as "legalized prostitution." Was there anything more outrageous, she asked in a 1910 lecture, "than the idea that the healthy, grown woman full of life and passion must deny nature's demand, must subdue her most intense craving, undermine her health, and break her spirit, must stunt her vision, abstain from the depth and glory of sex experience until a 'good' man comes along to take her unto himself as a wife? That is precisely what marriage means."

Her avant-garde views on sex were shaped from attending Freud's lectures in Vienna in 1896 and from immersing herself in the writings of Havelock Ellis and Edward Carpenter. She never promoted promiscuity but maintained that whatever two people did in the privacy of their home was their own personal business. This included homosexuality, which she defended. In one of her popular lectures, "Sex, the Great Element of Creative Art," she echoed Freud by stressing how sexuality, which she saw as the key to understanding human existence, also played a pivotal role in the creative process. In another lecture, "Vice," she lambasted both the Church and the State for their futile efforts to establish moral standards. No fan of Anthony Comstock, she questioned the meaning of vice and the government's right to enforce it. "What is usually hastily condemned as vice by thoughtless individuals, such as homosexuality, masturbation, etc," she stated, "should be considered from a scientific viewpoint, and not in a moralizing way."

She met Ben Reitman in Chicago in 1908. He was twenty-nine years old; she was nearly thirty-nine. He was a former hobo from the Midwest who still enjoyed hopping the trains. Reitman had settled down long enough to obtain a medical degree from the College of Physicians and Surgeons of Chicago in 1904. He taught hygiene and public health at the Chicago Nurses' School, administered medical care to the poor, and campaigned for the prevention of venereal disease. From Goldman's perspective, he was also a good-looking man – charming, suave, and slightly naughty. The attraction was mutual, and for the next decade he consumed her. "I was caught in the torrent of an elemental passion I have never dreamed any man could rouse in me," she later wrote in her autobiography. "I responded shamelessly to its primitive call, its naked beauty, its ecstatic joy." He had shown her, as she put it, "the sublime madness of sex."

Often away from Reitman on her lecture tours, she wrote him steamy love letters. They developed their own lovers' code: "W" was for Reitman's "Willie," "t-b" for her "treasure box," "t" for tongue, and "M" for mountains – her breasts – nicknamed "Mount Blanc and Jura." She wrote to him in the summer of 1910, for example, as follows: "The day seems unbearable if I do not talk to you. I would prefer to do something else to you, to run a red hot velvety 't' over 'W' and the bushes, so Hobo would go mad with joy and ecstasy. . . . Oh for one s[uck] at that beautiful head of his, for one drink from that fountain of life. How I would press my lips to the fountain and drink every drop." In another letter written some months later, she told him she wished "I could love you as wildly as I please, as wildly as you make me when you drink the 't-b' dew and pluck the petal of the 'M' and give 'W' juice."

Her "savage passion" for Reitman also caused her much heartache. He refused to commit himself to her totally, and she refused to see that he could not be trusted. He shamelessly seduced other women, lied to her, and even stole money from funds raised at her lectures. At first, she dismissed his infidelity as a "disease for women" and a "pathological craving" that could be overlooked, perhaps cured. But he hurt her deeply. Goldman supported "free love," but not of the kind Reitman practised. Sex for her was tied to love, tenderness, and mutual respect, yet also without jealousy or recrimination. With Reitman, however, her passion was in constant conflict with her principles. On discovering that he had romanced women in every city and town they had visited together when he accompanied her on the lecture circuit, she was devastated. In time, these conflicted feelings drove her finally to separate from Reitman, although he remained in her heart for the rest of her life.

There was, as Goldman's biographer Alice Wexler observes, a fair degree of irony in her relationship with Reitman. "Publicly proclaiming the necessity of love and freedom in love," writes Wexler, "privately Emma took a certain pleasure in her erotic dependence on Reitman, even while fighting against it. . . . Portraying herself in her letters as 'weak and dependent,' she nonetheless remained in many respects the dominant partner in the relationship, socially, financially, and intellectually." Like the other Greenwich Village radicals, she was far more clear-headed on the subject of birth control.

To Free the Motherhood of the World

Margaret Sanger was born in 1883 in Corning, New York, to Anne and Michael Hennessy Higgins, the sixth of eleven children. She was only seventeen years old when her mother (who was forty-nine years old) died of tuberculosis and cervical cancer. Margaret always believed that poverty and long years of child-bearing caused her mother's early death. She became a nurse and began working with impoverished families in New York City's Lower East Side. "Very early in my childhood," she later recalled, "I associated poverty, toil, unemployment, drunkenness, cruelty, quarrelling, fighting, debts, jails with large families." She soon discovered there was a direct correlation between socio-economic status and knowledge about contraception: the less well off the woman, the more ignorant she was about the methods to prevent pregnancy. How, Sanger asked, could such a women experience sexual freedom and survive?

In 1902, following a brief courtship, she married William Sanger, a talented architect. During the next decade, they moved out of the city to the chic suburb of Hastings-on-the-Hudson and had three children. Such a middle-class lifestyle, however, did not suit her, and by 1911 the Sangers were back in New York in an apartment on 135th Street. Margaret immediately resumed her work as a nurse and entered the intellectual circle of the Greenwich Village radicals.

In those days, as later, she was irresistible. "Her green eyes were flecked with amber, her hair a shiny auburn hue, her smile always warm and charming, her hands perpetually in motion, beckoning even to strangers," historian Ellen Chesler says. "She had a quick Irish wit, high spirits, and radiant common sense. Men adored her."

And she welcomed the attention, eventually having affairs that created discord in her marriage.

The defining moment in her career, she said, took place in 1912 and involved a poor Russian-Jewish immigrant woman named Sadie Sachs and her husband, Jake. Sadie did not want any more children, and when she became pregnant again she tried to abort it herself. Jake found her bleeding and called the physician with whom Sanger worked. After Sadie had recovered, she asked the doctor what she could do to prevent another pregnancy. His reply: "Tell Jake to sleep on the roof!" Sanger was dumbfounded at the doctor's response. Three months later, Sadie, pregnant again, tried to abort using knitting needles. This time it was fatal. The doctor and Sanger could not save her; she contracted an infection and died.

That night, Sanger committed herself to confronting the desperate situation of women like Sadie Sachs. "I went to bed, knowing that no matter what it might cost, I was finished with palliatives and superficial cures," she remembered. "I was resolved to seek out the root of evil, to do something to change the destiny of mothers whose miseries were as vast as the sky." She later claimed dramatically that she intended to "awaken the womanhood of America to free the motherhood of the world!"

On the advice of Bill Haywood of the IWW, Sanger and her family visited Paris in late 1913 to learn more about European contraceptive methods. She returned to New York in 1914 with her children – her husband, William, remained in France to pursue his art career and they eventually divorced – and established a journal she called *The Woman Rebel*. On its masthead was her clarion call: "No Gods, No Masters!"

In its first issue in March 1914, "eight pages on cheap paper," she defined a woman's duty as follows: "To look the world in the face with a go-to-hell look in the eyes; to have an idea; to speak and act in defiance of convention." She encouraged her female readers to take charge of their own bodies. Two issues later, she coined the term "birth control" to describe her main goal. Almost overnight her name was inseparable from the cause she so passionately espoused.

By then she had run afoul of the post office and her chief nemesis, Anthony Comstock, at seventy years old still the post office's special agent and as determined as ever to impose his moral views on the new generation. In his mind, contraception was linked to "unbridled sexuality" and thus he continued to personally harass Sanger until the day he died in 1915.

Providing information to any woman, rich or poor, about contraception and unwanted pregnancies was a challenge. In 1912, abortion was illegal in every state. It was still regarded, as it had been for decades, as the great "evil of the age" – and the only way to obtain one was to risk a visit to a back-alley doctor or a discreet midwife.* More problematic for Sanger, however, was the Comstock Law of 1873, which made it illegal to send anything relating to contraception (considered obscene) through the mail. Almost immediately, she received official notification that articles on contraception in *The Woman Rebel* were in violation of the law and that the journal was therefore "unmailable." Sanger was outraged that "information regarding motherhood, which was so generally called sacred" was "classed with pornography."

Not a person to be intimidated, Sanger pushed forward, composing a pamphlet on birth control entitled *Family Limitation*. Before

---

* Many married and single women, from all classes and ethnic groups, had abortions, and for a variety of reasons. Before "quickening" – usually about the fourth month of pregnancy, when a woman could feel the fetus moving – it was much easier to obtain an abortion. If complications arose, or if the woman died as a result of the procedure, the full weight of the law was often brought to bear on the abortionist. If the woman was single, her boyfriend was frequently arrested and jailed. As historian Leslie Reagan notes, "the state punished young men for the moral offense of engaging in premarital intercourse and then failing to fulfill the implicit engagement by marrying the women whom they impregnated. Police routinely arrested and incarcerated unmarried men as accomplices in the crime of abortion, and the state's attorney sometimes prosecuted them. In contrast . . . it was rare for a husband to be arrested or prosecuted."

she could have it distributed, the federal government indicted her on nine counts for publishing *The Woman Rebel*. If she was found guilty, she faced a sentence of up to forty-five years in jail. The legal proceedings in *The People v. Margaret Sanger* had only begun when she decided to flee to gain some time. "I was not afraid of penitentiary," she explained many years later. "I was not afraid of anything except being misunderstood." By the next day, she was in Montreal and within a week she had sailed to England. There, she learned more about diaphragms, condoms, and "planned parenthood," and fell in love with Havelock Ellis.

Meanwhile, more than a hundred thousand copies of *Family Limitation* were distributed. Days later, William Sanger, who had returned to New York, was paid a visit by a man claiming to need a copy of the pamphlet for his ailing wife. Sanger found one of the few he had left and gave it to the individual, who was actually an agent for Comstock's Society for the Suppression of Vice. Soon after, Comstock himself arrived at the studio with an arrest warrant, and Sanger was charged with distributing obscene literature. His trial was held in September 1915. Comstock was in fine form. He told the press that *Family Limitation* was written by "a heinous criminal who sought to turn every home into a brothel." The judge concurred, condemning Margaret Sanger's work as "indecent, immoral, and a menace to society." William Sanger, who was denied his attempt to use a defence of free speech, was found guilty and sentenced to thirty days in jail or a fine of $150. He opted for jail. It was at this point that Emma Goldman took a more active role in the fight and began distributing Sanger's pamphlet at her lectures. She, too, was arrested and fined.[*]

---

[*] Sanger and Goldman had their differences, since Emma regarded Margaret as too "middle-class." As Sanger wrote in her autobiography, "[Goldman] was never satisfied until people had arrived at her own doorstep and accepted the dogma she had woven for herself. Short, stocky, even stout, a true Russian peasant type, her figure

Hearing the news of William's conviction, Sanger decided to return to the United States and deal with her legal problems. The government initially refused to quash the indictment against her and rescheduled her trial for the fall. In the interim, her case became a *cause célèbre* and the government was inundated with appeals from across North America and England to drop the charges against her. As the trial began, the district attorney had second thoughts, and at the last moment the proceedings in *The People v. Margaret Sanger* were halted. Sanger and her supporters were relieved and delighted, but her struggle for birth control remained illegal, subject to the "mutton-headed restrictions of some post office clerk and the complaisant persecution of the federal district attorney," as the *New York Globe* put it.

On the morning of October 16, 1916, Sanger opened a birth-control clinic in the Brownsville section of Brooklyn. It was the first in the United States and indeed, the first outside of Holland. Although she had advertised it with leaflets in English, Yiddish, and Italian, Sanger was concerned that few women would make use of her services. On that first morning, when she peered out the front door, she was stunned. "Halfway to the corner," she recalled, "they were standing in line, at least one hundred and fifty, some shawled, some hatless, their red hands clasping the cold, chapped, smaller ones of their children." Now her life's work began in earnest. She saw the women in groups of seven and ten. "To each group we explained simply what contraception was," she adds, "that abortion was the wrong way – no matter how early it was performed it was taking life; that contraception was the better way, the safer way – it took a little time, a little trouble, but was well worth while in the long run, because life had not yet begun."

---

indicated strength of body and strength of character, and this impression was enhanced by her firm step and reliant walk. Though I disliked both her ideas and her methods I admired her; she was really like a spring house-cleaning to the sloppy thinking of the average American."

During the next decade, Sanger was arrested nine more times and spent thirty days in a workhouse, where she took the opportunity to teach her fellow inmates about birth control. The Roman Catholic Church and an array of moral crusaders denounced her. She ignored her numerous critics in the medical community – who argued as late as 1927 that contraception was "unnatural in terms of ethics and unphysiological in terms of biology" and was of "the same character as murder and sexual perversion" – and fought each and every legal challenge. Her first book, *Woman and the New Race* (1920), sold more than 250,000 copies. A year later, she organized the American Birth Control League, which two decades later became the Planned Parenthood Federation of America. For a brief time, she also considered linking her cause with the eugenics movement, "defining birth control at one point as 'more children from the fit, less from the unfit.'"

As contraception became somewhat more acceptable in the 1920s (at least in private), she toured the world to lecture and teach. A talk she gave in Vancouver in 1923 inspired women there to establish the Canadian Birth Control League. An Ontario branch was organized two years later, chaired by eugenicist and physician Dr. O.C.J. Withrow, though both groups remained small and ineffective. (It was not until 1931 that the Birth Control League of Canada was created, supported by Protestant church officials and representatives of the National Committee on Mental Hygiene.)

Sanger's second husband, business tycoon J. Noah Slee, the head of the Three-in-One Oil Company, assisted her in her many endeavours. Despite his basically conservative views, Slee was so devoted to Sanger that he financed her birth-control campaign (paying ten thousand dollars annually to the well-respected physician Dr. James F. Cooper to speak on contraception) and even acted as her bootlegger, smuggling German-made diaphragms into the United States via his plant in Montreal hidden in oil drums.

*

Birth control remained a taboo subject for much of the twenties. It was rarely featured in magazine articles or discussed on radio programs. There were fears, as the feminist writer Charlotte Perkins Gilman warned, that its widespread use would lead to "a degree of sexual indulgence without parallel in nature." Reliable information on contraception was still not easy for lower-class women to obtain. Yet by any measure, Sanger had made a difference. It took until the late 1930s and 1940s, but birth-control clinics based on her model eventually opened throughout the United States and Canada.

"Whether or not birth control is eugenic, hygienic and economic, it is the most revolutionary practice in the history of sexual morals," claimed Walter Lippmann in 1929. That same year, social worker Katharine Bement Davis's ten-year study on the sex lives of 2,200 American women was published. She found, among other fascinating facts, that in her sample of one thousand educated women, 74 per cent said they used contraceptives, and most "believed that its use was morally right."[*]

Sanger must have been pleased. Her attitude towards sex always had been progressive. "The need of women's lives is not repression," she wrote in *Woman and the New Race*, "but the greatest possible expression and fulfillment of their desires upon the highest possible plane. . . . Sex life must be stripped of its fear. This is one of the great functions of contraceptives." Or, as her friend Mabel Dodge Luhan put it, "Margaret Sanger was the first person I ever knew who was openly an ardent propagandist for the joys of the flesh." No one could deny that Sanger was indeed a full-fledged

---

[*] Katharine Bement Davis was born in Buffalo, New York, in 1860. She attended Vassar College and Columbia University and later worked as a social worker in Philadelphia. In 1900, she obtained her Ph.D. in political economy, one of the first women in the United States to do so. For nearly fifteen years, she was the superintendent of the Reformatory for Women at Bedford, New York. In 1917 she became the general secretary of the Bureau of Social Hygiene, funded by the Rockefeller Foundation, and conducted studies on public health, prostitution, and sexual attitudes.

modernist. Her attitude exemplified the generation that came of age during the years of the First World War, when jazz, orgiastic dancing, and risqué fashions seemed to turn the respectable world upside down.

Sex O'clock in America

Blame it on jazz. Almost everyone else did. It was sinful "Negro" music that was corrupting America's youth. "Anyone who says the 'youths of both sexes can mingle in close embrace' – with limbs intertwined and torso in contact – without suffering harm lies," wrote one commentator in a 1927 magazine article. "Add to this position the wriggling movement and sensuous stimulation of the abominable jazz orchestra with its voodoo-born minors and its direct appeal to the sensory centre, and if you can believe that youth is the same after this experience as before, then God help your child." Jazz and the dancing it prompted were both denounced, said Frederick Allen, as "impure, polluting, corrupting, debasing, destroying spirituality, [and] increasing carnality." When a clergyman in Whitby, Ontario, east of Toronto suggested in 1921 that supervised dancing at his church was acceptable, there was an outcry in the community. "Churches that entertain sin and Satan in their parlours," one congregant wrote in a letter to the *Toronto Star*, "don't find God in their auditoriums."

From the beginning, the mood and rhythm of the music were irresistible. Jazz was born in New Orleans at the turn of the century where the dynamic interaction of black (both Creoles and "American Negroes") and white musicians produced several new captivating sounds. It was in the brothels of Storyville, the city's infamous red-light district (named after the city official who conceived of the area), where New Orleans–style jazz, ragtime, and Dixieland took root. When they were not relaxing in the brothels' backrooms spending time with the ladies, patrons could sit back with a whisky and a cigar and be entertained by such greats as pianist "Jelly Roll" Morton. A Creole who had been born in New Orleans, Morton preferred the company of whites, earning the disdain of some of his fellow black musicians. Still, with his gold rings, expensive clothes, and celebrated skill with women, few could deny that Morton had a lot of style and talent. Jazz, he said, "was not what you played, but how you played it." It was intense, emotional, and exhilarating. In a word, "hot," and it made you want to get up and dance.

The connection between jazz and sex was a natural one. "The word jazz in its progress toward respectability has meant first sex, then dancing, then music," said novelist F. Scott Fitzgerald, who used jazz to define his generation in the 1920s. "It is associated with a state of nervous stimulation, not unlike that of big cities behind the lines of a war." Yet well before Fitzgerald discovered jazz's magical allure, New Orleans musicians – particularly after the U.S. Navy, fearful of an outbreak of venereal disease among its sailors, had shut down Storyville in 1917 – had brought it north with them first to Chicago and then to New York. Joseph "King" Oliver led the way in 1920 with his popular Creole Jazz Band, soon featuring a remarkable young trumpet player named Louis "Satchmo" Armstrong. Before long jazz was forever linked with speakeasies, cabarets like the Cotton Club in New York's Harlem, where the immortal bandleader Edward Kennedy "Duke" Ellington held court, and intimate dancing that was cause for concern of moralists everywhere.

It was true, as Paul Whiteman, the most popular of the white big band leaders in the twenties, put it in a 1927 *New York Times* article, that jazz "loosened libidos and corsets and there seemed to be no end to the variety of dances that the flapper could do. From the intimate waltz to the sultry black bottom, the Charleston, and the shimmy, to the endless series of animal dances, experimentation was the order of the day." In truth, the concerns about dancing had been around for more than a decade, even before jazz took hold.

The first dance craze broke out in 1912, when young middle- and working-class men and women disobeyed their parents and frequented dance halls. There they did the foxtrot, turkey trot, "shaking the shimmy," and the grizzly bear. "Mother said I shouldn't dare," one popular song of the era went, "to try and do the Grizzly Bear." The bunny hug, which required dance partners to embrace, was perceived to be the worst of the lot. "Couples stand very close together," complained one moral reformer, "the girl with her arms around the man's neck, the man with both his arms around the girl or on her hips; their cheeks are pressed together, their bodies touch each other." The title of a 1913 article in the journal *Current Opinion* summed up for many this offending turn of events: Regrettably, it had struck "Sex O'clock in America."

Flappers Are Brave and Gay and Beautiful

Many young women were not content merely to dance – although they soon made the Charleston their trademark jive. They began wearing looser and shorter dresses, using cosmetics, smoking in public (which could have led to an arrest in some states before 1912), driving alone in their automobiles, attending hops, proms, and ball games, and talking openly about sex. And like Bernice in one of F. Scott Fitzgerald's most admired short stories from 1920, they "bobbed" their hair.

"Do you think I ought to bob my hair?" Bernice asks Charley Paulson.

Charley looks up in surprise. "Why?"

"Because I'm considering it. It's such a sure and easy way of attracting attention. . . . I want to be a society vampire, you see."

In Winnipeg, Vivian Maw, a young and single stenographer who worked at the Inland Shipping Company, impulsively bobbed her hair one lunch hour in December 1922. Her return to her office with her new coiffure sent shockwaves through the Winnipeg Grain

Exchange Building that lasted for days. Her female friends soon followed her lead. Their short hair – a visible challenge to traditional
styles and authority – underlined that real change was in the air.

Such women as Vivian or the fictional Bernice were more independent than their mothers and determined to enjoy life's pleasures.
"What a gulf separates even two generations," claimed sociologist
William Ogburn in his 1929 book on changing American morality.
"Mothers and daughters often understand each other's viewpoints
so little that it seems as though they [are not] speaking the same lan-
guage." The daughters modelled themselves after silent film stars
Gloria Swanson, whose "bob" was adroitly "pressed around her head
and not carefully curled," and Louise Brooks, a former *Ziegfeld
Follies* dancer, whose "sleek look and signature bob" were made
famous in advertisements, photographs, and magazine sketches.
Swanson and Brooks were the antithesis of "Gibson Girls."

As depicted in *LIFE* magazine by Charles Dana Gibson in the
1890s, "Gibson Girls" were full-figured and tightly corseted, secure
of their social position, and happy to be their husbands' chief adorn-
ment. By the twenties, they were a vanishing breed. The new
modern women were flat-chested, and in the words of London's
Daily Mail "as slim as a lamp post."

Writer H.L. Mencken took note of this radical transformation
in fashion, look, and attitude as early as 1915. He called these new
women "flappers" (although the term was likely used earlier than
this to describe women who wore slit-skirts and rode in automobiles). "Observe, then, this nameless one, this American
Flapper," he declared. "Her skirts have just reached her very trim
and pretty ankles: her hair, newly coiled upon her skull, has just
exposed the ravishing whiteness of her neck. . . . She is opposed to
the double standard of morality and favours a law prohibiting it."

Or, put slightly differently a few years later by Fitzgerald's fun-
loving and debonair wife, Zelda, a flapper if there ever was one, "I
think a woman gets more happiness out of being gay, light-hearted,

unconventional, mistress of her own fate, than out of a career that calls for hard work, intellectual pessimism and loneliness," she said. "I don't want Pat [her daughter] to be a genius. I want her to be a flapper, because flappers are brave and gay and beautiful." Zelda's enemy, and the enemy of every flapper, was the symbolic Mrs. Grundy, who epitomized "prudery and sacrifice as opposed to the new standards of pleasure and consumption."

Transforming oneself into a flapper was, nevertheless, hard work. "I wonder if it ever occurred to any of you," asked Ellen Welles Page, a self-proclaimed flapper, in a 1922 *Outlook* magazine article, "that it required brains to become and remain a successful flapper? Indeed it does! It requires an enormous amount of cleverness and energy to keep going at the proper pace. It requires self-knowledge and self-analysis. We must know our capabilities and limitations. We must be constantly on the alert. Attainment of flapperhood is a big and serious undertaking!" In Page's view, it was her advanced education, confidence, and desire for self-fulfillment and improvement that set her apart from her parents and grandparents.

Shorter hemlines attracted the most critical attention. In 1919, the hems of women's dresses were about six inches from the ground, and then to the horror of many traditionalists they began to rise. "The American woman," affirmed a *New York Times* fashion writer, "has lifted her skirts far beyond any modest limitation." The Young Women's Christian Association published a booklet entitled *Modesty Appeal* and strongly recommended that women show some good taste and restraint. Legislators in Utah and Virginia introduced bills in their state assemblies setting restrictions on women's fashions. Had they passed, women in Utah could have been fined or imprisoned for publicly wearing skirts that were a few inches above the ankle, while in Virginia politicians wanted to stop women from wearing dresses which displayed their bare necks.

In the summer, some women started wearing what were considered revealing bathing suits. The authorities clamped down.

On a beach close to Chicago, the police scoured the area, relates historian Carolyn Johnston, "measuring swimsuits' armpits and necklines and arresting bathers in one-piece knitted suits with shoulder straps and short legs." During the first Miss America pageant held in Atlantic City in 1921, the audience "gasped" when Margaret Gorman, Miss Washington, D.C., walked across the stage wearing a bathing suit that displayed her knees. "With above-the-knee skirts, bathing-beauty contests, one-piece bathing suits," decried one Christian educator, "the female form divine is clad in little more than the circumambient atmosphere. Everywhere you go, everywhere you read, everywhere you look, there is the ever protrusive, everlasting sex-appeal. You see it on the billboards . . . in the Sunday supplements . . . in the advertisements . . . in the magazines – low class and high – everywhere . . . sex, sex, sex!"

Some flappers wondered what all the fuss was about. "Are we as bad as we're painted?" asked one young female student at Ohio State University. "We are. We do all the things that our mothers, fathers, aunts and uncles do not sanction, and we do them knowingly. We are not young innocents – we've got the dope at our finger ends and we use it wisely for our own protection." She added, however, that this new style did not justify the tremendous condemnation. "She kisses the boys, she smokes with them, drinks with them, and why? Because the feeling of comradeship is running rampant. . . . The girl does not stand aloof – she and the man meet on common ground, and yet can she not retain her moral integrity? The criticism of immorality directed toward her is undeserved and unjustified."

Dorothy Parker, the witty and cynical literary critic, saw it slightly differently. "The playful flapper here we see," she wrote in her poem about the new woman, "The fairest of the fair. / She's not what Grandma used to be – / you might say, *au contraire*. / Her girlish ways may make a stir, / Her manners cause a scene, / But there is no more harm in her / Than in a submarine."

The flapper was not an obvious danger, but she was subversive. The young women depicted in Fitzgerald's first big novel, *This Side of Paradise*, published in the spring of 1920, enjoyed kissing and petting. "I've kissed dozens of men," says one female character. "I suppose I'll kiss dozens more." (*This Side of Paradise* was considered very up to date: Freud was mentioned by page six.) "Petting parties" were all the rage, and there was an element of sexual freedom never before experienced. "Sex had not yet become as available as tap water for everyone, or even for the majority," writes historian Geoffrey Perrett in his history of America during this era. "But the sexual liberty of the Twenties is nothing less than amazing when compared with the sexual repression only a decade or so earlier. . . . A generation earlier a teenager who would have wanted to lose his virginity would have gone to the local whorehouse. These days he was far more likely to try to seduce his high school sweetheart."*

There was no denying that teenagers and young adults had a lot more fun than their parents ever did. But whether more women were losing their virginity before they got married is more difficult to determine. Several key studies completed in the United States, for instance, differ widely in their conclusions. Asked if premarital sex for a woman was "ever justified," only 20 per cent of the 1,200 unmarried women Katharine Bement Davis surveyed during the late twenties answered in the affirmative. Only 7 per cent of the one thousand married women she interviewed admitted to having had sex before their wedding day. Other research by Gilbert Hamilton and Lewis Terman published in 1929 and 1938 respectively showed much higher figures: Hamilton found that 61 per cent of the women

---

* This was a situation not lost on the YMCA and American Social Hygiene Council. During the mid-twenties, these organizations distributed throughout the United States and Canada booklets entitled *The Rational Sex Life of Man* and *The Question of Petting*, both by Dr. M.J. Exner. In the latter work, young readers were warned "that the degenerate effects of promiscuity blighted the possibility of a happy marriage in the same way that an early addiction to jazz rendered a person incapable of enjoying a symphony."

in his study born in 1891 or later had had premarital sex; while Terman reported that of his eight hundred female subjects, "12 per cent of the women married before 1912 were not virgins at the time, and the percentage rose to 32 per cent in the years 1932–37." (The difference in the two studies suggests that the women Terman interviewed may have been less than candid.)

Relations between husbands and wives in the bedroom were, it seemed, becoming less routine and more modern. This was the result of a number of factors: the faster pace of life, a wider circulation and acceptance of Freudian thinking about healthy sex – even if a majority of Americans and Canadians could not explain precisely what Freud was really about – the popularity of birth control, and a greater degree of egalitarianism gradually taking hold in North America. "I remember a perfectly mated, contented young mother," F. Scott Fitzgerald recalled, "asking my wife's advice about 'having an affair right away,' though she had no one specifically in mind, 'because don't you think it's sort of undignified when you get much over thirty?'" Yet it was equally true that most couples likely agreed with Bertrand Russell's dictum from his 1929 book *Marriage and Morals* that "children rather than sexual intercourse are the true purpose of marriage." That did not mean, however, that there was no place for pleasure in this equation. In Katharine Bement Davis's study, for example, the majority of married women said they had sex twice or more a week. Sixty per cent also stated that the experience was gratifying.[*]

It is significant, as well, that the most popular sex manual of all time, *Ideal Marriage*, by the Dutch gynaecologist Theodoor Hendrick van de Velde, was a huge success in Europe and North America. Translated into English in 1930 (it was published in Dutch and German in 1926), it sold in the hundreds of thousands and kept

---

[*] Traditionalists also bemoaned the rising divorce rate during the twenties. According to William Ogburn, the divorce rate in the U.S. had doubled from 8.8 per 100 marriages in 1910 to 16.5 by 1928 – approximately one divorce for every six marriages.

on selling right up until 1970. (In Germany it went through forty-two printings between 1926 and 1932 alone, before being banned by the Nazis in 1933.) Not only did van de Velde provide couples with a how-to guide for experimenting with different sexual positions, oral sex, and the "techniques to achieve the desired mutual orgasm," he also advised women to take the lead.

"A certain feminine initiative and aggression brings a refreshing variety," he recommended. "Let her be the wooer sometimes, not always the wooed. She can be so while quite retaining her distinctive dignity and sweetness. This role of wooer can express her love in a very desirable way and be intensely gratifying to the husband who feels that he not only feels desire, but inspires it, too."

This new open approach to sex was reflected in a number of popular novels. In Ernest Hemingway's *The Sun Also Rises*, sex was a destructive force as Hemingway wrestled with his own anxieties about strong, sexually independent women. Quite different, Sherwood Anderson's *Winesburg, Ohio* offered a sympathetic portrayal of homosexuality, while Radclyffe Hall's *The Well of Loneliness* included an introduction from Havelock Ellis and a lesbian (albeit, a guilt-ridden one) as the heroine. Pressured by the Society for the Suppression of Vice, now led by John Sumner (who had succeeded Anthony Comstock) copies of *The Well of Loneliness* were seized by the New York police. The novel was declared obscene in a New York City courtroom in 1929, despite the judge's comments that it was "a well written, carefully constructed piece of fiction" with "no unclean words." The legal system was similarly vigilant on Broadway – as the indomitable Mae West, who fashioned her celebrated career personifying raw sexual power, was to learn in the spring of 1927.

I Expect It Will Be the Making of Me

SEX, the play that is, went on trial in a jammed New York courtroom at the end of March 1927, along with its thirty-four-year-old writer and up-and-coming star, Mae West. With her curvaceous, full-figured body, she was no flapper. Yet no one tested the bounds of sexual mores in the late twenties more than Mae West. The moralists successfully (if only temporarily) drove her off the stage on several occasions, yet she ultimately won the day. It was her candid attitude to sex that prevailed.

In many ways West had been heading for her day in court from the time she was a teenager starting out on the vaudeville circuit. Her ambitious mother, Tillie, decided early on that Mae – born in 1892 in Brooklyn – would make something of herself. Her father, Jack, the son of Irish-Catholic immigrants, was a one-time bare-knuckle prizefighter who never made much of a living. By the age of ten, Mae was starring in vaudeville talent shows, following her mother's directions by using her feminine charm and wooing audiences with sexual double entendres. She was only sixteen years old when she made her debut in a burlesque theatre and performed a seductive fan dance wearing nothing but white powder. "The fan was big and red and she shook her bare body behind it," one enthusiastic male spectator recalled. "When she shook herself the powder would fly all over the stage, down onto us in the front rows. We loved that."

Gradually, she moved up the vaudeville ranks to a role in a Broadway revue in 1918 opposite comedian Ed Wynn in an Arthur Hammerstein production called *Sometime*. West was cast as a chorus girl "in search of temptation but never finding it." The reviews were excellent, but it was West's soon-to-be famous shimmy strut that drew the crowd's undivided attention. "All I had to do, I discovered," she later said, "was to wander around that stage like so much bait while the boys kept the audience happy with laughs." An astute and seasoned enough talent, she soon billed herself the "Shimadonna."

Determined to be both the best and the most outrageous star on Broadway, West composed a racy three-act play about the exploits of a prostitute named Margy. She initially called it *The Albatross*. By the time it opened in a small theatre in nearby Waterbury, Connecticut, in early 1926 its title had changed to *SEX*. It debuted at the off-Broadway Daly Theatre in April 1926 to mixed, even harsh reviews. "We were shown not sex but lust," wrote one critic, "stark naked lust." The more conservative *New York Times*, no fan of West, dismissed the play as "feeble and disjointed." *The New Yorker* said it was "a poor balderdash of street sweepings and cabaret sentimentality unexpurgated in tone."

Regardless, the city's theatre crowd took a liking to it and to West's classic double-entendre dialogue.

"Oh, I've got something for you," the actor playing the part of Lieutenant Gregg told West as Margy. "Wait until you see this, wait until you see this."

"Well, come on," said Margy.

"You'll get it. I don't mind telling you I had an awful time saving it for you," he added. "Why all the women were fighting for it."

"It better be good," said Margy.

"It's good alright. It's the best you could get, but you've got to be very careful not to bend it." As the audience howled, Gregg handed Margy a bird of paradise.

John Sumner and his group at the Society for the Suppression of Vice were far less amused. At the first performance he attended, West knew he was present so she toned down the production. But it was to no avail. Sumner labelled *SEX* "moral poison" and declared that he would shut it down. Somewhat ironically, Sumner was supported by William Randolph Hearst's tabloid, the *Daily Mirror*. Hearst and his editors were concerned about censorship, and despite their own salacious stories they aimed to show Sumner that the *Mirror* was a morally worthy institution. The best way to do this, they felt, was to join in the anti-*SEX* chorus. The paper castigated the play as, "a monstrosity plucked from the garbage can, destined for the sewer." Other drama critics and theatre producers were less supportive of censorship, even if they did not particularly like West's production.

Things escalated when West, in the midst of the controversy over *SEX*, produced and directed a new play about homosexuality, *The Drag*. Manhattan theatregoers had never seen anything like it. With a cast of gay actors, singers, and drag queens, the play tested the limits of official tolerance. Few critics had much good to say about it. After watching a rehearsal at the Daly Theatre, a *Variety* writer condemned it as a "sex perversion exposition." Fearing the wrath of the authorities, most Broadway producers did not want it to open in New York. "*The Drag*, I believe," declared William de Lignemare, echoing sentiments shared by many producers, "is the worst possible play I have ever heard of contemplating an invasion of New York. That production . . . strikes at the decency of manhood."

Despite West's attempts to placate city officials – by giving them a private preview – grave concern over *The Drag*'s possible Broadway opening, plus intensive lobbying by Sumner, forced the district attorney's office to act. On the evening of February 8, 1927, West and the rest of the cast of *SEX* were arrested, as were casts in two other controversial plays, *The Captive*, about lesbianism, and *The Virgin Man*, which recounted the relationship between a college student and a "female seductress." West and her cast members were charged with violating New York's obscenity law, including "corrupting the morals of youth and others." Immediately her lawyers had everyone released on bail and obtained an injunction for *SEX* to continue its run.

Before West's case came to trial, New York State's Senate passed the Wales Padlock Law. The district attorney was compelled to prosecute the producers and actors involved in any indecent show and close for one year the theatre where the performance took place. Despite his well-known views against such censorship, Governor Al Smith, vying for the Democratic presidential nomination (which he did not win) and wanting to be perceived as a moral guardian of public interest, signed the Senate's bill into law at the end of April.

*

The *SEX* trial began in New York City in March 1927. It was Deputy District Attorney James Wallace's job to show that the play was immoral and obscene. One of his witnesses, Harry Cohen, who had helped finance the production, testified how he had argued with West about its offensive language. He explained how West had assured him that such dialogue sold tickets at the box office. Wallace later pointed out that it was not only West's words which were at issue, it was also how she delivered her lines. In short, the actress was being condemned, as she later claimed, for her suggestive personality, mannerisms, and walk.

Another key witness, Sergeant Patrick Keneally of the midtown vice squad, who had watched *SEX* on three occasions, listed for the jury the various "indecent" moments in the play, among them West's "prolonged" kisses and what Keneally described as a "muscle dance." "Miss West moved her navel up and down and from right to left," the police officer testified. On cross-examination, West's lawyers asked the sergeant to demonstrate the dance, but the judge, George Donnellan, amidst titters in the courtroom, would not allow it.

In his closing argument, Deputy District Attorney Wallace pleaded with the members of the jury to consider the moral ramifications of permitting *SEX* to continue. "We have cleaned up the red-light district of New York," he claimed. "It's a pretty clean town. But we've got red lights on the stage." The members of the jury, however, were not convinced and after several hours voted nine to three to acquit. Then the judge intervened, explaining that according to the law if any part of the production was obscene, no matter how minor, the entire play must be ruled obscene.

On April 5 the jury did their legal and moral duty and found West and the other defendants guilty as charged. West declared she would take the case to the Supreme Court. A few weeks later, she and several key cast members were fined five hundred dollars and sentenced to ten days in jail. Judge Donnellan stated that *SEX* was "obscene, immoral, and indecent" and that West and her friends had tarnished New York City's reputation – "the most moral city in the universe." West accepted the judgment coolly, but as she left the courtroom she turned and told the assembled journalists, "I expect it will be the making of me."

In a sense, she was correct. As her notoriety grew, so too did her career. Her fame spread to Hollywood. Following eight days of incarceration at Welfare Island Penitentiary – she was let out early for good behaviour – she returned to work. In the months ahead, she starred as Lou in the play *Diamond Lil*, one of her most famous roles. It was a story about a 1890s Bowery Queen in which West sang the show-stopping tune "Frankie and Johnny."

Undeterred by her recent incarceration, she set New York buzzing again with another new play, *The Pleasure Man*. It had, like *The Drag*, a homosexual theme, and for good measure a reference to a castration. *Variety* hailed it as "the queerest show you've ever seen. All the Queens are in it." The *New York Times* was more critical, declaring that it was "coarse, vulgar and objectionable specimen of its author's theatrical writings." The audiences loved it, and the authorities took notice. Early in October 1928, after it had run for two weeks, the police raided the Biltmore Theater and arrested the cast. West quickly bailed them out of jail. "We shall not have disgusting or revolting degenerate shows for exhibition in this city," stated the city's mayor, Jimmy Gray, a few days later.

The play had been closed, but the politicians, police, and lawyers dithered about how to deal with *The Pleasure Man* for more than a year. A trial was finally convened in mid-March 1930 with James Wallace again leading the prosecution. Early on he stated that he would "prove that it would take the most confirmed pervert to write such a play." As in the *SEX* trial, he mainly used police officers to marshal his case of obscenity. They singled out for condemnation one song in the production, "I'm Queen of the Bitches" – which defence lawyers claimed was actually "I'm Queen of the Beaches."

The judge, Amedeo Bertini, charged the jury members to heed testimony about "innuendoes and double-meanings." "The greater danger lies in an appeal to the imagination," he said, echoing the judge in the *SEX* trial, "and when the suggestion is immoral, the more that is left to the imagination, the more subtle and seductive the influence." Yet in the end, without having seen the play, the jury had a next-to-impossible decision. Following hours of discussion, they finally told the judge that they could not agree on a verdict. The case was dismissed and the district attorney opted not to retry it.

West later claimed to have been vindicated by the outcome, and certainly New York's obscenity laws were wanting. Her fans hailed her as a champion of free speech, while her detractors said she was just in it for the money. Her biographer Jill Watts says that the trial "indicated she was a little of both." Had *The Pleasure Man* continued, she would have made a significant sum. But given the conservative attitude of the authorities, she was also risking a lot, including another jail sentence.

She continued to take creative risks with the publication of her novel, *Babe Gordon* (later reissued as *The Constant Sinner*), the story of a white prostitute who worked in black Harlem and had an African-American lover. "If any man can have as many women as he wants," says Babe, sounding like a liberated woman of the twenties, "there is no reason why a woman should not do the same thing."

Clearly, Mae West was a different type of "new woman," doing what she wanted, when she wanted. "The modern girl is like Lindbergh, built for speed," declared the former *Ziegfeld Follies* dancer and film star Dorothy Mackaill in a 1930 interview. "We have tremendous vitality of body and complete emancipation of mind. None of the old taboos . . . mean a damn to us. We don't care." That was the attitude West would carry with her to Hollywood. The censors, however, as always, were ready for her and all others like her.

CHAPTER EIGHT

The Sins of Hollywood

Previous page: The indomitable Mae West, c. 1940. She fashioned her celebrated career personifying raw sexual power on the stage and in the movies, encountering strong resistance from the moralists and censors who ran Hollywood in the 1920s and 1930s.

The motion picture does not present the audience with tastes and manners and views and morals; it reflects those they already have.

        – Irving Thalberg, 1930

Nickel Delirium

It was a pivotal event in Hollywood history, although few appreciated it at the time. On February 21, 1901, nearly every vaudeville performer in New York City went out on strike to protest low wages and demand recognition of a newly formed union called the "White Rats" (named after the London actors' union). Theatre owners refused to budge, but instead of shutting down their establishments they offered their clientele a selection of silent movies. Most of the owners had already incorporated films into their repertoires of song, dance, comedy, and acrobatics, yet merely as "chasers" to push one audience out and play another one in; now, they advertised the movies as the only show on the bill. The public loved it and lined up at every theatre that ran motion pictures.

Knowing a profitable venture when they saw it, many astute businessmen opened stand-alone movie theatres, "nickelets," or "nickelodeons," as they were called (derived from combining the word *nickel*, the price of admission, with *odeon*, the Greek word for theatre). The industry's growth was astounding. Soon motion-picture theatres

313

were everywhere, from New York to Chicago to San Francisco, and north to Toronto, Montreal, and Winnipeg. The fixed costs were low – the biggest expense was the rental of films, about fifty dollars a week in 1907 – and the profits high. One operator in New York's Lower East Side in 1907, for instance, was taking in $1,800 a week, with fixed expenses of $500 for a very respectable weekly profit of $1,300. It was a veritable gold mine.

By 1910, there were more than four hundred movie theatres in Manhattan alone, with a weekly attendance estimated at nine hundred thousand paying customers. Across the United States that year, ten thousand nickelodeons sprang up. The average one could seat between 100 and 250 patrons for each show. The country, declared journalist Barton W. Currie in an article in *Harper's Weekly* in August 1907, had succumbed to "nickel delirium." (The industry continued to expand at a rapid rate. By 1927 there were 743 new movies playing in 21,660 theatres in the United States with an average weekly attendance of fifty-seven million.) Throughout North America, everyone, it seemed, was following the advice of an early advertisement: "If you're sick of troubles rife, go to the picture show; you'll forget your unpaid bills, rheumatism and other ills, if you'll stow away your pills, and go the picture show."

As movies became part of daily life, increasingly large theatres, so-called picture palaces, were built to accommodate the crowds. None was as luxurious and ostentatious as Samuel Lionel Rathapfel's Strand Theater in New York, which could seat more than three thousand people. "Going to the Strand," wrote the *New York Times* drama critic Victor Watson in 1914, soon after it opened, "was very much like going to a Presidential reception, a first night at the opera or the opening of the horse show."

A decade later, Rathapfel surpassed the Strand with the Roxy, a $12 million edifice known as "The Cathedral of the Motion Picture." It had seating for 6,200 along with a five-storey rotunda, and was tricked out in an exotic amalgam of Renaissance, Gothic, and Moorish decorative themes. In its first week of operation in mid-March 1927, it showed *The Love of Sunja*, starring Gloria Swanson, and grossed $135,000.

Part of the allure of going to the movies was that it was (and still is) a shared experience, even if you spoke no English or had little money in the bank. In fact, because the admission fee was only a nickel, less well off immigrants and workers flocked to the theatres. "The popularity of these cheap amusement-palaces with the new population of New York is not to be wondered at," explained Barton Currie. "The newly arrived immigrant from Transylvania can get as much enjoyment out of them as the native. The imagination is appealed to directly and without any circumlocution." Or, as another writer noted a little more eloquently a few years later in *American Magazine*, inside the theatre "there is no bar of language for the alien or the ignorant, but here the masses of mankind enter through the rhythm of vivid motion the light that flies before and the beauty that calls the spirit of the race. For a mere nickel, the wasted man, whose life hitherto has been toil and sleep, is kindled with wonder."

Immigrants not only patronized the motion-picture theatres, they also owned them. Many newcomers were attracted by the low overhead costs, plus the promise of attaining the "American Dream." For a variety of reasons – already-established links with vaudeville, family connections, timing, good business sense, and sheer luck – several of the key movie pioneers were Jewish, a fact not lost on the press. As early as 1901, for example, *LIFE* magazine used blatantly anti-Semitic caricatures to lampoon Jewish involvement in the entertainment business. Cartoon sketches showed greedy Jews counting their nickels and manipulating actors and actresses like puppets.

There were in later years non-Jewish movie moguls, too. William Randolph Hearst ran Cosmopolitan Pictures in the twenties, primarily as a vehicle for his mistress, Marion Davies. And young and ambitious Joseph P. Kennedy, before he moved on to intrigues in Washington and elsewhere, made a lot of money with investments in three major studios from 1926 to 1930, the most important of which was Radio-Keith-Orpheum or RKO (with his main partner David Sarnoff of RCA). He had a brief but passionate love affair with Gloria Swanson and pocketed a $5 million fortune when he sold out in 1931.[*]

Yet it was Adolph Zukor, Marcus Loew, William Fox, Carl Laemmle, Samuel Goldwyn (born Schmuel Gelbfisz), Louis B. Mayer, and Jack and Sam Warner who really created Hollywood.[**]

The irony was that these Jewish moguls, nearly all of whom came from poor eastern European families, wanted desperately to be seen as "American" (Mayer, who was not certain of his actual birthday chose to celebrate it on July 4). Yet no matter what they accomplished or how wealthy they became, to the rest of the world, inside and outside of Hollywood, they were first and foremost Jews. Their prominence gave ammunition to their numerous critics, who blamed them for Hollywood's immorality and for corrupting the minds of young Americans.

They were the "enemies of mankind," declared Canon William Sheafe Chase of Christ Church in Brooklyn, an ardent opponent of

---

[*] As a Boston financial executive, Kennedy was able to study the financial books of a prominent New England motion-picture company and immediately realized that there was a "gold mine in moving pictures." Noting the strong Jewish presence in Hollywood, he told a fellow broker, "Look at the bunch of pants pressers in Hollywood making themselves millionaires. I could take the whole business away from them."

[**] In 1901, Carl Laemmle, then head of Independent Motion Pictures Company, came up with the idea for a high-profile publicity campaign of a young actress named Florence Lawrence – and the Hollywood star system was born. "Other independents," writes film historian Garth Jowett, "soon realized the tremendous value of the free publicity that could be obtained from a news-hungry press, and began to turn their own performers into public figures. . . . Of course, the more public attention and favour a performer received the more money he or she could command, and the motion-picture industry's economic structure was peculiarly suited to providing the larger salaries demanded and received by its performers."

the movies. At a 1923 New York State hearing convened to discuss movie censorship, Ellen O'Grady, a former police commissioner, referred to the studio heads as "money-mad men" presenting a "pagan" view of America. The stereotype was powerful and lasting.

The Triumph of Virtue and the Overthrow of Wickedness

Some of the earliest nickelodeons played non-stop ten hours a day. A typical film in the early days was a fifteen-minute or so comedy or melodrama on a single reel. Canadian-born Mack Sennett's "Keystone Kops" capers and other silly spoofs starring Fatty Arbuckle and Charlie Chaplin were especially crowd favourites. As longer and more meaningful narrative films were produced – the first was *The Great Train Robbery* in 1903 – movies delivered clear messages about life in which good always vanquished evil. Hollywood adhered to the formula for decades. Ben Hecht, a journalist and novelist who became a talented screenwriter for MGM in the mid-twenties, quickly discovered that there was only one basic movie plot: "the triumph of virtue and the overthrow of wickedness." Upon arriving in Los Angeles, he was instructed by Herman Mankiewicz, also a MGM writer. "I want to point out to you," Mankiewicz told him, "that in a novel a hero can lay 10 girls and marry a virgin for a finish. In a movie this is not allowed. The hero, as well as the heroine, has to be a virgin. The villain can lay anybody he wants, have as much fun as he wants cheating and stealing, getting rich and whipping the servants. But you have to shoot him in the end."

This approach made no difference to Anthony Comstock and the other moral reformers who followed in his footsteps. They condemned the nickelodeons and movie theatres, denouncing them for corrupting children, harbouring pickpockets, fleecing patrons, and providing clandestine spots where prostitutes hunted for new prey. (When vaudeville was starting out in the mid-nineteenth century, it was fairly common in many theatres for prostitutes to have sex with their clients in the balcony or backstage, literally "behind the scenes.")

Mostly, though, they objected to the controversial subjects that the films raised and the manner in which they were presented. Motion pictures with such suggestive titles as *Eternal Sin*, *Purgatory*, *The Forbidden Path*, and *She-Devil* deliberately insinuated (even if the finished product did not deliver on the promise) that there was something dangerous and risqué about going to the movies. *Traffic in Souls*, a 1913 film from Carl Laemmle's studio, was based on a real report about white slavery and billed itself in advertising as "a sensational motion picture dramatization . . . a $200,000 spectacle [actually $5,700] in 700 scenes with 800 players, showing the traps cunningly laid for young girls by vice agents."

In the 1920 movie *Why Change Your Wife?*, the lovely and seductive Gloria Swanson exuded sex appeal without even trying. She played a "frumpy housewife" about to lose her husband to an even more glamorous vamp. Much to the dissatisfaction of the moralists, her example taught young women that appearances mattered and that in order to hold on to a man any tactic was fair.

Even Charlie Chaplin's films were censured for their "grotesque and vulgar antics." The brilliant comedian was always lusting after some beauty or other, only to be thwarted by a returning father, husband, or boyfriend – or in a few cases the entire family.*

---

* Chaplin was the first international star to emerge from Hollywood. It was said that when he went abroad he did not require a passport "for his face was known everywhere." In 1916, he signed a deal with the Mutual Film Corporation for a one-year contract worth $670,000 – an astounding amount that was, as newspapers pointed out, "equal to 94 per cent of the payroll of the entire U.S. Senate." Only steel magnate Charles Schwab made more money that year. Chaplin's private life, particularly his well-known affection for young girls, became the gossip of Hollywood. His first two marriages (and divorces) were to actresses Mildred Harris and Lita Grey, both of whom were about sixteen years old at the time of their weddings. Chaplin was twenty-eight years old when he married Harris and thirty-five years old with Grey. He also had a rather public affair with William Randolph Hearst's mistress, Marion Davies.

For fans and critics alike, movies came of age with D.W. Griffith's classic 1915 film *The Birth of a Nation*, one of the most significant motion pictures ever made. Its impact went far beyond the theatre. Griffith, who pioneered the "close-up" and the "fade out," adapted Thomas Dixon's bestselling novel *The Clansman* about life in the United States during the post–Civil War era. Today, his three-hour film is mostly remembered for how it glorified the Ku Klux Klan.

There were two controversial scenes that drew critical comments and outright hostility from the most important African-American organization of the day, the National Association for the Advancement of Colored People (NAACP). In the first, a young white woman, played by Lillian Gish, was locked in a room by a "gorilla-like black politician," scheming to force marriage on her. Southern as well as the Northern audiences actually stood up and cheered as the Klan rode to save her. The second scene was even worse from the NAACP's point of view, since it reinforced a stereotype of black men as rapists. In a moment of sheer terror, the actress Mae Marsh jumped to her death off a cliff rather than submit to the sexual advances of "a slavering, animalistic black man" who had caught her.

From the day it was released, loud protests were heard from black leaders and reformers like Jane Addams, who called the picture "vicious." In Boston, the black journalist William Monroe Trotter led a march on a movie theatre where a stink bomb was detonated and fighting erupted between black activists and white patrons. None of this stopped moviegoers from flocking to cinemas to watch the picture. In New York City alone in 1915, nearly one million people saw the movie and within two years it had earned more than $60 million across the country and in Canada. When questioned about the fuss he had caused, Griffith defended his right to make motion pictures as an act of free speech. What made *The Birth of a Nation* stand apart from other films of the day, however, was that Griffith had shown – as his biographer Robert Henderson has noted – "that an audience would accept fiction as reality." This was Hollywood's true power to mould North American values.

The Greatest Enemy of Civilization

The storm that engulfed *The Birth of a Nation* came as less of a surprise to the moralists, reformers, and critics who had eyed the motion-picture industry from its earliest days. "To some observers movies offered 'limitless potential' for serving humanity," explains historian Stephen Vaughn. "They promised to stimulate local business and world trade, promote international understanding and good will, and transmit great literature and the latest medical techniques to the hinterlands. To others this new medium, which had emerged from the urban ghettoes . . . presented a corrupting potential."

In 1896, dramatic theatre actors May Irwin and John Rice filmed an intimate scene from the play *Widow Jones*. The short film of fifty seconds was entitled *The Kiss*, and it caused uproar among audiences. It was one thing to see an intimate embrace between a man and a woman on the stage, but quite another to witness it on a large screen. "The spectacle of the prolonged pasturing on each other's lips [was] beastly," one drama critic wrote. The motion picture *Orange Blossoms*, released a year later, received an even more negative reaction. It had one scene in which an actress playing a bride pretended to change into her nightgown. New York police raided the movie theatre and arrested its owner. "The evil results of the immoral pictures shown in the slot machines have not been at all overestimated," a 1900 editorial in the *New York Journal* stated. "Many of the pictures were incentives to immorality. Through their agency debauchery was dressed in tempting spangles and glitter."

From Hull-House in Chicago in 1909, Jane Addams derided movie theatres as a "house of dreams." She accepted the allure for young people of "going to the show" – as opposed to the playground – and conceded that it was "the only possible road to the realms of mystery and romance." The theatre, she said, "is the only place where they can satisfy that craving for a conception of life higher than that which the actual world offers them." But in her view the heavy concentration in the movies of sex and crime threatened America's "moral codes" and physical well-being. Sounding very much like today's critics who point to video games as the cause of youth violence, Addams related the story, as reported by a Chicago physician, of three boys, aged nine, eleven, and thirteen years, who, after seeing a Wild West motion picture, "spent weeks planning to lasso, murder and rob a neighbourhood milkman." The boys purchased a gun and attacked the milkman and his horse-drawn delivery wagon, but their scheme went awry and the man was unharmed.

At universities, social scientists studied the psychological impact of motion pictures. One notable 1916 study by Harvard psychologist Hugo Munsterberg warned that prolonged viewing of crime and vice could have "disastrous results." "The normal resistance breaks down," he wrote, "and the moral balance, which would have been kept under the habitual stimuli of the narrow routine life, may be lost under the pressure of the realistic suggestions." Reverend Wilbur Crafts, an outspoken Christian lobbyist and reformer in Washington, D.C., was more strident, condemning movies as "schools of vice and crime . . . offering trips to hell for [a] nickel." Likewise Canon William Sheafe Chase, who fought against the motion picture for much of his adult life, declared films to be "the greatest enemy of civilization."

The campaign to censor movies began early, and for more than four decades it never really relented. Starting in Chicago in 1907, exhibitors had to clear movies with police-department censors, whose personal preferences dictated what they approved or rejected. Sergeant Charles O'Donnell stated that he would only approve of films that he regarded as "proper for women and children to witness." Movie-theatre owners challenged the arbitrary rulings in court, yet the law backed the authorities; "immoral" and "obscene" productions were contrary to the public good and therefore legally forbidden. The courts did not deal with the more significant issue of the precise determination of acceptable moral standards, other than to note that the "average person of healthy and wholesome mind" knew, as Sergeant O'Donnell did, what was obscene and what was not.

These legal decisions stood the test of time. In 1915, the U.S. Supreme Court ruled – in a suit brought by the Mutual Film Corporation against the Industrial Commission of Ohio, which wanted to censor films before they were shown – that making and showing movies was "a business pure and simple, originated and conducted for profit" and subject to censorship. The argument used by Mutual Films that under the U.S. Constitution it had the same special rights of freedom of expression as a newspaper was rejected. In a classic statement of contemporary moral thinking, the judges stated that motion pictures "are mere representations of events, of ideas and sentiments published and known; vivid, useful, and entertaining no doubt, but . . . capable of evil, having power for it, the greater because of their attractiveness and manner of exhibition."

Taking the high ground, much of the press sided with the moralists. A *Chicago Tribune* editorial of March 1907, for instance, stated that the city's nickelodeons were "without a redeeming feature to warrant their existence . . . ministering to the lowest passions of childhood." Two years later, the *Pittsburgh Post* suggested that many movies were "not fit to be seen by self-respecting adults." They joined the chorus of voices demanding government censorship. There were also insinuations that it was the Jewish studio owners and producers who were to blame for this swelling corruption.

In Canada, interestingly enough, officials and moralists not only drew attention to the sex and vice portrayed in U.S. films, they also ensured that government censors dealt with overt Americanism and American flag-waving in newsreels and movies. Only seduction and infidelity were ranked higher than "American flag-waving" by Canadian officials as offences committed in films.

In New York on Christmas Eve 1908, Mayor George B. McClellan (the son of the Civil War Union general) – acting on a recommendation from the police commissioner and after a round of rowdy public hearings – boldly revoked every movie-theatre licence in the city (many were vaudeville theatres) thereby shutting them down. New licences were granted only after exhibitors agreed to close their establishments on Sundays – a particular sore point among moralists. Within two days, movie-theatre owners led by William Fox got an injunction to stop the mayor's actions and city officials backed off. But the first shots had been fired in a censorship battle that dragged on for decades.

A Symbol of All the Vice

His closest friends never called him "Fatty," yet that's who he was to his legions of adoring fans. There was likely no more popular motion-picture celebrity in 1921 than Roscoe "Fatty" Arbuckle – five-foot-ten and close to three hundred pounds. He detested the nickname, a reminder of the bullying taunts he had been subjected to as a child. But he loved show business and knew how to play to a crowd. If moviegoers wanted him to be a jolly and slightly goofy fat man in farm overalls and a bowler hat, so be it.

He had recently signed a lucrative three-year contract with Adolph Zukor, the shrewd and successful president of Famous Players–Lasky (soon renamed Paramount Pictures) and the reigning king of Hollywood moguls.[*] For Arbuckle, the complex deal of cash, stock options, and bonuses was potentially worth $1 million and at

---

[*] As film historian Gregory Black points out, Zukor "was an organizational genius. He perfected the concept of vertical monopoly in the industry – production – distribution – exhibition – which allowed film companies to control their product from inception to final presentation. Zukor also understood, perhaps more so than any of the other original moguls, that stars sold films." Besides Roscoe Arbuckle, he had under contract cowboy William Hart, Mary Pickford, Douglas Fairbanks, Gloria Swanson, and Rudolph Valentino.

a minimum he was earning $250,000 annually – an enormous salary for the times. Only Arbuckle's fellow comedian and silent film star Charlie Chaplin, as talented a businessman as he was an entertainer, was earning more.* Like Chaplin, the baby-faced Arbuckle had started on the vaudeville circuit at a young age and come from an impoverished background. His mother had died when he was only twelve, and his alcoholic father had abandoned him. Somehow, he made it on his own, becoming a versatile performer and then by 1914 one of Mack Sennett's stable of stars at Keystone Film Company studios in Edendale (now Glendale) in Southern California. Shy and gentle in private, Arbuckle was a talented song-and-dance man. He possessed a beautiful tenor voice and was surprisingly agile for a man of his large size. Film actress Louise Brooks later recalled that when she danced with Arbuckle she felt as if she were "in the embrace of a floating doughnut."

He was a comedic wizard on stage and in the movies. One of his many claims to fame was that he had conceived the gag of the thrown cream pie, used on many occasions in Sennett's silent films. Arbuckle had been on the receiving end of a pie hurled at him by his friend, the brilliant and striking Mabel Normand. It was a crowd-pleaser. "The longer I worked with Roscoe the more I liked him," remembered comedian Buster Keaton. "He took falls no other man his weight ever attempted, had a wonderful mind for gags, which he could devise on the spot. . . . He had no meanness, malice or jealousy in him. Everything seemed to amuse and delight him. He was

---

* Arbuckle's extravagance with money was legendary. In 1921, he purchased a mansion in Los Angeles for $250,000 cash. "The house was ornately furnished," notes his biographer Andy Edmonds, "and Roscoe added hundreds of thousands of dollars in furnishings and knickknacks to the décor. He had a cellar stacked floor to ceiling with liquor (which became the most valuable asset when Prohibition was enacted on January 16, 1920, making his parties the most popular in town). He bought imported paneling, crystal chandeliers, Oriental rugs, marble counters, gold-leaved bathtubs, rare oil paintings, and antique china and crystal services. He had a butler, a chauffeur, and six cars."

free with advice and too free in spending and lending money. I could not have found a better-natured man to teach me the movie business, or a more knowledgeable one." Added Charlie Chaplin, "I knew Roscoe to be a genial, easy-going type who would not harm a fly." Arbuckle, however, did have one other major flaw – besides spending more money than he earned – and it ultimately destroyed his first marriage, to the actress Minta Durfree. He had inherited from his father an unhealthy appetite for liquor, and, like William Arbuckle, Roscoe was a nasty drunk.

Arbuckle, often accompanied by Buster Keaton, liked to unwind after working on a film with a brief excursion to San Francisco. The city in the early twenties was livelier than Los Angeles and the bootleg liquor of higher quality. Many film stars used San Francisco as a "party town," and its more refined citizens did not like it. The "rogues and ruffians from Hollywood" disrupted their "peaceful city with their ill-mannered ways," in the opinion of the *San Francisco Examiner*. "They behave like children who had yet experienced the back hand of a parent, they spend money wildly, and expect their conduct to be forgiven with the wave of a dollar bill." Gossip about movie stars with one-thousand-dollar-a-week cocaine habits participating in wild sex orgies added fuel to the fire.

Such was the mood when Arbuckle opted to spend the 1921 Labor Day weekend at the St. Francis Hotel in San Francisco with a few film friends rather than promote his new Paramount comedy *Gasoline Gus* as Adolph Zukor expected him to do. He should have listened to Zukor. Instead, Arbuckle's weekend jaunt in San Francisco altered his life forever, plunging him and the entire Hollywood community into a devastating scandal.

For the first two days of the trip, things remained unusually calm, although the group – Arbuckle, comedy director Fred Fischbach, and actor Lowell Sherman – had had a local bootlegger deliver a few bottles of gin and bourbon to their hotel rooms. The trouble started on Monday morning, September 5, with a drinking party that soon attracted about twenty people. The guests included Virginia Rappé (formerly Rapp), a model and chorus girl with a long list of Hollywood boyfriends (the most influential of whom was Keystone director Henry Lehrman), and Maude Delmont, a well-known con woman, professional correspondent, who would tell any story in divorce court she was asked to relate, as long as she was paid for it. Rappé that September weekend was likely recovering from a botched abortion she had undergone in San Francisco. Arbuckle did not like either woman, but Fischbach, after meeting them on the street, had invited Delmont and Rappé to the intimate gathering.

As the party continued into the late afternoon, Rappé, who had consumed a considerable amount of alcohol, became ill and slightly hysterical. She tore at her clothes, obviously in pain. It is possible (according to Arbuckle's biographer Andy Edmonds) that during a bit of horseplay Arbuckle, who had also drunk a lot, accidentally kneed Rappé in the stomach, triggering the attack. This was, however, never revealed at his subsequent trials. Arbuckle attempted to help Rappé and cool her high temperature with a bath of ice. Physicians were eventually called, and after heated discussions and much turmoil, Rappé was taken to hospital. Arbuckle checked out of the hotel and returned to Los Angeles. Several days later, Rappé died from a ruptured bladder leading to peritonitis likely caused by complications brought on by a recent abortion.

Maude Delmont – possibly out of spite or perhaps as part of a conspiracy to "get" Arbuckle, as Edmonds suggests – told the San Francisco police that Arbuckle had raped and assaulted Rappé.[*] The

---

* Edmonds's thesis, not much more than speculation, is that Zukor, who believed Arbuckle was overpaid, was upset with him for disobeying his orders and not attending a Paramount promotional gathering. He supposedly told Fred Fischbach to arrange to have Arbuckle photographed having sex with a woman – which explains the invitation to Rappé and Delmont – so that he could use the photos to renegotiate Arbuckle's contract. But the plan went awry when Rappé became ill. At the Hollywood Museum Archives, Edmonds also discovered a cheque signed by Zukor for ten thousand dollars that was made out to Matthew Brady, the San

police and San Francisco district attorney Matthew Brady, a man with political ambitions and an outspoken critic of Hollywood's low morals, had no trouble believing Delmont's convoluted tale. Damaging testimony by several other party guests – merely uncorroborated innuendo – and mutterings made by Rappé to nurses in the hospital, which Brady conveniently twisted, sealed Arbuckle's fate. He was arrested and charged with murder.

The newspapers quickly convicted him. "Torture of Virginia Rappé Charged," blared the *San Francisco Examiner*. "Arbuckle Dragged Girl to Room, Woman Testifies," declared the *New York Times*. "Ice on Actress Big Joke to Arbuckle," added the *Los Angeles Examiner*. The outrageous story, which later became an accepted part of Hollywood folklore, was that Arbuckle, sex-crazed and drunk, had viciously assaulted Rappé with a Coca-Cola bottle. The comedian suffered through three trials. The juries could not arrive at a decision in the first two, and at the third, held in early-March 1922, they finally saw through the web of lies spun by Delmont and acquitted Arbuckle.

Hollywood's collective reputation was stained further when William Desmond Taylor, a prominent director who worked for Paramount, was murdered while Arbuckle's second trial was under way. Although the perpetrator was never apprehended, the Los Angeles Police interrogated film stars Mabel Normand and Mary Miles Minter. Both had had intimate relations with Taylor. There were also sordid stories of excessive drug use, sexual escapades, and allegations that Taylor was a bisexual. One of his homosexual liaisons, it was speculated, had led to his death.

The gossip columns were still raging, too, about "America's Sweetheart," Mary Pickford. She had divorced her husband, actor Owen Moore, and married her long-time lover, the dashing Douglas

---

Francisco district attorney who went after Arbuckle. Although as Edmonds concedes, "the purpose of the check is not clear and it will never be known if this was the only other check sent to Brady."

Fairbanks, Jr. As one anonymous Hollywood reporter stated in a 1922 pamphlet entitled *The Sins of Hollywood* (published a month after Arbuckle's third trial), "There is something about the pictures which seem to make men and women less human, more animal like." Without naming names, the author offered an insider's look at Hollywood life: a catalogue of sin and depravity highlighted by orgies, dope smoking, and other examples of debauchery. "If the screen is to be cleaned up," the author wrote, "the sores must be cut open – the pus and corruption removed – This always hurts! But it is the only known way!"

Keen to be regarded as moral men, the movie moguls agreed. But they needed a scapegoat and they chose Roscoe "Fatty" Arbuckle. He was blamed for the ill will and resentment that had been building against Hollywood for many years. Arbuckle's legal proceedings had been costly. He owed more than $750,000 and became bankrupt. He was also fined $850 for violating Prohibition's Volstead Act after the federal government determined he had purchased illegal whisky in San Francisco. The Internal Revenue Service claimed he owed close to $100,000 in back taxes. His films were banned across the United States and Canada, and his reputation destroyed. The California District Attorney's office portrayed him as a degenerate and a pervert. The only people who stood by him were a handful of his fellow Hollywood actors.

His acquittal made no difference to Zukor and Jesse Lasky. They refused to pay his salary while he was charged and then had him blacklisted using the new power they had given to Will Hays, the head of the recently organized Motion Picture Producers and Distributors Association (MPPDA). As the *New York Times* editors wrote following the last trial, "Arbuckle has become, through mischance, a symbol of all the vice that has been indulged in by movie people . . . [and] the only thing to do with a scapegoat is to chase him into the wilderness."

Arbuckle did work again in Hollywood, as a director – using the alias William Goodrich or, as Buster Keaton cleverly called him, "Will B. Good" – and as a mentor for such up-and-coming young comedians as Bob Hope. Arbuckle's many fans welcomed him back. But for an array of politicians and religious officials, Arbuckle, no matter how repentant he was, remained forever linked to vice and sin. * Following two more marriages and a fairly successful attempt to re-establish himself, he died on June 29, 1933, from heart disease. By then, Hollywood had experienced a decade of moral guidance from Will Hays, although few people were satisfied.

The Czar of All the Rushes

Even before Roscoe Arbuckle's San Francisco fiasco, Adolph Zukor, Jesse Lasky, Carl Laemmle of Universal Pictures, William Fox of Fox Films, and Marcus Loew of Metro – which in a 1924 merger with Goldwyn Pictures and Louis B. Mayer became the giant Metro-Goldwyn-Mayer or MGM – realized that they had to take action to stem the growing public demand for federal government censorship. As it was, four states already had censorship boards, as did nearly every Canadian province – and they had been operating for nearly a decade in Pennsylvania, Ohio, Kansas, Ontario, and Manitoba. In 1921 and 1922, censorship legislation was introduced in thirty-seven states and five succeeded in passing it, including New York, which was of the greatest concern to Hollywood executives given New York City's status as the cultural capital of North America (the other states were Virginia, Florida,

---

* In 1925, for example, Arbuckle was scheduled to appear with Keaton and other dancers and singers in a comedy revue entitled *Public Revels*. The group was to perform at the Hollywood High School auditorium. At the last moment members of the school board, upon learning of Arbuckle's participation, refused to allow it. "In the interest of the school children of Los Angeles," the school board's secretary stated, Arbuckle "should not be permitted to appear on the school stage in view of the unenviable notoriety which has been attached to the former comedian."

Massachusetts, and Nebraska, although in the last two the bills were never implemented).

Within weeks of Arbuckle's acquittal, the major film companies quickly established an industry code, known as the "Thirteen Points." They pledged to stay away from such taboo subjects as white slavery and "illicit love affairs," not to glorify gambling, drunkenness, or the use of narcotics, and keep nudity, bloodshed, and violence out of their motion pictures. Despite their promises, New York governor Nathan Miller signed the censorship bill, declaring that the public had "heard that old story before." The governor had been especially upset about a scene in the film *Way Down East* (1920) from the brilliant and pioneering director D.W. Griffith. In the movie, the heroine gives birth to a baby with the accompanying words, "Maternity: Woman's Gethsemane (or agony)." On its first day of operation, the New York Commission cut scenes from a western that showed the inside of a saloon and from another that displayed too much of an actress's leg.

On top of this, the federal trade commission was investigating Zukor and Lasky's ingenious "block booking" system, which forced movie exhibitors to purchase a block of the studio's films – including ones they did not want – in order to obtain rights to show the movies starring popular actors and actresses. Zukor feared that the government interference might impede the necessary Wall Street financing for expansion plans he and the other studio heads were contemplating. As the 1920s began, Hollywood was about to grow rapidly into a multi-million dollar industry and the moguls needed cash and lots of it to fulfill their dreams. No one, particularly a former vaudeville comedian like Fatty Arbuckle, was going to stand in the way.

All of these various factors led to the creation of the Motion Picture Producers and Distributors Association (MPPDA) in the spring of 1922. To head it, the movie executives had wanted Herbert Hoover, then Secretary of Commerce in the Republican administration of

Warren Harding, but he turned them down. They settled for his colleague, the postmaster general, Will Hays.

For such a successful politician, Hays was an unremarkable-looking man. His most distinguishing feature was his large jug ears (he half-jokingly requested that photographers use "an ear-reduction lens" when taking a picture of him). He was a small-town lawyer from Indiana, who had worked his way up the ranks of the Republican Party and was respected for his superb organizational skills. Two other qualities made him the perfect candidate for the MPPDA. First, he staunchly opposed government censorship of motion pictures, maintaining that self-regulation was preferable by far. And second, and more importantly, he was a bit of a saint. Hays did not smoke, drink, or fool around with bad women. He was also an elder of his Presbyterian church. "Hays brought the respectability of mainstream middle America to a Jewish-dominated film industry," says film historian Gregory Black. "He symbolized the figurative Puritan in Babylon."

The movie moguls dangled an annual salary of $100,000-plus in front of him, and he agreed to their terms. Then, they held a gala dinner for him at the Waldorf-Astoria Hotel in New York and publicly showered him with praise. Never one to miss an opportunity to make a point, Zukor, as serious as ever, instructed Hays that he should never "permit our enemies to malign us on account of the action of any individual." Everyone in the ballroom knew that he was referring to Arbuckle.

Zukor and the other executives then returned to Los Angeles to oversee their empires, while Hays remained based in a New York office. Soon he was being promoted as "the Czar of all the Rushes."*

---

* Some time later, when Hays visited Hollywood, another dinner was held for him at a large hotel. Sam Marx, a MGM story editor attended. Hays delivered a speech about how wonderful he found Hollywood and how "sober" it was. He added, Marx recalled, "how he would do everything possible to give the public faith in the soundness of Hollywood and the moviemakers." Prohibition was still in effect at the time and he failed to notice that, "all around the moguls are sipping tea cups full of whiskey."

The question remained, however, whether Hays, essentially an employee of the movie moguls, could actually influence the content of their films.

The Don'ts and Be Carefuls

No one could ever have accused Will Hays of not being idealistic enough – despite the control the heads of the studios had over him. "Evil pictures have been produced, yes – but incalculable good has been accomplished," he argued in an article in January 1923. "The motion picture has carried the silent call for virtue, honesty, ambition, patriotism, hope, love of country and of home, to audiences speaking twenty different languages but understanding in common the universal language of pictures." He further believed that the film business was not only "one of the great industries in the country," but was also "an instrument and means of immeasurable education and moral influence; and we must not forget that even as we serve the leisure hours of the people with right diversion so do we rivet the girders of society." Pointing to the defeat of government censorship in the recent Massachusetts referendum – in the course of campaigning for which his office had spent three hundred thousand dollars – he argued that, in the final analysis, the American public would be "the real censor" and stay away from immoral movies.

As inspiring as he could be, Hays remained nothing more than the studio executives "employee," unable to control or dictate to his bosses how to make movies or what to put in them. "As a public relations agent, he was an unqualified success," says Gregory Black. But "as a censor or regulator of movie content during the 1920s, he was a failure. From his offices in New York, Hays had little contact with the Los Angeles studios and even less control over the content of films. The moguls had hired a spokesperson and lobbyist; they were reluctant to allow Hays to interfere with their producers in Hollywood."

Almost immediately, Hays's narrower definition of morality clashed with creative geniuses and trendsetters like director Cecile B. De Mille, who produced some of his best and most controversial work during the twenties. By the age of forty, in 1921, the muscular and handsome De Mille was Hollywood's most innovative film director. His strict father, an Episcopalian clergyman who also taught English at Columbia University, had wanted him to go into the military. De Mille was intent on being an actor and then a director. His entrée into the movies was through his friend Jesse Lasky, Adolph Zukor's partner. Except for a few years, De Mille remained connected to Lasky, Zukor, and Paramount for most of his long career. His success, notes film historian Garth Jowett, "lay in his uncanny ability to gauge which way the public's interest seemed to be shifting, and to pattern his productions accordingly by extending these shifting moods to almost illogical conclusions. The audience loved it."

De Mille wore only the most stylish clothes and he cut a dashing figure on the set and around Hollywood. Starting with such movies as *Joan the Woman*, his first real epic, and *The Little American* with Mary Pickford, he ensured that his films had the best set designers, costumers, hairstylists, and, above all, the most popular and sexy actors and actresses. He used sex appeal and the suggestion of sexual pleasure like no other director before him. "Cecil B. De Mille converted the bedroom into a boudoir," wrote cultural historian Lloyd Morris in 1949, "divorcing it from its familiar and literal associations with sleep. Largely because of him, the verb itself, as used by Americans, shed all suggestions of dormancy."

In *Male and Female* (1919) he had Gloria Swanson appear in one memorable bath scene more or less naked, and *Manslaughter* (1922) included a shocking Roman orgy, complete with nude actresses. Naked or near-naked women were mandatory for him. "I wear twenty-eight costumes and if I put them on all at once, I couldn't keep warm," declared Betty Blythe, the star of *Queen of Sheba* (1921). Many of De Mille's films had eye-opening titles, which kept his audiences guessing right up until after they paid the price of admission – *Why Change Your Wife?*, *The Golden Bed*, and *Forbidden Fruit*. He understood that even the hint of something sinful on the screen would produce lineups at the movie theatres. Then in 1923 he produced his first (silent) version of *The Ten Commandments* with a healthy dose of sex added to the Biblical saga. This was followed four years later with *The King of Kings*, a daring film about the life of Christ that upset a large number of Protestants, Catholics, and Jews.

De Mille's audacious productions proved problematic for Will Hays. Hays had appointed a public relations committee – headed by Colonel Jason Joy, the former national secretary of the American Red Cross – composed of representatives from women's groups, churches, the YMCA, Boy Scouts of America, and the American Library Association. De Mille's daring work, or that of other innovative Hollywood directors, did not impress them. Hays's hands were tied. A few months after his New York office opened, he tried to reinstate Fatty Arbuckle, but the committee was intensely hostile to the idea and he was forced to devise another solution to that problem. Confronted with the failure of Prohibition and the rapid decline in public morals, the members of these citizen organizations were impatient with Hays's plodding approach.

Still, Hays must get credit for trying to appease both the moralists and the moguls. In 1924, he unveiled "The Formula," a measure supported, on paper at least, by the members of the MPPDA. Under this plan, studios were to forward synopses and scripts to the Hays's office prior to filming so that any potential controversies could be detected early. Hays later claimed that in 1925 "The Formula" stopped 160 "prevalent books and plays" from being adapted for motion pictures. Yet such decisions were purposely kept confidential, so the public rarely knew how diligently Hays was advancing the cause of decency in movies. More significantly, if a studio wanted to make a racy film, such as The Famous Players–Lasky 1924 production *West of the Water Tower* – which "portrayed small town life as petty and repressed, and included the character of a 'dissolute clergyman'" – there was not much Hays could do about it.

The following year, he formalized Joy's committee into the Department of Public Relations, which was supposed to have more direct contact between his office, representing "the moral forces of the country," as he said, and movie producers. Joy ran the department until 1932 and was then replaced by Carl Milliken, the former governor of Maine. Nevertheless, the cries for tougher censorship of movies grew louder, and more than one hundred bills were soon pending in forty-four state legislatures demanding stricter rules and more rigid enforcement.

It was Col. Joy's turn next to tackle the problem. In 1927, he helped create a more comprehensive set of guidelines, which he fittingly entitled, "The Don'ts and Be Carefuls." It consisted of eleven "don'ts" and twenty-six "be carefuls" that movie producers and directors were to avoid. Like the earlier "Thirteen Points," the "don'ts" included "Pointed profanity," references to Jesus or God, "any licentious or suggestive nudity" (not even in silhouette), illegal traffic in drugs, white slavery, miscegenation (sexual relations between white and black races), sex hygiene, venereal disease, and ridicule of the clergy. The "be carefuls," on the other hand, warned about the improper use of the flag, the depiction of crime, sympathy for criminals, cruelty to children and animals, rape or attempted rape, deliberate seduction of girls, double occupancy of a bed, and "excessive lustful kissing," particularly when one or other character was a villain.

The adoption of "The Don'ts and Be Carefuls" coincided with the advent of sound in movies and thus took on even greater significance. Warner Brothers' release in October 1927 of *The Jazz Singer*, starring Al Jolson, inaugurated the age of the "talkies" and transformed the industry. Skeptics, like the usually astute MGM producer Irving Thalberg, considered sound pictures a fad, but when moviegoers heard Jolson utter the immortal lines "Wait a minute.

Wait a minute. You ain't heard nothin' yet," audiences across North America applauded. From the perspective of Hays and Joy, however, sound also gave new meaning to the double entendre. Now, what Mae West and others had been saying for years on the stage would be heard in movie theatres. The result was both thrilling and potentially dangerous.

If the moralists were unhappy, so too were the studio executives, but for a different reason. Those who had tried to go along with Hays and Joy were losing money to competitors who did what they pleased. The head of Universal, Carl Laemmle, had tried to follow the guidelines, but his reputation, as he stated in a letter to Hays, for making "namby-pamby" movies was costing him money. "Invariably," he wrote, "they are too damned clean, and [the public] stay away on account of it."

The public had flocked to MGM's *Ben-Hur*, which apart from the famous chariot race also, movie journalist Mick LaSalle notes, "featured naked nymphs (in long shot) strewing flower petals in the path of the hero." They also loved it when a "sweaty Joan Crawford dropped her skirt for a hot Charleston in *Our Dancing Daughters*," and watched Renée Adorée in *Mating Call* swimming in a "sheer chemise."

The criticism and problems aside, Hays maintained his faith in self-regulation over government regulation of the industry. It was dangerous, he argued, to tamper with creativity of human thought. State censorship boards took a contrary view and demanded cuts. In New York in 1928, for instance, the state censorship board deleted four thousand scenes from more than six hundred films its members reviewed. Most dealt with portrayals of crime and sex.

Protestant and Catholic groups intensified their lobbying in Washington for more censorship, not less. "The moving picture might be a very practical vehicle of education and amusement," stated Archbishop Michael J. Curley, the Bishop of Maryland, at a hearing to consider federal regulation of films in 1926, "but as a matter of fact . . . the major impression made by the movies of today is that they are more destructive than constructive. They tend to dissipate the mind, to cripple its power of concentration on serious work by our young people, and worst of all, they have little, if any, moral-uplifting effect. They treat of illegitimate love affairs, of triangular situations, of marital infidelity, and of sex problems, ad nauseam." Rabbi William Rosenau from Baltimore said he did not want to be an "uplifter" of morality, yet agreed with the Bishop that movies were "fast becoming a menace to society."

Meanwhile the *Churchman*, a prominent Methodist journal, attacked the MPPDA and accused Hays of being "a smoke screen to mask [the] meretricious methods . . . [of] shrew Hebrews who make the big money by selling crime and shame." Hays was also labelled a "seller of swill and an office boy" and was criticized in 1929 for divorcing his wife after twenty-seven years of marriage.

The Curse of the Modern World

On the eve of the Depression, the mood in some quarters was decidedly anti-Hollywood.[*] William Randolph Hearst used his newspapers to push for federal government intervention. And in March 1929, Iowa senator Smith Bookhart introduced a bill to have the Federal Trade Commission regulate the film industry.

Around this time, Hays received an urgent telephone call from Martin Quigley. Born in Cleveland in 1890, Quigley had married the wealthy Gertrude Schofield of Chicago in 1913. This enabled him to become the editor and then publisher of the *Exhibitor's-Herald*, which

---

[*] At least one notable commentator, H.L. Mencken, typically took a different view. Writing about Hollywood's alleged immorality for his magazine *American Mercury* in 1927, he observed in his inimitable style after a visit to California that "Hollywood, despite the smell of patchouli and rattle of revolver fire, seemed to me to be one of the most respectable towns in America. . . . The notion that actors are immoral fellows is a delusion that comes down to us from Puritan days, just as the delusion that rum is a viper will go down to posterity from our days. There is no truth in it."

he merged with *Moving Picture World* in 1931 to form the *Motion Picture Herald*, the largest trade journal in Hollywood. He had attended Catholic University of America and was closely aligned with the Catholic hierarchy in Chicago. He had little faith in Hays's "don'ts and be carefuls." He wanted to implement strict regulations that would finally stop objectionable movies from being made and make censorship unnecessary. As he wrote in his 1937 book *Decency in Motion Pictures*, "The overall depiction of evil [which he classified as "sin, crime and sordidness"] must be weighed, insuring that the end results in audience reaction will not amount to an invasion of the ideas and ideals of morality which the audience entertains." If films were not severely controlled, he warned, they would become "the curse of the modern world."

In 1929, there were twenty million Catholics in the United States and more than two million more in Canada. Most lived in big urban centres on the east coast and in Chicago. In short, they represented a large number of moviegoers. Talk of unified action, even a boycott, rightly concerned the studios.

On the recommendation of Quigley and Father FitzGeorge Dinneen, a Jesuit pastor from Chicago and a member of Chicago's Board of Censorship, Hays gave the task of coming up with a new movie code to Reverend Daniel A. Lord, who had worked as a consultant on De Mille's *King of Kings*. Like Dinneen, Lord was a Jesuit priest, but also a professor of dramatics at St. Louis University and a prolific and popular religious writer – of some 227 pamphlets, 30 books, 12 booklets, 48 volumes for children, 12 pageants, 3 musicals, and 5 other pieces of music. He was known for his frank opinions on a wide range of controversial issues, including abortion, communism, Darwinism, sex, and literature.

In general, he railed against the "joys of sin" and had a healthy skepticism of Hollywood while recognizing its tremendous influence. More than a decade earlier, he had seen Griffith's *The Birth of a Nation* and understood at once that such films had potential, as he said, to "change our whole attitude toward life, civilization and established custom."

In completing his assignment, Lord was advised by George Cardinal Mundelein of Chicago, MPPDA lawyer Charles Pettijohn, and Joseph I. Breen, a politically conservative Catholic layman from Philadelphia who had worked as a reporter for the *North American*. Breen was experienced in public relations but was notoriously anti-Semitic. He made little attempt to hide his disdain for the Jewish movie moguls. Nevertheless, he would eventually be appointed director of the Production Code Administration in 1934 and become responsible for instituting Hollywood morality for more than two decades.

Lord relished his task. "Here was a chance," he later recalled, "to tie the *Ten Commandments* in with the newest and most widespread form of entertainment. Here was an opportunity to read morality and decency into mass recreation." His "Production Code," as it became known, adopted in 1930, had the usual restrictions on profanity, crime, sin, blasphemy, adultery, obscenity, suggestive dancing, and nudity. "The more intimate parts of the human body are male and female organs and the breasts of a woman," Lord had deemed. "They should never be uncovered." A distinction was also made between pure and impure love. It was all far more thorough than anything that had come out of Hays's office during the twenties.

Lord recognized that motion pictures were a form of entertainment, but maintained that this entertainment had a unique "moral importance." He linked motion pictures to the entire moral fabric of American life. His basic premise, as he explained, was that "correct entertainment raised the whole standard of a nation. Wrong entertainment lowers the whole living condition and moral ideals of a race."

Hays later said that he was elated when he first saw Lord's draft code. "My eyes nearly popped out when I read it," he wrote in his memoirs. "This was the very thing I had been looking for." The studio executives and producers were more dubious.

In early February 1930, only a few months after the stock market crash (which had not yet had its full impact on Hollywood) Hays and Joy met with a number of representatives from the major studios, including Jesse Lasky, Irving Thalberg, and Jack Warner. At issue was how much "special moral responsibility," as Lord had phrased it, did the industry have. Thalberg of MGM said little and attempted to convince the group that the motion picture did not present movie audiences with morals and values, it merely reflected those they already had. Hays knew that Lord vehemently disagreed with this position. As he subsequently told Thalberg, "You set the standards; you inculcate an idea of customs; you create fashions in dress."

Thalberg and his colleagues saw no reason to accept the code, but after Lord travelled to Los Angeles to present his case the executives had reversed their position within twenty-four hours. The Production Code was approved and announced to the public on April 1, 1930.

Why did they change their minds? It was more for practical reasons than a sudden conversion to Lord's way of thinking.[*] They feared that if they did not take a more decisive step towards true self-regulation, the federal government would take over the industry. As well, they had incurred heavy expenses converting thousands of theatres to sound and depended on huge financing from the banks. Given the drastic economic climate, they needed to ensure that operations ran smoothly, since the banks demanded a "stabilized industry." As it was, William Fox was the first to suffer from the crash. He had lost control of his company in late 1929 (after dropping $50 million in the stock markets) and would declare personal

---

[*] At the same time, this was how most of them likely felt. Louis B. Mayer, for instance, who regarded himself a man of sound moral character, believed like Lord that motion pictures should be above reproach.

bankruptcy a few years later. Thus, no one wanted a Catholic boycott of the movies. Who knew where that could lead?

As in the past, however, adherence to the code, no matter how clear the code was, demanded complete compliance, and not surprisingly that proved extremely difficult. The studios continued to churn out movies that Lord and others felt went far beyond the bounds of the code and good taste. Whereas in Canada, the public and the press were more accepting of censorship, recognizing its moral value and trusting the provincial governments' authority in this matter, U.S. newspapers and commentators were more critical of attempts to legislate morality – at least when it came to the movies. And the American public, whose welfare everyone was so concerned about, continued to go to the picture shows. The only point upon which all interested parties could agree was that instituting the Production Code without also imposing severe punishment for violations would be next to impossible.

While many scripts were vetted by Joy – of the nearly 1,400 feature-film scripts the MPPDA scrutinized between 1931 and 1933, it rejected almost 280, or 20 per cent of them – many more films were produced that broke the code. This greatly distressed Lord, who believed this lack of enforcement led to movies adopting a "fundamentally dangerous . . . philosophy of life."

The list of motion pictures that had gone too far, in the view of Lord and his colleagues, was a lengthy one. In *No Man of Her Own* (1932), Clark Gable, who played a conniving gambler, brilliantly seduced actress Carole Lombard. Joy had seen the script of this film and approved it; Lord thought it was a "filthy" movie. In Howard Hughes's *Hell's Angels* (1930), Jean Harlow tried to seduce a pilot, while in Paramount's *Confessions of a Co-Ed* (1931), two men chased the same woman. James Cagney gave such a memorable performance in *Public Enemy* (1931) that he turned gangsters into heroes.

Contributing to the tension was Mae West. She had arrived in Hollywood in 1932 and reworked her controversial Broadway play

Diamond Lil into the movie *She Done Him Wrong*, complete with all the double entendres that had made her so infamous. In one legendary scene, West's character, Lou, was arrested by an undercover agent named Captain Cummings, played by a youthful Cary Grant. He held out a set of handcuffs for her: "Are those absolutely necessary? You know, I wasn't born with 'em," said West.

"No. A lot of men would've been safer if you had," replied Grant.

"Oh, I don't know. Hands ain't everything," West retorted.

Censor boards hated the film, but the fans loved it. *She Done Him Wrong* earned more than two million dollars in three months. It was so successful that it helped lift Paramount out of serious financial problems caused by the economic downturn.

Just as controversial was De Mille's *The Sign of the Cross*, a $650,000 Roman-Christian saga he produced in 1932. It included scenes of seductive dancing, blood and gore, group sex, references to homosexuality, and beautiful Claudette Colbert naked in a milk bath. The hot lighting curdled the milk but despite the stench Colbert looked sexier than ever. Predictably religious officials denounced the movie as "highly offensive," "repellent," and "nauseating." The *New York Times* was much kinder, calling it a "striking pictorial spectacle."[*]

Joseph Breen, now working with Hays on improving public relations, blamed in general the immorality that he believed permeated Hollywood society, and in particular the Jewish moguls. "This burg is probably the mad house of the universe," he had informed Hays from Hollywood in August 1931. A year later, around the time *The Sign of the Cross* was released, he confided

---

[*] During production, Hays had called De Mille and told him that there was one particular dance sequence that presented a problem. At the time Martin Quigley was visiting Hays. As the conversation proceeded, Hays asked De Mille what he planned to do about it. "Will, listen carefully to my words because you might want to quote them. Not a damn thing."

his true feelings in a letter to his friend Father Wilfrid Parsons, the editor of the Catholic publication *America*. He wrote that Hays lacked "guts" and that the Jews who managed most of the studios were contemptible. "Hays sold us a first-class bill of good when he put over the Code on us," he told Parsons. "It may be that Hays thought these lousy Jews out here would abide by the Code's provisions but if he did then he should be censured for his lack of proper knowledge of the breed." The Jewish studio owners, he added, "are simply a rotten bunch of vile people with no respect for anything beyond the making of money. . . . Here we have Paganism rampant and in its most virulent form. . . . These Jews seem to think of nothing but money making and sexual indulgence. . . . They are probably the scum of the scum of the earth."

The moguls may not have been fully aware of Breen's anti-Semitic venom, but they had a good enough idea how he felt. For a variety of reasons – most notably their view that they were Americans before they were Jews – they chose to ignore it. Breen, moreover, had the ear of the well-organized Catholic community, whose leaders were determined to win this battle. They soon organized the Catholic Legion of Decency – with chapters in the U.S. and Canada, the League represented more than nine million Catholics – and threatened a nationwide Catholic boycott if the Production Code was not properly enforced.

The worsening economic climate and the concern over negative publicity led the studio executives to capitulate. Breen was appointed head of the new Production Code Administration in early July 1934 with the power to fine studios twenty-five thousand dollars for not complying with the regulations. He became the movie "czar" that Hays had always wanted to be. *Film Weekly* called him "The Hitler of Hollywood." For the next two decades, he wielded power and considerable influence, imposing his superior and exalted sense of morality on the rest of the movie community and, in a broader way, much of North America.[*]

Modern life would proceed, but not without substantial input from moralists like Breen and his friends, whose vision of purity and a healthy America would continue to shape the society. Their faith in the future demanded nothing less.

---

[*] Breen did not win every battle. When he first saw the script for the film *Gone with the Wind*, he did not approve of Clark Gable's immortal line at the end of movie, "Frankly, my dear, I don't give a damn." He wanted it changed to "My dear, I don't care." Producer David Selznick won that argument.

CONCLUSION

Fear and Progress

We don't know . . . we aren't sure . . . we're wondering.
— Archibald MacLeish, *Land of the Free*, 1938

In the End the Truth Is Bound to Prevail

Hollywood's indiscretions may have received a lot of attention from moral crusaders, yet they paled when compared to those of Wall Street. If morality in America was under attack in the twenties, it was not in fact in Los Angeles but in New York where greed, corruption, and unscrupulous behaviour were routine.

One of the few who saw the true crisis looming was William Ripley, a professor of political economy at Harvard University. In 1927, Ripley wrote *Main Street and Wall Street*, a highly critical account of American corporate business practices. In the book, he denounced the high-risk speculation, secrecy, and nepotism that characterized the operations of many companies. President Calvin Coolidge, who was also skeptical of the bull market and inflated stock prices, sent for the Harvard economist, and in a private interview at the White House, Ripley painted a harsh picture of Wall Street as a place dominated by self-interest and dishonesty. Stock speculation was out of control, and a crash, he claimed, was inevitable. "Prosperity, not real but specious, may indeed be unduly protracted by artificial means," he wrote, "but in the end, the truth is bound to prevail." Ripley's book sold fifty thousand copies and received a lot of press, yet on Wall Street nothing changed. "It was," writes historian Geoffrey Perrett, "as though the stock market led a life all its own."

That was what Michael J. Meehan would have argued, at any rate. He was exactly the type of Wall Street operator who Ripley scorned. Meehan was the son of poor Irish Catholic immigrants and had arrived in New York City early in the twentieth century when he was still a young boy. A natural salesman, he found work peddling cigarettes for the United Cigar Store Company and was a store manager by the time he was eighteen. He moved on to a job selling Broadway theatre tickets, but his sights were set on Wall Street.

In 1920, Meehan became a stockbroker and despite a few set-backs quickly made a name for himself as a man who knew when to buy and, more importantly, at what moment to sell. It allowed him to make a great deal of money for his clients and for himself. By 1929, when he was thirty-seven years old, he owned a brokerage house with close to four hundred employees and boasted of having an annual payroll of six hundred thousand dollars. His firm had eight seats on the New York Stock Exchange; the last one had cost him nearly half a million dollars. Money, he had told newspaper reporters, "was there for the spending and making." He was short, wore steel-rimmed glasses, was slightly chubby, and smoked too many cigarettes. On Wall Street, he was known for his ruthlessness and bravado. His eyes and ears were everywhere.

In the spring of 1929, his instincts told him that a stock to buy was the Radio Corporation of America, or RCA. A decade earlier, "Radio," as RCA was called around the Exchange, then its infancy, was selling at $2.50 a share; in early 1929 it had reached $85, and

Meehan knew it could go higher still. All that was required was a little push.

He amassed his pool of investors. John Jacob Raskob, a director of General Motors, who was planning the construction of the Empire State Building, put in $1 million. Walter Chrysler, a brilliant automobile industrialist from Detroit, who was also set to unveil his magnificent seventy-seven-storey skyscraper on the east side of 42nd Street, gave Meehan $500,000. Others, like Billy Durant, Percy Rockefeller, and Joseph Tumulty, formerly President Woodrow Wilson's executive secretary, advanced amounts ranging from $75,000 to $400,000. Meehan's wife, Elizabeth, was marked down for $1 million.

By the first week of March, sixty-eight investors had presented Meehan with a total of $12.7 million with which to gamble. He tapped his regular sources in the financial press, at the *Wall Street Journal* and the New York *Daily News*, and positive if vague stories soon appeared touting RCA stock. Like magic, Radio began climbing above ninety dollars a share and Meehan began accumulating large amounts of it. The hype quickly spread across the country; in San Francisco, Chicago, Boston, and St. Louis, speculators could not buy RCA fast enough.

Within a week, using a host of questionable if not unethical strategies, Meehan and his team of brokers managed to push the RCA stock price up to a hugely inflated $109 a share, at which point Meehan started unloading his group's stock, and RCA gradually dropped back down to $87. By the end of it, he had a $4.9 million profit to divide among his satisfied investors. (Raskob, for example, got his million dollars back along with $291,710.80.) Between his wife's share of the pot and his 10 per cent commission, Meehan walked away with more than one million. It was all in a week's work on Wall Street – and he had not broken one rule or regulation of the New York Stock Exchange.

Meehan's manipulations were typical. When it came to making money, morality took a back seat.[*] In the years leading up to the great crash of October 1929, Wall Street was, as Walter Ripley argued, a place where swindles, embezzlement, fraud, and corruption occurred almost daily. At the same time, bankers caught up in the fervour loaned millions of dollars to brokers, who in turn loaned this money to their clients to accumulate more and more stocks. In most cases, these stock speculators put down as little as 10 per cent of the purchase price. If the stock dropped, they would be forced to cover the total cost of a losing venture. It was a tenuous and risky arrangement, yet greed won out over common sense.

Less-than-honest bankers and brokers devised a variety of ways to beat the system. Once the market collapsed, these various schemes were exposed, and thousands of ordinary depositors discovered that they had been bilked out of their hard-earned savings. They were soon astonished to learn that their trusted bankers had been using their money to speculate on the stock market and had lost it all. The biggest failure was the New York–based Bank of the United States, an institution with close to sixty branches and four hundred thousand customers. As the market collapsed, its president, Bernard K. Marcus, and his executives suffered huge losses. Most of the money they squandered had been taken from their clients' accounts. Marcus ended up in jail, but that was little comfort to the bank's customers, who were left with nothing.

October 29, 1929, otherwise known as Black Tuesday, was the worst day in Wall Street history to that point. It destroyed any chance for a recovery. Millions of North Americans soon felt the sting of the Great Depression.

---

[*] Meehan suffered from the stock market crash like everyone else. In total, he lost an estimated $40 million. The newly organized Securities Exchange Commission investigated him in 1936. He was accused of impropriety and was eventually expelled from the NYSE. He died at the age of fifty-six in 1948, still proclaiming his innocence.

The Only Thing We Have to Fear Is Fear Itself

The economic crisis of the 1930s was not caused solely by crooked bankers and brokers, or even by the frantic materialism that had come to symbolize modern life.[*] The factors were far more complex – a combination of poor business and government practices, overproduction, harmful protective tariffs, a drop in foreign trade in the United States, the drastic decline in world agricultural prices, and a period of horrendous weather that devastated the agricultural economies of the American Midwest and Canadian prairies. Added to this were the governments of President Herbert Hoover in United States and Prime Minister Richard B. Bennett in Canada, neither of which truly grasped the magnitude of disaster. As unemployment soared, people ran out of money, stifling consumer spending and crippling the finances of both countries.

Franklin Delano Roosevelt, who replaced Hoover as president after the election of November 1932, tried to reassure Americans in his inaugural address that the "only thing we have to fear is fear itself." But they were fearful nevertheless. And who could blame them?

"Fear was the great leveller of the Great Depression," journalist and editor T.H. Watkins writes in his chronicle of America in the thirties. "It haunted the dreams of the African-American sharecropper in the South who held a fistful of barren dust in his hand and wondered what the system would do now to cheat him and his family of life. It stalked the middle-class white merchant in Idaho who had seen decades of work destroyed when his once-friendly banker forced him into bankruptcy. . . . Fear shattered all the fine Anglo-Saxon certitudes of the Great Plains farm wife who watched black clouds of dust roll up on the edge of the horizon."

---

[*] Few individuals epitomized the desire to win at any cost more than Albert Wiggin, the president of the Chase National Bank. Late in 1929 he made four million dollars, as historian Ferdinand Pecora points out, "by selling short the stock of his own bank."

Many people had lost everything – their jobs, families, dignity, and hope. In New York City alone, three hundred thousand workers were unemployed in 1931, and the numbers kept rising. Millions across North America became destitute. For a good two years, governments were helpless and people literally starved. "We saw the city at its worst," Louise Armstrong writes in her memoir of those years. "Our vivid, gruesome moment of those dark days we shall never forget. We saw a crowd of some fifty men fighting over a barrel of garbage which had been set outside the back door of a restaurant. American citizens fighting for scraps of food like animals!"

Being "on the dole," or accepting government relief, was not an option for most people. The stigma was too devastating. Indeed, for many there was something morally repugnant about living off state and provincial handouts. "The dole smacked of helplessness," writes Geoffrey Perrett, "once dependent, always dependent."

The unemployed were blamed for the terrible predicament they found themselves in, as if they were responsible for their destitution. The message delivered nearly six decades earlier by the outspoken New York preacher Henry Ward Beecher continued to hold true. "Looking comprehensively through city and town," he had repeatedly told his congregation, "the general truth will stand, that no man in this land suffers from poverty unless it be more than his fault – unless it be his sin. . . . There is enough and to spare thrice over; and if men have not enough of it, it is owing to the want of provident care, and foresight, and industry and frugality and wise saving. This is the general truth."[*] But provident care and foresight were not always enough, and thousands of single men were compelled to adopt the life of hobos. They rode the rails in search of work yet were depicted by governments and the press as potential agitators, even radicals, who were a threat to law and order.

---

[*] This idea was even conveyed in Walt Disney's 1933 animated version of *The Three Little Pigs*, which, says historian Paul Johnson, "presented hard work as the only protection from the Big Bad Wolf of despair."

In the devastated cities and across the drought-ridden prairies, fear was endemic and the future grim. The uncertainty made people cautious, more conservative, and less tolerant, and it was this mood of anxiety and insecurity that the American poet and playwright Archibald MacLeish later captured so brilliantly in his long poem *Land of the Free*.

North Americans had always viewed immigrants, particularly those from eastern and southern Europe and Asia, with a measure of suspicion and contempt. The United States had shut its doors in 1924; Canada followed in 1931, when the federal government instituted a restrictive policy banning everyone except British subjects and U.S. citizens with sufficient means to fend for themselves.

Later in the decade, both countries, but especially Canada, refused to receive large numbers of Jewish refugees fleeing Nazi Germany. From 1933 to 1945, the United States admitted two hundred thousand European Jews, while Canada found room for only five thousand – the lowest of any western country; even Chile and Bolivia each accepted more. In Ottawa, Canadian officials saw nothing to apologize for. "Pressure on the part of the Jewish people to get into Canada has never been greater than it is now," reported Frederick Blair, the deputy minister of immigration in Ottawa, "and I am glad to be able to add after thirty-five years experience here, that it was never so well controlled."

William Lyon Mackenzie King, who defeated Bennett in the 1935 general election, was an anti-Semite, a typical member of the Canadian Anglo-Saxon elite, willing to conduct business with Jews but keen to exclude them from social clubs, resorts, and universities. Jewish immigration was particularly unpopular in Quebec, where the Catholic Church was strong and vocal and King was fearful of losing political support. He also purchased all of the land around his country property outside of Ottawa so that Jews would not be able to buy it. Echoing sentiments expressed by Madison Grant and other proponents of eugenics, he wrote in his diary in March 1938, "We must seek to keep this part of the continent free from unrest and from too great an intermixture of foreign strains of blood."

As economic conditions worsened, prejudice, discrimination, and bigotry increased. While Father Charles Coughlin continued to berate Jews in his radio broadcasts, white mobs, often led by the Ku Klux Klan, took out their frustration on African-Americans. Nearly 120 black people were lynched between 1930 and 1938.

The moral and racial implications were clear: accusations of sexual misconduct would be dealt with viciously. At the end of May 1930, for example, a nineteen-year-old African-American named Henry Argo from Chickasha in rural Oklahoma was alleged to have raped the wife of a white farmer. Despite the lack of hard evidence, a white mob broke into the jail where Argo was being detained and shot him. He did not die immediately. Three hours later, as Chickasha's sheriff stood by, the husband of the woman Argo had supposedly assaulted stabbed him to death. No one was ever brought to trial for the murder.

In 1934, in Jackson County, Florida, a twenty-three-year-old married black man named Claude Neal was accused of raping and killing Lola Cannidy, a nineteen-year-old white woman. Neal often worked on the farm where Cannidy lived. Again without any real evidence, Neal was arrested and charged with the crime. The authorities moved him across the state line to a jail in Alabama to protect him, but a mob of fifteen men soon abducted Neal and brought him back to Florida. Before they hanged him, he was tortured and mutilated. His body was strung up on a tree beside the local courthouse. "What America needs today," declared one Jackson County newspaper, "is men who are willing to defend virtue and womanhood not only against the brute Negro, but the social temptations of today that are placed around our girls."

In nearby Fort Lauderdale on July 19, 1935, Rubin Stacey, an African-American, was lynched for merely looking at a white woman the wrong way. Franklin Roosevelt had called lynching "a vile form of collective murder," yet time and again, attempts to pass an anti-lynching bill in Congress were defeated by the stiff resolve of politicians from the segregated South.

The fear generated by the Depression turned equally on those who dared challenge the rule of law and order. As strikes and labour demonstrations erupted across North America and unemployed men demanded work, the hostility that equated unions and working-class rights with a communist revolution was revived. The demon of the "Red Menace" had returned with a vengeance.

In the United States the small Communist Party, now reorganized as the Trade Union Unity League under the leadership of William Z. Foster, saw the stock market crash as a sure sign of capitalism's demise. Their attempts to lead the unemployed in parades and marches in New York, Philadelphia, Cleveland, Chicago, and other cities brought down upon them the full wrath of paranoid police forces. "Thousands of terrified people scattered rushing for safety from the flailing police, shouting, stumbling, stepping over one another in their fear and haste to get away," reported the *New York Times* after thousands of peaceful protestors were attacked near Union Square on March 6, 1930. "Hundreds of policemen and detectives, swinging nightsticks, blackjacks, and bare fists, rushed into the crowd, hitting out at all with whom they came into contact."

The League spent most of its efforts supporting union activity and strikes. But even when Foster and his colleagues were only marginally involved, labour disputes in the United States during the early thirties were regarded as Bolshevik-inspired revolutions and dealt with harshly. As in 1919, the protection of civil liberties was one of the first casualties of the Depression.

In September 1930, state militia confronted textile workers on strike in Virginia. Coal miners in West Virginia, Pennsylvania, and

Ohio walked off their jobs in the summer of 1931, and when communist groups joined the picket lines and set up soup kitchens, there
were violent attacks on the strikers and union men were murdered.
It was the same in Harlan County, Kentucky. Non-unionized coal
miners asked the communist-run National Mineworkers Union
(NMU) for assistance after their wages were drastically cut. The
NMU's presence exacerbated the situation and led to bloody confrontations between the miners and the company and police. A NMU
soup kitchen was blown up and opponents of the miners even
attacked reporters covering the story.

Thousands of unemployed veterans, soldiers who had fought for
the country during the First World War, decided to take their cause
to the White House. In June 1932, they made their way to
Washington to protest the lack of a proper military pension. They set
up twenty-seven camps in and around the city, including inside several
vacant government-owned buildings. The House of Representatives
passed a much-needed bill granting a bonus to the veterans, but then
it stalled in the Senate. At that point, President Hoover decided that
the squatters posed a threat and had to be removed. After the police
failed to accomplish this, Hoover called in General Douglas
MacArthur, the chief of staff of the Army, to get the job done. He was
instructed to work with the police and clear the men out.

The president did not want to start a war, yet MacArthur had
other ideas. Like many others, he believed the massing of homeless
men, veterans or not, was the beginning of a revolution. Readying
himself for the battle, he brought in the cavalry and tanks. With
their swords held high, his troops advanced toward the first crowd
of unemployed men as they would any dangerous enemy. They used
tear gas and set fire to the protestors' shanties. The veterans tried to
resist the onslaught and the war that Hoover had tried to avoid
broke out. Watching from a distance, General MacArthur, "his chest
glittering with medals," as journalist Thomas Stokes later recalled,

"strode up and down the middle of Pennsylvania Avenue, flipping a riding crop against his neatly pressed breeches." By the next morning, the veterans had been dispersed.

In Canada, protests by Communists and the unemployed produced the same reaction. Even before the October crash, the police in Toronto assaulted activists taking part in what was intended to be a peaceful communist rally in front of the Ontario legislature. Denny Draper, the chief of police, had boasted that he would teach the Communists a lesson they would not forget. As the police waded into the crowd with their truncheons, kicking those who had fallen down, they shouted at the marchers to "get back to Russia." Most of the city's newspapers concurred. "SEND THE BOLSHEVIKS BACK," blared the headline of the *Globe* the next day.

The pattern was repeated throughout the decade, as local authorities from Winnipeg to Windsor, fearful of a revolution, dealt harshly with any activity they suspected involved Communists. If there were troubles with the unemployed, so the official thinking went, it had to be part of a Bolshevik conspiracy to overthrow the government. "If we could get rid of [the Communists]," declared Major-General James MacBrien, commissioner of the RCMP, "there would be no unemployment."

The Canadian federal government still had at its disposal Section 98 of the Criminal Code, implemented in 1919 to quash the leaders of the Winnipeg General Strike (it would be not repealed until 1936). It allowed the authorities to arrest any member of an organization, or anyone linked to it, no matter how tenuously, who "sought by acts or threats of force, violence or injury to bring about any government, industrial, or economic change in Canada." In mid-August 1931, the government raided the home of Tim Buck, the outspoken communist leader. He was arrested along with eight of his comrades, put on trial, and convicted largely on circumstantial evidence supplied by an undercover Mountie operative. Buck received a five-year jail term, although he was released after serving only three years.

Despite the crackdown, communist groups continued to defend the rights of unemployed men placed in work-relief camps, where for room and board and twenty cents a day they hauled rocks, cut wood, and pushed dirt. In June 1935, men in the camps located in British Columbia decided they had had enough. They hopped trains and headed for Ottawa for what was intended as a massive, but peaceful, protest. As the trains proceeded east, more and more men joined in the On to Ottawa Trek. Prime Minister Bennett became frightened, ordered the RCMP to stop the convoy, and a bloody riot ensued as the police attacked the crowd and anyone else in the vicinity. An official inquiry later blamed communist agitators for the riot and absolved the police from any responsibility. The government maintained that the participants in the trek had wanted "to break down the forces that represent law and order"; the men claimed they merely wanted a job and their dignity back.

Deportation was another option available to the government. Any person who was not a Canadian citizen and deemed by the government to be a troublemaker or a burden could be expelled from the country. This included immigrants who had been in Canada for less than five years, many of whom had been specifically recruited in the late twenties by various businesses in need of inexpensive unskilled workers. "Russians and other European people who have only been in this country a short time," said Senator Gideon Robertson, "should not be allowed to work . . . while hundreds of Canadians are standing in the breadline."

A simple application for relief was sufficient grounds for deportation proceedings to begin. Close to twenty-three thousand people were deported from 1930 to 1934 as a way to clear Canada of "undesirables." Many of these unfortunate individuals had come to Canada when they were children and had not been back to their European homelands for decades. It made no difference to the government or to the Canadian people, most of whom supported the policy.

A Chase Up Into the Sky

It was in New York City, fittingly, that two skyscrapers provided a measure of hope during the worst years of the Depression. And ironically, the two men responsible for their appearance were both party to Michael Meehan's stock scheme in 1929: Walter Chrysler and John Jacob Raskob.

Chrysler was one of the great pioneers of the automobile industry. He had begun his long career as a machinist's apprentice and worked his way up to become an executive with General Motors and eventually head of his own corporation. In 1929, he had more money than he knew what to do with. His head office was in Detroit, but he wanted to provide his sons with adequate office space in Manhattan, so he decided to embark on an ambitious project: to erect a skyscraper taller than the Woolworth Building. The spot he chose was at 42nd Street and Lexington Avenue.

The Chrysler Building was opened to great fanfare during the last week of May in 1930. New Yorkers were not only impressed by architect William Van Alen's Gothic and Art Deco design; they were also tantalized by the 185-foot, seven-storey steel spire he had added so that the seventy-seven-storey building could exceed one thousand feet. His fellow architects, among others, praised its "dazzling" and "exotic" style. "It grasps and holds at least for a moment the attention of the passerby below," the journal *Architectural Forum* noted, "as well as the amazed interest of the countryside and distant seafarers for miles around."

From its dome and tower to its eight large nickel-chrome steel gargoyles to its exquisite interior, everything about the Chrysler Building was first-rate. While he never moved his head office to

Manhattan, Walter Chrysler kept a lavish office and personal suite on the top floor.[*]

Nine months later, with the completion of the Empire State Building, the Chrysler's reign as the world's tallest building was over. Located at 34th Street and Fifth Avenue, on the site of the old Waldorf-Astoria Hotel, the new record-holder was far from the financial business district. The skyscraper was the brainchild of John Jacob Raskob, the wily chairman of General Motors Finance Committee, and his hand-picked president of the Empire State Corporation, Al Smith, the former governor of New York and Democratic presidential candidate.

It was not merely the planned height of the Empire State Building that excited the imagination of the crowd of spectators who gathered each day at the construction site; it was also the speed at which the skyscraper rose, "like an immense metal phoenix in the middle of Manhattan island," in the words of Ric Burns and James Sanders. Raskob and Smith employed thousands of workmen, who often toiled twelve hours a day or more, to finish the job in only eleven months. In one ten-day period in 1930, fourteen storeys were added, an unheard-of feat of labour power and engineering ingenuity. "The whole effect is of a chase up into the sky," the *New York Times* said in July of that year, "with the steel workers going first and all others following madly after them."

It hardly mattered when it finally opened; Raskob and Smith could not possibly fill up the thousands of square feet of office space, especially in the midst of the Depression. And anyone who still had money wanted to be near Wall Street, not in midtown Manhattan. Nonetheless, to the thousands of unemployed Americans forced to

---

[*] As Marc Eliot notes in his history of 42nd Street, Chrysler had instructed his builders to ensure that the toilet in the suite "was the highest toilet in Manhattan, so that he could look down upon the city from his porcelain throne and, as one observer put it, 'shit on Henry Ford and the rest of the world.'"

stand in line for soup and bread each day, the Empire State and the Chrysler Building were reassuring signs that all was not lost. If businessmen like Raskob and Chrysler were prepared to invest in New York, then surely there was hope for the future.

The march of progress could not be halted.

A New Time of Restlessness

The combined forces of urbanization and industrialization at the dawn of the twentieth century, which triggered a mass immigration movement across the Atlantic, led to a complex social upheaval that seemingly threatened everything white upper- and middle-class North Americans cherished. By 1930 it was difficult to dispute the fact that North American society had, for good or bad, been dramatically transformed. The fears generated by these radical changes were genuine – even if from our perspective many of them were wrong-headed. Giving women the vote did not ruin the family or destroy marriages. Granting labour a true voice did not lead to revolution. And allowing nudity in movies did not corrupt the young.

Relations between men and women in the office as well as the family home were permanently altered. Invention and innovation advanced communications and transportation technology and with it daily life. Religious observance was in decline, even if many people questioned Darwin's secular view of the world. If truth be told, going for a ride in a car or listening to the radio adventures of Amos 'n' Andy was far more entertaining than attending church services. Attitudes to sex had changed, too. A 1936 survey by *Fortune* magazine found, for instance, that U.S. college students were having sex at a younger age; they were, however, no longer talking about it quite as much as the preceding generation. "As for sex, it is, of course, still with us," the magazine's editors concluded. "But the campus takes it more casually than it did ten years ago. Sex is no longer in the news. And the fact that it is no longer news is news."*

Having a glass of wine or beer at dinner was no longer sinful. Once Prohibition ended in 1933, moderate drinking was acceptable in the United States. "There is no prohibition law to defy," a writer at *Fortune* pointed out, "hence one can drink in peace."

The traditionalists had not surrendered. In Hollywood and elsewhere, they continued to push their interpretation of morality. Moreover, democratic governments are typically cautious when it comes to altering laws dealing with social issues. Hence, in 1936 you could still be arrested and put on trial in Canada for distributing or promoting birth-control devices. Another three decades would pass and many more battles would be waged before abortion was widely (though by no means universally) and legally available. Likewise, women and men would not be paid the same salary for the same job until the struggles of the 1960s were a memory.

Entrenched notions about race did not vanish overnight. Cultural tolerance is a recent ideal. It would take the horror of the Holocaust and the hard-fought civil rights battles of Martin Luther King, Jr., and his followers during the fifties and sixties to make a real difference. Many lives were lost before much of the world abandoned the racial theories that gave rise to Hitler and his regime.

Racism, in public at least, is now no longer tolerated. Most Americans like to think they are colour-blind, yet issues of race,

---

* On the other hand, some things took a little longer than others to change. As popular historian Pierre Berton relates, in 1934 in Toronto, "when the distinguished British actor Maurice Colbourne appeared at the Royal Alexandra Theatre in *Reunion in Vienna*, a Robert Sherwood play, the censors were in full cry. Thanks to the vigilance of Mrs. Henry Cody, wife of the president of the University of Toronto, the police forced a number of script changes. The word 'bathroom' was deleted, an eight-second kiss was reduced to five seconds, the word 'damn' was cut out, and a love scene was toned down. And when the wildly successful new picture magazine *LIFE* published a photographic essay on the birth of a baby that year, the issue was denied entry into Canada."

whether to do with the conduct of the police, employment opportunities, or the problems of urban ghettos, continue to define
day-to-day life in much of the United States and Canada.

Canadians claim to embrace multiculturalism, yet they still
preach conformity, albeit a subtler version than that of old. In 1991,
a national survey commissioned by the Canadian Council of
Christians and Jews indicated that 72 per cent of Canadians rejected
"the notion of [their] country as a multicultural mosaic." The
message for new immigrants, especially those who are members of
visible minorities, does not seem to differ much from James S.
Woodsworth's day: adapt, conform, or leave. The gap between the
rich and poor still often splits along racial lines. "We may not be
calling people nigger or Chink or kike or raghead on the street,"
writes Toronto journalist Margaret Cannon, "but we make it clear
that the values we want enshrined in our institutions are the values
of the founding races – white, Catholic, Protestant, European
culture, Western philosophy."

But Canada and the United States are certainly more equal and
less racist societies than they were a century ago, and today's moral
struggles have moved to new yet similar territory. The millions of
traditionalists who helped U.S. president George W. Bush win two
terms in office bemoan the disappearance of religion from public
education and condemn same-sex marriage and stem-cell research.
They denounce the proliferation of violence and sex on television,
the easy accessibility of pornography on the Internet, and the
manner in which greed, lying, and materialism seem to dominate
our culture. On these latter issues, they might have a point. Decades
from now, what will future generations think of reality television
shows such as *Survivor*, *Big Brother*, and *For Love or Money*, in which
backstabbing and cheating are considered admirable qualities? Even
the most liberal and radical thinkers of the past – Emma Goldman,
Havelock Ellis, Margaret Sanger, and others – might consider
current culture and values bordering on the depraved.

The truth is that moral conflicts are part of every age. Morality always has been in a state of flux, and new philosophical and practical debates arise as each generation attempts to define for itself what is proper, acceptable, and modern. Think of the furor caused in 1956 when Elvis Presley performed on *The Ed Sullivan Show*. Or of the raging debates over miniskirts, the length of men's hair, J.D. Salinger's *The Catcher in the Rye* (now taught in high schools), and the birth-control pill? As late as 1992, then U.S. vice-president Dan Quayle set off a stormy debate over "family values" after he publicly condemned the television character Murphy Brown for deciding to have a baby even though she was not married on the show. Years later, these controversies seem mildly amusing, yet at the time they generated heated and serious discussion.

Debating these issues, no matter how painful or divisive, remains part of the human condition. "Many of us are looking forward to a new time of restlessness," reflected American playwright Sherwood Anderson in 1932 at the low point of the Depression. "There is much hidden just under the surface. There may well come soon now . . . a time of protest, of wide discussion, of seeking. There may be new literature, a new romantic movement, new religious impulses. If the machine has really made for us a new world we may at any time now begin the movement of trying to go into the new world. God grant it may be a better world."

Notes

INTRODUCTION: THE CITY

3 "The city is not all bad": Helen Campbell, *Darkness and Daylight; or, Lights and Shadows of New York Life* (Hartford: A.D. Worthington & Company, 1892), 40–42; **4 At that moment**: *New York Times*, April 25, 1913; Ric Burns and James Sanders, *New York: An Illustrated History* (New York: Alfred A. Knopf, 2003), 293; **4 Towering sixty stories**: Burns and Sanders, ibid., 293; **4 "The Woolworth Building"**: Ibid., 293; **5 With its giant masonry towers**: Ibid., 181; **5 Thereafter, the bridge**: Edward R. Ellis, *The Epic of New York City* (New York: Coward-McCann, 1966), 375; **5 The library graced**: Marc Eliot, *Down 42nd Street: Sex, Money, Culture, and Politics at the Crossroads of the World* (New York: Warner Books, 2001), 65; **5 Almost overnight**: Ibid., 17; **5 "Broadway had been waiting"**: *New York Times*, January 1, 1905; **5 Ochs installed**: Eliot, *Down 42nd Street*, 25; **6 Owing mainly to the efforts**: Ibid., 14–15; Burns and Sanders, *Illustrated History*, 255–56; **6 Nearly a million people**: *New York Times*, October 28, 1904; Burns and Sanders, ibid., 257; **6 "The skyline of New York"**: Cited in Burns and Sanders, ibid., 230; **6 Hence, as Steffens**: Ibid., 231; **6 "The skyscraper"**: Paul Johnson, *A History of the American People* (London: Phoenix, 1997), 587–88; **7 "It is as if some"**: Cited in Burns and Sanders, ibid., 231; **7 One visitor "stepped off"**: Ellis, *Epic of New York*, 408; **7 From the right**: George H. Douglas, *Skyscrapers: A Social History in America* (Jefferson, N.C.: McFarland & Company, 1996), 38; **7 Two years after that**: Burns and Sanders, *Illustrated History*, 233; **9 "[Is] New York"**: Cited in ibid., 293; **8 "It's only a matter of"**: Cited in ibid., 182; **9 "Material progress does"**: Henry George, *Progress and Poverty* (New York: Wynkoop & Hallenbeck, 1884), 6; **9 His talent and energy**: Roy Lubove, *The Progressives and the Slums* (Pittsburgh: University of Pittsburgh Press, 1962), 57; **9 Day after day**: Francesco Cordasco, ed., *Jacob Riis Revisited* (Garden City, N.Y.: Anchor Books, 1968), xvi; **10 Lincoln Steffens, who**: Lincoln Steffens, *The Autobiography of Lincoln Steffens* (New York: Harcourt, Brace and Company, 1931), 203–06; **10 In the same period**: Jacob Riis, *How the Other Half Lives* (New York: Charles Scribner's Sons, 1912), 242; **10 "If 'Mr. Millions' had"**: Charles F. Wingate, "The Moral Side of the

Tenement-House Problem," *The Catholic World* XLI (1885), 162; **10 In their report**: Cited in Moses Rischin, *The Promised City* (Cambridge, Mass.: Harvard University Press, 1962), 199; **10 "Typhus fever"**: Riis, *Other Half*, 109; **11 "Physical evils produce"**: Cited in Lubove, *Progressives*, 6; **11 The city**: See Arthur M. Schlesinger, *The Rise of the City 1878–1898* (New York: The Macmillan Company, 1933), 80; **11 Footnote: New York City's Tammany**: Ibid., 391; **12 It was the "jungle"**: Upton Sinclair, *The Jungle* (Memphis, Tenn.: Peachtree Publishers, 1988), 28–40; Harold Bloom, ed., *Upton Sinclair's The Jungle* (Philadelphia: Chelsea House Publishers, 2002), 8–10; **12 Politician and crusader**: Justin Kaplan, *Lincoln Steffens: A Biography* (New York: Simon & Schuster, 1974), 61; Neil Baldwin, *Henry Ford and the Jews: The Mass Production of Hate* (New York: Public Affairs, 2001), 86; **12 In his novel**: Edward Bellamy, *Looking Backward* (New York: New American Library, 1960), 213; **12 Footnote: The most daunting**: Edwin G. Burrows and Mike Wallace, *Gotham: A History of New York City to 1898* (New York: Oxford University Press, 1999), 757; **13 By 1890, for example**: James West Davidson and Mark H. Lytle, *The United States: A History of the Republic* (Englewood, N.J.: Prentice-Hall, 1990), 468–71; **13 As one writer**: Cited in Schlesinger, *The Rise of the City*, 65; **13 "This place is the"**: Cited in Anselm S. Strauss, ed., *The American City: A Sourcebook of Urban Imagery* (Chicago: Aldine Publishing Company, 1968), 41; **13 The city's commercial elite**: See Jean Bethke Elshtain, *Jane Addams and the Dream of American Democracy* (New York: Basic Books, 2002), 164; Alan F.J. Artibise, *Winnipeg: A Social History of Urban Growth 1874–1914* (Montreal: McGill-Queen's University Press, 1975), 223–28; *Winnipeg Telegram*, January 5, 1905; **13 However, civic leaders, social reformers**: Mariana Valverde, *The Age of Light, Soap, and Water: Moral Reform in English Canada, 1885–1925* (Toronto: McClelland & Stewart, 1991), 132–33; **14 "Underneath the seemingly moral"**: Cited in Valverde, ibid., 132; **14 For Reverend S.W. Dean**: S.W. Dean, "The Church and the Slum," *Social Service Council of Canada Congress* (Ottawa, 1914), 127; Valverde, ibid., 134; **14 Even someone as sensible**: *Report of the Medical Officer on Slum Conditions in Toronto* (Toronto, 1911), 3; Valverde, ibid., 133; **14 In Dr. Hastings's opinion**: *Report of the Medical Officer*, 4, 24; Valverde, ibid., 133; **17 "The central paradox"**: Cited in Paul A. Carter, *The Twenties in America* (New York: Thomas Y. Crowell Company, 1968), 8; **18 The challenge facing**: Cited in Henry F. May, *The End of American Innocence* (London: Jonathan Cape, 1959), 20–1; David R. Colburn and George E. Pozzetta, eds., *Reform and Reformers in the Progressive Era* (Westport, Conn.: Greenwood Press, 1983), vii–viii; **18 In the years after 1880**: Valverde, *Age of Light*, 79, 131; **18 Or, put slightly more eloquently**: Cited in Valverde, ibid., 131; **18 "We are now witnessing**: John Roach Straton, *The Menace of Immorality in Church and State: Messages of Wrath and*

Judgment (New York: George H. Doran, 1920), 12; **18 As the *New Republic* magazine**: Cited in Douglas Carl Abrams, *Selling the Old-Time Religion: American Fundamentalists and Mass Culture, 1920–1940* (Athens, Ga.: University of Georgia Press, 2001), 1; **19 He bemoaned the greed**: See John Roach Straton, *Fighting the Devil in Modern Babylon* (Boston: The Stratford Company, 1929); **19 "We must either Americanize**: Ibid., 5; **19 As historian Alison Parker**: Alison M. Parker, *Purifying America: Women, Cultural Reform, and Pro-Censorship Activism, 1873–1933* (Chicago: University of Illinois Press, 1997), 112.

CHAPTER ONE: STRANGERS AND REFORMERS

23 "Out of the remote": James D. Whelpley, "The Problem of the Immigrant" (London, 1905) in J.S. Woodsworth, *Strangers Within Our Gates* (Toronto: University of Toronto Press, 1972), 12; **23 They came wave**: Woodsworth, ibid., 13; **23 Among the multitude**: Pierre Berton, *The Promised Land: Settling the West 1896–1914* (Toronto: McClelland & Stewart, 1984), 42–3, 52–3; Gregg Shilliday, ed., *Manitoba 125: Gateway to the West*, vol. 2 (Winnipeg: Great Plains Publications, 1994), 84; Peter Morton Coan, *Ellis Island Interviews: In Their Own Words* (New York: Facts On File, 1997), 43–4, 244–45; **24 Between 1870 and 1914**: Walter Nugent, *Crossings: The Great Transatlantic Migrations, 1870–1914* (Bloomington, Ind.: Indiana University Press, 1992), 14; **24 In the fifty-year period**: Ibid., 12, 94; **24 In *The Promised City***: Rischin, *The Promised City*, xi; **25 "This great city of ours"**: Cited in Burns and Sanders, *Illustrated History*, 254; **26 By taking on back-breaking**: Robert F. Harney and Harold Troper, *Immigrants: A Portrait of the Urban Experience, 1890–1930* (Toronto: Van Nostrand Reinhold, 1975), 52; **26 Aiding the steamship companies**: Ibid., 4–5; **26 "America was in everybody's mouth"**: Mary Antin, *From Plotzk to Boston* (Boston: W.B. Clarke, 1899), 12; **26 Footnote: In the late nineteenth century**: John Zucchi, *Italians in Toronto: Development of a National Identity, 1875–1935* (Montreal: McGill-Queen's University Press, 1988), 79–80; **27 "People used to jump"**: Cited in Franc Sturino, *Forging the Chain: A Case Study of Italian Migration to North America, 1880–1930* (Toronto: Multicultural History Society of Ontario, 1990), 68; **27 Seemingly friendly *landsmann***: Harney and Troper, *Immigrants*, 5; **27 Abraham Cahan**: Allan Levine, *Scattered Among the Peoples: The Jewish Diaspora in Ten Portraits* (Toronto: McClelland & Stewart, 2002), 240; **27 In January 1910**: *New York Times*, January 30, 1910; **28 In the great hall**: Irving Howe, *World of Our Fathers* (New York: Harcourt Brace Jovanovich, 1976), 43–5; Levine, *Scattered Among the Peoples*, 240; **28 In his novel**: Abraham Cahan, *The Rise of David Levinsky* (1917 reprint, New York: Penguin Books, 1993), 93; **29 "Little idea can"**: Cited in Sturino, *Forging the Chain*, 125;

29 Prostitution was (and is) a highly: Valverde, *Age of Light*, 77;
29 Married men: Nicola Beisel, *Imperiled Innocents: Anthony Comstock and Family Reproduction in Victorian America* (Princeton, N.J.: Princeton University Press, 1997), 34; **29 North American cities**: Ibid., 24; Timothy Gilfoyle, *City of Eros* (New York: W.W. Norton, 1992), 198; **29 In New York, brothels**: Lubove, *Progressives*, 69; **30 Novelist Michael Gold**: Michael Gold, *Jews Without Money* (New York: Carroll and Graf, 1958), 15; **30 The women helped**: Beisel, *Imperiled Innocents*, 24; **30 One madam later**: Schlesinger, *The Rise of the City*, 116; **30 Parkhurst, described by journalist**: Steffens, *Autobiography*, 215; **30 In sermon after sermon**: Kaplan, *Lincoln Steffens*, 67–8; **30 To prove his point**: Burrows and Wallace, *Gotham*, 1168; **30 At one of the fancier**: Kaplan, *Lincoln Steffens*, 68; **30 At another, a scantily clad**: Burrows and Wallace, *Gotham*, 1168; **31 Further north in Montreal**: Andrée Lévesque, *Making and Breaking the Rules: Women in Quebec, 1919–1939* (Toronto: McClelland & Stewart, 1994), 62; **31 In the end**: Ibid., 70; **31 "There is no city"**: Cited in Valverde, *Age of Light*, 84; **32 The Canadian federal government**: Valverde, *Age of Light*, 97–8; **32 Once involved in the trade**: Arthur Weinberg and Lila Weinberg, eds., *The Muckrakers* (New York: Simon & Schuster, 1961), 394–96; **32 None of these efforts**: Wendy Kline, *Building a Better Race: Gender, Sexuality, and Eugenics from the Turn of the Century to the Baby Boom* (Berkeley, Calif.: University of California Press, 2001), 46; **32 Footnote: This included San Francisco's**: See Lisa Archer, "Barbary Coast Walking Tour," May 23, 2001, www.sfbg.com; **33 This was a point**: Robert Hunter, *Poverty* (New York: The Macmillan Company, 1912); cited in Strauss, *The American City*, 142; **33 So powerful was this image**: E. Allen Richardson, *Strangers in This Land* (New York: The Pilgrim Press, 1988), 22, 68; Ronald Sanders, *The Downtown Jews: Portraits of an Immigrant Generation* (New York: Harper & Row, 1969), 136–7; **33 Detested most of all**: Richardson, *Strangers in This Land*, 84. See also Peter W. Ward, *White Canada Forever* (Montreal: McGill-Queen's University Press, 1978); **33 Footnote: In 1897, Clifford Sifton**: Clifford Sifton, "The Immigrants Canada Wants," *Maclean's*, April 1, 1922, 16; cited in Howard Palmer, ed., *Immigration and the Rise of Multiculturalism* (Toronto: Copp Clark Publishing, 1975), 35; **34 In the eyes of many politicians**: See Marilyn Barber, Introduction, Woodsworth, *Strangers Within Our Gates*, xii; Valverde, *Age of Light*, 127; Angus McLaren, *Our Own Master Race: Eugenics in Canada 1885–1945* (Toronto: McClelland & Stewart, 1990), 47–8; **34 "Many of our non-Anglosaxon"**: Cited in Valverde, *Age of Light*, 53; **34 Speaking in the House of Commons**: Canada House of Commons, *Debates*, January 23, 1914, 140; **35 "Thousands [of immigrants]"**: Charles Hastings, "Medical Inspection of Public Schools," *Canadian Journal of Medicine and Surgery*, 21 (1907), 73; **35 Clearly, mixing races**: See Abraham

J. Karp, *Haven and Home: A History of Jews in America* (New York: Schocken Books, 1985), 175; John Higham, *Strangers in the Land: Patterns of American Nativism 1860–1925* (New York: Antheneum, 1978), 90–2; Salvatore Mondello, *The Italian Immigrant in Urban America, 1880–1920* (New York: Arno Press, 1980), 147–50; **35 Reverend Samuel D. Chown**: Cited in Valverde, *Age of Light*, 106; **36 Even more alarming**: Woodsworth, *Strangers Within Our Gates*, xvi; **36 "We are overwhelmed"**: Cited in Laurence Bergreen, *Capone: The Man and the Era* (New York: Simon & Schuster, 1994), 21; **36 Earlier, the *Calgary Herald***: *Calgary Herald*, January 18, 1899, cited in Palmer, *Immigration and the Rise of Multiculturalism*, 45; **36 One of the worst**: S.T. Joshi, ed., *Documents of American Prejudice: An Anthology of Writings on Race from Thomas Jefferson to David Duke* (New York: Basic Books, 1999) 254–58; **37 "Now understand that America"**: Israel Zangwill, *The Melting Pot* (New York: Macmillan Company, 1917), 33; Karp, *Haven and Home*, 362; **37 The play had a lengthy**: Richardson, *Strangers in This Land*, 111; **37 "America does not"**: Howe, *World of Our Fathers*, 411; **38 In a study done**: Emory S. Bogardus, Immigration and Race (Boston: D.C. Heath, 1928), 23–6; John W. Briggs, *An Italian Passage: Immigrants to Three American Cities, 1890–1930* (New Haven, Conn.: Yale University Press, 1978), 331 n.7; **38 It was next to impossible**: Howe, *World of Our Fathers*, 411–12; **38 Footnote: "As historian Salvatore Mondello points**: Mondello, *Italian Immigrant*, 217; **39 The Jewish answer**: Levine, *Scattered Among the Peoples*, 237–38; **39 According to the report**: Nugent, *Crossings*, 160; **39 "They form, on their arrival"**: Government of Canada, *Report of the Royal Commission on Chinese and Japanese Immigration* (Ottawa, 1902), 278; Ward, *White Canada Forever*, 60; **40 Their goal, in theory**: Valverde, *Age of Light*, 22; Parker, *Purifying America*, 90; **40 This meant shaping**: Valverde, ibid., 19; **40 As one Toronto public school**: Harney and Troper, *Immigrants*, 110; **40 Canadian teachers**: Ibid., 109; **40 Education was seen**: Ibid., 110; **40 In an investigation**: Artibise, *Winnipeg*, 203; **40 Several years later**: Ibid., 203; **41 These "alien" youngsters**: "City Children and the Library," *Library Journal* 25 (April 1900), 170; cited in Parker, *Purifying America*, 90; **41 To the librarians**: Mary E. Comstock, "The Library as an Educational Factor, *Library Journal* 21 (April 1896), 147–49; cited in Parker, ibid., 90; **41 "Shearer comes closer"**: Valverde, *Age of Light*, 54–5; **41 There was much**: John G. Shearer, "Right Kind of Puritanism," *Dominion Presbyterian* (May 6, 1906) 9; cited in ibid., 56; **42 "Is it too much to ask"**: Cited in ibid., 56; **42 Then, on a rampage**: "Social Evil Runs Riot in Winnipeg," *Globe* (Toronto), November 12, 1910; **42 Newspapers hailed her**: Allen F. Davis, *American Heroine: The Life and Legend of Jane Addams* (New York: Oxford University Press, 1973), 201; Mary Kittredge, *Jane Addams* (New York: Chelsea House Publishers, 1988), 82; **42 A century** later: Elshtain, *Jane Addams*, xix; **42 "She was larger than life"**: Cited in ibid., 9; **42 One newspaper profile**: Cited in Davis, *American Heroine*, 103; **43 Mary Jo Deegan**: Mary Jo Deegan, *Jane Addams and the Men of the Chicago School 1892–1928* (New Brunswick, N.J.: Transaction Books, 1990), 3; **43 He was also a friend**: Jane Addams, *Twenty Years at Hull-House* (New York: The Macmillan Company, 1926), 31; **43 The disease**: Kittredge, *Jane Addams*, 25–6; **43 She attended the Rockford**: Elshtain, *Jane Addams*, 15; **44 Footnote: "Let's love each"**: Cited in Davis, *American Heroine*, 45–6. See also K.A. McKenzie, *Edith Simcox and George Eliot* (London: Oxford University Press, 1961), xv. Introduction by Gordon Haight; **44 Originally it was called**: Rischin, *Promised City*, 206; **44 His small apartment**: Howe, *World of Our Fathers*, 401; **45 Returning to the United States**: See Addams, *Twenty Years*, 97; **45 "The streets are inexpressibly dirty"**: Ibid., 98–100; **45 On their first night**: Ibid., 95–6; **45 Like Toynbee Hall**: Cited in Elshtain, *Jane Addams*, 92; **46 Hull-House offered**: Kittredge, *Jane Addams*, 19; **46 In one case**: Ibid., 53–5. See also Elshtain, *Jane Addams*, 74; **46 Into Hull-House**: Cited in Kittredge, ibid., 60; **46 Following a visit to the city**: Ibid., 60–1; **46 Footnote: The residents at Hull-House**: See Davis, *American Heroine*, 75, 81; **47 "I remember a little girl"**: Addams, *Twenty Years*, 199–200; **47 It was one**: Kittredge, *Jane Addams*, 63; **47 She exposed their incompetence**: Ibid., 64; **47 "The image of the brave"**: Davis, *American Heroine*, 121; **48 She constantly bemoaned**: Elshtain, *Jane Addams*, 145; **48 Although, as sociologist Mary Jo Deegan**: Deegan, *Jane Addams*, 295; **48 She thought of the newcomers**: Elshtain, *Jane Addams*, 20–1; **48 She understood writes**: John C. Farrell, *Beloved Lady* (Baltimore: Johns Hopkins University Press, 1967), 65; **48 Ahead of her time**: Elshtain, *Jane Addams*, 203; **49 "In our assertive"**: Cited in Deegan, *Jane Addams*, 294; **49 Its objective, she explained**: Addams, *Twenty Years*, 235–45; **49 She also helped create**: Elshtain, *Jane Addams*, 196; **49 Chief Shippy met Averbuch**: Walter Roth and Joe Kraus, *An Accidental Anarchist* (San Francisco: Rudi Publishers, 1998), 13–16, 80–1, 181–82; **50 Shippy testified that**: Ibid., 13–16; **50 The official investigation**: Ibid., 154; **50 He uncovered several inconsistencies**: Ibid., 62; **51 "The more excited"**: Cited in Angelina Corsale and Mary Ann Johnson, "Multiculturalism in Chicago: Lazar Averbuch Case, 1908," Illinois Periodical Online, www.lib.niu.edu/ipo/iht29525.html; **51 If she had a fault**: Elshtain, *Jane Addams*, 219; **51 She condemned**: Jane Addams, *The Second Twenty Years at Hull-House* (New York: The Macmillan Company, 1930), 278, 296; **51 When comments she**: Kittredge, *Jane Addams*, 86–7; **51 Even her former friend**: Ibid., 87; **52 Only then was she praised**: Cited in ibid., 100; **52 It was a clarion call**: Richard Allen, *The Social Passion: Religion and Social Reform in Canada 1914–28* (Toronto: University of Toronto Press, 1971), 4; **53 He was** appointed: Robert T. Handy, ed., *The Social Gospel in America 1879–1920* (New York: Oxford University Press, 1966), 253. See also Paul Minus, *Walter Rauschenbusch: American Reformer* (New York: Macmillan, 1988); **53 His experience**: Handy, ibid., 255; **53 "Competitive commerce exalts"**: Walter Rauschenbusch, *Christianity and the Social Crisis* (New York: The Macmillan Company, 1907), 265; **53 Influenced by the British Fabians**: Charles H. Hopkins, *The Rise of the Social Gospel in American Protestantism 1865–1915* (New Haven, Conn.: Yale University Press, 1940), 217; **53 As he explained**: Walter Rauschenbusch, *Christianizing the Social Order* (New York: The Macmillan Company, 1913), 49; **53 In the social gospel**: Ibid., 93; **54 His beliefs had**: Martin Luther King, "Pilgrimage to Nonviolence" *The Christian Century* LXXVII (April 1960), 439; Handy, *Social Gospel*, 259; **54 As the Methodist *Christian Guardian***: Marilyn Barber, "Nationalism, Nativism and the Social Gospel" in Richard Allen, ed., *The Social Gospel in Canada* (Ottawa: National Museums of Canada, 1975), 221; **54 "If from this North American"**: Cited in Woodsworth, *Strangers Within Our Gates*, xix; **55 He was a serious and sober**: J.S. Woodsworth, *My Neighbour* (Toronto: University of Toronto Press, 1972), xv; **55 Though he had some doubts**: See Kenneth McNaught, *A Prophet in Politics: A Biography of J.S. Woodsworth* (Toronto: University of Toronto Press, 1959), 3–11; **55 This exposure to**: Ibid., 15; **55 "Surely," he wrote, "there"**: Cited in ibid., 15; **56 "I fear that in our own city"**: Cited in ibid., 25; **57 "If it is right to help"**: Cited in ibid., 26; **58 "It is true that they may"**: See Woodsworth, *Strangers Within Our Gates*, 154–55; **58 On "the Negro,"**: Woodsworth, ibid., 158; **58 Like Prescott Hall**: Ibid., 192; **58 Yet, while he included**: Ibid., 206; **58 "The coming of the immigrant"**: J.S. Woodsworth, "National Building," *University Magazine* (February 1917), 97–9.

CHAPTER TWO: SUFFRAGETTES

63 "Another mistake that": Cited in Andrew Rosen, *Rise Up, Women! The Militant Campaign of the Women's Social and Political Union 1903–1914* (London: Routledge & Kegan Paul, 1974), 77; **64 "The thought in my"**: Cited in Antonia Raeburn, *The Militant Suffragettes* (London: Michael Joseph, 1973), 128; **64 "The idea in my mind"**: Cited in Gertrude Colmore, *The Life of Emily Davison* (London: The Women's Press, 1913), 45; **65 "I was watching her"**: Cited in Midge Mackenzie, *Shoulder to Shoulder: A Documentary* (New York: Alfred A. Knopf, 1975), 242; **65 "I hope you suffer"**: Women's Library, London, Emily Davison Papers, File A7/1, Letter of June 15, 1913; **66 "The glorious and inscrutable"**: Ibid., Box 554, "The Price of Liberty," undated; **67 Footnote: Late nineteenth and early twentieth**: Eleanor Flexner and Ellen Fitzpatrick, *Century of Struggle: The Women's Rights Movement in the United States* (Cambridge, Mass.: Harvard University

Press, 1975), 171; **68 In one of the first major**: Cited in Rosen, *Rise Up*, 97; **68 As the nineteenth-century adage**: Cited in Raeburn, *Militant Suffragettes*, 1; **68 Women, after all**: Rosen, *Rise Up*, 1; **68 Even with changes**: Sophia A. van Wingerden, *The Women's Suffrage Movement in Britain, 1866–1928* (London: MacMillan Press, 1999), 4–5; **69 The law regarded**: David Morgan, *Suffragists and Liberals* (Totowa, N.J.: Rowman and Littlefield, 1975), 20; **69 In 1900 in Pennsylvania**: Flexner and Fitzpatrick, *Century of Struggle*, 221; **69 A Canadian mother**: Deborah Goreham, "Singing Up the Hill," *Canadian Dimension*, vol. 10 (Winnipeg, 1975), 28; **69 Furthermore, in Manitoba in 1913**: Ramsay Cook and Wendy Mitchinson, eds.,*The Proper Sphere: Woman's Place in Canadian Society* (Toronto: Oxford University Press, 1976), 115–16; **69 "There is much more difference"**: Cited in Brian Harrison, *Separate Spheres: The Opposition to Women's Suffrage in Britain* (New York: Holmes & Meier Publishers, 1978), 60; **70 Emily Davison's behaviour**: Lucia Zedner, *Women, Crime and Custody in Victorian England* (Oxford: Clarendon Press, 1991), 2; **70 As Violet Markham**: Cited in Lisa Tickner, *The Spectacle of Women: Imagery of the Suffrage Campaign 1907–14* (Chicago: University of Chicago Press, 1988), 155; **70 The *New York Times* editorialized**: Cited in Sherna Gluck, ed., *From Parlor to Prison: Five American Suffragists Talk about their Lives* (New York: Vintage Books, 1976), 192–94; **70 Or, put another way**: Nellie McClung, *The Stream Runs Fast* (Toronto: Thomas Allen & Son, 1945), 109; **70 When it came to**: Sara Hunter Graham, *Woman Suffrage and the New Democracy* (New Haven, Conn.: Yale University Press, 1996), 12; Laura L. Behling, *The Masculine Woman in America 1890–1935* (Chicago: University of Illinois Press, 2001), 2; Lyman Abbot, "Why Women Do Not Wish Suffrage," *Atlantic Monthly* (September 1903), 289–96; **70 "I think that I am"**: Cited in Behling, ibid., 45–6; **71 Time and again**: Ibid., 3, 61–3; **71 Carrie Chapman Catt**: Ibid., 36; Mary Sumner Boyd, *The Woman Citizen* (New York: Frederick A. Stokes Company, 1918), 8–9. With an Introduction by Carrie Chapman Catt; **71 As British historian**: Tickner, *Spectacle of Women*, 153; **72 "One is forced to the conclusion"**: Cited in Rosen, *Rise Up*, 203; **72 She also claimed**: van Wingerden, *The Women's Suffrage Movement*, 145; **72 Almost immediately**: Tickner, *Spectacle of Women*, 223; **72 "Christabel is not like"**: Cited in Martin Pugh, *The Pankhursts* (London: The Penguin Press, 2001), 95; **72 At the age of forty-four**: Rosen, *Rise Up*, 14–15; **72 Besides Christabel**: Pugh, *The Pankhursts*, 38; **73 Mrs. Pankhurst was**: Cited in Rosen, *Rise Up*, 168; **73 Another contemporary remembered**: Dame Christabel Pankhurst, *Unshackled: The Story of How We Won the Vote* (London: Hutchinson, 1959), 130; **73 The Pankhursts might have**: E. Sylvia Pankhurst, *The Suffragette Movement* (New York: Longmans, Green, 1931), 182; **74 "Deeds, not words"**: Emmeline Pankhurst, *My Own*

Story (New York: Hearst's International Library, 1971), 38; **74 "This was the first militant"**: Christabel Pankhurst, *Unshackled*, 46; **75 When she entered a room**: Ibid., 12. The book was annotated and edited by Frederick Pethick Lawrence; **75 More than one suffragette**: Martin Pugh, *The March of the Women* (Oxford: Oxford University Press, 2000), 178; **76 Mary Richardson**: Mary R. Richardson, *Laugh of Defiance* (London: George Weidenfeld & Nicholson, 1953), 50; **76 Dunlop did not seek permission**: Pugh, *March of the Women*, 180; **76 The point of the WSPU**: Tickner, *Spectacle of Women*, 9; **77 They courted editors**: Ibid., 59; **77 "I feel that the action"**: Cited in Pugh, *March of the Women*, 182; **77 "I want to say here"**: Cited in Jane Marcus, ed., *Suffrage and the Pankhursts* (London: Routledge and Kegan Paul, 1987), 156; **78 Likewise, from her hideaway**: Cited in Raeburn, *Militant Suffragettes*, 170; **78 "Though the suffragettes"**: Pugh, *March of the Women*, 216; **78 Many of the women**: Rosen, *Rise Up*, 139; Mackenzie, *Shoulder to Shoulder*, 140, 162–69; **79 The *Times* published**: *Times of London*, October 7, 1909; **79 Footnote: The most memorable case**: Tickner, *Spectacle of Women*, 107; Rosen, *Rise Up*, 129–30; Christabel Pankhurst, *Unshackled*, 146; **80 As Christabel explained**: *Daily Telegraph* (London), September 4, 1914; Rosen, ibid., 249–50; **81 In her impassioned speech**: Rosen, ibid., 250; **82 "Women at last"**: Ibid., 294; **82 Women, as historian Lisa Tickner**: Tickner, *Spectacle of Women*, 236–7; **82 Footnote: As late as 1960**: Pugh, *March of the Women*, 154; **83 Women had not automatically**: Tickner, *Spectacle of Women*, 237; **83 "Some of us"**: Christabel Pankhurst, *Pressing Problems of the Closing Age* (London: Morgan & Scott, 1924), 38; **83 As a representative of the modern era**: Ibid., 35–6; **84 In an era when**: Linda J. Lumsden, *Rampant Women* (Knoxville, Tenn.: University of Tennessee Press, 1997), xxvi; **84 They were more**: Flexner and Fitzpatrick, *Century of Struggle*, 138–39; **85 Footnote: As Carrie Chapman Catt later**: Carrie Chapman Catt and Nettie Rogers Shuler, *Woman Suffrage and Politics: The Inner Story of the Suffrage Movement* (New York: Charles Scribner's Sons, 1923), 107; Flexner and Fitzpatrick, ibid., 165; **85 The movement was**: Harriot Stanton Blatch and Alma Lutz, *Challenging Years: The Memoirs of Harriot Stanton Blatch* (New York: G.P. Putnam's Sons, 1940), 92; **86 The police intervened**: Lumsden, *Rampant Women*, 35–9; **86 She left education**: Robert Booth Fowler and Spencer Jones, "Carrie Chapman Catt and the Last Years of the Struggle for Woman Suffrage," in Jean H. Baker, ed., *Votes for Women: The Struggle for Suffrage Revisited* (New York: Oxford University Press, 2002), 131; **86 Footnote: Harriot Stanton Blatch also**: Lumsden, *Rampant Women*, 108; Ellen Carol Dubois, "The Next Generation" in Baker, ibid., 167; **87 In later years**: Fowler and Jones, "Carrie Chapman Catt," 133; **87 While some suffragists**: Graham, *Woman Suffrage*, 150; **87 "I know of no other woman"**: Fowler and Jones, "Carrie

Chapman Catt," 133; **87 He died in 1905**: Graham, *Woman Suffrage*, 81; **88 She did so in 1916**: Fowler and Jones, "Carrie Chapman Catt," 134–35; **88 While she believed**: Lumsden, *Rampant Women*, 16; **89 "There was no division"**: Cited in ibid., 79; **89 According to later**: *New York Post*, March 4, 1913; ibid., 79–80; **89 The *New York Times*, a long-time**: *New York Times*, March 5, 1913; **90 Solemnly the women stood**: Flexner and Fitzpatrick, *Century of Struggle*, 275; **90 Footnote: Inez Milholland, a suffragist**: See Lumsden, *Rampant Women*, 117; **90 For the most part, President Wilson**: *New York Times*, January 11, 1917; Gluck, *From Parlor to Prison*, 238–39; **90 It is hard to dispute**: Flexner and Fitzpatrick, *Century of Struggle*, 277; **91 This was, by all accounts**: Doris Stevens, *Jailed for Freedom: The Story of the Militant American Suffragist Movement* (New York: Schocken Books, 1976), 107–21; **91 The food was terrible**: Ibid., 109, 155; **91 More than a little conservative**: Ibid., xxv; **91 Footnote: On August 14, 1917**: Ibid., 128–29; Lumsden, *Rampant Women*, 125; **92 The federal appeals court**: Lumsden, ibid., 135; **92 By this time**: Ibid., 139; **92 As in Britain**: Flexner and Fitzpatrick, *Century of Struggle*, 318; **93 Only twenty-four hours**: *Winnipeg Tribune*, January 28, 1914; **93 Referring to the violence**: Mary Hallett and Marilyn Davis, *Firing the Heather: The Life and Times of Nellie McClung* (Saskatoon: Fifth House, 1993), 121–22; **94 Throughout the premier's speech**: The details of the Mock Parliament are found in the *Manitoba Free Press*, January 29, 1914. This scene is similarly described in my novel *Sins of the Suffragette* (Winnipeg: Great Plains Publications, 2000), 8–10; **96 With the vote**: Carol Lee Bacchi, *Liberation Deferred? The Ideas of the English-Canadian Suffragists, 1877–1918* (Toronto: University of Toronto Press, 1983), 39–57; **96 The aim of the club**: E. Luke, "Women's Suffrage in Canada," *Canadian Magazine* (Toronto, 1895), 329; **96 Footnote: As historian Carol Lee Bacchi points**: Ibid., 3; **97 A fairly radical feminist**: Linda Kealey, ed., *A Not Unreasonable Claim: Women and Reform in Canada, 1880s–1920s* (Toronto: The Women's Press, 1979), 28–9, 62–3; **97 Flora Macdonald Denison**: *Toronto World*, December 14, 1913; Bacchi, *Liberation Deferred*, 33; **97 Ironically, some of the social**: Bacchi, ibid., 36; **97 "Without doubt the democracy"**: *Grain Growers' Guide* (Winnipeg), February 14, 1914; **98 "A woman's place is in the home"**: Cited at "Maternal Feminism," timelinks.merlin.mb.ca; **98 On another occasion**: *Canadian Home Journal*, January 5, 1920, 5; **98 Yet the novels**: Candace Savage, *Our Nell: A Scrapbook Biography of Nellie L. McClung* (Saskatoon: Western Producer Prairie Books, 1979), 18–20; **99 "No one can deny"**: McClung, *The Stream Runs Fast*, 59–60; **99 Her son Mark**: Savage, *Our Nell*, 104–05; **99 They burned her in effigy**: May L. Armitage, "Mrs. Nellie McClung," *Maclean's*, July 1915, 38; Savage, ibid., 98, 103; **99 "Never retract, never explain"**: Veronica Strong-Boag and Anita Clair Fellman,

eds., *Rethinking Canada: The Promise of Women's History*, First Edition
(Toronto: Copp Clark Pitman, 1986), 178; **100 Conformity and assimila-
tion**: Nellie McClung, *In Times Like These* (Toronto: University of Toronto
Press, 1972), 54–5; "The Problem of our New Canadians," (1920) in Savage,
Our Nell, 92; **100 The injustice rankled**: Savage, ibid., 91–2, 134–35,
169–70, Hallett and Davis, *Firing the Heather*, 129–30; **100 Nellie
McClung, for one**: *Grain Growers' Guide* (Winnipeg), January 26, 1916;
Bacchi, *Liberation Deferred*, 140; **101 Writing about the extension**: Cited in
Savage, *Our Nell*, 137–38.

CHAPTER THREE: SURVIVAL OF THE FITTEST

105 While scrutinizing the islands': Edward Caudill, *Darwinian Myths:
The Legends and Misuses of a Theory* (Knoxville, Tenn.: University of Tennessee,
1997), 6–7; Peter J. Bowler, *Charles Darwin: The Man and His Influence*
(Cambridge, Mass.: Cambridge University Press, 1990), 113; **106 The
London publisher**: Bowler, ibid., 114; **107 (An example might be**: Cynthia
Eagle Russett, *Darwin in America: The Intellectual Response 1865–1912* (San
Francisco: W.H. Freeman and Company, 1976), 6; **107 From the start**:
Bowler, *Darwin*, 150; **107 Natural selection**: Russett, *Darwin in America*, 33;
107 Or, explained more aptly: Ibid., 33; **107 Darwin himself
complicated**: Ibid., 12–13; Charles Darwin, *The Descent of Man and Selection
in Relation to Sex* (London: John Murray, 1871), 372; **107 Where were the
so-called**: Bowler, *Darwin*, 184–85; **107 "I do not carry the doctrine"**:
Cited in Edward J. Larson, *Summer For the Gods: The Scopes Trial and
America's Continuing Debate Over Science and Religion* (Cambridge, Mass.:
Harvard University Press, 1997), 20; William Jennings Bryan, "The Prince
of Peace," in William Jennings Bryan, ed., *Speeches of William Jennings Bryan*
vol. 2 (New York: Funk & Wagnalls, 1909), 266–67; **108 Applied to the
history of human**: Bryan, ibid., 268; **108 Trained as a civil engineer**:
Russett, *Darwin in America*, 14; **108 Unlike Darwin, he**: Caudill, *Darwinian
Myths*, 135; **109 His *Study of Sociology***: William H. Tucker, *The Science and
Politics of Racial Research* (Chicago: University of Illinois Press, 1994), 27;
109 In particular, Spencer's vision of liberty: Ibid., 27; **109 Spencer,
more than anyone else**: Caudill, *Darwinian Myths*, 135, 77; **109 As
Rockefeller stated**: Cited in Richard Hofstader, *Social Darwinism in
American Thought* (New York: George Braziller, 1959), 45; **109 Footnote:
While Darwin included the term**: Cited in ibid., 65; **110 Nature,
asserted**: Cited in Caudill, *Darwinian Myths*, 75; **110 Bryan enjoyed enter-
taining**: Larson, *Summer For the Gods*, 42; **110 "Every honest man knows"**:
Cited in Willard B. Gatewood, ed., *Controversy in the Twenties:
Fundamentalism, Modernism, and Evolution* (Nashville, Tenn.: Vanderbilt
University Press, 1969), 19; **111 For them evolution signified**: James

Robertson, *American Myth, American Reality* (New York: Hill & Wang, 1980), 288; **111 Yet by the time he died**: Bowler, *Darwin*, 2; **111 "In their vocabulary"**: Gatewood, *Controversy in the Twenties*, 20; **112 And that, given the right opportunity**: Bowler, *Darwin*, 199; **112 The wealthy and educated**: Ibid., 199–200; **112 "With savages"**: Charles Darwin, *The Descent of Man and Selection in Relation to Sex*, 2nd ed. (London: John Murray, 1874), 151, 207–08; **113 Eugenics was, he said**: Cited in Tucker, *Science and Politics*, 45–6; **113 So convinced was he**: Francis Galton, *Memories of My Life* (London: Methuen and Company, 1908), 322; **113 Mendel's Law of Segregation**: Daniel J. Kevles, *In the Name of Eugenics: Genetics and the Uses of Human Heredity* (New York: Alfred A. Knopf, 1985), 41; **114 Thereafter Pearson was**: Cited in ibid., 40; **114 In 1877, Richard Dugdale**: See Ian Robert Dowbiggin, *Keeping America Sane* (Ithaca: Cornell University Press, 1997), 74–5; R.L. Dugdale, *The Jukes: A Study in Crime, Pauperism and Heredity*, 4th ed., (New York: Putnam's, 1910); **115 A follow-up study**: Arthur A. Estabrook, *The Jukes in 1915* (Washington, D.C.: Carnegie Institution of Washington, 1916), iii; Kevles, *In the Name of Eugenics*, 71; **115 At the bottom of the scale**: Kevles, ibid., 77–8; Kline, *Building a Better Race*, 23; **115 Feeble-mindedness**: Stefan Kühl, *The Nazi Connection: Eugenics, American Racism, and German National Socialism* (New York: Oxford University Press, 1994), 39–40; Henry Herbert Goddard, *The Kallikak Family: A Study in Feeble-Mindedness: Its Causes and Consequences* (New York: The Macmillan Company, 1912); **116 According to one estimate**: Higham, *Strangers in the Land*, 150–51. See also Kline, *Building a Better Race*, 14–15 and Kevles, *In the Name of Eugenics*, 58; **116 One of its early pamphlets**: Caudill, *Darwinian Myths*, 100; **116 Eugenics had become**: Higham, *Strangers in the Land*, 150; **116 "We know enough about"**: Cited in M.H. Haller, *Eugenics: Hereditarian Attitudes in American Thought* (New Brunswick, N.J.: Rutgers University Press, 1963), 76; **117 Then the First World War**: Tucker, *Science and Politics*, 56; Kevles, *In the Name of Eugenics*, 72–3; **117 In London, George Bernard Shaw**: Donald J. Childs, *Modernism and Eugenics* (Cambridge, Mass.: Cambridge University Press, 2001), 9; **117 "Their characteristic weaknesses"**: H.G. Wells, *Anticipations* (London: Chapman and Hall, 1901), 287–90, 298–99; Childs, ibid., 9; **118 In a letter**: James Boulton, ed., *The Letters of D.H. Lawrence* (Cambridge, Mass.: Cambridge University Press, 1979), vol. 1, 81; **118 His father, Amzi**: For the biographical material on Davenport, see Kevles, *In the Name of Eugenics*, 49–52; **119 During the latter part of the 1890s**: Ibid., 45, 54–6; **119 Hundreds of physicians**: Ibid., 58; **119 He participated in international**: Kühl, *Nazi Connection*, 13–14; **120 For the thousands of people**: Kline, *Building a Better Race*, 15; **120 At the Kansas State Fair**: Kevles, *In the Name of Eugenics*, 62; **120 "Science knows no way"**: Cited in Steven Selden,

Inheriting Shame: The Story of Eugenics and Racism in America (New York: Teachers College, Columbia University, 1999), 11; **120 Footnote: "More hard-hitting"**: Ibid., 23–4; **121 "Man is an animal"**: Cited in ibid., 49; **121 That progress, in his view**: Tucker, *Science and Politics*, 63; **121 These were the key components**: Charles Davenport, "State Laws Limiting Marriage Selection in Light of Eugenics," *Eugenics Record Office Bulletin* No. 9 (Cold Spring Harbor, N.Y.: Eugenics Records Office, 1913), 36; cited in Selden, *Inheriting Shame*, 53; Kevles, *In the Name of Eugenics*, 47; **121 President Theodore Roosevelt**: Kline, *Building a Better Race*, 11; **121 Davenport, like others**: Selden, *Inheriting Shame*, 51; Kevles, *In the Name of Eugenics*, 47; **122 In particular, interracial marriages**: Charles Davenport, "The Effects of Race Intermingling," *Proceedings of the American Philosophical Society* 56 (1917), 367; Tucker, *Science and Politics*, 65; **122 Despite occasional criticism**: Kevles, *In the Name of Eugenics*, 48–9; **122 "I believe in striving"**: Selden, *Inheriting Shame*, 12; **122 Footnote: In his brilliant study**: Kevles, *In the Name of Eugenics*, 48–9; **123 Footnote: It was Count Joseph Arthur de Gobineau**: See Howard M. Sachar, *The Course of Modern Jewish History* (Cleveland, OH: The World Publishing Company, 1958), 233; **124 "Nothing is convincing"**: Houston Stewart Chamberlain, *The Foundations of the Nineteenth Century*, vol. 1 (London: John Lane Company, 1913), 269; **124 Despite the condescending**: Theodore Roosevelt, *History as Literature* (New York: Charles Scribner's Sons, 1913) cited at Bartleby.com, 1998; George Bernard Shaw, *Misalliance, The Dark Lady of the Sonnets, and Fanny's First Play, With a Treatise on Parents and Children* (New York: Brentano's, 1926), chapter 58; **124 Indeed, Julius Streicher**: Ashley Montagu, *Man's Most Dangerous Myth: The Fallacy of Race* (Walnut Creek, Calif.: Altamira Press, 1997), 79; Ian Kershaw, *Hitler 1889–1936: Hubris* (London: Penguin, 1998), 151; **124 In North America**: Caudill, *Darwinian Myths*, 91; J.L.M. Curry, "The Negro Question," *Popular Science Monthly* 55 (June 1899), 177–85; Tucker, *Science and Politics*, 88–9; **124 When Frederick Douglass**: *New York Times*, February 27, 1895; Tucker, *Science and Politics*, 30; **124 Yet, as historian**: Higham, *Strangers in the Land*, 135; **125 Once he discovered**: Brian Regal, *Henry Fairfield Osborn: Race, and the Search for the Origins of Man* (Aldershot, England: Ashgate Publishing House, 2002), 108–10; **125 Between 1920 and 1939**: Caudill, *Darwinian Myths*, 125; **125 Grant later sent**: Ibid., 125; **126 "The Nordics are"**: Madison Grant, *The Passing of the Great Race* (New York: Charles Scribner's Sons, 1916), 167, 228; **126 But the part of the book**: Ibid., 16, 79, 85; **126 "The cross between a white"**: Ibid., 18, 60; Tucker, *Science and Politics*, 90–1; **126 Now, it was not only**: Higham, *Strangers in the Land*, 286–96; **127 Emphasizing that Grant's work**: "The Great American Myth," Editorial, *Saturday Evening Post*, May 7, 1921; **127 In his review**:

Selden, *Inheriting Shame*, 57; **127 Parroting Grant**: Calvin Coolidge, "Whose Country Is This?" *Good Housekeeping*, February 1921, 14; Tucker, *Science and Politics*, 93; **127 (On the other hand**: Franz Boas, "Inventing a Great Race," *New Republic* 51, (1917), 305; Tucker, ibid., 91; **128 As devoted and fanatical**: Higham, *Strangers in the Land*, 313; **128 The future "germ plasm"**: Kevles, *In the Name of Eugenics*, 103; **128 Nordics and eugenicists**: *Los Angeles Times*, April 13, 1924; Juan F. Pera, ed., *Immigrants Out: The New Nativism and the Anti-Immigrant Impulse in the United States* (New York: New York University Press, 1997), 24–5; **129 Most people in the region**: Dowbiggin, *Keeping America Sane*, 76; **129 Within a few years**: Ibid., 76–7; **129 More states passed**: Ibid., 78; **130 In 1914, Goddard**: Henry H. Goddard, *Feeble-Mindedness: Its Causes and Consequences* (New York: The Macmillan Company, 1914), 582; Kevles, *In the Name of Eugenics*, 106–7; **130 Writing at the end of the twenties**: Edward M. East, *Heredity and Human Affairs* (New York: Charles Scribner's Sons, 1929), 189; Tucker, *Science and Politics*, 69; **130 Sterilization legislation**: East, *Heredity and Human Affairs*, 238, 300; Tucker, ibid., 69; **130 Footnote: It is significant**: Tucker, ibid., 123, 129–31; **130 That was the opinion**: Charles Davenport, "Report of the Committee on Eugenics," *American Breeders' Magazine* 1 (1910), 27; Tucker, ibid., 69; **131 To protect the rapist**: Selden, *Inheriting Shame*, 129–31; **131 To test the act's validity**: Robert J. Cynkar, *"Buck v. Bell*: Felt Necessities v. Fundamental Values?" *Columbia Law Review* 81, (November 1981), 1435; "Three Generations, No Imbeciles: New Light on *Buck v. Bell*," *New York University Law Review* (1985), 60; **131 A local Red Cross**: D.J. Smith and K.R. Nelson, *The Sterilization of Carrie Buck* (Far Hills, N.J.: New Horizons Press, 1989), 108; **131 Several years later**: Selden, *Inheriting Shame*, 131; **131 After a cursory study**: Kevles, *In the Name of Eugenics*, 110; **132 That legal process took**: Ibid., 111; **132 "We have seen more"**: Supreme Court of the United States, 200, *"Buck v. Bell,"* 274 (1927); **132 Many doubted**: Angus McLaren, *Our Own Master Race: Eugenics in Canada 1885–1945* (Toronto: McClelland & Stewart, 1990), 38; **133 As early as 1901**: "Report of the Eighth Annual Meeting," *National Council of Women* (Ottawa: Taylor and Clarke, 1901), 141; cited in ibid., 38; **133 Influenced by the work**: Cited in ibid., 31; **133 Returning to Canada**: Dowbiggin, *Keeping America Sane*, 162–3; **133 Footnote: These fears were realized**: W.G. Smith, *A Study in Canadian Immigration* (Toronto: Ryerson, 1920), 242; **134 "It is the age"**: Helen MacMurchy, *The Almosts: A Study of the Feeble-Minded* (Boston: Houghton Mifflin, 1920), 173; **135 The feeble-minded might**: McLaren, *Our Own Master Race*, 40; **135 Quoting from the work**: Tim Christian, *The Mentally Ill and Human Rights in Alberta* (Edmonton: Alberta Law Foundation, 1974), 12; **135 Birth control, in her**: Helen MacMurchy, *Sterilization? Birth Control? A Book for Family Welfare and*

Safety (Toronto: Macmillan, 1934), 5; **135 Sensing that the public**:
Winnipeg Free Press, November 15, 1916, 11; **135 "Katie was well"**:
McClung, *The Stream Runs Fast*, 180; **136 "We protect the"**: *Vancouver Sun*,
May 25, 1927, 8; **136 Asked Margaret Gunn**: Christian, *The Mentally Ill*, 9;
137 "Are we animals": *Edmonton Journal*, February 28, 1928; **137 The gov-
ernment passed**: *Edmonton Bulletin*, March 6, 1928; **137 Alberta's steriliza-
tion act**: Christian, *The Mentally Ill*, 30; **137 By then, 2,822 Albertans**:
Gerald Hallowell, ed., *The Oxford Companion to Canadian History* (Toronto:
Oxford University Press, 2004), 580; **138 The Eugenics Society of Canada**:
McLaren, *Our Own Master Race*, 113; **138 According to a January 1936**:
"Sterilization of the Unfit," *Canadian Doctor* 2 (January 1936), 16–17, 43;
McLaren, ibid., 119; **138 It was, he noted**: Kevles, *In the Name of Eugenics*,
118; **138 At one mental institution**: Tucker, *Science and Politics*, 133; **138 In
1946, at the trial**: Kühl, *The Nazi Connection*, 101–02; **139 A national poll**:
"Old Faith Still Strong in America," *Literary Digest*, vol. 92, January 15,
1927, 30–1; **139 The book was banned**: "The Storm over 'Elmer Gantry,'"
Literary Digest, vol. 93, April 16, 1927, 28; **139 The evangelical preacher**:
Cited in Gerald Leinwand, *1927: High Tide of the Twenties* (New York: Four
Walls Eight Windows, 2001), 28; **139 Neither side, it should be**: See
Gatewood, *Controversy in the Twenties*, 6; Regal, *Henry Fairfield Osborn*, 155;
140 "The moral decline": Cited in Sprague L. De Camp, *The Great Monkey
Trial* (Garden City, N.Y.: Doubleday & Company, 1968), 30; **140 In his
sermons**: Regal, *Henry Fairfield Osborn*, 157; *New York Times*, March 9, 10,
17, 23, 1924; **140 And, Albert S. Johnson**: *Daily Observer* (Charlotte, N.C.),
February 24, 1925; Gatewood, *Controversy in the Twenties*, 24; **140 Footnote:
Bryan was also a lot**: Larson, *Summer For the Gods*, 38–9; **141 His legion
of supporters**: De Camp, *The Great Monkey Trial*, 36–7; **141 The chief culprits**: Larson, *Summer For the Gods*, 41; William Jennings Bryan, "Darwin's
Christ was Nobody," *The Forum* LXX (July 1923), 1675–80; **141 He filled
halls**: *New York Times*, February 26, 1922, March 5, 1922, March 14, 1922;
141 Although Osborn marshalled: Ibid., February 26, 1922; *Chicago
Tribune*, June 20, 1923; Larson, *Summer For the Gods*, 47; **142 In Kentucky
where Bryan**: Lawrence Levine, *Defender of Faith: William Jennings Bryan
1915–1925* (New York: Oxford University Press, 1965), 277; **142 Then,
following intense**: Larson, *Summer For the Gods*, 58–9; **142 Nevertheless,
as of the end of March**: Chapter 27, House Bill 185, *Public Acts of Tennessee
1925*, cited in Sheldon N. Grebstein, ed., *Monkey Trial: The State of Tennessee
vs. John Thomas Scopes* (Boston: Houghton Mifflin Company, 1960), 3;
144 Scopes later recalled: John T. Scopes, *The Center of the Storm:
Memoirs of John T. Scopes* (New York: Henry Holt, 1967), 58–9; **144 Yet
what propelled**: Cited in Gatewood, *Controversy in the Twenties*, 333;
145 When Sue Hicks: See Larson, *Summer For the Gods*, 97–100, 172;

H.L. Mencken, "The Monkey Trial: A Reporter's Account,"
July 14, 1925, University of Missouri–Kansas City Law School,
www.law.umkc.edu/faculty/projects/ftrials/scopes/menk.htm; **145 As an
agnostic**: George Shadroui, "Monkey Business," *Memphis Flyer*, February 7,
2000; Kevin Tierney, *Darrow: A Biography* (New York: Croswell, 1979), 85;
145 "Scopes is not": "Darrow loud in his protest," *Nashville Banner*, July 8,
1925, cited in Larson, *Summer For the Gods*, 146; **145 It was not long**:
Commercial Appeal (Memphis), July 15, 1925, cited in ibid., 166; **146 By
then, Dayton**: Clarence Darrow, *The Story of My Life* (New York: Charles
Scribner's Sons, 1932), 261; **146 Footnote: As an easterner**: Mencken,
"The Monkey Trial," July 9, 1925; **147 The "Great Commoner"
intended**: Larson, *Summer For the Gods*, 116; **147 "We feel we stand"**:
Scopes, *The Center of the Storm*, 154–56; Joseph Wood Krutch, "Dayton:
Then and Now" in Gatewood, *Controversy in the Twenties*, 365; "Darrow
Scores Ignorance and Bigotry Seeking to Quash Scopes Indictment," *New
York Times*, July 14, 1925; Mencken, "The Monkey Trial," July 14, 1925;
147 Footnote: Defence lawyer Dudley Field Malone: "Malone Glad Trial
Starts on a Friday," *Chattanooga Times*, July 10, 1925, cited in ibid., 145;
148 By the time Raulston: Darrow to Mencken August 15, 1925, cited in
Larson, *Summer For the Gods*, 190; **148 "Darrow succeeded in showing"**:
Sterling Tracy, "Darrow Quizzes Bryan; Agnosticism in Clash with
Fundamentalism," *Commercial Appeal* (Memphis), July 21, 1925, cited in ibid.,
190; **148 "I think this case"**: Cited in Larson, ibid., 193; **149 Indeed,
Tennessee's state legislature**: Shadroui, "Monkey Business"; **149 On the
seventy-fifth anniversary**: Doug Linder, "Speech on the Occasion of the
75th Anniversary of the Opening of the Scopes Trial," Kansas City, July 10,
2000, www.law.umkc.edu/faculty/projects/ftrials/scopes/confspeech.html;
149 Footnote: In a 1991 Gallup: "Public Beliefs About Evolution and
Creation," www.religioustolerance.org/ev_publ.htm. See also "Textbook
Warning Draws Lawsuit in Georgia," *USA Today*, November 8, 2004.

CHAPTER FOUR: THE RED SCARE
153 "The 'Red' movement": A. Mitchell Palmer, "Extent of Bolshevik
Infection Here," *The Literary Digest*, vol. 64, January 17, 1920, 13; **154 A
devout Quaker**: Cited in Curt J. Gentry, *Edgar Hoover: The Man and the
Secrets* (New York: W.W. Norton & Company, 1991), 75; **154 Officers at
the scene**: Stanley A. Coben, *A. Mitchell Palmer: Politician* (New York: Da
Capo Press, 1972), 205–06; **154 "A time has come"**: Charles H.
McCormick, *Seeing Reds: Federal Surveillance of Radicals in the Pittsburgh Mill
District, 1917–1921* (Pittsburgh: University of Pittsburgh Press, 1997), 91;
155 In April explosives: Robert K. Murray, *Red Scare: A Study in National
Hysteria, 1919–1920* (Minneapolis: University of Minnesota, 1955), 70;

156 A lawyer, former congressman: Coben, *A. Mitchell Palmer*, 197;
156 His biographer, historian: Ibid., viii; **156 "The morning after"**: Cited
in ibid., 206–07; **157 Evidence found by the police**: Richard Gid Powers,
Not Without Honor: The History of American Anticommunism (New York: The
Free Press, 1995), 22; McCormick, *Seeing Reds*, 112–16; **157 Flynn, whom
Palmer**: McCormick, ibid., 113; **157 Footnote: Luigi Galleani**: See Paul
Avrich, *Anarchist Portraits* (Princeton, N.J.: Princeton University Press,
1988), 167–71; **158 Two more key members**: Robert J. Goldstein, *Political
Repression in Modern America: From 1870 to the Present* (Cambridge, Mass.:
Schenkman Publishing Company, 1978), 149; **158 A self-professed "avid
student"**: Gentry, *Edgar Hoover*, 62–4; **159 His conservative attitudes**:
Ibid., 63; **159 As he studied communism**: Powers, *Not Without Honor*, 23;
159 As U.S. writer Richard Powers notes: Ibid., 23; **159 "Like a prairie
fire"**: A. Mitchell Palmer, "The Case Against the Reds," *Forum*, February
1920, in David F. Trask (ed.), *World War I at Home: Readings on American Life,
1914–1920* (New York: Wiley, 1969), 185–186; **160 They had "wild eyes"**:
Harry Gutkin and Mildred Gutkin, *Profiles in Dissent: The Shaping of Radical
Thought in the Canadian West* (Edmonton: NeWest Publishers, 1997), 121;
160 Their every move occupied: Margaret MacMillan, *Paris 1919: Six
Months that Changed the World* (New York: Random House, 2002), 65–7;
161 In an open letter: Powers, *Not Without Honor*, 20; **161 Ironically,
success in Russia**: Murray, *Red Scare*, 51; Goldstein, *Political Repression*,
140–41; **161 They cheered because**: Western Labour Press, August 9,
1918; A. Ross McCormack, *Reformers, Rebels, and Revolutionaries: The Western
Canadian Radical Movement 1899–1919* (Toronto: University of Toronto
Press, 1977), 141; **162 The lecture she presented**: Alice Wexler, *Emma
Goldman: An Intimate Life* (New York: Pantheon Books, 1984), 242; **162 And,
from a jail cell**: Cited in Powers, *Not Without Honor*, 8; **163 As a result the
United States**: Cited in Goldstein, *Political Repression*, 3; **163 If that did not
work**: Ibid., 54; **163 From its inception**: Cited in Sachar, *The Course of
Modern Jewish History*, 179–80; Murray, *Red Scare*, 109; **164 "I saw how pro-
fessions"**: Cited in Goldstein, *Political Repression*, 57; **164 He dismissed the
idea**: McCormick, *Seeing Reds*, 35; Murray, *Red Scare*, 114; Gentry, *Edgar
Hoover*, 104; **165 The gathering was peaceful**: Wexler, *Emma Goldman*, 34;
Paul Avrich, *The Haymarket Tragedy* (Princeton, N.J.: Princeton University
Press, 1984), 57; **165 Footnote: As the noose was placed**: Avrich, *The
Haymarket Tragedy*, 393–401; **166 Workers throughout the world**: Avrich,
ibid., 428; **166 "For years, the memory"**: Higham, *Strangers in the Land*,
55; **166 "I read about their"**: Emma Goldman, *Living My Life*, vol. 1 (New
York: Dover Publications, 1970), 9–10; **167 The authorities had tried**:
Wexler, *Emma Goldman*, 65–6; **167 Goldman was arrested**: Ibid., 103–111;
168 It was rumoured: Murray, *Red Scare*, 27; **168 The decision to create**:

McCormick, *Seeing Reds*, 32; **168 From the start, the IWW**: Ibid., 32;
168 At its peak in 1917: Goldstein, *Political Repression*, 98; **168 "When a
Wobbly comes to town"**: Cited in ibid., 83; **168 A San Diego *Tribune*
editor**: Cited in Gibbs M. Smith, *Labor Martyr Joe Hill* (New York: Grosset
and Dunlap, 1969), 9–10; **169 Before the war**: Goldstein, *Political Repression*,
89; **170 The WMA allowed**: J.M. Bumsted, *The Winnipeg General Strike of
1919: An Illustrated History* (Winnipeg: Watson & Dwyer, 1994), 3;
170 "Don't be a Soldier": Murray, *Red Scare*, 29; **171 Newspaper editors
referred**: See ibid., 30; **171 In private, President Wilson**: Goldstein,
Political Repression, 106; **171 Footnote: On one occasion**: See ibid., 113–14;
172 Both were eventually: Wexler, *Emma Goldman*, 235; **172 The New
York Times called**: *New York Times*, July 11, 1917; ibid., 236; **172 In March
1919**: Murray, *Red Scare*, 23; **172 "Do not worry over"**: Ibid., 23–6; **173
"Every strike is"**: Cited in Powers, *Not Without Honor*, 19; **173 Two days
before**: *Seattle Star*, February 14, 1919; Robert L. Friedheim, *The Seattle
General Strike* (Seattle: University of Washington Press, 1964), 108–09;
174 "There will be many": Cited in Friedheim, ibid., 110–11; **174 And,
indeed, across**: See Murray, *Red Scare*, 65; **174 He later maintained**: Ibid.,
63; **174 "The time has come"**: Cited in Friedheim, *Seattle General Strike*,
131; **175 Hanson, however, made the most**: Ibid., 147; **175 Again, newspapers portrayed**: See McCormick, *Seeing Reds*, 121–23; William K.
Klingaman, *1919: The Year Our World Began* (New York: St. Martin's Press,
1987), 549–52; **175 J. Edgar Hoover considered**: McCormick, ibid., 120;
175 A Senate Committee: Murray, *Red Scare*, 151; **176 At the local army**:
Bumsted, *The Winnipeg General Strike*, 28–9; **177 "What they did not see"**:
David Jay Bercuson, *Confrontation at Winnipeg* (Montreal: McGill-Queen's
University Press, 1974), 178; **177 The decision to allow**: Ibid., 130; **177
Under the heading**: *New York Times*, May 22, 1919; **178 Closer to home**:
Cited in Bumsted, *The Winnipeg General Strike*, 34; **178 A downturn in
the economy**: Bercuson, *Confrontation at Winnipeg*, 191; **178 "Let every
hostile"**: *Winnipeg Telegram*, January 28, 1919; **178 Footnote: According to
the *Western Labour News***: *Western Labour News*, May 2, 1919, cited in
Norman Penner, ed., *Winnipeg 1919: The Strikers' Own History of the
Winnipeg General Strike* (Toronto: James Lewis & Samuel, 1973), 31–3;
179 "God gave me this plant": "The Winnipeg General Strike,"
timelinks.merlin.mb; **179 Yet they also came**: Bumsted, *The Winnipeg
General Strike*, 5–6; **179 By the time he settled**: Gutkin, and Gutkin.
Profiles in Dissent, 140; **179 Footnote: "Years later when"**: Ibid., 3; **180 In
December 1918**: Ibid., 153, 165; **180 Indeed, the OBU**: Penner, *Winnipeg
1919*, 29; **180 Organizers made little**: Bumsted, *The Winnipeg General
Strike*, 25; **180 Some months earlier**: Cited in ibid., 14; **181 During the
past few months**: Ibid., 20; Penner, *Winnipeg 1919*, 16; **181 There were**

scuffles: Bercuson, *Confrontation at Winnipeg*, 86–7; **182 In fact, the RNWMP**: Ibid., 88; **182 On May 13, 1919**: *Western Labour News*, May 16, 1919; Penner, *Winnipeg 1919*, 42–4; **183 "It is a fine spectacle"**: Cited in Gutkin, and Gutkin, *Profiles in Dissent*, 158; **183 But to John W. Dafoe**: *Manitoba Free Press*, May 16, 1919; **183 Footnote: Russell also liked**: Gutkin, and Gutkin, *Profiles in Dissent*, 158; **184 First was Winnipeg City Council's**: Bumsted, *The Winnipeg General Strike*, 40; **184 The pro-strike mob**: Ibid., 88; **184 This unprecedented legal action**: Ibid., 55; **185 But his voice**: Penner, *Winnipeg 1919*, 189; **185 While this was taking place**: See ibid., 57; Bercuson, *Confrontation at Winnipeg*, 174; **185 Footnote: The photograph**: Ibid., 191; Bumsted, *The Winnipeg General Strike*, 57; **186 The metal-workers**: Bercuson, ibid., 177; **186 In early May**: Coben, *A. Mitchell Palmer*, 196; **187 During the steel strike**: Murray B. Levin, *Political Hysteria in America* (New York: Basic Books, 1971), 28; **187 The worst incident of vigilantism**: See ibid., 51–2; Murray, *Red Scare*, 183–84; **187 Washington senator Wesley L. Jones**: Cited in Murray, ibid., 185; **188 Some were later released**: Gentry, *Edgar Hoover*, 83; **188 Footnote: When attorney Isaac Schorr**: Ibid., 84; **189 Hoover later remembered**: Ibid., 86; **189 Goldman, on the other hand**: Goldman, *Living My Life*, vol. 2, 717; **189 Footnote: Emma Goldman remained**: Paul Avrich, *Anarchist Voices: An Oral History of Anarchism in America* (Princeton, N.J.: Princeton University Press, 1995), 47–9; **189 Without proper arrest or search warrants**: Ibid., 27; Coben, *A. Mitchell Palmer*, 225–26; **189 Hoover had cleverly instructed**: Powers, *Not Without Honor*, 27; **190 It "defeats the ends"**: Gentry, *Edgar Hoover*, 94; **190 At first, the public cheered**: *New York Times*, January 5, 1920; *Chicago Tribune*, January 3, 1919; **190 No dynamite was discovered**: Gentry, *Edgar Hoover*, 94; **190 "Undoubtedly these raids"**: McCormick, *Seeing Reds*, 167; **190 "My one desire is"**: Cited in Levin, *Political Hysteria*, 195; **190 And, for a brief time**: See Powers, *Not Without Honor*, 30–1; **191 Hoover opened a file**: Gentry, *Edgar Hoover*, 99; ibid., 32–3; **191 Footnote: During the period from**: McCormick, *Seeing Reds*, 148; **192 Property damage was extensive**: James Adams, "The Day Wall Street Exploded," *Globe and Mail* (Toronto), September 15, 2001; **192 More than likely, the culprit in question**: Ibid.; See also Beverly Gage, *The Day Wall Street Exploded* (New York: Oxford University Press, 2003; **192 Five months earlier**: Leinwand, *1927*, 85; **192 Three weeks later**: Ibid., 85–7; **192 According to historian Paul Avrich**: Avrich, *Anarchist Voices*, 88; **192 Judge Webster Thayer**: Leinwand, *1927*, 87; **193 New evidence revealed**: Avrich, *Anarchist Voices*, 88; **193 There were demonstrations**: Powers, *Not Without Honor*, 94; **193 The two anarchists became symbols**: Ibid., 94–5; **193 The trio concluded**: Avrich, *Anarchist Voices*, 89; **193 Sacco's last words**: Leinwand, ibid., 89; **193 Footnote:**

According to Curt Gentry,: Gentry, *Edgar Hoover*, 105; Leinwand, *1927*, 90; **194 Footnote: In 1977, on the fiftieth**: Cited in ibid., 92; Brian Jackson, *The Black Flag: A Look at the Strange Case of Nicola Sacco and Bartolomew Vanzetti* (Boston: Routledge and Kegan Paul, 1981), 90.

CHAPTER FIVE: BOOZE

197 "I make my money": Cited in Dennis Eisenberg, Uri Dan and Eli Landau, *Meyer Lansky: Mogul of the Mob* (London: Paddington Press, 1979), 86; **197 "Undoubtedly the historian"**: *Manitoba Free Press*, March 11, 1916; Craig Heron, *Booze: A Distilled History* (Toronto: Between the Lines, 2003), 235; **198 The amendment would abolish**: Cited in Norman H. Clark, *Deliver Us From Evil: An Interpretation of American Prohibition* (New York: W.W. Norton & Company, 1976), 140; **198 More moderate reformers**: Cited in Eisenberg, et. al, *Meyer Lansky*, 77; **198 "The reign of tears is over"**: Cited in Mark Thornton, "Alcoholic Prohibition Was a Failure," *Policy Analysis* (no. 157) Cato Institute, (July 17, 1991), 6; **198 At best**: Clark, *Deliver Us From Evil*, 165; **199 As the great vaudeville**: Cited in Peter C. Newman, *Bronfman Dynasty* (Toronto: McClelland & Stewart, 1978), 83; **199 Similarly, historian**: Charles Merz, *The Dry Decade* (Seattle: University of Washington Press, 1969), 162–63; **199 Thomas Jefferson**: Clark, *Deliver Us From Evil*, 23; **199 By 1873, there**: Ibid., 50; **200 In 1914 in Winnipeg**: James Gray, *Booze: The Impact of Whisky on the Prairie West* (Toronto: Signet Books, 1972), 93; **200 David Murray**: Ibid., 93–4; **200 Saloons probably were**: Heron, *Booze*, 107–108, 116; **200 After all, the main**: Ibid., 123–24. As Heron points out, government investigators in 1913 found that at closing time a high percentage of bar patrons in Hamilton and London, Ontario, for example, would not have been considered to be intoxicated; **200 As Albert Kennedy**: Cited in John Kobler, *Ardent Spirits: The Rise and Fall of Prohibition* (New York: G.P. Putnam's Sons, 1973), 176; **200 Bar floors were covered**: Gray, *Booze*, 70; **201 "The names of Karl Marx"**: Cited in John J. Rumbarger, *Profits, Power and Prohibition* (Albany, N.Y.: State University of New York Press, 1989), 117; **201 "There was never a moment"**: Merz, *The Dry Decade*, 5; **202 As historian John Rumbarger**: Rumbarger, *Profits, Power and Prohibition*, x–ix; **202 "It is within the knowledge"**: Cited in ibid., 130; **203 The Woman's Christian Temperance Union**: See Sara M. Evans, *Born for Liberty: A History of Women in America* (New York: The Free Press, 1989), 128–29; **203 "I hereby promise"**: Cited in Wendy Mitchinson, "The WCTU: 'For God, Home and Native Land': A Study in Nineteenth-Century Feminism," in Linda Kealey, ed., *A Not Unreasonable Claim: Women and Reform in Canada, 1880s–1920s* (Toronto: The Women's Press, 1979), 165; **203 McClung and her WCTU sisters**: Cited in Gerald A Hallowell, *Prohibition in Ontario, 1919–1923* (Ottawa: Ontario Historical

Society, 1972), 15; **203 Footnote: One of the more radical**: Clark, *Deliver Us From Evil*, 81–2; **204 "No one, of course"**: Michael Marrus, *Mr. Sam: The Life and Times of Samuel Bronfman* (Toronto: Viking, 1991), 59; **204 Its members were**: Rumbarger, *Profits, Power and Prohibition*, 184; **205 In one of his more celebrated**: Billy Sunday, "Booze" sermon can be found at www.biblebelievers.com; **205 He regarded the campaign**: Darrow, *The Story of My Life*, 285; **205 In June 1909, both Sunday and Darrow**: See Clark, *Deliver Us From Evil*, 100–01; **206 "When we find ourselves"**: McClung, *In Times Like These*, 99; **206 "The dealings of the liquor"**: Cited in Marrus, *Mr. Sam*, 63; **206 Prohibitionists implored Canadians**: National Archives Documents, Ottawa, http://www.archives.ca/05/0529/052930/05293053-e.htm; **206 A few years later**: Kobler, *Ardent Spirits*, 207; Higham, *Strangers in the Land*, 207–08; **207 The bartender's union**: Gray, *Booze*, 79–80; **207 According to writer**: James Gray, *The Roar of the Twenties* (Toronto: Macmillan of Canada, 1975), 139; **207 To acquire a bottle**: Hallowell, *Prohibition in Ontario*, 108; **208 The Bronfman family arrived**: See Marrus, *Mr. Sam*, 35–57; **208 Their first establishment**: Ibid., 59; **208 Footnote: Naturally enough, there**: Ibid., 59; **209 Sam, in particular**: Ibid., 66–8; **209 According to testimony**: Newman, *Bronfman Dynasty*, 84; **210 Footnote: Harry Bronfman's first attempt**: Ibid., 85–6; **210 "The only wealthy"**: Cited in Savage, *Our Nell*, 154; **210 Likewise, Stephen Leacock**: Cited in C.W. Hunt, *Booze, Boats and Billions* (Toronto: McClelland & Stewart, 1988), 41; **211 Prohibition might be**: Cited in Savage, *Our Nell*, 154; **211 Across Canada**: Gray, *Booze*, 142; **211 As Charles Merz noted**: Merz, *The Dry Decade*, 19; **212 In May 1919**: Kobler, *Ardent Spirits*, 212–13; **212 "Let the church bells"**: Cited in ibid., 11; **213 It is likely**: Clark, *Deliver Us From Evil*, 163; **213 By 1926, the forty-eight state legislatures**: Clark, *Deliver Us From Evil*, 163; **213 Footnote: As James Gray explains**: Gray, *Booze*, 197; **214 In his 1926 report**: Ibid., 165; **214 The *Chicago Tribune* estimated**: See Merz, *The Dry Decade*, 138; **214 They found it in**: Kobler, *Ardent Spirits*, 234–35; **214 The fashionable speakeasies**: Ibid., 232–33; **214 Footnote: Liquor was abundant**: Kobler, *Ardent Spirits*, 242; **215 Thousands more died**: Ibid., 302; **215 "People who drink bootleg"**: "Prohibition After Wheeler," *Literary Digest* vol. 94 (September 1927), 6; **215 "In order to enforce Prohibition"**: Cited in ibid., 223; **215 For a time**: Hunt, *Booze, Boats and Billions*, 96–7; **216 During a five-year period**: See Kobler, *Ardent Spirits*, 294–98; **216 Footnote: Detroit was the**: Ibid., 298; **217 Footnote: According to Eliot Asinof**: Eliot Asinof, *Eight Men Out: The Black Sox and the 1919 World Series* (New York: Holt, Rinehart and Winston, 1977), 291–346; **218 "He stood there"**: Cited in Eisenberg, et. al, *Meyer Lansky*, 129–31; **219 Other key members**: Rich Cohen, *Tough Jews*

(New York: Simon & Schuster, 1998), 161. See also Mark A. Stuart, *Gangster #2: Longy Zwillman, the Man Who Invented Organized Crime* (Seacus, N.J.: Lyle Stuart, Inc., 1985); **219 "Prohibition is going"**: Cited in Eisenberg, et. al, *Meyer Lansky*, 82; **219 The Bronfmans did not**: Marrus, *Mr. Sam*, 147; **219 Canadian liquor was**: Eisenberg, et. al, *Meyer Lansky*, 79; Howard M. Sachar, *A History of the Jews in America* (New York: Alfred A. Knopf, 1992), 347; **219 The only way to stop**: Allan S. Everest, *Rum Across the Border* (Syracuse, N.Y.: Syracuse University Press, 1978), 11; **219 Footnote: In the mid-1940s**: Ibid., 237–40; **220 Ethically, Canadian entrepreneurs**: See Marrus, *Mr. Sam*, 129, 151–57; **220 In 1935, after the RCMP**: See ibid., 202–11; **220 At the same time**: Ibid., 77; **220 The value of all liquor**: Kobler, *Ardent Spirits*, 254; **220 "Rum Running," the** Toronto Financial Post: Cited in Newman, *Bronfman Dynasty*, 87; **221 Dubbed by the press**: See Hunt, *Booze, Boats and Billions*, 125–26, 145–47; **221 The Bronfmans set up**: Marrus, *Mr. Sam*, 141–43; **221 Starting in 1921, McCoy**: Kobler, *Ardent Spirits*, 257; **221 Meanwhile, on the Canadian prairies**: Marrus, *Mr. Sam*, 75; Newman, *Bronfman Dynasty*, 98; **221 Footnote: According to Michael Marrus**: Marrus, ibid., 141; **222 The gangsters also mounted**: Ibid., 76; **222 Some of the more inventive**: Everest, *Rum Across the Border*, 27–8; **222 In 1922, Paul Matoff**: See Newman, *Bronfman Dynasty*, 101; **223 As Arnold Rothstein had predicted**: Eisenberg, et. al, *Meyer Lansky*, 91–2; **223 Born Alphonse Capone**: See Bergreen, *Capone*, 27–37; **224 Ironically, syphilis**: Ibid., 46; **224 In 1917, a confrontation**: Robert J. Schoenberg, *Mr. Capone* (New York: William Morrow and Company, 1992), 33–4; **224 At first, he managed**: Bergreen, *Capone*, 82–9; **224 "He was atavistic"**: Ibid., 19; **225 He gave freely**: Leinwand, *1927*, 137–38; **225 When the popular comedian**: Schoenberg, *Mr. Capone*, 294; **225 McGurn was also the mastermind**: See Bergreen, *Capone*, 306–15; **225 Footnote: On one infamous occasion**: Leinwand, *1927*, 132–33; **226 According to the U.S. Attorney General's office**: Schoenberg, *Mr. Capone*, 177; **226 Justice Oliver Wendell Holmes**: Leinwand, *1927*, 138–39; **226 Footnote: Near the end of his turbulent life**: Bergreen, *Capone*, 344; **227 On the morning of December 12, 1927**: Ibid., 84; **227 Moreover, from an economic standpoint**: Clark, *Deliver Us From Evil*, 200; **227 "Fed by war psychology"**: "Prohibition After Wheeler," *Literary Digest* vol. 94 (September 1927), 7; **227 "This convention wants"**: Cited in Clark, *Deliver Us From Evil*, 205.

CHAPTER SIX: INNOVATORS AND INNOVATIONS

231 "I will build a motor car": Cited in Warren Susman, *Culture as History: The Transformation of American Society in the Twentieth Century* (New York: Pantheon Books, 1984), 136; **231 Ford, who for about five years**: See

Douglas Brinkley, *Wheels for the World: Henry Ford, His Company, and a Century of Progress* (New York: Viking, 2003), 21–3; Daniel Gross, ed., *Forbes Greatest Business Stories Of All Time* (New York: John Wiley & Sons, 1996), 77–8; **232 As Will Rogers put it**: Cited in David E. Kyvig, *Daily Life in the United States, 1920–1939: Decades of Promise and Pain* (Westport, Conn.: Greenwood Press, 2002), 37; **232 Despite the excitement**: Gross, *Forbes Greatest Business Stories*, 74–5; **232 It took Ford several attempts**: Carol Gelderman, *Henry Ford: The Wayward Capitalist* (New York: The Dial Press, 1981), 19–23; **233 Even Ransom Olds's**: Kyvig, *Daily Life*, 23; **233 "I'm going to democratize"**: Cited in Gross, *Forbes Greatest Business Stories*, 81; **233 Later he visited an abattoir**: Heather Robertson, *Driving Force: The McLaughlin Family and the Age of the Car* (Toronto: McClelland & Stewart, 1995), 128; **233 By utilizing similar methods**: Gelderman, *Henry Ford*, 50; **233 (As a comparison**: Gross, *Forbes Greatest Business Stories*, 83; **233 By the early twenties**: Gelderman, *Henry Ford*, 223, 251; **233 Whereas in 1905**: Gross, *Forbes Greatest Business Stories*, 76; **234 "You know, Henry"**: Cited in Reynold M. Wik, *Henry Ford and Grass-roots America* (Ann Arbor, Mich.: University of Michigan Press, 1973), 1; **234 Ironically, Ford himself**: Gelderman, *Henry Ford*, 243; **234 "Until your father"**: Cited in ibid., 25; **234 Footnote: In 1929, sociologists Robert and Helen Lynd**: Robert S. Lynd and Helen Merrell Lynd, *Middletown: A Study in Contemporary America* (New York: Harcourt, Brace and Company, 1929); Frederick Lewis Allen, *Only Yesterday: An Informal History of the 1920s* (New York: Harper & Row Publishers, 1964), 136; **235 As one Oldsmobile ad**: Cited in Robertson, *Driving Force*, 116; **235 Women whose slit-skirts**: Ibid., 121; **235 "The automobile was the quintessential"**: Ibid., 140; **235 Liberated from the supervision**: Peter Ling, "Sex and the Automobile in the Jazz Age," *History Today* (November 1989), 18; **235 "Automobiles have become"**: Cited in Robertson, *Driving Force*, 184; Ling, ibid., 18, 22; **235 Footnote: According to historian**: Kyvig, *Daily Life*, 23. See also Burrows and Wallace, *Gotham*, 948; **236 Eighteen people were**: Robertson, *Driving Force*, 161, 238–9; **236 "My friend, you're mistaken"**: Cited in Gelderman, *Henry Ford*, 38; **236 Footnote: Next to Henry Ford**: Robertson, *Driving Force*, 133–34; **237 He scorned the**: Gelderman, *Henry Ford*, 243; **237 His motto was**: Henry Ford, *My Life and Work* (Garden City, N.Y.: Doubleday, Page & Company, 1922), 128; **237 According to *Forbes* magazine**: Gross, *Forbes Greatest Business Stories*, 83; **237 The *Wall Street Journal* criticized**: *Wall Street Journal*, January 12, 1914; **238 Typical of Ford**: Gelderman, *Henry Ford*, 57; **238 According to a company**: Neil Baldwin, *Henry Ford and the Jews: The Mass Production of Hate* (New York: Public Affairs, 2001), 37; **238 The department was led**: Ibid., 38; **238 "I want you"**: Ibid., 38; **239 "We used to say"**: Cited in ibid., 76; **239 Footnote: Even in the**

1930s: See Gelderman, *Henry Ford*, 207–09; **240 The depiction of Ford**: Ibid., 86–7; **240 "He speaks at times"**: Cited in ibid., 230; **240 "He has the way of discoursing"**: Cited in Baldwin, *Henry Ford and the Jews*, 230; **240 To counter what**: Ibid., 69; **240 One historian has**: Donald Warren, *Radio Priest: Charles Coughlin, the Father of Hate Radio* (New York: The Free Press, 1996), 145; **240 Liebold was Prussian**: See Baldwin, *Henry Ford and the Jews*, 51–2; **241 "Henry Ford holds"**: Cited in S.T. Joshi, ed., *Documents of American Prejudice: An Anthology of Writings on Race from Thomas Jefferson to David Duke* (New York: Basic Books, 1999), 387–90; **241 Footnote: In 1905, a Russian**: Sachar, *Modern Jewish History*, 312; Baldwin, *Henry Ford and the Jews*, 82–5; **242 Later, another friend**: Baldwin, ibid., 235; **242 Footnote: The Nazis, in the early twenties**: See Gelderman, *Henry Ford*, 224–27, 240–41; Adolf Hitler, *Mein Kampf* (Boston: Houghton Mifflin Company, 1971), 639; **243 This apology was a complete**: *New York Herald Tribune*, July 9, 1927; Gelderman, ibid., 233; **243 It is, however, debatable**: See Baldwin, *Henry Ford and the Jews*, 241–319; **243 "I have in mind"**: Cited in Knowlton Nash, *The Microphone Wars: A History of Triumph and Betrayal at the CBC* (Toronto: McClelland & Stewart, 1994), 26–7; "Sarnoff, David," www.museum.tv/archives; **244 With Marconi's encouragement**: "Sarnoff, David," ibid; **244 Taking full advantage**: Kyvig, *Daily Life*, 61–2; Susan Smulyan, *Selling Radio: The Commercialization of American Broadcasting 1920–1934* (Washington, D.C.: Smithsonian Institute Press, 1994), 14; **245 This included close**: "July 2nd Fight Described by Radiophone," *The Wireless Age*, July 1921; Smulyan, ibid., 28–9; **245 With the added hype**: See Allen, *Only Yesterday*, 174–75; **246 As the game went**: Nash, *The Microphone Wars*, 33; **246 Within a decade of its introduction**: Allen, *Only Yesterday*, 137; **246 In 1925, approximately**: Allan Levine, *Scrum Wars: The Prime Ministers and the Media* (Toronto: Dundurn Press, 1993), 168; **246 A September 1923 story**: J.H. Morecroft, "The March of Radio: Preparing for Long Distance," *Radio Broadcast* 3 (September 1923), 361; Smulyan, *Selling Radio*, 12; **246 A year earlier in Toronto**: Nash, *The Microphone Wars*, 30–1; **247 "The radio is turned"**: Ibid., 35; **247 Millions of Americans and Canadians**: Kyvig, *Daily Life*, 72; **247 White audiences adored**: Smulyan, *Selling Radio*, 115; **247 When Pepsodent sponsored**: David Halberstam, *The Powers That Be* (New York: Alfred A. Knopf, 1979), 15; **248 Large-scale advertising campaigns**: Kyvig, *Daily Life*, 161–64; **248 He was the "first"**: Halberstam, *The Powers That Be*, 15; Levine, *Scrum Wars*, 169; **248 In 1928, the Canadian federal**: See Levine, ibid., 168; **249 *Collier's* magazine suggested**: Cited in Smulyan, *Selling Radio*, 32; **249 The editors of the**: *Globe* (Toronto) July 2, 1927; **249 That memorable night**: Dennis N. Voskuil, "The Power of the Air: Evangelicals and the Rise of Religious Broadcasting" in Quentin J. Schultze, ed., *American*

Evangelicals and the Mass Media (Grand Rapids, Mich.: Zondervan Corporation, 1973), 70–1; **250 The church's senior pastor**: Ibid., 71; **250 Charles Fuller, for instance**: Tona J. Hangen, *Redeeming the Dial* (Chapel Hill, N.C.: University of North Carolina Press, 2002), 5; **250 "We believe"**: Cited in Nash, *The Microphone Wars*, 50–1; **251 "The rise of radio"**: Hangen, *Redeeming the Dial*, 11; **251 A farmer in Saskatchewan**: Cited in Warren, *Radio Priest*, 49; **252 Aberhart's motto was**: See David R. Elliott, and Iris Miller, *Bible Bill: A Biography of William Aberhart* (Edmonton: Reidmore Books, 1987), 31–6; **252 "He commanded attention"**: Ibid., 55–6; **252 "He did not then"**: Ibid., 73; **253 At the height**: John Irving, *The Social Credit Movement in Alberta* (Toronto: University of Toronto Press, 1959), 31–2; **253 Footnote: Social Credit was based**: See Daniel Francis and Sonia Riddoch, *Our Canada: A Social and Political History* (Toronto: McClelland & Stewart, 1985), 192–93; **253 At the end of the show**: Irving, *The Social Credit Movement*, 110–11; **254 Based in Los Angeles**: Hangen, *Redeeming the Dial*, 58, 78; **254 She gave "the old-time religion"**: William G. McLoughlin, "Aimee Semple McPherson: 'Your Sister in the King's Glad Service,'" *Journal of Popular Culture* 1 (Winter, 1967), 207; **254 "She remains"**: Hangen, *Redeeming the Dial*, 78; **254 Her performances on stage**: Ibid., 58; **254 When she appeared**: Carey McWilliams, "Aimee Semple McPherson: 'Sunlight in My Soul'" in Isabel Leighton, ed., *The Aspirin Age, 1919–1941* (New York: Simon & Schuster, 1949), 77–8; **255 As a teenager**: Robert Bahr, *The Least of All Saints: The Story of Aimee Semple McPherson* (Englewood Cliffs, N.J.: Prentice-Hall, 1979), 285–86; **255 By the end of the evening**: Aimee Semple McPherson, *The Story of My Life* (Waco, Tex.: Word Books, 1973), 46; **255 With her husband's support**: Leinwand, *1927*, 201; **255 A Bible College soon**: See Hangen, *Redeeming the Dial*, 60–71; Leinwand, ibid., 201; **256 She rode in a float**: Leinwand, ibid., 201; **256 Her broadcasts were so moving**: Bahr, *The Least of All Saints*, 292; **256 "These are the days of invention"**: Cited in Hangen, *Redeeming the Dial*, 65–6; **256 "Please order your minions"**: Cited in Kyvig, *Daily Life*, 67; **257 "Her voice is a full-throated"**: Cited in Daniel Mark Epstein, *Sister Aimee: The Life of Aimee Semple McPherson* (New York: Harcourt Brace Jovanovich, 1993), 320; **257 The critic H.L. Mencken**: Cited in Hangen, *Redeeming the Dial*, 76; **257 He portrayed himself**: See Warren, *Radio Priest*, 1–2, 20; **258 He was born in Hamilton**: See ibid., 9–16; **259 "Within three weeks"**: Ibid., 34; **259 Many of those letters contained**: Ibid., 27, 34; **259 When critics complained**: Ibid., 34; **259 Coughlin was a brilliant**: Wallace Stenger, "The Radio Priest and His Flock," in Leighton, *The Aspirin Age*, 234; **260 Radio, he said**: Louis B. Ward, *Father Charles E. Coughlin: An Authorized Biography* (Detroit: Tower Publications, 1933), 38, 42; **260 "What occurred"**: Warren, *Radio Priest*, 26;

260 First, it was the "Red Menace": Ibid., 35, 150–55; **260 "One of the great problems before our Civilization"**: *Detroit Free Press*, April 1, 1933; **261 Journalists and radio broadcasters**: See Kenneth S. Davis, *The Hero: Charles A. Lindbergh and the American Dream* (Garden City, N.Y.: Doubleday and Company, 1959), 213; **262 "What is the greatest story of all time?"**: *New York Times*, May 22, 1927; **262 More than 250,000**: Herbert Ashbury, "The Year of the Big Shriek," in *Mirrors of the Year 1927–1928* (New York: Frederick Stokes and Company, 1928), 204; Leinwand, *1927*, 247; **262 Instead, he governed**: W.A. Swanberg, *Citizen Hearst* (New York: Bantam Books, 1963), 436–37; **263 He lived in a spectacular**: Ibid., 464–67; **263 Yet from about 1919 onward**: David Nasaw, *The Chief: The Life of William Randolph Hearst* (Boston: Houghton Mifflin Company, 2000), 254–55, 279–86. See also Marion Davies, *The Times We Had: Life with William Randolph Hearst* (New York: The Bobbs-Merrill Company, 1975); **263 "The public"**: *New York Journal*, November 8, 1896, cited in Swanberg, *Citizen Hearst*, 107; **263 Footnote: Millicent Hearst learned**: See David Niven, *The Moon's a Balloon: Reminiscences* (London: Hamilton, 1971), 276–77; **264 "An ideal morning edition"**: *Collier's*, September 29, 1906, cited in ibid., 232; **264 In the circulation war**: Nasaw, *The Chief*, 108; **264 "Everything is quiet"**: Cited in Swanberg, *Citizen Hearst*, 127; **265 "Hearst's coverage"**: Ibid., 162; **265 By 1909, the most**: Nasaw, *The Chief*, 321; **265 "Think in terms"**: John D. Stevens, *Sensationalism and the New York Press* (New York: Columbia University Press, 1991), 119–20; **265 Footnote: In 1925, the *Mirror* sponsored**: Stevens, ibid., 135; **266 Owned by Bernarr Macfadden**: See Leinwand, *1927*, 252; Stevens, ibid., 137–42; **266 "Sensationalism is nothing"**: Cited in ibid., 140; **266 Nevertheless, it was at the *Graphic***: Lester Cohen, *The New York Graphic: The World's Zaniest Newspaper* (Philadelphia: Chilton Books, 1964), 25, 35; **266 Here, for example, was how**: Cited in Bob Thomas, *Winchell* (Garden City, N.Y.: Doubleday and Company, 1971), 37; **266 Footnote: In 1927, the New York Society**: Stevens, *Sensationalism*, 141; **267 The tabloids tried**: Ibid., 123; **267 The blatant distortion**: "Tabloid Poison," *Saturday Review of Literature* vol. 3 (February 19, 1927), 589–91; **267 "Please Phil be"**: Cited in Nasaw, *The Chief*, 379; **267 Footnote: During the time**: Nasaw, *The Chief*, 381; **268 In one, as the tabloids**: Stevens, *Sensationalism*, 146; **268 Yet Hearst's readers**: Leinwand, *1927*, 251; **268 One fan of the tabloids**: Martin Weyrauch, "The Why of the Tabloids," *Forum* vol. 77 (April, 1927), 496; Leinwand, ibid., 253–54; **268 A sure sign**: Oliver H.P. Garrett, "The Gods Confused," *American Mercury* vol. 12 (November, 1927): 331–2; Leinwand, ibid., 251; **268 Not satisfied and sensing**: Ibid., 147–48; **269 "I have told the truth"**: Allen, *Only Yesterday*, 177–78; **269 Footnote: After extensive research**: Stevens, *Sensationalism*, 152. See also William

Kunstler, *The Hall-Mills Murder Case: The Minister and the Choir Singer*
(New Brunswick, N.J.: Rutgers University Press, 1980); **270 "Peaches'
Shame"**: See Cohen, *The New York Graphic*, 129; **270 There were stories**:
Allen, *Only Yesterday*, 179; **270 Remarkably, the editors**: Ibid., 179;
270 On the first day: Stevens, *Sensationalism*, 153–54; **270 It began on**: See
ibid., 153; Cohen, *The New York Graphic*, 119; **271 Runyon and others**:
Leinwand, *1927*, 248.

CHAPTER SEVEN: SEX, FLAPPERS, AND A SHIMMY

275 "Babbitt had heard": Sinclair Lewis, *Babbitt* (New York: Harcourt,
Brace & World, 1950), 227–28; **275 After discovering "love" letters**:
Jeffrey Weeks, *Sex, Politics and Society* (London: Longman, 1981), 100; **275 In
St. Louis, the city's chief**: Jonathan N. Katz, *Gay/Lesbian Almanac: A New
Documentary* (New York: Harper & Row, 1983), 263–64; **276 Sexual inver-
sion was**: Ibid., 309–10, 358; **276 Even Sigmund Freud**: Paul Robinson,
The Modernization of Sex (New York: Harper & Row, 1976), 5; **276 The
typical middle-class**: Katz, *Gay/Lesbian Almanac*, 140–41; **276 If a
husband**: John D'Emilio and Estelle B. Freedman, *Intimate Matters: A
History of Sexuality in America* (New York: Harper & Row, 1988), 181–82;
276 Footnote: In some parts of the United States: See "U.S. Awaits
Landmark Sodomy Ruling," *Globe and Mail*, June 23, 2003; "U.S. Supreme
Court Lifts Ban On Sodomy," *Globe and Mail*, June 27, 2003; **277 Comstock
was born**: Nicola Beisel, *Imperiled Innocents: Anthony Comstock and Family
Reproduction in Victorian America* (Princeton, N.J.: Princeton University Press,
1997), 37; **277 It was the classic**: Ibid., 41, 65–7; **278 As he explained**:
Cited in Parker, *Purifying America*, 24; **278 He detested the city**: Beisel,
Imperiled Innocents, 44; **278 And boasted that**: Schlesinger, *The Rise of the
City*, 271; **278 In the same period**: Beisel, *Imperiled Innocents*, 45; **279 He
remained vigilant**: Ann Douglas, *Terrible Honesty: Mongrel Manhattan in the
1920s* (New York: Farrar, Straus and Giroux, 1995), 47; **279 But his main
failing**: Schlesinger, *The Rise of the City*, 271; **279 In one case, Comstock**:
Douglas, *Terrible Honesty*, 47; **279 It was a broad cross-section**: Beisel,
Imperiled Innocents, 50–4; **279 Progress, in this case**: Parker, *Purifying
America*, 4; **279 Often working side by side**: Ibid., 7, 21–49, 134–57;
279 "This Department of Purity": Marian W. Wark, "Purity in Literature
and Art," *New Hampshire Annual Review* (1908), 72, cited in ibid., 26;
280 Immorality in art: Parker, ibid., 22–3; **280 Hence reading a**: Cited in
ibid., 52; **280 In 1912, Comstock**: Douglas, *Terrible Honesty*, 47; **280 One
New York City school superintendent**: D'Emilio and Freedman, *Intimate
Matters*, 207; **280 Footnote: The public relations pioneer**: Harry
Reichenbach, *Phantom Fame: Anatomy of Ballyhoo* (New York: Simon &
Schuster, 1931), cited at www.snigglenet/septmorn.php; **281 A eugenics**

advocate: McLaren, *Our Own Master Race*, 70–1; **281 Still, as U.S. writer**: Douglas, *Terrible Honesty*, 133; **281 Footnote: One of Beall's favourite stories**: McLaren, *Our Own Master Race*, 71; **282 It took until**: D'Emilio and Freedman, *Intimate Matters*, 224; **282 Freud was very evident**: Douglas, *Terrible Honesty*, 125; **282 Soon, too, the middle-class**: Nathan Hale, *Freud and the Americans: The Beginnings of Psychoanalysis in the United States, 1876–1917* (New York: Oxford University Press, 1971), 405; **282 More than anyone**: D'Emilio and Freedman, *Intimate Matters*, 225–26; Kline, *Building a Better Race*, 62; **282 Sex was not immoral**: Phyllis Grosskurth, *Havelock Ellis: A Biography* (New York: Alfred A. Knopf, 1980), 225; **283 When he returned**: Ibid., 122; **283 Above all, he viewed**: Robinson, *The Modernization of Sex*, 17–18; **283 Women, suggested Ellis**: Grosskurth, *Havelock Ellis*, 231; **283 Footnote: Ellis could not entirely**: Robinson, *The Modernization of Sex*, 14; **284 His volumes on sex**: Katz, *Gay/Lesbian Almanac*, 513–14; **284 Still, he always considered**: Grosskurth, *Havelock Ellis*, xv–xvi, 216–17; **284 "He seemed a"**: Margaret Sanger, *An Autobiography* (New York: W.W. Norton & Company, 1938), 133–34; **284 They made New York's Greenwich**: Carolyn Johnston, *Sexual Power: Feminism and the Family in America* (Tuscaloosa, Ala.: University of Alabama Press, 1992), 83; **285 "Feminism," declared Henrietta Rodman**: Ibid., 83; **285 Both the men and the women**: D'Emilio and Freedman, *Intimate Matters*, 229; **285 When she separated from**: Johnston, *Sexual Power*, 85; **285 "Reed & I love"**: Cited in Lois Palken Rudnick, *Mabel Dodge Luhan: New Woman, New World* (Albuquerque, N.M.: University of New Mexico Press, 1984), 96–7; **286 "Both Hutch and I"**: Cited in Johnston, *Sexual Power*, 84; **286 "I have an abiding love"**: Cited in D'Emilio and Freedman, *Intimate Matters*, 230; **286 She had several lovers**: Ibid., 80; **286 Was there anything more**: Emma Goldman, *Anarchism and Other Essays* (New York: Mother Earth, 1910), 237; **287 In one of her popular**: Cited in Wexler, *Emma Goldman*, 94; **287 From Goldman's perspective**: Ibid., 142; **287 "I was caught in the torrent"**: Goldman, *Living My Life*, vol. 1, 420; **287 He had shown**: Wexler, *Emma Goldman*, 146; **287 They developed their**: See ibid., 147–48; **288 Her "savage passion"**: Ibid., 153; **288 At first, she dismissed**: Ibid., 155; **288 There was, as Goldman's**: Ibid., 160; **289 "Very early in my"**: Margaret Sanger, *My Fight For Birth Control* (New York: Farrar & Rinehart, 1931), 5; **289 "Her green eyes"**: Ellen Chesler, *Woman of Valor: Margaret Sanger and the Birth Control Movement in America* (New York: Simon & Schuster, 1992), 16; **290 The defining moment**: See Sanger, *An Autobiography*, 89–92; **290 "I went to bed"**: Ibid., 92; **290 She later claimed**: Sanger, *My Fight For Birth Control*, 55–6; **290 In its first issue**: Beisel, *Imperiled Innocents*, 40; **291 By then, she had**: Ibid., 40; **291 Almost immediately**: Sanger, *An Autobiography*, 109–11; **291 Footnote: Many**

married and single women: Leslie J. Reagan, *When Abortion Was a Crime* (Berkeley, Calif.: University of California Press, 1997), 8, 127; See also James C. Mohr, *Abortion in America* (New York: Oxford University Press, 1978); **292 "I was not afraid of"**: Ibid., 119–21; **292 Soon after, Comstock**: Emily Taft Douglas, *Margaret Sanger: Pioneer of the Future* (New York: Holt, Rinehart and Winston, 1970), 80; **292 He told the press**: Ibid., 85; **293 As the trial began**: Douglas, *Margaret Sanger*, 90–3; **292 Footnote: Sanger and Goldman**: Sanger, *An Autobiography*, 72; **293 "Halfway to the corner"**: Sanger, *An Autobiography*, 216; **293 "To each group"**: Ibid., 216–17; **294 She ignored her**: Halliday Sutherland, "The Fallacies of Birth Control," *Forum* vol. 77 (May 1927), 841; Leinwand, *1927*, 186–87; **294 For a brief time**: Kline, *Building a Better Race*, 64–5; **294 A talk she gave**: McLaren, *Our Own Master Race*, 82–3; **294 Sanger's second husband**: Leinwand, *1927*, 187; **295 There were fears**: Charlotte Perkins Gilman, "Progress Through Birth Control," *North American Review* vol. 224 (December 1927), 622–29; ibid., 188; **295 "Whether or not birth control"**: Walter Lippmann, *A Preface to Morals* (New York: The Macmillan Company, 1929), 291; **295 She found, among**: Katharine Bement Davis, *Factors in the Sex Life of Twenty-Two Hundred Women* (New York: Harper & Brothers, 1929), 14; **295 "The need of women's lives"**: Margaret Sanger, *Women and the New Race* (New York: Brentano's, 1920), 117; **295 Or, as her friend**: Mabel Dodge Luhan, *Intimate Memories, Movers and Shakers* vol. 3 (New York: Harcourt Brace Jovanovich, 1936), 69–71; **296 "Anyone who says"**: John R. McMahon "Unspeakable Jazz Must Go," *Ladies Home Journal*, (December, 1921), 116, cited in Johnston, *Sexual Power*, 122; **296 Jazz and the dancing**: Allen, *Only Yesterday*, 76; **296 "Churches that entertain"**: "Letter to Editor," *Toronto Star*, September 1, 1921; **297 A Creole who had**: Geoffrey Perrett, *America in the Twenties: A History* (New York: Simon & Schuster, 1982), 232–33; **297 Jazz, he said**: Ibid., 233; **297 "It is associated with"**: F. Scott Fitzgerald, "Echoes of the Jazz Age," *Scribner's* (November 1931) in Edmund Wilson, ed., *The Crack-Up* (New York: J. Laughlin, 1945), 16; **297 Joseph "King" Oliver**: Arnold Shaw, *The Jazz Age: Popular Music in the 1920s* (New York: Oxford University Press, 1987), 2–3; **297 It was true**: Paul Whiteman, "In Defense of Jazz," *New York Times*, March 13, 1927; Leinwand, *1927*, 266–67; **298 "Mother said I"**: Cited in Joan Hoff Wilson, ed., *The Twenties: The Critical Issues* (Boston: Little, Brown and Company, 1972), 132; **298 "Couples stand very"**: Cited in D'Emilio and Freedman, *Intimate Matters*, 195–96; **298 The title of a 1913**: "Sex O'clock in America," *Current Opinion*, vol. 55 (1913) cited in Evans, *Born for Liberty*, 161. See also Kathy Peiss, "Dance Madness: New York City Dance Halls and Working-Class Sexuality, 1900–1920," in Charles Stephenson, ed., *Life and Labor: Dimensions of American Working-Class History* (Albany, N.Y.: State

University Press, 1986), 150–76; Abrams, *Selling the Old-Time Religion*, 73–4; **298 "Do you think I ought"**: F. Scott Fitzgerald, *Flappers and Philosophers* (Cambridge: Cambridge University Press, 2000), 121; **298 In Winnipeg, Vivian Maw**: Gray, *The Roar of the Twenties*, 183; **299 "What a gulf separates"**: William Ogburn, *Recent Social Change in the United States Since the War and Particularly in 1927* (Chicago: University of Chicago Press, 1929), xii; **299 As depicted in *LIFE* magazine**: Leinwand, *1927*, 172–73; **299 "Observe, then, this nameless"**: Cited in Wilson, *The Twenties*, 133; **299 Or, put slightly differently**: Cited in Shaw, *The Jazz Age*, 8; **300 Zelda's enemy**: Evans, *Born for Liberty*, 175; **300 "I wonder if it ever occurred"**: Ellen Welles Page, "A Flapper's Appeal to Parents," *Outlook*, December 6, 1922: www.geocities.com/flapper_culture/appeal.html; **300 "The American woman"**: Cited in Allen, *Only Yesterday*, 74; **300 Had they passed**: Ibid., 77; **301 On a beach close**: Johnston, *Sexual Power*, 120; **301 "With above-the-knee skirts"**: Cited in Abrams, *Selling the Old-Time Religion*, 104; **301 "Are we as bad"**: *Ohio State Lantern*, January 9, 1922, cited in Paula S. Fass, *The Damned and the Beautiful: American Youth in the 1920s* (New York: Oxford University Press, 1977), 307; **301 Dorothy Parker, the witty**: "The Jazz Age: Flapper Culture and Style," www.geocities.com/flapper_culture/; **302 The young women**: Cited in Leinwand, *1927*, 175; **302 *This Side of Paradise* was**: Perrett, *America in the Twenties*, 270–71; **302 "Sex had not yet"**: Ibid., 156; **302 Asked if premarital sex**: Davis, *Factors in the Sex Life*, 351; **302 Only 7 per cent of**: Ibid., 19; **302 Other research by Gilbert Hamilton**: Gilbert Van Tassel Hamilton, *A Research in Marriage* (New York: Albert & Charles Boni, 1929); Lewis M. Terman, *Psychological Factors in Marital Happiness* (New York: McGraw Hill, 1938); Johnston, *Sexual Power*, 121; **302 Footnote: This was a situation not**: McLaren, *Our Own Master Race*, 75–6; **303 This was the result**: Wilson, *The Twenties*, 131; Perrett, *America in the Twenties*, 156; **303 "I remember a perfectly"**: Cited in Allen, *Only Yesterday*, 95; **303 Yet it was equally true**: Weeks, *Sex, Politics and Society*, 206; **303 Footnote: Traditionalists also bemoaned**: William F. Ogburn, "Divorce: A Menace that Grows," *New York Times Magazine*, December 18, 1927, 1–2, 21; Allen, *Only Yesterday*, 95; Leinwand, *1927*, 190; **304 Not only did van de Velde**: Ibid., 206–07; **304 "A certain feminine initiative"**: Theodoor H. van de Velde, *Ideal Marriage; Its Physiology and Technique* (New York: Random House, 1965), 156; **304 This new open approach**: Allen, *Only Yesterday*, 93; **304 The novel was declared**: Jonathon Green, *The Encyclopedia of Censorship* (New York: Facts on File, 1990), 3–4; **305 By the age of ten**: Jill Watts, *Mae West: An Icon in Black and White* (New York: Oxford University Press, 2001), 14–17; **305 "The fan was big and red"**: Cited in ibid., 28; **305 "All I had to do"**: Cited in ibid., 53–4; **306 "We were shown"**: *New York Times*,

April 27, 1926; **306 *The New Yorker* said**: "At the Theatre," *New Yorker*, May 8, 1926, 26; **306 "Oh, I've got something"**: Cited in Watts, *Mae West*, 77–8; **306 Sumner labelled**: Ibid., 79; **306 The best way to**: *New York Daily Mirror*, April 30, 1926; ibid., 80; **307 After watching a rehearsal**: Cited in ibid., 83; **307 "*The Drag*, I believe"**: Cited in ibid., 85–6; **308 West and her cast**: Ibid., 89; **307 Before West's case**: Ibid., 90; **308 One of his witnesses**: *New York Times*, March 31; April 1, 20, 1927; **308 Another key witness**: Ibid., April 1, 1927; **308 "We have cleaned"**: *New York Herald Tribune*, April 2, 1927; Watts, *Mae West*, 91; **308 Judge Donnellan stated**: *New York Times*, April 20, 1927; **309 *Variety* hailed it**: *Variety*, September 19, 1928; *New York Times*, October 2, 1928; Watts, *Mae West*, 114; **309 "We shall not"**: *New York Times*, October 5, 1928; Watts, ibid. 114; **309 Early on he stated**: *New York Times*, March 21, 1930; **310 The judge, Amedeo Bertini, charged**: Ibid., April 3, 1930; Watts, *Mae West*, 121; **310 Her biographer Jill Watts says**: Watts, ibid., 121; **310 "If any man can"**: Mae West, *The Constant Sinner* (New York: Macaulay, 1931), 15; **310 "The modern girl is like"**: Cited in Mick LaSalle, *Complicated Women: Sex and Power in Pre-Code Hollywood* (New York: St. Martin's Press, 2000), 76.

CHAPTER EIGHT: THE SINS OF HOLLYWOOD

313 "The motion picture": Cited in LaSalle, *Complicated Women*, 64; **313 On February 21, 1901 nearly**: Garth Jowett, *Film: The Democratic Art* (Boston: Little, Brown and Company, 1976), 29; **313 Knowing a profitable venture**: Kyvig, *Daily Life*, 77–8; **314 One operator in**: Ibid., 77–8; **314 The country, declared journalist**: Gerald Mast, ed., *The Movies in Our Midst* (Chicago: University of Chicago Press, 1982), 46–8; **314 Throughout North America**: Cited in Frank Walsh, *Sin and Censorship: The Catholic Church and the Motion Picture Industry* (New Haven, Conn.: Yale University Press, 1996), 4; **314 "Going to the Strand"**: *New York Times*, April 1, 1914; Jowett, *Film: The Democratic Art*, 59; **315 "The popularity of these cheap"**: Mast, *The Movies in Our Midst*, 49; **315 Or, as another writer**: "The Ubiquitous Moving Picture," *American Magazine* (July 1913), 105, cited in Jowett, *Film: The Democratic Art*, 42; **315 As early as 1901**: Steven Carr, *Hollywood and Anti-Semitism: A Cultural History Up to World War ii* (Cambridge: Cambridge University Press, 2001), 46–9; **315 And young and ambitious**: Carl Beauchamp, "The Mogul in Mr. Kennedy," *Vanity Fair* (April 2002), 406–07; **316 The irony was**: Neal Gabler, *An Empire of Their Own: How the Jews Invented Hollywood* (New York: Crown Publishers, 1988), 3–4; **316 They were the "enemies of mankind"**: Carr, *Hollywood and Anti-Semitism*, 71; **316 Footnote 1: As a Boston financial executive**: Ibid., 399; Peter Collier and David Horowitz, *The Kennedys: An American Drama* (New York: Summit Books, 1984), 47; **316 Footnote 2: In 1901, Carl Laemmle**:

Jowett, *Film: The Democratic Art*, 55–6; **317 At a 1923 New York**: Ruth
Vasey, *The World According to Hollywood, 1918–1939* (Madison: University of
Wisconsin Press, 1997), 25; **317 As longer and more meaningful**: Jowett,
Film: The Democratic Art, 62; **317 Hollywood adhered to the**: Ben Hecht, *A
Child of the Century* (New York: Simon & Schuster, 1954), 469; **317 "I want
to point"**: Ibid., 469; **317 (When vaudeville was**: Pizzitola, *Hearst Over
Hollywood*, 7; **318 Mostly, though, they objected**: Mast, *The Movies in Our
Midst*, 69; **318 *Traffic in Souls*, a 1913**: Cited in Jowett, *Film: The Democratic
Art*, 63; **318 In the 1920 movie**: Kyvig, *Daily Life*, 82; **318 The brilliant
comedian**: Kenneth S. Lynn, *Charlie Chaplin and His Times* (New York:
Simon & Schuster, 1997), 130–31; **318 Footnote: Chaplin was the first**:
See ibid., 211–15; Chaplin, *My Autobiography*, 247; Joyce Milton, *Tramp: The
Life of Charlie Chaplin* (New York: HarperCollins, 1996), 100–2, 226–7,
235–37, 242–43, 275–76; **319 There were two controversial**: Lynn, ibid.,
132; **319 From the day**: Ibid., 132–33; **319 In New York City**: Ibid., 133;
319 When questioned about: Mast, *The Movies in Our Midst*, 132–35;
319 What made *The Birth of a Nation*: Robert M. Henderson, *D.W.
Griffith: His Life and Work* (New York: Oxford University Press, 1972), 158;
320 "To some observers movies": Stephen Vaughn, "Morality and
Entertainment: The Origins of the Motion Picture Production Code,"
Journal of American History 77:1 (June 1990), 40; **320 "The spectacle of"**:
Cited in Walsh, *Sin and Censorship*, 6; **320 The motion picture *Orange
Blossoms***: Ibid., 6; **320 "The evil results"**: Cited in Pizzitola, *Hearst Over
Hollywood*, 78; **320 From Hull-House in Chicago**: See Mast, *The Movies in
Our Midst*, 72–7; **321 One notable 1916 study**: Hugo Munsterberg, *The
Photoplay: A Psychological Study* (New York: Dover Publications, 1970), 95;
321 Reverend Wilbur Crafts: Black, *Hollywood Censored*, 10; **321 Sergeant
Charles O'Donnell**: Ibid., 10–11; **322 The courts did not deal**: Walsh, *Sin
and Censorship*, 7; **322 The argument used**: Mast, *The Movies in Our Midst*,
142; **322 A *Chicago Tribune* editorial**: Black, *Hollywood Censored*, 11;
322 There were also insinuations: Vaughn, "Morality and Entertainment,"
40; **322 Only seduction and infidelity**: Malcolm Dean, *Censored! Only in
Canada: The History of Film Censorship – the Scandal Off the Screen* (Toronto:
Virgo Press, 1981), 21; **323 In New York on Christmas Eve**: *New York
Times*, December 25, 1908; Jowett, *Film: The Democratic Art*, 111–12;
323 For Arbuckle, the complex deal: Andy Edmonds, *Frame Up: The
Untold Story of Roscoe "Fatty" Arbuckle* (New York: William Morrow and
Company, 1991), 95–7; **323 Footnote: As film historian Gregory Black
points**: Black, *Hollywood Censored*, 23; **324 Film actress Louise Brooks**:
Cited in Lynn, 112; **324 "The longer I worked"**: Buster Keaton, *My
Wonderful Life of Slapstick* (New York: Da Capo Press, 1982), 95;
324 Footnote: Arbuckle's extravagance with: Edmonds, *Frame Up*, 137;

325 Added Charlie Chaplin: Charles Chaplin, *My Autobiography* (London: The Bodley Head, 1964), 294; **325 Arbuckle, however, did have one**: Edmonds, *Frame Up*, 46–8, 101–02, 149; **325 Many film stars used**: Ibid., 142–44; **325 For the first two**: See ibid., 154–59; **326 As the party continued**: See ibid., 250–53; See also Keaton, *My Wonderful Life of Slapstick*, 156–61; **326 Arbuckle attempted to help**: Edmonds, ibid., 161–70; **326 Footnote: Edmonds's thesis, not much**: Ibid., 252–53; **327 The newspapers quickly**: See Lynn, *Charlie Chaplin*, 113–14; **327 There were also sordid stories**: Perrett, *America in the Twenties*, 226; **327 The gossip columns**: Lynn, *Charlie Chaplin*, 190–92; **328 As one anonymous Hollywood**: Cited in Walsh, *Sin and Censorship*, 26. See also Mast, *Movies in Our Midst*, 176–83; **328 The California District Attorney's**: Edmonds, *Frame Up*, 239; **328 As the *New York Times* editors**: Cited in Lynn, *Charlie Chaplin*, 113; **329 Arbuckle did work**: Edmonds, *Frame Up*, 267; **329 Footnote: In 1925, for example, Arbuckle**: Ibid., 264; **329 In 1921 and 1922, censorship**: Black, *Hollywood Censored*, 32; Jowett, *Film: The Democratic Art*, 118–19; **330 They pledged to**: See "The Thirteen Points, 1921" in Jowett, ibid., 465; **330 Despite their promises**: Walsh, *Sin and Censorship*, 25; **330 The governor had been**: Ibid., 25; **331 For such a successful**: Leonard J. Leff and Jerold L. Simmons, *Dame in the Kimono: Hollywood, Censorship and the Production Code* (Lexington, Ky.: University of Kentucky Press, 2001), 4; **331 "Hays brought the"**: Black, *Hollywood Censored*, 31; **331 Never one to miss**: Louis Pizzitola, *Hearst Over Hollywood* (New York: Columbia University Press, 2002), 202; **331 Footnote: Some time later, when Hays**: See Patricia Elito Tobais, "Who Put the Sin in Cinema?" *Written By* (November 1999), cited at: www.wga.org/; **332 "Evil pictures have been"**: Will Hays, "The Motion Picture Industry," *American Review of Reviews*, January 23, 1923, in Mast, *The Movies in Our Midst*, 206, 210–211; **332 "As a public relations agent"**: Black, *Hollywood Censored*, 31–2; **333 His success, notes film**: Jowett, *Film: The Democratic Art*, 188; **333 De Mille wore only**: Perrett, *America in the Twenties*, 227–8; **333 "Cecil B. De Mille converted"**: Lloyd Morris, *Not So Long Ago* (New York: Random House, 1949), 174; **333 In *Male and Female***: Black, *Hollywood Censored*, 27–8; **333 "I wear twenty-eight"**: Cited in ibid., 29; **333 Many of De Mille's films**: Perrett, *America in the Twenties*, 227; **334 De Mille's daring work**: Black, *Hollywood Censored*, 29–30; **334 Hays later claimed**: Francis G. Couvares, ed., *Movie Censorship and American Culture* (Washington, D.C.: Smithsonian Institution Press, 1996), 104; **334 More significantly, if a studio**: Ibid., 135; **335 The following year, he formalized**: Walsh, *Sin and Censorship*, 73–4; **335 Nevertheless, the cries for tougher**: Couvares, *Movie Censorship*, 136–37; **335 In 1927, he helped create**: Mast, *The Movies in Our Midst*, 213–14; **335 Skeptics, like the**

usually astute: See Leinwand, *1927*, 259; ibid., 282–302; Perrett, *America in the Twenties*, 297; **336 The head of Universal**: Cited in Leff and Simmons, *Dame in the Kimono*, 6; **336 The public had flocked**: LaSalle, *Complicated Women*, 62; **336 They also loved it**: Ibid., 8; **336 It was dangerous**: Jowett, *Film: The Democratic Art*, 235; **336 In New York in 1928**: Black, *Hollywood Censored*, 34; Walsh, *Sin and Censorship*, 48; **336 "The moving picture might"**: Cited in Jowett, *Film: The Democratic Art*, 174; **337 Meanwhile the Churchman**: Cited in Vaughn, "Morality and Entertainment," 46; **337 Hays was also labelled**: Walsh, *Sin and Censorship*, 49; **337 And in March 1929**: Ibid., 55; **337 Footnote: At least one notable commentator**: H.L. Mencken, "Interlude in the Socratic Manner" in *Prejudices: Sixth Series* (New York: Alfred A. Knopf, 1927), in Mast, *The Movies in Our Midst*, 228–33; **338 As he wrote in his 1937 book**: Martin Quigley, *Decency in Motion Pictures* (New York: Macmillan, 1937) excerpted in ibid., 341; **338 On the recommendation of Quigley**: Couvares, *Movie Censorship*, 144; **338 Like Dinneen, Lord was**: Vaughn, "Morality and Entertainment," 49; **338 He was known for**: Lynn, *Charlie Chaplin*, 363; **338 In general, he railed**: See Vaughn, "Morality and Entertainment," 51; Daniel Lord, *Played by Ear: The Autobiography of Daniel A. Lord, S.J.* (Chicago: Loyola University Press, 1956), 269–77, 284–91; **339 Breen was experienced**: See Walsh, *Sin and Censorship*, 55–60; **339 Nevertheless, he would eventually**: Black, *Hollywood Censored*, 39; **339 "Here was a chance"**: Lord, *Played by Ear*, 298; **339 His "Production Code"**: "General Principals of Motion Picture Production Code of 1930" in Mast, *The Movies in Our Midst*, 321–33; **339 His basic premise**: Ibid., 321; **339 "My eyes nearly popped"**: Cited in Will Hays, *Memoirs* (Garden City, N.Y.: Doubleday, 1955), 439; Lynn, *Charlie Chaplin*, 363; **340 At issue was how much**: LaSalle, *Complicated Women*, 64; **340 As he subsequently told Thalberg**: Ibid., 64; Vaughn, "Morality and Entertainment," 56; **340 It was more for practical**: See Vaughn, ibid., 56–60; **340 Footnote: At the same time**: Black, *Hollywood Censored*, 43; See also Charles Higham, *Merchant of Dreams: Louis B. Mayer, M.G.M., and the Secret Hollywood* (New York: Donald I. Fine, Inc., 1993), 49–50, 105–08, 126–27, 177, 182; **341 While many scripts**: Cited in Vaughn, "Morality and Entertainment," 60; **341 The list of motion pictures**: See Walsh, *Sin and Censorship*, 76; Black, *Hollywood Censored*, 64; **342 He held out a set of handcuffs**: Cited in Leff and Simmons, *Dame in the Kimono*, 30–1; **342 It included scenes of seductive dancing**: Black, *Hollywood Censored*, 66; **342 Predictably religious officials**: *New York Times*, December 1, 1932; ibid., 68–9; **342 "This burg is probably"**: Cited in Vaughn, "Morality and Entertainment," 62–3; **342 Footnote: During production, Hays**: Cecil B. De Mille, *The Autobiography of Cecil B. De Mille* (Englewood Cliffs, N.J.: Prentice-Hall, 1959), 324; **343 *Film Weekly* called**

him: Cited in LaSalle, *Complicated Women*, 201; **344 Footnote: Breen did not win every battle**: See Leff and Simmons, *Dame in the Kimono*, 100–01.

CONCLUSION: FEAR AND PROGRESS

347 In the book: Perrett, *America in the Twenties*, 369; **348 "Prosperity, not real"**: William Z. Ripley, *Main Street and Wall Street* (Lawrence, Kans.: Scholars Book Company, 1972), 352; **348 Ripley's book**: Perrett, *America in the Twenties*, 369; **348 By 1929, when he**: Gordon Thomas and Max Morgan-Witts, *The Day the Bubble Burst* (New York: Doubleday & Company, 1979), 6–7; **349 He amassed his pool**: See ibid., 122–23; **349 Within a week**: Ibid., 130–31; **350 They were soon**: See Perrett, *America in the Twenties*, 439–40; **350 Marcus ended up**: Ibid., 440; **351 "Fear was the great leveller"**: T.H. Watkins, *The Great Depression: America in the 1930s* (Boston: Little, Brown and Company, 1993), 13; **351 Footnote: Few individuals epitomized**: Ibid., 381, Ferdinand Pecora, *Wall Street Under Oath: The Story of Our Modern Money Changers* (New York: Simon & Schuster, 1939), 153; **352 "We saw the city"**: Cited in ibid., 56; **352 "The dole smacked"**: Perrett, *America in the Twenties*, 450; **352 "Looking comprehensively through city"**: Cited in Johnson, *A History of the American People*, 623; **352 Footnote: This idea was even**: Ibid., 712; **352 The uncertainty made people**: Louis Filler, ed. *The Anxious Years: America in the Nineteen Thirties* (New York: Capricorn Books, 1964), 175; **353 From 1933 to 1945**: Irving Abella and Harold Troper, *None Is Too Many* (Toronto: Lester & Orpen Dennys, 1982), x; **353 "Pressure on the part"**: Cited in ibid., 8; **353 Echoing sentiments expressed**: Cited in Jonathon Gatehouse, "Pride and Prejudice," *Maclean's*, August 2, 2004, 48; **354 Nearly 120 Black people**: Archives of Tuskegee Institute, www.law.umkc.edu; **354 "What America needs today"**: Cited in "Hate Crimes, Lynching in America," www.crf-usa.org; **354 In nearby Fort Lauderdale**: Watkins, *The Great Depression*, 227; **355 Franklin Roosevelt had**: Ibid., 223–24, 323–24; **355 The demon of the**: Perrett, *America in the Twenties*, 456–7; **355 In the United States**: Watkins, *The Great Depression*, 82; **355 "Thousands of terrified people"**: T.H. Watkins, *The Hungry Years: A Narrative History of the Great Depression in America* (New York: Henry Holt and Company, 1999), 118–120; *New York Times*, March 7, 1930; **356 It was the same in Harlan County**: Watkins, *The Great Depression*, 83; Perrett, *America in the Twenties*, 456–58; **356 They set up twenty-seven camps**: Watkins, ibid., 98–102; **356 Like many others**: Ibid., 102–03; **356 Watching from a distance**: Cited in ibid., 103; **357 As the police waded**: Pierre Berton, *The Great Depression, 1929–1939* (Toronto: McClelland & Stewart, 1990), 21–2; *Globe* (Toronto), August 14, 1929; **357 If there were troubles**: Berton, ibid., 94–5; Michiel Horn, ed., *The Dirty Thirties* (Toronto: Copp Clark

Publishing, 1972), 425–28; **357 "If we could get"**: Cited in Berton, ibid., 96; **357 He was arrested along**: Max Braithwaite, *The Hungry Thirties* (Toronto: Natural Science of Canada, 1977), 38; **358 As the trains proceeded**: See Berton *The Great Depression*, 325–38; **358 "Russians and other European people"**: Cited in ibid., 145; **359 New Yorkers were**: Douglas, *Skyscrapers*, 95; **359 His fellow architects**: Cited in Burns and Sanders, *Illustrated History*, 371; **360 It was not merely**: Ibid., 378; **360 Raskob and Smith employed**: Douglas, *Skyscrapers*, 111; **360 "The whole effect"**: *New York Times*, July 27, 1930; **360 Footnote: As Marc Eliot notes**: Eliot, *Down 42nd Street*, 32; **361 If truth be told**: Allen, *Only Yesterday*, 157; **361 A 1936 survey by** Fortune **magazine**: Ibid., 134; **362 "There is no prohibition law"**: Cited in Allen, *Only Yesterday*, 143; **362 Hence, in 1936**: Berton, *The Great Depression*, 368–70; **362 Footnote: On the other hand**: Ibid., 368; **363 In 1991, a national survey**: Margaret Cannon, *The Invisible Empire: Racism in Canada* (Toronto: Random House, 1995), 269; **363 "We may not be calling"**: Ibid., 271; **364 "Many of us are looking"**: Cited in Watkins, *The Great Depression*, 18.

Bibliography

INTRODUCTION: THE CITY

Artibise, Alan F.J. *Winnipeg: A Social History of Urban Growth 1874–1914*. Montreal: McGill-Queen's University Press, 1975.

Bloom, Harold, ed. *Upton Sinclair's The Jungle*. Philadelphia: Chelsea House Publishers, 2002.

Colburn, David R., and George E. Pozzetta, eds. *Reform and Reformers in the Progressive Era*. Westport, Conn.: Greenwood Press, 1983.

Copp, Terry. *The Anatomy of Poverty*. Toronto: McClelland & Stewart, 1974.

Cordasco, Francesco, ed. *Jacob Riis Revisited*. Garden City, N.Y.: Anchor Books, 1968.

Elshtain, Jean Bethke. *Jane Addams and the Dream of American Democracy*. New York: Basic Books, 2002.

Filler, Louis. *The Muckrakers*. University Park, Pa.: Pennsylvania State University Press, 1976.

Kaplan, Justin. *Lincoln Steffens: A Biography*. New York: Simon & Schuster, 1974.

Lubove, Roy. *The Progressives and the Slums*. Pittsburgh: University of Pittsburgh Press, 1962.

Madison, Charles. *Critics and Crusaders*. New York: Henry Holt and Company, 1947.

Nordau, Max. *Degeneration*. New York: D. Appleton and Company, 1895.

Regier, C.C. *The Era of the Muckrakers*. Gloucester, Mass.: Peter Smith, 1957.

Richardson, E. Allen. *Strangers in This Land*. New York: The Pilgrim Press, 1988.

Riis, Jacob. *How the Other Half Lives*. New York: Charles Scribner's Sons, 1912. (Originally published 1890.)

Rischin, Moses. *The Promised City: New York's Jews, 1870–1914*. Cambridge, Mass.: Harvard University Press, 1962.

Schlesinger, Arthur M. *The Rise of the City 1878–1898*. New York: The Macmillan Company, 1933.

Sinclair, Upton. *The Jungle*. Memphis, Tenn.: Peachtree Publishers, 1988. (Originally published 1906.)

Steffens, Lincoln. *The Shame of the Cities*. New York: Hill and Wang, 1957. (Originally published 1904.)

———. *The Autobiography of Lincoln Steffens*. New York: Harcourt Brace & Company, 1931.

Stelter, Gilbert A., and Alan F.J. Artibise, eds. *The Canadian City: Essays in Urban History*. Toronto: McClelland & Stewart, 1977.

Strauss, Anselm S., ed. *The American City: A Sourcebook of Urban Imagery*. Chicago: Aldine Publishing Company, 1968.

Weinberg, Arthur, and Lila Weinberg, eds. *The Muckrakers*. New York: Simon & Schuster, 1961.

Wiebe, Robert H. *The Search for Order 1877–1920*. New York: Hill and Wang, 1967.

Woodsworth, J.S. *My Neighbour*. Toronto: University of Toronto Press, 1972. (Originally published 1911.)

CHAPTER ONE: STRANGERS AND REFORMERS

Addams, Jane. *Twenty Years at Hull-House*. New York: The Macmillan Company, 1926.

———. *The Second Twenty Years at Hull-House*. New York: The Macmillan Company, 1930.

Allen, Richard. *The Social Passion: Religion and Social Reform in Canada 1914–28*. Toronto: University of Toronto Press, 1971.

Artibise, Alan F.J. *Winnipeg: A Social History of Urban Growth 1874–1914*. Montreal: McGill-Queen's University Press, 1975.

Avery, Donald. *"Dangerous Foreigners": European Immigrant Workers and Labour Radicalism in Canada, 1896–1932*. Toronto: McClelland & Stewart, 1979.

Berton, Pierre. *The Promised Land: Settling the West 1896–1914*. Toronto: McClelland & Stewart, 1984.

Briggs, John W. *An Italian Passage: Immigrants to Three American Cities, 1890–1930*. New Haven, Conn.: Yale University Press, 1978.

Coan, Peter Morton. *Ellis Island Interviews: In Their Own Words*. New York: Facts On File, 1997.

Cose, Ellis. *A Nation of Strangers*. New York: William Morrow and Company, 1992.

Cordasco, Francesco, ed. *Jacob Riis Revisited*. Garden City, N.Y.: Anchor Books, 1968.

Davis, Allen F. *American Heroine: The Life and Legend of Jane Addams*. New York: Oxford University Press, 1973.

Deegan, Mary Jo. *Jane Addams and the Men of the Chicago School 1892–1928*. New Brunswick, N.J.: Transaction Books, 1990.

Elshtain, Jean Bethke. *Jane Addams and the Dream of American Democracy*. New York: Basic Books, 2002.

Farrell, John C. *Beloved Lady*. Baltimore: Johns Hopkins University Press, 1967.

Johnson, Emily Cooper, ed. *Jane Addams: A Centennial Reader*. New York: The Macmillan Company, 1960.

Handy, Robert T., ed. *The Social Gospel in America 1879–1920*. New York: Oxford University Press, 1966.

Harney, Robert F., and Harold Troper. *Immigrants: A Portrait of the Urban Experience, 1890–1930*. Toronto: Van Nostrand Reinhold, 1975.

Higham, John. *Strangers in the Land: Patterns of American Nativism 1860–1925*. New York: Antheneum, 1978.

Hopkins, Charles Howard. *The Rise of the Social Gospel in American Protestantism 1865–1915*. New Haven, Conn.: Yale University Press, 1940.

Howe, Irving. *World of Our Fathers*. New York: Harcourt Brace Jovanovich, 1976.

Karp, Abraham J. *Haven and Home: A History of Jews in America*. New York: Schocken Books, 1985.

Kittredge, Mary. *Jane Addams*. New York: Chelsea House Publishers, 1988.

McLaren, Angus. *Our Own Master Race: Eugenics in Canada 1885–1945*. Toronto: McClelland & Stewart, 1990.

McNaught, Kenneth. *A Prophet in Politics: A Biography of J.S. Woodsworth*. Toronto: University of Toronto Press, 1959.

Minus, Paul. *Walter Rauschenbusch: American Reformer*. New York: Macmillan, 1988.

Mondello, Salvatore. *The Italian Immigrant in Urban America, 1880–1920*. New York: Arno Press, 1980.

Moquin, Wayne, and Charles Van Doren, eds. *A Documentary History of the Italian Americans*. New York: Praeger Publishers, 1974.

Nugent, Walter. *Crossings: The Great Transatlantic Migrations, 1870–1914*. Bloomington, Ind.: Indiana University Press, 1992.

Palmer, Howard, ed. *Immigration and the Rise of Multiculturalism*. Toronto: Copp Clark Publishing, 1975.

Parker, Alison M. *Purifying America: Women, Cultural Reform, and Pro-Censorship Activism, 1873–1933*. Chicago: University of Illinois Press, 1997.

Richardson, E. Allen. *Strangers in This Land*. New York: The Pilgrim Press, 1988.

Rischin, Moses. *The Promised City: New York's Jews, 1870–1914*. Cambridge, Mass.: Harvard University Press, 1962.

Rose, Peter I., ed. *Nation of Nations: The Ethnic Experience and the Racial Crisis*. New York: Random House, 1972.

Sanders, Ronald. *Shores of Refuge: A Hundred Years of Jewish Emigration*. New York: Henry Holt and Company, 1988.

Sturino, Franc. *Forging the Chain: A Case Study of Italian Migration to North America, 1880–1930*. Toronto: Multicultural History Society of Ontario, 1990.

Tsai, Shih-Shan Henry. *The Chinese Experience in America*. Bloomington, Ind.: Indiana University Press, 1986.

Valverde, Mariana. *The Age of Light, Soap, and Water: Moral Reform in English Canada, 1885–1925*. Toronto: McClelland & Stewart, 1991.

Ward, W. Peter. *White Canada Forever*. Montreal: McGill-Queen's University Press, 1978.

Woodsworth, J.S. *Strangers Within Our Gates*. Toronto: University of Toronto Press, 1972. (Originally published 1909.)

———. *My Neighbour*. Toronto: University of Toronto Press, 1972. (Originally published 1911.)

Zucchi, John E. *Italians in Toronto: Development of a National Identity, 1875–1935*. Montreal: McGill-Queen's University Press, 1988.

CHAPTER TWO: SUFFRAGETTES

Bacchi, Carol Lee. *Liberation Deferred? The Ideas of the English-Canadian Suffragists, 1877–1918*. Toronto: University of Toronto Press, 1983.

Baker, Jean H., ed. *Votes for Women: The Struggle for Suffrage Revisited*. New York: Oxford University Press, 2002.

Bax, Ernest Belfort. *The Legal Subjection of Men*. London: New Age Press, 1908.

Behling, Laura L. *The Masculine Woman in America 1890–1935*. Chicago: University of Illinois Press, 2001.

Buhle, Mari Jo, and Paul Buhle, eds. *The Concise History of Woman Suffrage: Selections from the Classic Work of Stanton, Anthony, Gage, and Harper*. Chicago: University of Illinois Press, 1978.

Cleverdon, Catherine L. *The Woman Suffrage Movement in Canada*. Toronto: University of Toronto Press, 1974. (Originally published 1940.)

Colmore, Gertrude. *The Life of Emily Davison*. London: The Women's Press, 1913.

Cook, Ramsay, and Wendy Mitchinson, eds. *The Proper Sphere: Woman's Place in Canadian Society*. Toronto: Oxford University Press, 1976.

DuBois, Ellen Carol. *Harriot Stanton Blatch and the Winning of Woman Suffrage*. New Haven, Conn.: Yale University Press, 1997.

Eustance, Claire, Joan Ryan, and Laura Ugolini, eds. *A Suffrage Reader*. London: Leicester University Press, 2000.

Evans, Sara M. *Born for Liberty: A History of Women in America*. New York: The Free Press, 1989.

Finnegan, Margaret. *Selling Suffrage*. New York: Columbia University Press, 1999.

Flexner, Eleanor, and Ellen Fitzpatrick. *Century of Struggle: The Woman's Rights Movement in the United States*. Cambridge, Mass.: Harvard University Press, 1975.

Gluck, Sherna, ed. *From Parlor to Prison: Five American Suffragists Talk about their Lives*. New York: Vintage Books, 1976.

Graham, Sara Hunter. *Woman Suffrage and the New Democracy*. New Haven, Conn.: Yale University Press, 1996.

Hallett, Mary, and Marilyn Davis. *Firing the Heather: The Life and Times of Nellie McClung*. Saskatoon: Fifth House, 1993.

Harrison, Brian. *Separate Spheres: The Opposition to Women's Suffrage in Britain*. New York: Holmes & Meier Publishers, 1978.

Holton, Sandra Stanley. *Suffrage Days*. London: Routledge and Kegan Paul, 1996.

Johnston, Carolyn. *Sexual Power: Feminism and Family in America*. Tuscaloosa, Ala.: University of Alabama Press, 1992.

Jorgensen-Earp, Cheryl R. *"The Transfiguring Sword": The Just War of the Women's Social and Political Union*. Tuscaloosa, Ala.: University of Alabama Press, 1997.

——, ed. *Speeches and Trials of the Militant Suffragettes*. London: Associated University Presses, 1999.

Kealey, Linda, ed. *A Not Unreasonable Claim: Women and Reform in Canada, 1880s–1920s*. Toronto: The Women's Press, 1979.

Kraditor, Aileen S. *The Ideas of the Woman Suffrage Movement 1890–1920*. New York: W.W. Norton & Company, 1981.

Liddington, Jill, and Jill Norris. *One Hand Tied Behind Us: The Rise of the Women's Suffrage Movement*. London: Virago, 1978.

Lumsden, Linda J. *Rampant Women*. Knoxville, Tenn.: University of Tennessee Press, 1997.

Mackenzie, Midge. *Shoulder to Shoulder: A Documentary*. New York: Alfred A. Knopf, 1975.

Marcus, Jane, ed. *Suffrage and the Pankhursts*. London: Routledge and Kegan Paul, 1987.

Marshall, Susan E. *Gender and Class in the Campaign against Woman Suffrage*. Madison, Wisc.: University of Wisconsin Press, 1997.

McClung, Nellie. *Clearing in the West*. Toronto: Thomas Allen & Son, 1965. (Originally published 1935.)

——. *The Stream Runs Fast*. Toronto: Thomas Allen & Son, 1945.

——. *In Times Like These*. Toronto: University of Toronto Press, 1972. (Originally published 1915.)

Mitchell, David. *The Fighting Pankhursts*. London: Jonathan Cape, 1967.

Morgan, David. *Suffragists and Liberals*. Totowa, N.J.: Rowman and Littlefield, 1975.

Pankhurst, Dame Christabel. *Unshackled: The Story of How We Won the Vote*. London: Hutchinson, 1959.

Pankhurst, Emmeline. *My Own Story*. New York: Hearst's International Library, 1971.

Pankhurst, E. Sylvia. *The Suffragette*. New York: Source Book Press, 1970. (Originally published 1911.)

Purvis, June, and Sandra Stanley Holton, eds. *Votes for Women*. London: Routledge, 2000.

Pugh, Martin. *The March of the Women*. Oxford: Oxford University Press, 2000.

———. *Women and the Women's Movement in Britain, 1914–1999*. New York: St. Martin's Press, 2000.

———. *The Pankhursts*. London: Penguin Books Ltd., 2001.

Raeburn, Antonia. *The Militant Suffragettes*. London: Michael Joseph, 1973.

Rosen, Andrew. *Rise Up, Women! The Militant Campaign of the Women's Social and Political Union 1903–1914*. London: Routledge and Kegan Paul, 1974.

Savage, Candace. *Our Nell: A Scrapbook Biography of Nellie L. McClung*. Saskatoon: Western Producer Prairie Books, 1979.

Stevens, Doris. *Jailed for Freedom: The Story of the Militant American Suffragist Movement*. New York: Schocken Books, 1976. (Originally published 1920.)

Strong-Boag, Veronica, and Anita Clair Fellman, eds. *Rethinking Canada: The Promise of Women's History*. First Edition. Toronto: Copp Clark Pitman, 1986.

Strong-Boag, Veronica, Mona Gleason, and Adele Perry, eds. *Rethinking Canada: The Promise of Women's History*. Fourth Edition. Toronto: Oxford University Press, 2002.

Tickner, Lisa. *The Spectacle of Women: Imagery of the Suffrage Campaign 1907–14*. Chicago: University of Chicago Press, 1988.

The Trial of the Suffragette Leaders. London: The Women's Press, 1908.

Van Voris, Jacqueline. *Carrie Chapman Catt: A Public Life*. New York: The Feminist Press at the City University of New York, 1987.

van Wingerden, Sophia A. *The Women's Suffrage Movement in Britain, 1866–1928*. London: Macmillan Press, 1999.

CHAPTER THREE: SURVIVAL OF THE FITTEST

Bowler, Peter J. *Charles Darwin: The Man and His Influence*. Cambridge: Cambridge University Press, 1990.

Brumbaugh, Robert S., ed. *Six Trials*. New York: Thomas Y. Crowell, 1969.

Caudill, Edward. *Darwinian Myths: The Legends and Misuses of a Theory*. Knoxville, Tenn.: University of Tennessee, 1997.

Childs, Donald J. *Modernism and Eugenics*. Cambridge: Cambridge University Press, 2001.

Christian, Tim. *The Mentally Ill and Human Rights in Alberta*. Edmonton: Alberta Law Foundation, 1974.

De Camp, L. Sprague. *The Great Monkey Trial*. Garden City, N.Y.: Doubleday & Company, 1968.

Dowbiggin, Ian Robert. *Keeping America Sane*. Ithaca: Cornell University Press, 1997.

Gatewood, Willard B., ed. *Controversy in the Twenties: Fundamentalism, Modernism, and Evolution*. Nashville, Tenn.: Vanderbilt University Press, 1969.

Grebstein, Sheldon N., ed. *Monkey Trial: The State of Tennessee vs. John Thomas Scopes*. Boston: Houghton Mifflin Company, 1960.

Haller, M.H. *Eugenics: Hereditarian Attitudes in American Thought*. New Brunswick, N.J.: Rutgers University Press, 1963.

Holmes, Samuel J. *The Trend of Race*. New York: Harcourt Brace & Company, 1921.

Kevles, Daniel J. *In the Name of Eugenics: Genetics and the Uses of Human Heredity*. New York: Alfred A. Knopf, 1985.

Kline, Wendy. *Building a Better Race: Gender, Sexuality, and Eugenics from the Turn of the Century to the Baby Boom*. Berkeley, Calif.: University of California Press, 2001.

Kühl, Stefan. *The Nazi Connection: Eugenics, American Racism, and German National Socialism*. New York: Oxford University Press, 1994.

Larson, Edward J. *Summer For the Gods: The Scopes Trial and America's Continuing Debate Over Science and Religion*. Cambridge, Mass.: Harvard University Press, 1997.

McDougall, William. *Is America Safe for Democracy?* New York: Charles Scribner's Sons, 1921.

Marsden, George M. *Fundamentalism and American Culture*. New York: Oxford University Press, 1980.

McConnachie, Kathleen Janet. "Methodology in the Study of Women in History: A Case Study of Helen MacMurchy." *Ontario History* 75 (1983): 61–70.

———. "Science and Ideology: The Mental Hygiene and Eugenics Movements in the Inter-War Years, 1919–1939." Ph.D. dissertation, University of Toronto, 1987.

McLaren, Angus. *Our Own Master Race: Eugenics in Canada 1885–1945*. Toronto: McClelland & Stewart, 1990.

Montagu, Ashley. *Man's Most Dangerous Myth: The Fallacy of Race*. Walnut Creek, Calif.: Altamira Press, 1997.

Pera, Juan F., ed. *Immigrants Out: The New Nativism and the Anti-Immigrant Impulse in the United States*. New York: New York University Press, 1997.

Regal, Brian. *Henry Fairfield Osborn: Race, and the Search for the Origins of Man*. Aldershot, England: Ashgate Publishing House, 2002.

Russett, Cynthia Eagle. *Darwin in America: The Intellectual Response 1865–1912*. San Francisco: W.H. Freeman and Company, 1976.

Selden, Steven. *Inheriting Shame: The Story of Eugenics and Racism in America*. New York: Teachers College, Columbia University, 1999.

Tucker, William H. *The Science and Politics of Racial Research*. Chicago: University of Illinois Press, 1994.

CHAPTER FOUR: THE RED SCARE

Avery, Donald. *"Dangerous Foreigners": European Immigrant Workers and Labour Radicalism in Canada, 1896–1932*. Toronto: McClelland & Stewart, 1979.

Avrich, Paul. *Anarchist Portraits*. Princeton, N.J.: Princeton University Press, 1988.

———. *Anarchist Voices: An Oral History of Anarchism in America*. Princeton, N.J.: Princeton University Press, 1995.

———. *The Haymarket Tragedy*. Princeton, N.J.: Princeton University Press, 1984.

Bercuson, David Jay. *Confrontation at Winnipeg*. Montreal: McGill-Queen's University Press, 1974.

Bumsted, J.M. *The Winnipeg General Strike of 1919: An Illustrated History*. Winnipeg: Watson & Dwyer, 1994.

Coben, Stanley. *A. Mitchell Palmer: Politician*. New York: Da Capo Press, 1972.

De Toledano, Ralph. *J. Edgar Hoover: The Man In His Time*. New Rochelle, N.Y.: Arlington House, 1973.

Demaris, Ovid. *The Director: An Oral Biography of J. Edgar Hoover*. New York: Harper & Row, 1975.

Figes, Orlando. *A People's Tragedy: The Russian Revolution 1891–1924*. London: Jonathan Cape, 1996.

Frankfurter, Felix. *The Case of Sacco and Vanzetti*. Stanford: Academic Reprints, 1954.

Friedheim, Robert L. *The Seattle General Strike*. Seattle: University of Washington Press, 1964.

Gentry, Curt. *J. Edgar Hoover: The Man and the Secrets*. New York: W.W. Norton & Company, 1991.

Goldman, Emma. *Living My Life*. 2 vols. New York: Dover Publications, 1970. (Originally published 1931.)

Goldstein, Robert J. *Political Repression in Modern America: From 1870 to the Present*. Cambridge, Mass.: Schenkman Publishing Company, 1978.

Gutkin, Harry, and Mildred Gutkin. *Profiles in Dissent: The Shaping of Radical Thought in the Canadian West*. Edmonton: NeWest Publishers, 1997.

Higham, John. *Strangers in the Land: Patterns of American Nativism 1860–1925*. New York: Antheneum, 1978.

Jaffe, Julian F. *Crusade Against Radicalism: New York During the Red Scare, 1914–1924*. Port Washington, N.Y.: Kennikat Press, 1972.

Klingaman, William K. *1919: The Year Our World Began*. New York: St. Martin's Press, 1987.

Levin, Murray B. *Political Hysteria in America*. New York: Basic Books, 1971.

MacMillan, Margaret. *Paris 1919: Six Months that Changed the World*. New York: Random House, 2002.

McCormack, A. Ross. *Reformers, Rebels and Revolutionaries: The Western Canadian Radical Movement 1899–1919*. Toronto: University of Toronto Press, 1977.

McCormick, Charles H. *Seeing Reds: Federal Surveillance of Radicals in the Pittsburgh Mill District, 1917–1921*. Pittsburgh: University of Pittsburgh Press, 1997.

Murray, Robert K. *Red Scare: A Study in National Hysteria, 1919–1920*. Minneapolis: University of Minnesota, 1955.

Penner, Norman, ed. *Winnipeg 1919: The Strikers' Own History of the Winnipeg General Strike*. Toronto: James Lewis & Samuel, 1973.

Powers, Richard Gid. *Not Without Honor: The History of American Anticommunism*. New York: The Free Press, 1995.

Shulman, Alix Kates, ed. *Red Emma Speaks*. New York: Random House, 1972.

Theoharis, Athan, ed. *From the Secret Files of J. Edgar Hoover*. Chicago: Ivan R. Dee, 1991.

Usiskin, Roz. "'The Alien and the Bolshevik in our Midst': The 1919 Winnipeg General Strike," *Jewish Life and Times*, vol. 5. Winnipeg: Jewish Historical Society of Western Canada, 1988, 28–49.

Wexler, Alice. *Emma Goldman: An Intimate Life*. New York: Pantheon Books, 1984.

———. *Emma Goldman in Exile*. Boston: Beacon Press, 1989.

CHAPTER FIVE: BOOZE

Bergreen, Laurence. *Capone: The Man and the Era*. New York: Simon & Schuster, 1994.

Blocker, Jack S. *Retreat From Reform: The Prohibition Movement in the United States 1890–1913*. Westport, Conn.: Greenwood Press, 1976.

Campbell, Robert A. *Demon Rum or Easy Money*. Ottawa: Carleton University Press, 1991.

Clark, Norman H. *Deliver Us From Evil: An Interpretation of American Prohibition*. New York: W.W. Norton & Company, 1976.

Coffey, Thomas. *The Long Thirst: Prohibition in America 1920–1933*. New York: W.W. Norton & Company, 1975.

Cohen, Rich. *Tough Jews*. New York: Simon & Schuster, 1998.

Eisenberg, Dennis, Uri Dan, and Eli Landau. *Meyer Lansky: Mogul of the Mob*. London: Paddington Press, 1979.

Everest, Allan S. *Rum Across the Border*. Syracuse, N.Y.: Syracuse University Press, 1978.

Grant, B.J. *When Rum Was King: The Story of the Prohibition Era in New Brunswick*. Fredericton, N.B.: Fiddlehead Poetry Books, 1984.

Gray, James. *Booze: The Impact of Whisky on the Prairie West*. Toronto: Signet Books, 1972.

Hoffman, Dennis E. *Scarface Al Capone and the Crime Crusaders*. Carbondale, Ill.: Southern Illinois University Press, 1993.

———. *The Roar of the Twenties*. Toronto: Macmillan of Canada, 1975.

Hunt, C.W. *Booze, Boats and Billions*. Toronto: McClelland & Stewart, 1988.

Kobler, John. *Ardent Spirits: The Rise and Fall of Prohibition*. New York: G.P. Putnam's Sons, 1973.

Landesco, John. *Organized Crime in Chicago*. Chicago: University of Chicago Press, 1968. (Originally published 1929.)

Leinwand, Gerald. *1927: High Tide of the Twenties*. New York: Four Walls Eight Windows, 2001.

Marrus, Michael. *Mr. Sam: The Life and Times of Samuel Bronfman*. Toronto: Viking, 1991.

Merz, Charles. *The Dry Decade*. Seattle: University of Washington Press, 1969. (Originally published 1931.)

Mitchinson, Wendy. "The WCTU: 'For God, Home and Native Land': A Study in Nineteenth-Century Feminism." In Linda Kealey, ed. *A Not Unreasonable Claim: Women and Reform in Canada, 1880s–1920s*. Toronto: The Women's Press, 1979, 151–229.

Newman, Peter C. *Bronfman Dynasty*. Toronto: McClelland & Stewart, 1978.

Parker, Marion, and Robert Tyrrell. *Rumrunner: The Life and Times of Johnny Schnarr*. Victoria, B.C.: Orca Book Publishers, 1988.

Rumbarger, John J. *Profits, Power and Prohibition*. Albany, N.Y.: State University of New York Press, 1989.

Schoenberg, Robert J. *Mr. Capone*. New York: William Morrow and Company, 1992.

Sneath, Allen Winn. *Brewed in Canada*. Toronto: The Dundurn Group, 2001.

Stuart, Mark A. *Gangster #2: Longy Zwillman, the Man Who Invented Organized Crime*. Seacus, N.J.: Lyle Stuart, Inc., 1985.

Thornton, Mark. "Alcoholic Prohibition Was a Failure." *Policy Analysis*
(no. 157) Cato Institute, July 17, 1991, 1–14.

Warsh Krasnick, Cheryl, ed. *Drink in Canada: Historical Essays*. Montreal:
McGill-Queen's University Press, 1993.

Yablonsky, Lewis. *Gangsters: Fifty Years of Madness, Drugs, and Death on the
Streets of America*. New York: New York University Press, 1997.

CHAPTER SIX: INNOVATORS AND INNOVATIONS

Allen, Frederick Lewis. *Only Yesterday: An Informal History of the 1920s*. New
York: Harper & Row Publishers, 1964. (Originally published 1931.)

Bahr, Robert. *The Least of All Saints: The Story of Aimee Semple McPherson*.
Englewood Cliffs, N.J.: Prentice-Hall, 1979.

Baldwin, Neil. *Henry Ford and the Jews: The Mass Production of Hate*. New
York: Public Affairs, 2001.

Brinkley, Douglas. *Wheels for the World: Henry Ford, His Company, and a
Century of Progress*. New York: Viking, 2003.

Burlingame, Roger. *Henry Ford*. New York: Alfred A. Knopf, 1954.

Carter, Paul A. *The Twenties in America*. New York: Thomas Y. Crowell
Company, 1968.

Cohen, Lester. *The New York Graphic: The World's Zaniest Newspaper*.
Philadelphia: Chilton Books, 1964.

Davies, Marion. *The Times We Had: Life with William Randolph Hearst*. New
York: The Bobbs-Merrill Company, 1975.

Elliott, David R., and Miller, Iris. *Bible Bill: A Biography of William Aberhart*.
Edmonton: Reidmore Books, 1987.

Epstein, Daniel Mark. *Sister Aimee: The Life of Aimee Semple McPherson*. New
York: Harcourt Brace Jovanovich, 1993.

Gelderman, Carol. *Henry Ford: The Wayward Capitalist*. New York: The Dial
Press, 1981.

Halberstam, David. *The Powers That Be*. New York: Alfred A. Knopf, 1979.

Hangen, Tona J. *Redeeming the Dial*. Chapel Hill, N.C.: University of North
Carolina Press, 2002.

Irving, John. *The Social Credit Movement in Alberta*. Toronto: University of
Toronto Press, 1959.

Joshi, S.T., ed. *Documents of American Prejudice: An Anthology of Writings on
Race from Thomas Jefferson to David Duke*. New York: Basic Books, 1999.

Kyvig, David E. *Daily Life in the United States, 1920–1939: Decades of Promise
and Pain*. Westport, Conn.: Greenwood Press, 2002.

Levine, Allan. *Scrum Wars: The Prime Ministers and the Media*. Toronto:
Dundurn Press, 1993.

Ling, Peter. "Sex and the Automobile in the Jazz Age." *History Today*
(November 1989), 18–24.

McPherson, Aimee Semple. *The Story of My Life*. Waco, Tex.: Word Books, 1973.

Nasaw, David. *The Chief: The Life of William Randolph Hearst*. Boston: Houghton Mifflin Company, 2000.

Nash, Knowlton. *The Microphone Wars: A History of Triumph and Betrayal at the CBC*. Toronto: McClelland & Stewart, 1994.

Robertson, Heather. *Driving Force: The McLaughlin Family and the Age of the Car*. Toronto: McClelland & Stewart, 1995.

Schultze, Quentin J., ed. *American Evangelicals and the Mass Media*. Grand Rapids, Mich.: Zondervan Corporation, 1973.

Smulyan, Susan. *Selling Radio: The Commercialization of American Broadcasting 1920–1934*. Washington, D.C.: Smithsonian Institute Press, 1994.

Stevens, John D. *Sensationalism and the New York Press*. New York: Columbia University Press, 1991.

Swanberg, W.A. *Citizen Hearst*. New York: Bantam Books, 1963.

Tull, Charles J. *Father Coughlin and the New Deal*. Syracuse, N.Y.: Syracuse University Press, 1965.

Warren, Donald. *Radio Priest: Charles Coughlin, the Father of Hate Radio*. New York: The Free Press, 1996.

Wik, Reynold M. *Henry Ford and Grass-roots America*. Ann Arbor, Mich.: The University of Michigan Press, 1973.

CHAPTER SEVEN: SEX, FLAPPERS, AND A SHIMMY

Beisel, Nicola. *Imperiled Innocents: Anthony Comstock and Family Reproduction in Victorian America*. Princeton, N.J.: Princeton University Press, 1997.

Davis, Katharine Bement. *Factors in the Sex Life of Twenty-Two Hundred Women*. New York: Harper & Brothers, 1929.

D'Emilio, John, and Estelle B. Freedman. *Intimate Matters: A History of Sexuality in America*. New York: Harper & Row, 1988.

Douglas, Ann. *Terrible Honesty: Mongrel Manhattan in the 1920s*. New York: Farrar, Straus and Giroux, 1995.

Douglas, Emily Taft. *Margaret Sanger: Pioneer of the Future*. New York: Holt, Rinehart and Winston, 1970.

Ellis, Havelock. *The Dance of Life*. Boston: Houghton Mifflin Company, 1929.

Evans, Sara M. *Born for Liberty: A History of Women in America*. New York: The Free Press, 1989.

Fass, Paula S. *The Damned and the Beautiful: American Youth in the 1920s*. New York: Oxford University Press, 1977.

Fitzgerald, F. Scott. *Flappers and Philosophers*. Cambridge: Cambridge University Press, 2000.

Gray, James H. *The Roar of the Twenties*. Toronto: Macmillan of Canada, 1975.

Grosskurth, Phyllis. *Havelock Ellis: A Biography*. New York: Alfred A. Knopf, 1980.

Haaland, Bonnie. *Emma Goldman: Sexuality and the Impurity of the State*. Montreal: Black Rose Books, 1993.

Higham, Charles. *Ziegfeld*. Chicago: Henry Regnery Company, 1972.

Johnston, Carolyn. *Sexual Power: Feminism and the Family in America*. Tuscaloosa, Ala.: University of Alabama Press, 1992.

Katz, Jonathan N. *Gay/Lesbian Almanac: A New Documentary*. New York: Harper & Row, 1983.

Kinney, Arthur F. *Dorothy Parker*. Boston: Twayne Publishers, 1978.

Kline, Wendy. *Building a Better Race: Gender, Sexuality, and Eugenics from the Turn of the Century to the Baby Boom*. Berkeley, Calif.: University of California Press, 2001.

Lévesque, Andrée. *Making and Breaking the Rules: Women in Quebec, 1919–1939*. Toronto: McClelland & Stewart, 1994.

Lippmann, Walter. *A Preface to Morals*. New York: The Macmillan Company, 1929.

Little, Margaret Jane Hillyard. *"No Car, No Radio, No Liquor Permit": The Moral Regulation of Single Mothers in Ontario, 1920–1997*. Toronto: Oxford University Press, 1998.

May, Henry F. *The End of American Innocence*. London: Jonathan Cape, 1959.

Melman, Billie. *Women and the Popular Imagination in the Twenties*. New York: St. Martin's Press, 1988.

Mencken, H.L. *The American Scene: A Reader*. Edited by Huntington Cairns. New York: Alfred A. Knopf, 1965.

Mizejewski, Linda. *Ziegfeld Girl: Image and Icon in Culture and Cinema*. Durham, N.C.: Duke University Press, 1999.

Perrett, Geoffrey. *America in the Twenties: A History*. New York: Simon & Schuster, 1982.

Pugh, Martin. *Women and the Women's Movement in Britain, 1914–1999*. New York: St. Martin's Press, 2000.

Robinson, Paul. *The Modernization of Sex*. New York: Harper & Row, 1976.

Sanger, Margaret. *My Fight For Birth Control*. New York: Farrar & Rinehart, 1931.

———. *An Autobiography*. New York: W.W. Norton & Company, 1938.

Shaw, Arnold. *The Jazz Age: Popular Music in the 1920s*. New York: Oxford University Press, 1987.

Stearns, Marshall W. *The Story of Jazz*. New York: Oxford University Press, 1958.

Valverde, Mariana. *The Age of Light, Soap, and Water: Moral Reform in English Canada, 1885–1925*. Toronto: McClelland & Stewart, 1991.

Weeks, Jeffrey. *Sex, Politics and Society*. London: Longman, 1981.

Wexler, Alice. *Emma Goldman: An Intimate Life*. New York: Pantheon Books, 1984.
Wilson, Joan Hoff, ed. *The Twenties: The Critical Issues*. Boston: Little, Brown and Company, 1972.

CHAPTER EIGHT: THE SINS OF HOLLYWOOD
Berg, A. Scott. *Goldwyn: A Biography*. New York: Alfred A. Knopf, 1989.
Bernstein, Matthew, ed. *Controlling Hollywood: Censorship and Regulation in the Studio Era*. New Brunswick, N.J.: Rutgers University Press, 1999.
Black, Gregory D. *Hollywood Censored: Morality Codes, Catholics and the Movies*. Cambridge: Cambridge University Press, 1994.
Carr, Steven. *Hollywood and Anti-Semitism: A Cultural History Up to World War II*. Cambridge: Cambridge University Press, 2001.
Chaplin, Charles. *My Autobiography*. London: The Bodley Head, 1964.
Collier, Peter, and David Horowitz. *The Kennedys: An American Drama*. New York: Summit Books, 1984.
Cooper, Mark Garrett. *Love Rules: Silent Hollywood and the Rise of the Managerial Class*. Minneapolis: University of Minnesota Press, 2003.
Couvares, Francis G., ed. *Movie Censorship and American Culture*. Washington, D.C.: Smithsonian Institution Press, 1996.
Dean, Malcolm. *Censored! Only in Canada: The History of Film Censorship – the Scandal Off the Screen*. Toronto: Virgo Press, 1981.
Doherty, Thomas. *Pre-Code Hollywood: Sex, Immorality, and Insurrection in American Cinema, 1930–1934*. New York: Columbia University Press, 1999.
Edmonds, Andy. *Frame Up: The Untold Story of Roscoe "Fatty" Arbuckle*. New York: William Morrow and Company, 1991.
Gabler, Neal. *An Empire of Their Own: How the Jews Invented Hollywood*. New York: Crown Publishers, 1988.
Higham, Charles. *Ziegfeld*. Chicago: Henry Regnery Company, 1972.
———. *Merchant of Dreams: Louis B. Mayer, M.G.M., and the Secret Hollywood*. New York: Donald I. Fine, Inc., 1993.
Jowett, Garth. *Film: The Democratic Art*. Boston: Little, Brown and Company, 1976.
Langman, Larry. *American Film Cycles: The Silent Era*. Westport, Conn.: Greenwood Press, 1998.
LaSalle, Mick. *Complicated Women: Sex and Power in Pre-Code Hollywood*. New York: St. Martin's Press, 2000.
Leff, Leonard J., and Jerold L. Simmons. *Dame in the Kimono: Hollywood, Censorship and the Production Code*. Lexington, Ky.: University of Kentucky Press, 2001.
Lynn, Kenneth S. *Charlie Chaplin and His Times*. New York: Simon & Schuster, 1997.

Mast, Gerald, ed. *The Movies in Our Midst*. Chicago: University of Chicago Press, 1982.

Milton, Joyce. *Tramp: The Life of Charlie Chaplin*. New York: HarperCollins, 1996.

Perrett, Geoffrey. *America in the Twenties: A History*. New York: Simon & Schuster, 1982.

Pizzitola, Louis. *Hearst Over Hollywood*. New York: Columbia University Press, 2002.

Vasey, Ruth. *The World According to Hollywood, 1918–1939*. Madison: University of Wisconsin Press, 1997.

Vaughn, Stephen. "Morality and Entertainment: The Origins of the Motion Picture Production Code." *Journal of American History* 77:1 (June 1990), 39–65.

Walsh, Frank. *Sin and Censorship: The Catholic Church and the Motion Picture Industry*. New Haven, Conn.: Yale University Press, 1996.

Watts, Jill. *Mae West: An Icon in Black and White*. New York: Oxford University Press, 2001.

CONCLUSION: FEAR AND PROGRESS

Abella, Irving, and Harold Troper. *None Is Too Many*. Toronto: Lester & Orpen Dennys, 1982.

Allen, Frederick Lewis. *Since Yesterday: The Nineteen-Thirties in America*. New York: Harper & Brothers, 1939.

Berton, Pierre. *The Great Depression, 1929–1939*. Toronto: McClelland & Stewart, 1990.

Braithwaite, Max. *The Hungry Thirties*. Toronto: Natural Science of Canada, 1977.

Broadfoot, Barry. *Ten Lost Years 1929–1939*. Toronto: Doubleday Canada, 1973.

Filler, Louis, ed. *The Anxious Years: America in the Nineteen-Thirties*. New York: Capricorn Books, 1964.

Gray, James H. *The Roar of the Twenties*. Toronto: Macmillan of Canada, 1975.

Horn, Michiel, ed. *The Dirty Thirties*. Toronto: Copp Clark Publishing, 1972.

Johnson, Paul. *A History of the American People*. London: Weidenfeld & Nicolson, 1997.

Ogburn, William Fielding. *Social Change*. Gloucester, Mass.: Peter Smith, 1964.

Perrett, Geoffrey. *America in the Twenties: A History*. New York: Simon & Schuster, 1982.

Ripley, William Z. *Main Street and Wall Street*. Lawrence, Kans.: Scholars Book Company, 1972. (Originally published in 1927.)

Thomas, Gordon, and Max Morgan-Witts. *The Day the Bubble Burst*. New York: Doubleday & Company, 1979.

Thompson, John Herd. *Canada 1922–1939: Decades of Discord.* Toronto:
McClelland & Stewart, 1985.
Watkins, T.H. *The Great Depression: America in the 1930s.* Boston: Little,
Brown and Company, 1993.
———. *The Hungry Years: A Narrative History of the Great Depression in
America.* New York: Henry Holt and Company, 1999.

Picture Credits

Main text: (page ii) Library of Congress; (page 21) Museum of the City of
New York; (page 61) Library of Congress; (page 103) American Philosophical
Society; (page 151) Provincial Archives of Manitoba; (page 195) Library of
Congress; (page 229) From the Collections of the Henry Ford Museum;
(page 273) Library of Congress; (page 311) Library of Congress.

Photo section 1: (page 1) Museum of the City of New York; (page 2, all
photos) Library of Congress; (page 3, top) Library of Congress; (page 3,
bottom) Library and Archives Canada, C-055449; (page 4, top left and right)
Library of Congress; (page 4, bottom) photo by Cyril Jessop, Library and
Archives Canada, PA-030212; (page 5, top left) Cold Spring Harbor
Laboratory Archives; (page 5, top right) photo by "Pirie MacDonald,
Photographer-of-Men, New York," c. 1921, courtesy of Professor Jon Marks,
Department of Sociology and Anthropology, University of North Carolina;
(page 5, bottom) Arthur Estabrook Papers, M.E., Grenander Department
of Special Collections and Archives, University at Albany, State University of
New York; (page 6, top) University of Toronto Archives; (page 6, bottom)
Library of Congress; (page 7, all photos) Library of Congress; (page 8, all
photos) Library of Congress.

Photo section 2: (page 1, top) Library of Congress; (page 1, bottom) Pemco
Webster & Stevens Collection, Museum of History and Industry, Seattle;
(page 2, all photos) Provincial Archives of Manitoba; (page 3, top) Courtesy
of the Hagley Museum and Library, Wilmington, DE: (page 3, bottom)
© Bettmann/CORBIS/MAGMA; (page 4, top) Library of Congress; (page 4,
bottom) Glenbow Museum, Calgary; (page 5, top) Library of Congress;
(page 5, bottom) Wisconsin Historical Society; (page 6, top) Library of
Congress; (page 6, bottom) Tom Howard/*New York Daily News*; (page 7, top)
Library of Congress; (page 7, middle) Courtesy of sfmuseum.org. the San
Francisco Virtual Museum; (page 7, bottom) Library of Congress; (page 8,
top) © Bettmann/CORBIS/MAGMA; (page 8, bottom) Library of Congress.

Index